"This book strikingly unveils the staggering extent of China's grip on Canada and its hold on our politicians. It casts an unrelenting spotlight on the myriad of Canadian-Chinese entities that steadfastly pledge allegiance to China while exposing the ominous orchestration of the Triads, an Asian criminal juggernaut, in a pivotal, chilling role.

I dare every single Canadian politician to immerse themselves in the depths of this book and then, in a moment of introspection, confront the mirror and make the weighty choice: on which side of history shall you etch your name?"

**GARRY CLEMENT**, FORMER DIRECTOR OF PROCEED
OF CRIME, ROYAL CANADIAN MOUNTED POLICE
AND CLEMENT ADVISORY GROUP

'The Mosaic Effect *is dynamite, blowing wide-open the truth about a political and criminal collaboration between the Chinese Communist Party, Hong Kong's Triads and wealthy business tycoons that pose a direct and grave threat to Canada and its freedoms.*

*If this book was fictional it would be a gripping novel in the genre of Graham Greene or John le Carré, but the horrifying reality is it is fact, not fiction. What has come to light in recent years about the Chinese Communist Party regime's infiltration of Canada and how it has become the soft underbelly to infiltrate America is truly shocking. But in truth it has been going on extensively for over three decades – and was known to successive Canadian governments, which chose to cover up the evidence and do nothing."*

**BENEDICT ROGERS**, AUTHOR AND CEO
HONG KONG WATCH

D1561551

# THE MOSAIC EFFECT

## HOW THE CHINESE COMMUNIST PARTY STARTED A HYBRID WAR IN AMERICA'S BACKYARD

### SCOTT McGREGOR & INA MITCHELL

OPTIMUM
PUBLISHING
INTERNATIONAL
LONDON I MONTRÉAL I TORONTO

The Mosaic Effect, How the Chinese Communist Party Started a Hybrid War in America's Backyard © Toronto, 2023 Scott McGregor and Ina Mitchell

First Edition published in Canada and United States
Published by Optimum Publishing International

LIBRARY AND ARCHIVES CANADA CATALOGUING IN PUBLICATION
Title: The Mosaic Effect, How the Chinese Communist Party Started a Hybrid War in America's Backyard
Scott McGregor and Ina Mitchell, authors
Subjects: Espionage, Modern Warfare, Chinese Hegemony, Geo-politics
Transnational Repression
Description: Optimum Publishing International Canada edition

ISBN 978-0-88890-316-7 (Trade Paperback)
ISBN 978-0-88890-324-2 (Hardcover)
ISBN 978-0-88890-318-1 (ePub)

Printed and bound in Canada
MARQUIS PRINTING

For information on rights or any submissions, please e-mail:
deanb@opibooks.com
Optimum Publishing International
Dean Baxendale, President & CEO
Toronto, Canada

www.optimumpublishinginternational.com
www.opibooks.com
Twitter @opibooks | Instagram @opibooks

# CONTENTS

# FOREWORD

BY FINN LAU

*On July 4, 2023, the CCP's Hong Kong Authority announced a bounty had been placed on my head along with seven other Hong Kong freedom and democracy activists. 1,000,000 + dollars U.S. for all of us. As you read this foreword, remember that the Chinese Communist Party uses such tactics to instill fear and silence its critics worldwide. Transnational Repressions and the use of the United Front are all part of a well orchestrated Hybrid Warfare plan.*

Some observers nickname the United Front "Xi's secret weapon." In this foreword, I hope to provide readers with an understanding of the genesis, objectives and techniques of the United Front before you enter the world of counter-espionage and intelligence. The author's boots-on-the-ground investigation and various roles within law enforcement, military intelligence, and security threat analysis make this a unique and comprehensive expose.

"United Front" (統戰) is a technique different communist parties have mastered for over a century. It was one of the keys that led to the victory of the Chinese Communist Party (CCP) over Kuomintang (KMT), and hence the establishment of the authoritarian People's Republic of China (PRC) in 1949. While the Soviet Union collapsed in 1991, the CCP remained in power and continued to deploy such a manipulation technique at domestic and international stages, which paved the way for China (specifically the

PRC) to emerge as the second-largest economic power in the world. The essence of the United Front technique includes:

1. Identifying different factions of the party's enemy.
2. Uniting with some of the factions through monetary and/ or other forms of benefits.
3. Defeating the isolated faction(s) of the party's enemy.

Once the isolated faction(s) is undermined, the CCP would repeat steps 1 to 3 until the party's enemy destroyed.

Since the downfall of Shanghai in 1949, when it fell into the hands of the CCP, Hong Kong has become the only international city that has served as the bridge between the West and China for decades. As the intercepting point of geopolitics, Hong Kong almost perfectly blended the Cantonese culture with the British culture, together with a robust, independent judiciary system on par with other common law countries such as the United Kingdom, Canada, and Australia. It is also the only CCP-controlled city where English remains the official language. The unique background of Hong Kong implies that the city is an ideal testing ground for the application of the United Front tactic and hybrid warfare before the CCP intends to deploy the same overseas.

Two years after the 1997 Hong Kong Handover, two senior Chinese colonels at the time from the People's Liberation Army (PLA) published a Chinese book titled *Unrestricted Warfare* (超限戰). They openly discussed a wide range of tactics the Beijing regime could deploy to defeat "technologically superior opponents" like the United States. That book systematically classifies and explains the diversified tactics of the CCP's Hybrid War and breaks them into five categories. (1) Lawfare, (2) Economics Warfare, (3) Network Warfare, (4) Terrorism, and (5) Media Warfare. Even though the CCP's hybrid warfare has continuously evolved beyond the 1999 book, it still serves as an insightful, analytical framework to reflect on how the CCP has expanded the scope and breadth of operations outlined in *The Mosaic Effect*.

## TERRORISM

A terrorist attack is one of the tactics that has been and could be used to demand a concession from the national government. According to the two Chinese colonels, the advantage of launching a terrorist attack is that it could induce a disproportionate impact on the targeted country even though the terrorist attack fails to secure concession from the authority. With relatively limited resources, it could instil fear and impose dramatic pressure on the targeted population and its government.

Taking Hong Kong as an example, the CCP plotted and encouraged graduates from CCP-controlled schools and other underground communists to launch a terrorist attack in Hong Kong back in 1967. The CCP planted bombs all over Hong Kong's urban areas, which killed 15 people and injured at least 832 people. Although the British Hong Kong government successfully suppressed the CCP's terrorist attack, the 1967 Riot put tremendous pressure on the British government as it showcased the outreach of the CCP's influence in the city besides its military threat across the Shenzhen River. This paved the way for the United Nations Resolution No. 2908, which removed Hong Kong from the list of colonies in 1972, effectively depriving Hong Kong people of self-determination rights. The pressure created by the CCP's terrorist attack also gave the Beijing government an upper hand in negotiating with Britain and the PRC over Hong Kong's sovereignty in the 1980s. In the end, the British government reluctantly signed the Sino-British Joint Declaration in 1984 without holding a referendum.

## ECONOMIC WARFARE

The authors of "Unrestricted Warfare" emphasize the interdependence of economies among different countries in the age of globalization. With the introduction of the 1978 Open Door Policy by Deng Xiaoping, the PRC opened its market, attracting billions of foreign investments and becoming the world's factory due to its relatively low labour cost and loose environmental regulation. As such, almost all developed and developing countries have increasingly relied on imports of Chinese goods for decades. The potential purchasing power of the 12-billion Chinese population also attracted foreign businesses to explore the Chinese market. This resulted in high dependency on the PRC and trade deficits. The CCP is well aware of the lucrativeness of the Chinese market and the world's dependence on Chinese manufacturing. The CCP would often use the short-term economic benefits as bait in exchange for mid-to-long-term political and socio-economic influence. Under this context, the Belt and Road Initiative is a gigantic economic warfare initiative used to leverage other countries.

When we look at the case of Hong Kong, the Hong Kong government was short-sighted after the outbreak of SARS and the associated economic downturn in 2003. Instead of strengthening the local supply chain and rebuilding the Hong Kong economy by diversifying economic activities and attracting investment from the international community, the Hong Kong government agreed to receive economic stimulus from the Beijing regime. The introduction of the Individual Visit Scheme allows the residents of mainland China to visit Hong Kong on an individual basis. While the Scheme instantly injected hot money into Hong Kong's economy, it has resulted in a twisted economic structure heavily relies on the Chinese tourist market. On the one hand, the cityscape of Hong Kong was drastically reshaped with the emergence of luxury retailing businesses that targeted Chinese tourists; the Hong Kong property market, on the other hand, was dominated by speculative trading from the PRC. The Hong Kong government's figures showed that circa 57.5 million tourists visited Hong Kong in 2017, around 76% of which were Chinese tourists. That implies the rest of the world only added up to 24% of total tourists to Hong Kong before the 2019 Hong Kong Protest.

## NETWORK WARFARE

Network warfare means attacking and paralyzing different networks, especially the internet and telecommunication. The book discussed the possibility of paralyzing data exchange, local transportation and power supply via remote hacking and attacks on local networks. In July 2021, the United States and its allies, including the European Union, NATO, U.K., Australia, Japan, New Zealand and Canada, publicly criticized Beijing's cyberattack on the Microsoft Exchange Server.

In the case of Hong Kong, it is common knowledge among the protesters that we frequently suffer from suspicious hacking activities into personal internet services like email accounts and messengers like WhatsApp and Telegram. It is highly plausible that the cyberattacks originate from the CCP. However, it is almost impossible for journalists to trace the exact source of the attacks. Besides launching cyberattacks, the CCP's network warfare has evolved by constructing the "Great Firewall" in mainland China. Since 2020, many websites have been blocked by Internet Service

Providers (ISPs) as requested by the Hong Kong and Beijing authorities; that could be a prelude to the explicit introduction of the Great Firewall in Hong Kong which is now playing out in real time in 2023. Ironically, Russia, as the close ally of the PRC, launched repeated cyberattacks on Ukraine's power grid in January 2022—exactly the same as suggested by the Chinese book "Unrestricted Warfare". On February 15, 2022, authorities in Hong Kong started down this path by blocking access to content from Hong Kong Watch, run by Human Rights activist Ben Rogers.

## LAWFARE

There are two levels of lawfare—both using the legal system to take advantage of other countries and/or civil society and the Rule of Law. The first level of lawfare is misusing and finding loopholes in international law to build legitimacy and materialize one's diplomatic victory. As mentioned earlier, the CCP successfully removed Hong Kong from the U.N. decolonization list, which is subject to self-determination, by launching terrorist attacks in 1967 and threatening with potential military annexation. By influencing the U.N., the Hong Kong people were effectively deprived of the fundamental human rights of self-determination as entitled by people in other former colonies. Later, the Beijing regime took one step further to sign an international treaty, the Sino-British Joint Declaration, in 1984 to secure the 1997 Hong Kong Handover. Although the Joint Declaration is a UN-lodged treaty under which Hong Kong people shall be entitled to at least 50 years of autonomy and civil liberties after the 1997 Handover, there were no remedies in the treaty should the CCP violate the Joint Declaration. In 2017, the CCP claimed the international treaty was a "historical document". This is a perfect example of how Beijing misused international agreements to take advantage of its counterparts on the international level and changed the rules to suit its ends.

The second level of lawfare distorts the national and local judiciary system to deprive civil liberties. In 2019, the government's proposal for the draconian extradition bill sparked a large-scale protest in Hong Kong. The proposed extradition bill could enable the Beijing authority to freely persecute and extradite any dissidents from Hong Kong to China. In June 2020, the CCP decided to bypass Hong Kong's legislature and directly promulgated the notorious Hong Kong National Security Law (NSL). Since the promulgation of the NSL, more than 50 civil society organizations like the Hong Kong branch of Amnesty International had been forcibly dissolved; the top three pro-democracy or independent mass media in Hong Kong were shut down by the authority within seven months with journalists incarcerated in jails. Almost all prominent former lawmakers and activists are being prosecuted, imprisoned, or exiled. Since the 2019 Hong Kong pro-democracy movement outbreak, over 10,000 protestors have been arrested. These political purges are being legitimized in the name of the Rule of Law. However, it is Rule by law in reality. With sophisticated lawfare, Hong Kong's academic freedom, press freedom, freedom of assembly and other civil liberties are gone.

## MEDIA WARFARE

Media warfare is another critical tactic under hybrid and/or Unrestricted Warfare. It is a powerful instrument to control the press, which shapes public opinions and stifles people's voices against authority. The fundamental goal of media warfare is to undermine the press and media as the Fourth Estate, which monitors the Chinese government and politicians. The CCP deploys numerous techniques in media warfare, such as misinformation campaigns and commercial takeovers. Lawfare is another effective tool to eradicate press freedom.

With the downfall of the last pro-democracy newspaper—*Apple Daily*, in June 2021, the CCP has now taken control of all Chinese and English newspapers in Hong Kong. Alibaba, a quasi-state-owned Chinese corporation, acquired the city's most prominent English newspaper—*South China Morning Post*—with $266 million in 2015. It is widely considered an explicit measure by the CCP to takecontrol over press freedom of the city. Another notable example of how the CCP indirectly controls the media in Hong Kong would be the case of Sing Tao Daily. The Chairman of Sing Tao Daily, Charles Ho, simultaneously served as a National Committee Member of the Chinese People's Political Consultative Conference between 2001 and 2021.

The oldest active Chinese newspaper in Hong Kong, Ta Kung Pao ( 大公報), had also flipped from an independent pro-democracy newspaper into a state-owned newspaper that has served as a CCP propaganda machine since 1949. When the 2014 Umbrella Revolution and the 2019 Hong Kong Revolution broke out, almost all newspapers except Apple Daily assisted in spreading misinformation against the pro-democracy camp. For example, pro-democracy students were smeared as foreign agents sponsored by the West. At the same time, Hongkongers' calls for civil liberties were twisted as rioting. The Beijing Regime has secured a group of pro-CCP people who occasionally whitewash the totalitarian regime through well-coordinated misinformation campaigns that almost all local newspapers have orchestrated for years.

As to applying lawfare in media warfare, Jimmy Lai, the owner of Apple Daily and a pro-democracy tycoon, was arrested and imprisoned at 72 in 2020, alongside several senior executives and journalists of his newspaper. In June 2021, Apple Daily was forced to shut down as the authority cut off the cash flow, with $18 million in assets frozen under the draconian Hong Kong National Security Law. *Stand News*, the most prominent pro-democracy mass media after the downfall of Apple Daily, was also forcibly shut down in December 2021. The board members and senior executives of Stand News were arrested and charged with "publishing seditious materials"—a colonial law that has not been deployed for over five decades.

On the international level, the CCP has spread misinformation or even fake news. In August 2021, it was astounding to see multiple CCP state-owned media outlets fabricate fake news about an alleged Swiss biologist, Wilson Edwards, who defended the CCP regarding the origin of COVID-19 and the WHO's questionable independence during the COVID-19 pandemic. In response, the Swiss Embassy explicitly clarified that there is no registry of a Swiss citizen with the name "Wilson Edwards" and no academic articles under the name. This incident is only the tip of the iceberg of the misinformation and propaganda campaign of the CCP.

## UNITED FRONT

United Front work often begins with infiltration within academia, as it requires funding from time to time to survive and is the easiest one to be infiltrated. The private sector would be the next target as it is also profit-oriented instead of morally driven. Finally, the deeply penetrated academia and the business circle would encircle the political realm. Pro-Beijing public policy advisory from infiltrated think tanks, investment opportunities and donations to political parties would pave the way for the CCP to directly influence the parliament.

In the case of Hong Kong, the CCP was extremely keen on setting up schools in Hong Kong during the post-WWII period. However, the British government still governed Hong Kong at that time. The CCP-controlled schools quickly turned into a propaganda machine to brainwash and nurture groups of "patriotic" politicians and businessmen who are commonly known as "underground commies" like Jasper Tsang (who even became the second President of the Hong Kong Legislative Council between 2008 and 2016). In 1967, the graduates from these CCP-controlled schools were the primary force that launched terrorist attacks against Hong Kong civilians and the British Hong Kong authority.

In the late 1970s to 1990s, Hong Kong manufacturers and business people were highly encouraged and often invited by the CCP to invest in China. Some were even granted prestigious status and nominal positions in the National Congress of the PRC. On the grassroots level, Beijing secretly set up different satellite organizations, chambers and political parties that would actively organize trips to China in the name of "cultural exchange," "patriotism," and "field trips." As a remark, the same approach has been deployed by the CCP in the U.K. for recent decades. In 2020, *Daily Mail* investigated the 48 Club, which was effectively one of the entities controlled by the CCP. Optimum authors Clive Hamilton and Marieke Ohlberg first alerted the world in *Hidden Hand: How the Chinese Communist Party is Reshaping the World*. Scott's and Ina's *The Mosaic Effect* takes this further as they analyze and expose the CCP's hybrid warfare against different countries but that Canada has long been the preferred destination and staging grounds for attacks against their neighbours, the United States of America. Readers will be startled by the extent and complexity of the CCP's infiltration into Canada and how those techniques are currently being deployed in every major democracy worldwide.

The CCP's United Front works in Hong Kong were so successful that the CCP fully absorbed Hong Kong's major tycoons into its autocratic institution. After the 1997 Hong Kong Handover, Tung Chee-hwa, a billionaire businessman in the Chinese shipping industry, was appointed as the first Chief Executive of Hong Kong. With Hong Kong's sovereignty being transferred to the PRC, civil liberties, the Rule of Law and the autonomy of Hong Kong have been repeatedly hammered, eroded and dismantled by the repressive regime at an accelerating speed.

# FOREWORD

In 2020, Tung formed the largest United Front entity in Hong Kong history, the "Hong Kong Coalition." Its members include former senior government officials, legislators, judges, billionaires, principals, singers and even international movie actors like Jackie Chan. These 1,500 social elites jointly endorsed the crackdown by the Beijing and Hong Kong authorities in 2019 and 2020. However, under the United Front framework, it is only a matter of time before the CCP divides the Hong Kong Coalition into smaller groups of principal and non-principal enemies until Hong Kong is fully absorbed into China.

The time has come for Hongkongers to face the cold truth: it will be an uphill battle for us to fight against the resourceful dictatorship. Yet, there is still time for democratic governments and civil societies worldwide to wake up and take action. Everyone can play a paramount role in the resistance. Let's begin by taking a small step toward understanding the CCP's diversified tactics and infiltration.

The money, criminals and pro-Beijing agents started to move to Canada in earnest after Vancouver's Expo 86. RCMP investigators found high levels of fraud in the Hong Kong High Commission. With the aid of Canada's Investor Immigration Fund, thousands of suspect Chinese citizens entered the country under false pretenses and many with criminal ties to Triads and other organized crime groups. But many were Ministry of State Security agents or, as some of the characters in this book, the People's Liberation Army. Most Chinese or Hong Kong Citizens came here to escape the authoritarian clutches of the CCP. Still, as you will learn, Beijing exerts absolute control over most of the Chinese diaspora community.

Ambassadors and Chinese consular officials claim they speak for the entire Chinese community. This claim has become increasingly offensive to my colleagues and me worldwide. We want nothing to do with the United Front apparatus and seek freedom from oppression. Only when Canada and other nation-states realize how the United Front Works Department, the Ministry of State Security, and the PLA's cyber-espionage arm known as the Strategic Support Force (SSF) operate are we able to combat these threat actors. Once exposed, we trust governments will sanction and dismantle these operations so we can be free of Beijing's tyranny. This book has no contemporaries as the authors have infiltrated and exposed Canada's United Front Works Department apparatus and its global reach.

Please understand that the overwhelming majority of the citizens from China and Hong Kong are good, hardworking people. Their only desire was to escape from authoritarianism in their new country, but over the decades, they have seen firsthand that Beijing still exerts tremendous control over their lives. This book holds a key ingredient to understanding the CCP's ambitions and why they need to be combatted and held to account.

# THE CCP'S MAGIC BULLET

BY IVY LI

In the 1990s, I taught visual communication design in Oakville, Ontario. It was one of the most affluent cities in Canada, and nearly everyone was white. Downtown, there was a lovely English teahouse where my colleagues and I often dined. The food was good, and the staff was always courteous. One afternoon, I took two friends, a Chinese Canadian couple, there for dinner. To my surprise, the young white waitress ignored our table but served everyone who came after us. I was stunned. Later, I realized I had never been to that teahouse before without Caucasian company.

At first, I put that incident down to one bad experience in a country that had always welcomed me. But others followed. One peaceful sunny afternoon in the mid-2000s, I was strolling along the beaches of British Columbia's Okanagan Lake, deep in my own thoughts, when I heard someone behind me yell, "Go home!" I turned to see a middle-aged white man on a bike staring at me.

A few years later, an older white man on a packed bus in Toronto said the same thing to me.

Racism in Canada is real, and I have faced it squarely multiple times. Every time, it was hurtful, humiliating, and infuriating.

I came to Canada in 1989, but many Chinese immigrants who arrived decades before me faced even more blatant and frequent racist treatment. Those experiences cast a long and bitter shadow. Even though their Canadian-born children and grandchildren were more accepted, they still had to learn to be assertive and push back when needed. Today, fear of an upsurge in racism understandably persists among Chinese Canadians. Unfortunately, the Chinese Communist Party has exploited our legitimate concerns to strengthen its grip on diaspora communities and weaken Western democracies. To combat racism and defend our way of life, we need to understand how this strategy works.

Racism exists in all countries, and Western democracies are no exception. But China has a particularly atrocious track record. Racism against ethnic minorities at the hands of the CCP is systemic, large-scale, and often genocidal. Yet a peculiar quirk of China is that the dominant Han people—by far the racial majority, at more than 90 percent of the population—are not immune to it. In fact, most of the tens of millions who died in the numerous political upheavals and atrocities, including the Great Leap Forward, the Cultural Revolution and the unimaginable organ harvesting, were Han Chinese.

To impose communism onto a country of close to a billion people, the CCP eradicated the bedrock of its traditional culture. The party tortured and murdered untold numbers of writers and intellectuals, destroyed temples, uprooted young people and sent them to work in rural areas, censored information, distorted and rewrote history, and forced everyone to spy on and betray each other. After seven decades of lies, deceptions, purges, and human rights abuses, the values and behaviours of the Han people in mainland China have been drastically altered. The traditional Chinese virtues that many Westerners have admired and continue to romanticize are primarily gone. The CCP has remodelled the psyche of the Han people and turned them into tools for suppression and propaganda. Those who've dared to rebel have been silenced, imprisoned or disappeared.

Meanwhile, to control the Chinese diaspora, ethnic minorities, and those who are not members of the CCP, including foreigners, the party created the United Front Work Department (UFWD). The UFWD runs influence operations, co-opts individuals and organizations outside China, and attempts to shape public opinion to neutralize opposition to the CCP and its policies. China's leaders have called the UFW their magic weapon, and the magic bullet of this magic weapon is the racism card. Accusations of racism are a tactic that Beijing uses to muzzle criticism of its interests and to create internal turmoil in targeted groups or countries. It is especially effective in a multicultural society like Canada, where people are sensitive to such charges and generally have a genuine desire to combat racism and right historical wrongs. By accusing academics, journalists, and other critics of being racist, the CCP is able to shut down discourse and distract public attention from real issues like money laundering, drug trafficking, and election meddling.

In Canada, the COVID-19 pandemic showed us just how effective the racism card can be. In early 2019, the Wuhan outbreak ignited fear among people the world over. Some Canadian parents circulated petitions asking schools to force students whose families had just travelled back from China to stay away for seventeen days. Others called for a ban on all flights from China, and Chinese restaurants and malls were deserted across the country. These incidents were labelled racist by many and sparked concerns of stigmatization from politicians, media outlets, and human rights groups. Even the World Health Organization weighed in.

What few seemed to notice is that many of those who'd signed the parents' petition or raised the possibility of a travel ban had Chinese names, and most Chinese malls and restaurants are patronized largely by Chinese customers. Obviously, these were examples of people within the Chinese community trying to sound the alarm, but you would never have known that from the way these stories were framed.

The racism card arouses suspicions and stokes resentment within society. It is a divide-and-conquer tactic. Beijing wanted to stop Canada from banning flights from China, so it whipped out the racism card to help friendly politicians ward off demands that the CCP disapproved of. The racism card is the hard-striking bullet that cuts down all opponents in its path. Behind it comes the victimhood card. This card is played to ensure loyalty from all Chinese, but especially the Han, both within and outside China. It portrays the Chinese people as targets of endless bullying and subjugation by foreigners by constantly referencing historical humiliations like the Nanjing Massacre and the Boxer Rebellion. The goal of the victim card is to make people feel vulnerable and to prevent Overseas Chinese from developing a sense of belonging to their adopted countries. Alienated from their new homes, they will become ultra-patriotic about their mother country.

While inducing insecurity, the victimhood card also fosters a sense of superiority. The Chinese people are reminded they are the descendants of the dragon or the children of the Yellow Emperor. They are told that saintly blood is flowing in their veins. And since blood is thicker than water, they are told they must band together no matter where they are to regain their rightful place by the rejuvenation of their Middle Kingdom.

For the racism and victimhood cards to be effective, the CCP needs to keep racism alive, inflaming the fears of all Chinese people, especially the diaspora worldwide. This exaggerates the severity of anti-Asian racism today, but even worse, it prevents us from identifying and fighting real racism when it occurs.

The CCP excels at making unsuspecting people into its enthusiastic helpers in these endeavours. The push for a Nanjing Massacre Commemorative Day in Canada is just one example. The Canada Association for Learning & Preserving the History of WWII in Asia (Canada ALPHA) was founded in 1997 to foster awareness of the Second World War, said co-chair Thekla Lit in 2018, and to "further the value[s] of justice, peace, and reconciliation" and "activate historical memory, education in humanity, reconciliation, healing and closure, and cross-cultural understanding."

Since its inception, Canada ALPHA has been able to interview Nanjing Massacre survivors inside China. Without the permission and support of the government, it would be impossible for anyone outside the country to find and gain access to those people. Something of this nature would typically require assistance from the UFWD, the Civil Affairs Ministry, and assorted local departments to facilitate and even sponsor the trips of the survivors to travel to meet with foreign delegations. Naturally, such help would inspire gratitude and friendly feelings. This is how the UFWD builds relationships with community groups and Overseas Chinese.

In 2007, the Toronto chapter of Canada ALPHA published a bilingual (Chinese and English) book entitled *The Nanking Massacre: 70 Years of Amnesia*. Many people volunteered their time and skills to remind the world of the terrible suffering endured by the Chinese people during the Japanese occupation. Many pro-CCP media outlets and commentators applauded ALPHA and the book.

In 2018, New Democratic member of Parliament Jenny Kwan, who recalled learning about the massacre two decades earlier from a photo exhibition organized by Thekla Lit at the Vancouver Public Library— tabled a motion calling for an annual Nanjing Massacre Commemorative Day. Her motion was widely reported by CCP state media agencies such as Xinhua and *China Daily* and Canadian English- and Chinese-language media. Kwan's proposal was also endorsed by the Chinese embassy, various

PRC consulates, Canada ALPHA and its provincial chapters, and many federal MPs across the political spectrum.

Memorializing an atrocity to prevent it from ever happening again is a commendable act, which is presumably why Kwan's motion garnered such broad and enthusiastic support. But one fascinating detail seemed to go unnoticed. Of those so passionately championing the Nanjing Massacre Commemorative Day, no one has ever uttered a word about creating a similar day to remember the Tiananmen Square massacre.

And one critical and obvious question also went unasked: Why would a brutal dictatorial regime that has repeatedly tortured its own people and cares only about survival and power be so intent on commemorating the Nanjing Massacre? What is in this for the CCP?

To answer this question, we must turn back to the UFWD's influence operations—the racism and victimhood cards—used to protect or advance the regime's domestic and international agenda.

In Canada and throughout the West, the United Front uses Chinese-language news agencies and social media to promote the message that the Chinese people have been insulted, attacked, and disrespected for generations by inferior Western invaders. They are told that a strong motherland is the only defence against these continued abuses, and only the CCP can provide that strong motherland. To restore their dignity and regain their rightful place in the world, the Chinese people must make the CCP stronger.

White Canadians, meanwhile, are told they're racist and xenophobic. They're told they have no right to criticize China's human rights record because of Canada's history with its Indigenous peoples. They're accused of China bashing and Sinophobia and of victimizing the peaceful, civilized, and benign Chinese people.

So where does all this leave us? To defend ourselves effectively against authoritarianism, we need to understand the adversary we face. To flourish, democracy relies on engaged citizens who are independent, critical, and creative thinkers. A democracy imbues its people with fundamental rights and treats them as valued human beings. Autocracy needs people who are compliant and don't think for themselves. A dictatorship views its people as expendable and unworthy of respect—mere tools to be exploited. Human decency and morality are not a consideration. The only thing that matters is the party's survival.

The two political systems are fundamentally irreconcilable. If people in China begin to adopt the free-thinking mindset of those in democracies, the CCP's dictatorial rule will end. Mao Zedong and Deng Xiaoping knew this, and so does Xi Jinping. The majority of CCP leaders understand it. Since the Communist Party's inception, this collective understanding has been safeguarding this giant dictatorial organism. In the past seven decades, whenever the CCP flirts with opening up, even to a modest degree, it senses existential danger and suddenly slams shut again. It was no surprise when Deng brought in the tanks in 1989.

At the same time, if those living in democracies take on the attributes of those under dictatorial rule—follow orders blindly, uncritical of information received, and fearful of authority—democracy will wither and die. Our complacency as citizens has already led to the erosion of accountability of our elected officials in this country.

Make no mistake, the CCP is aggressively infiltrating Canada and remodelling our democratic system to serve its dictatorial interests. Many Hong Kongers, Taiwanese, and even Chinese mainlanders have seen first-hand what CCP rule looks like and have voted with their feet by immigrating to democratic Canada. I applaud this courageous effort by Scott McGregor and Ina Mitchell to expose those who work to undermine democracy. They are taking significant risks to advance this just and noble cause. But freedom and democracy are worth fighting for.

# INTRODUCTION

*"Every Canadian Prime Minister since Prime Minister Mulroney had been compromised by agents of influence of the Chinese Communist Party. Yes, every Prime Minister."*

— **MICHEL JUNEAU-KATSUYA**, FORMER DIRECTOR AT THE CANADIAN SECURITIES INTELLIGENCE SERVICE AND AUTHOR OF THE SIDEWINDER REPORT

A hybrid war is fought with ideas rather than bullets, using influence campaigns and other modern tactics, like lawfare, to defeat an enemy through economic, social, political, criminal operations, and cultural grounds. Unlike conventional warfare, hybrid war claims its victims slowly, over time, through infiltration, subversion, and disruption of a nation's critical infrastructure instead of military action, but it claims them nonetheless.

This book explores China's use of Canada as a staging ground in its hybrid war against the West. Our research shows that the Communist Party of China and its United Front Work Department, which is tasked with managing China's presence, reputation, and influence around the world, have run influence campaigns and continue to run unconventional operations and cultivate political candidates at every level of government in Canada, backing preferred candidates and leveraging influence in federal, provincial, and municipal elections, including Vancouver's latest mayoral race.

Along with revealing political interference, this book also explores the wider dimensions of China's attempts to infiltrate Canadian society for its own gain. Business tycoons with close ties to the CCP have bought up

PHOTO: A mosaic of Canada's Prime Ministers and some of their connections to CCP entities set against a backdrop of a "Link Chart."

whole towns and rescued dying industries in Canada, including the paper mills of Powell River, British Columbia, for reasons that benefit China and that may leave Canada exposed. We uncovered espionage operations in BC and built two case studies that raise serious questions about China's motivations for buying up Canadian aquaculture farms and aircraft industries in that province. Whether China is acquiring these interests in order to meet its growing resource needs or to be close to Canadian military installations (or both) remains unclear, but the questions need to be asked, and we raise them in the context of deep research into the contexts of each acquisition, including the political connections of the people behind those projects.

Although it bears our names, this book is the product of a multi-year research effort by a group of journalists, intelligence experts, and concerned citizens from Canada, China, Hong Kong, and the US, all of whom have become deeply concerned about China's interference in Western political and civilian life, and about what these incursions mean for the rest of the world.

As Public Safety Canada (the government agency that oversees the Canadian Security and Intelligence Service) informed the Canada-China Relations Committee in 2021, Canada has been a target of repeated and persistent interference by the People's Republic of China (PRC), which seeks to "advance [its] political, economic and security interests to the detriment of Canada's," and in so doing, "to advance its strategic objectives around the world."[1]

Foreign interference, according to Public Safety Canada, amounts to "hostile activity undertaken by foreign states that is purposely covert, malign, clandestine and deceptive," and can include "threats, harassment and intimidation" that is "directed at Canadians, or residents of Canada, or against Canadian institutions to advance their strategic interests at the expense of our national interest and values."

As far back as the mid-1990s, the United States was sufficiently concerned about foreign interference by the PRC in Canada to make it the focus of an intelligence operation, titled Operation Dragon Lord. Evidence we have of this project's existence is a report about its findings compiled by the US Department of Justice, and the sworn testimony of intelligence officer and manager at the Canadian Security Intelligence Service (CSIS), Michel Juneau-Katsuya.

Operation Dragon Lord found compelling reasons to believe that China was using Canada to achieve its larger aims in the West, and that immediate steps were needed to convince Canada to mount a robust defense against Chinese interference.

Since that time, China's influence and ambitions have expanded exponentially, and its presence in Canadian political and civilian life has only become more entrenched. President Xi Jinping has overseen a massive transformation within Chinese society since he took office in 2013, and he has been transparent about his goal to install China as the world's superpower by 2049. A hybrid war on the West that is designed to demote the US to follower status is well underway, and China has been able to use Canada's open, multicultural society as an entry point for its ambitious global reach.

Our research reveals that China has already made significant inroads in Canada and elsewhere, in the areas of culture, politics, education, and industry. By cultivating politicians and winning influence with powerful Canadians, China has infiltrated all three levels of Canadian political life, and has run or influenced candidates in municipal, provincial, and federal elections. By buying up large tracts of Canadian land and swooping in to buy or rescue dying Canadian industries, China has captured territory, won the trust and loyalty of local leaders with infusions of cash into their communities, and cultivated strategic partnerships across multiple industries. By funding educational initiatives, supporting student immigration as a path to Canadian citizenship, and working to make all Overseas Chinese feel connected and beholden to the motherland, China has also been able to infiltrate Canadian educational institutions, transfer talent and innovations back to China, and in some cases simply steal Canadian R&D.

Remarkably, all of this has been accomplished out in the open, through a complex web of seemingly benign hometown associations and friendship groups, many of which answer to the United Front Work Department of the CCP. Canadian politicians (and the quasi-governmental administrators who are often the real power brokers within government departments) have shown stunning levels of naivete, gullibility, and culpability when it comes to allowing China to curry favour, gain influence, and make tangible changes to Canadian culture and society. China has launched an unofficial Belt and Road Initiative within Canada, thanks to enthusiastic support from Canadian politicians, including former BC premier Christy Clark, among others. Canadian academics and investigators have aided China in hunting down so-called "corrupt" business tycoons and repatriating assets, and in doing so, have supported bounty hunting operations that are often based on outright fabrications by the CCP, which has used its anti-corruption program, Operation Fox Hunt, as a pretext for capturing political dissidents along with what China considers actual criminals. At the same time, Canada has become a safe haven for threat finance and money launderers from China, who buy up Canadian real estate with no intention of living in the homes they purchase, and fentanyl producers, who flood Canadian streets with drugs and precursors sourced primarily from China, fuelling a severe opioid crisis and driving up crime, homelessness, and health care costs.

When we began this project, Canadians were fully asleep when it came to understanding the threat faced by China. This state of affairs was being encouraged by the federal Liberals, whose leader, Justin Trudeau, comes by his admiration of China honestly, through his father, Pierre Elliot Trudeau. Trudeau Sr. made no secret of his support for China or his desire to improve relations between China, Canada, and the rest of the West. Recent events have shifted the tone of Canadian federal support for China, pushing even the Liberal government to acknowledge that China has exposed Canada to harm. Between the capture of the Two Michaels during the Huawei CFO, Meng Wanzhou, extradition trial and the intimidation campaigns waged against Canadian MP Michael Chong and his family in Hong Kong, Canadians, and even the Canadian government, appear to suddenly be aware of the threat represented by China's actions. Without sensationalism or hyperbole, this book painstakingly marshals the stories, evidence, and intelligence that is needed to help Canadians become fully awake and alive, to the actions that have already been taken by China within this country's too-trusting, multicultural milieu.

## A NOTE ON METHOD: THE MOSAIC THEORY OF INTELLIGENCE

Throughout this book, you will be presented with stories that illuminate the scope, methods, and threat level attached to myriad aspects of China's hybrid war on the West, and its use of Canada as a theatre in that larger conflict.

As an organizing principle and a method of processing the information that supports our conclusions in this book, we filter these stories through what's known as the mosaic theory of intelligence. As developed in a 2005 paper by David Pozen of Columbia Law School, the mosaic theory describes a basic precept of intelligence gathering—that disparate pieces of information only become useful for when they are combined and analyzed in context.[2] An official analysis tool already in use by the intelligence community, the mosaic theory can be thought of as a framework for understanding how varied information sources fit together into a whole. In this section, we'll talk a bit about how that works, and about the difference between evidence and intelligence.

Rarely does a single piece of information amount to much until it is correlated with other, related pieces of information. In the intelligence community, this usually means collecting information from various sources, and then verifying each one using a wide range of tools and tradecraft. Combining the items illuminates their interrelationships and breeds analytic synergies, so that the resulting mosaic of information is worth more than the sum of its parts. In the context of national security, the mosaic theory suggests the potential for an adversary to deduce from independently innocuous facts a strategic vulnerability, exploitable for malevolent ends.

The public has been trained to think about investigations in terms of a "smoking gun," or evidence that leads directly to incontrovertible proof of guilt. But intelligence doesn't always include a smoking gun, and even if there is one, it is not necessarily evidence of crime on its own as a single entity.

There is a distinct difference between information, intelligence, and evidence of crimes. Evidence is often elusive in espionage cases. This is why we say in the intelligence world that "Intelligence is not evidence." Intelligence deals in probabilities and the likelihood that an assessment will come to fruition. It is not designed, or intended, to prove to a court of law that an act of espionage occurred based on evidence collected for a prosecution. That's what law enforcement investigators do—collect evidence. Intelligence is meant to provide insight and create awareness so that those with authority to act can be better informed of the threats and the likelihood that those threats will take place. However, intelligence does much more than just provide threat assessments.

The real goal of intelligence is to help authorities see "the forest for the trees." It does this by capturing a complete picture that otherwise would not be understood as anything significant when viewed in isolation. It isn't until you assemble it with other pieces of intelligence that a more tangible picture of the possibilities emerges.

Let's say, for the sake of argument, that an intelligence assessment points to a potential threat. Law enforcement will take this assessment and conduct an investigation to collect evidence. This is called Intelligence-Led Policing. The FBI went to this form of policing some time ago, as they moved away from an older method called CompStat, which looked at the statistics of crime and targeted the areas the statistics identified as trouble areas. CompStat was a reactive way of addressing crime; it was not predictive in any way, and it forced law enforcement to focus on what had already happened instead of identifying root causes of criminal activity and using that knowledge to address crimes before they occur.

Crime prevention is undervalued and underutilized in many areas. Intelligence can help law enforcement to anticipate and prevent crime by gathering information from various sources and analyzing it in context. Intelligence may use evidence to better understand the environment, but intelligence is not the same as evidence. Instead, it's an assessment of information that has been analyzed. Some raw data collection might be used as evidence, but this information has not become intelligence until it has been collated, analyzed, and assessed, by a trained intelligence analyst.

The metaphor of the mosaic relies on an idea of perspective. If we stand too close to a mosaic, which is a type of image made of multi-coloured glass pieces of different shapes and sizes, stuck together in what seems to be a haphazard fashion, all we see is an abstract collection of colours and textures. Viewed up close, the pieces don't add up to anything that we can recognize from the world around us. Step back, however, and suddenly, those individual pieces of glass take on new meaning as a complete picture is revealed. It's this complete mosaic, composed of individual pieces of information that add up to a whole, that helps the intelligence community identify threat actors and security risks based on the balance of probabilities.

China's hybrid war against the West has been difficult to assess. It's a fast-moving threat that involves many different modes of infiltration that are almost always cloaked in plausible deniability. That's because so much of what happens occurs within friendship groups and hometown associations whose ties to the United Front Work Department are not always obvious. This book takes you deep into the mosaic, then steps back to show you what's really happening. We think you'll agree that there is much more to China's presence in the West—and in Canada, specifically—than meets the eye.

Controlling the narrative is the ultimate goal and winning at all costs defines China's unrestricted warfare.

# CHAPTER 1

# CHINA'S UNHOLY TRINITY

## A THREAT FROM WITHIN CANADA'S BORDERS

The words in the highly sensitive 1999 document were chilling. "Aggressive and long-overdue steps must be taken by U.S. authorities," said the document, purported to have come from a classified US Department of Justice task force working on Operation Dragon Lord, "including the U.S. Justice Department, State Department, and intelligence officials within the executive branch, to make it abundantly clear to their counterparts in Canada that the U.S. government can no longer tolerate such a threat emanating principally from within Canada's borders."[1]

The threat was multifaceted, ballooning, and undeniable, and it represented an imminent danger to US national security interests, as well as the interests of Canada and Australia, if something drastic wasn't done—and fast.

Operation Dragon Lord—which the document described as a combined initiative overseen by the DOJ and using data from the CIA, the NSA, the Defense Intelligence Agency (DIA), and the FBI—was formed to investigate and report on the nature and scope of the Chinese Communist

PHOTO: Officials from China and Canada attend the Vancouver Chinatown Spring Festival Parade every year.

regime's infiltration of Canada. It uncovered evidence of a political and criminal network involving Chinese military intelligence, ethnic triads, and business tycoons. This network was called China's Unholy Trinity. It was time, the document concluded, to fight back using a robust intelligence and a law enforcement campaign designed to "infiltrate and dismantle" China's Unholy Trinity throughout North America, but especially in Canada. This campaign, the sensitive DOJ document said, "must be fought with the same resolve and determination that has always defined America when it wages war. And make no mistake, this is a war."

## THREAT TRIFECTA

How did we get to a point where organizations as venerable as the DOJ, the CIA, and the FBI felt the need to put pen to paper and advise that the time was ripe for the US government to confront the Chinese Communist Party (CCP) on Canadian soil? To answer that question, we need to go back to when China's Unholy Trinity was formed.

In the early 1980s, China's senior security chief met with the heads of a Hong Kong crime syndicate called Sun Yee On to iron out the details of a joint partnership between the state, the triads, and the tycoons. This meeting was confirmed by a member of the Chinese intelligence service who later defected to Australia. In the 1990s, he told the Australian Secret Intelligence Service (ASIS) that his job was to go to Hong Kong to recruit triad members.[2] But for what purpose? It didn't seem as if this partnership could be entirely about money. After all, the triads were already earning boatloads of cash through illegal activities like gambling and prostitution, and the state not only owned pretty much everything and everyone in China but could also print its own currency on demand. There had to be another reason, but what was it?

For one, there was an existing relationship. The triads had acted as hired guns for Deng Xiaoping during his historic trip across the United States in 1979.[3] And in the early 1980s, as Deng grappled with how to manage the coming handover of Hong Kong from the British, the triads were called upon once more. The former deputy secretary-general of Xinhua, China's Hong Kong news agency, told a university audience in 1997 that he had been appointed to strike a deal with the triad bosses, if they would help maintain the peace after the transition. "I told them that if they did not disrupt Hong Kong's stability, we would not stop them from making money," he said.[4] So yes, it was a lucrative arrangement for all concerned, but what else did the triads get out of it?

Respectability, for a start. As just one example, China's state broadcaster began describing Stanley Ho, a billionaire tycoon and Communist Party member who was linked by both the RCMP and the FBI to the triads and numerous illegal activities, as a "patriotic entrepreneur," a major honour.[5] But above all else, the CCP needed the gangsters and tycoons to help invade the West so it could sow social chaos through political and economic subversion without drawing too much attention to itself.

Initially, the US intelligence community believed Canada was probably nothing more than a testing ground for the Unholy Trinity. But analysts soon came to the view that something more nefarious was going on. "[R] egrettably, it is apparent that Canada has become the gateway for [China's Unholy Trinity] operations throughout North America," the document speaking about Dragon Lord concluded.

Looking back on these events today, they almost seem like the plot of an international spy thriller. But the threat posed by the Unholy Trinity was very real indeed, with huge national security implications for both Canada and the US. Brian McAdam, a foreign affairs officer at the Canadian high commission in Hong Kong from 1991 to 1993, knew this better than most. He alerted Ottawa that triad members were getting into Canada through the country's business immigration program.[6] The triads, McAdam said, got access to visas by bribing commission employees and infiltrating the Computer-Assisted Immigration Processing System (CAIPS), which Canada used to administer visa applications in overseas offices. When McAdam figured out what was going on, he diligently filed report after report—over thirty-two of them—documenting how known gangsters had been able to obtain real Canadian visas. He hoped to light a fire under the bureaucrats on Parliament Hill, but instead he was silenced.

"I immediately became hated with a passion," he told the *Ottawa Citizen* in 2016.[7] His co-workers viewed him as a threat to their jobs, and his bosses labelled him a racist. McAdam was ordered to destroy his reports and return to Ottawa. He thought he would be given a new position with Foreign Affairs, but instead he was forced into early retirement at the age of fifty-one.

Why was McAdam treated as a pariah rather than a whistleblower who was acting in the best interests of Canadians? For one thing, Ottawa was embarrassed by what he'd uncovered and terrified of the political damage that would ensue if his reports were made public. There were rumours that McAdam had unearthed more than just an isolated problem at a single foreign mission, and some believed he may have exposed a scheme that reached all the way to the highest office in the land.

Another factor was that McAdam's reports flew in the face of the notion of Canada as a country of immigrants—a narrative that Ottawa had been promoting to its citizens since the 1970s. This embrace of multiculturalism was viewed by the Chinese regime as a weakness that could be exploited to gain a foothold in the West.

## A TANGLED WEB

In the late 1990s, just a few years after McAdam sounded his warning, Canada's spy agency, the Canadian Security Intelligence Service (CSIS), colloquially known as the Sisters, together with Canada's Royal Canadian Mounted Police (RCMP), got into a major dispute over the findings of Project Sidewinder, a joint task force looking into criminal operations in Canada involving the triads and China's intelligence services. The dispute erupted when the Mounties accused the Sisters of altering the report to the point of inaccuracy, possibly under political pressure.[8] In a 1998 letter to the spy agency, RCMP Chief Superintendent Richard Proulx complained that "a substantial amount of information contained in the original project has been altered . . . and in some cases removed completely."[9]

To call the Sidewinder report explosive would be an understatement. It alleged that the triads and the intelligence agencies represented a major threat to Canada and were working "in tandem on smuggling, nuclear espionage and other operations," including intellectual property theft and money laundering. It also asserted that the triads, the tycoons, and the intelligence agencies "have learned [that] the quick way to gain influence is to provide finance to the main political parties," and that Canadian companies owned by Chinese entrepreneurs had contributed thousands of dollars to both the Liberals and the Conservatives.[10] The report said bluntly that because of China's influence over Canadian politicians and the economy, it "remains one of the greatest ongoing threats to Canada's national security."

But that report was apparently not what the power brokers in Ottawa wanted to see just as they were making gains in Canada's relationship with China. Most copies of the strongly worded 1997 draft were destroyed, and in 1999, a sanitized report was produced instead. (Even this friendlier-to-China version was classified.) In 2000, however, a copy of the original draft was leaked to *The Globe and Mail*, which also published correspondence that showed how the disagreement between the Sisters and the Mounties had played out.

After the Sidewinder report was made public, other news organizations began to amplify its concerns. One 2005 article noted that Sidewinder had presented as a case study the China International Trust Investment Company (CITIC), an enormous state-owned investment agency that had a subsidiary in Canada. "CITIC has spent about $500 million to buy a Canadian pulp mill, a petrochemical company, vast real estate, and hotels," the article said. At the time of the Sidewinder report, CITIC was considering buying the Alberta tar sands in partnership with Toronto-based Noranda Mines—a deal worth more than $7 billion.[11]

Writing in India's *Sunday Guardian*, defence analyst Cleo Paskal described the high-level connections between Canadian politicians and major state-owned Chinese corporations like CITIC.[12] CITIC, Paskal noted, was involved in the Canada China Business Council (CCBC), which was founded in the late 1970s by ten large and influential companies, including the Montreal-based Power Corporation, Bombardier, and SNC-Lavalin, with the goal of gaining access to the lucrative Chinese market. CCBC also helped CITIC and other Chinese companies learn how to invest in the West. Power Corp., Paskal pointed out, had strong ties to four former Canadian prime ministers: Pierre Trudeau, Brian Mulroney, Jean Chrétien, and Paul Martin.

The Sidewinder report noted that CITIC was only one of an estimated two hundred Canadian companies under Chinese control. "These business [*sic*] are to be found in myriad sectors of the economy, ranging from multinationals to banking, high technology and real estate . . . At first site [*sic*], these individual cases do not seem to be a great threat [to Canadian security]. It becomes, however, more disturbing when the ownership links between various sectors of Canadian enterprises are revealed." This is really where we start to see the mosaic theory of intelligence-gathering take shape. When we link together individual pieces that on their own might seem insignificant, a picture begins to emerge of the Chinese regime as a serious national security threat.

CITIC is one of those pieces. From its modest beginnings, it has grown into an enormous conglomerate with one of the largest pools of foreign assets in the world. You will hear CITIC mentioned many times in this book—it's connected to all kinds of people and companies. Author Jonathan Manthorpe, in his 2019 exposé *Claws of the Panda*, described it as "the premier gatekeeper of [Canada's] formal relations with China."[13] He laid out the connections among Power Corp., the Desmarais family, and China Asset Management Co. (hereafter China AMC), one of the largest investment management firms in China. Power Corp. and its subsidiaries own a 27.8 percent stake in China AMC. CITIC owns 62.2 percent.

Billionaire businessman Paul Desmarais was the chairman and controlling shareholder of Power Corp.—and truly a master at what the Chinese call *guanxi*, or furthering business interests through social networks and personal relationships with people in power. "Desmarais has been personally consulted by prime ministers on every major federal economic and constitutional initiative since the 1970s," wrote Konrad Yakabuski in *The Globe and Mail* in 2006. (Desmarais died in 2013.) "Most of the time, they've taken his advice."[14]

Power Corp. has ties to both Liberal and Conservative politicians, but it's literally a family affair for former prime minister Jean Chrétien, whose daughter married Paul Desmarais's son André. (Their own son Olivier is currently the chair of the CCBC.) And the ties to the Liberal Party don't end there. After he left politics, Pierre Trudeau sat on the company's board. Michael Pitfield, who was the powerful clerk of the Privy Council under Trudeau, was once the vice-chairman. Paul Martin bought Canada Steamship Lines from Power Corp. in the 1980s. Quebec Liberal premier Daniel Johnson, Chrétien senior advisers Eddie Goldenberg and John Rae, and prominent Liberal supporter Maurice Strong also have ties to the company.

You may be thinking, Why does this matter? Don't politicians of all stripes leverage their connections to land lucrative private-sector jobs once they leave office? What's different here, though, is the degree of influence Paul Desmarais was alleged to have had on those politicians while they were still in office. In *Claws of the Panda*, Manthorpe tells one story involving Richmond MP Raymond Chan, who had just been put in charge of Asia-Pacific affairs for the newly elected Chrétien government in 1993. Before he'd even unpacked his office, Chan was told to get himself to Montreal to meet with André Desmarais. Once there, he and his aides were given a tour of the opulent Power Corp. offices, with special attention paid to the many valuable paintings adorning the walls. Desmarais stopped in front of one painting and told Chan it was a gift from his good friend Li Peng. Chan, who was born in Hong Kong, knew very well that Li was the Chinese premier who'd declared martial law on May 20, 1989, leading to the Tiananmen Square massacre. Manthorpe's source told him that they'd left Power Corp. "feeling we'd been told in no uncertain terms where Canada's China policy was made."[15]

## A HIGH-PROFILE TAKEDOWN

We can't prove that the tangled relationships among Liberal Party politicians, influential Canadian businesspeople, and Chinese Communist Party leaders resulted in Brian McAdam losing his job or the Sidewinder report getting suppressed, but there are plenty of indications that powerful people in Ottawa were helping the CCP gain a foothold in Canada. This was never more evident than in the 2010 takedown of then-Canadian Security Intelligence Service (CSIS) director Richard Fadden.

Fadden set off a firestorm when he appeared on CBC's *The National* and spoke bluntly about alleged foreign influence over Canada's political class. "There are several municipal politicians in British Columbia," he said, "and in at least two provinces, there are ministers of the Crown who we think are under at least the general influence of a foreign government."[16] He declined to identify the politicians, the two provinces, or the foreign countries, but it seems clear from the rest of his remarks that he was thinking primarily about China. He talked about foreign governments gaining influence with people early in their careers—through universities and social clubs, exactly as China likes to do—to foster a connection to the homeland. "Before you know it," he said, "you're being asked to think about things in a slightly different way . . . If the individual becomes in a position to make decisions that affect the country or the province or a municipality, all of sudden decisions aren't taken on the basis of the public good but on the basis of another country's preoccupations."[17] When the CBC's Brian Stewart suggested these people were effectively agents of influence, Fadden said, "In a manner of speaking, yes."

The reaction from the Chinese Canadian community was swift and painted Fadden's remarks as racist. George Chow, a Vancouver city councillor and the former president of the Chinese Benevolent Association of Vancouver (CBA), asked, "What was Mr. Fadden trying to say? Is this a form of McCarthyism? Or is this a new method of catching spies by public innuendo? How is this going to affect me in the ballot boxes, being an ethnic Canadian of Chinese heritage? How is this going to affect Chinese Canadians getting jobs in government, research centres and industry in general?"[18] He demanded that Fadden issue a public apology. The CBA, meanwhile, held a press conference together with the pro-Beijing National Congress of Chinese Canadians (NCCC). "When a federal agency makes a serious mistake," declared David Choi, national executive chair of the National Congress of Chinese Canadians (NCCC) and founder of a Vancouver-area real estate company that brags of having sold over 6.3 billion worth of real estate in one year, "we should demand that it be remedied right away."[19][20]

The public pressure campaign worked. Fadden was hauled before a House of Commons public safety committee and told that his allegations had created a climate of suspicion and planted doubts about the integrity of elected officials and the Chinese Canadian community as a whole. The committee urged the minister of public safety to force Fadden to resign, saying the action was necessary to restore Canadians' confidence in their elected officials.[21]

In the end, Fadden was severely reprimanded for speaking out but not fired or forced to resign. Nevertheless, former intelligence officer Michel Juneau-Katsuya, author of the Sidewinder report, felt that Fadden had been thrown under the bus by Prime Minister Stephen Harper. The decision-makers in Ottawa had rejected McAdam's information and the Sidewinder report, and now they didn't want to hear what their own spy chief had to say either. It was clear that anyone who dared to speak out about the CCP and foreign influence would suffer consequences.

Close to a decade later, President Xi Jinping met with overseas Chinese representatives, including David Choi, at a meeting of the Chinese Overseas Friendship Association (COFA), which is a branch of the United Front

Work Department of the Central Committee of the Chinese Communist Party (UFWD).[22] [23]

By now the party had rapidly gained power and influence in Canada, not only within the highest levels of government, but across all three levels of government, nationwide, and in key institutions, including law enforcement. And why would the CCP want to influence politicians in Canada? Three key reasons stand out: China's quest for global superpower status; demand for resources to support its "dream of national rejuvenation;" and its determination to control the narrative with respect to Taiwan.

Canada's proximity and strong trading relationships with the US make it an attractive place to set up shop. Every time a CCP-aligned business or individual makes an inroad into Canada—whether through land acquisitions or in the field of politics, business, social services, policing, or education—it arguably supports the CCP's goal of becoming the world's superpower by 2049. Support from public opinion makers in Canada can also help China avoid criticism for its treatment of minorities, human right abuses, and territorial claims with respect to Taiwan. Maintaining strong ties to Overseas Chinese who may be able to influence Canadian politicians in support for China's annexation of Taiwan can only help the CCP in the court of public opinion.

Then there is Xi Jinping's dream of national rejuvenation, which calls for China to reclaim past glory and achieve system-wide improvements, including the infrastructural polish to go along with its emerging superpower status.

And what does all of this mean for Canada? It means targeting Canada's abundant natural resources extraction, capturing food supply lines, stealing R&D, undermining Canada's sovereignty, compromising cyber infrastructure, and more. It means a hybrid war in the West, the end game of which is to import China's unofficial version of the Belt and Road Initiative (BRI) into the Americas through Northern BC (Pacific Gateway).

A cornerstone of Xi's foreign policy, the Belt and Road Initiative includes major investments by the Chinese government in infrastructure development in more than 150 countries and international organizations. While the Americas are not officially included in the BRI, transportation routes from China to Canada could be used to cause chaos by way of strangleholds in the supply chain, potentially creating an advantage for China in any future conflicts with the West.

We know that China is operating a shadow government in Canada. The friendship and hometown groups that have already been established in Canada, and that have direct links to the United Front Work Department, are organized in such a way that the CCP is able to control the activities being conducted in Canada. These groups are closely aligned with the Chinese consulates and embassy, which assist in providing direction and support to the United Front.

The next logical step would be to establish special authority style areas, predominantly controlled by CCP members, who would monitor and direct Overseas Chinese living in Canada as permanent residents. In China's estimation, Canadian permanent residents from China are still Chinese citizens who fall under the CCP's authority. Efforts are already underway to secure special authority style districts by landmarking areas, such as Chinatowns, with legal protection through an international convention like UNESCO.[24] Chinatowns in North America were formed by Cantonese-speaking Chinese who built the historic Chinese Clan association and society buildings. The CCP's United Front has coopted these groups and is using them as cover to advance Beijing's interests.

The CCP's goal with Overseas Chinese is to form an unbreakable bond to the motherland that will last for generations. They are cultivating this attachment with the installation of overseas service centers, police stations, and the infiltration of hometown associations. Hand in hand with this is the amplification of anti-Asian sentiment as a tool to further reinforce this bond.

The suggestion is that Overseas Chinese will never truly be safe or accepted in North America. Chinatowns are a symbol of the ongoing, enduring resilience of the motherland, and thus the need for special protection and preservation of cultural and heritage landmarks.[25]

As with anything the CCP has its handprint on, we need to look past the surface—past a bid by UFWD entities to seek a heritage designation. In a later chapter titled "The Rise of the Puppet Mayor at Ground Zero," we examine how a UNESCO designation is a backdoor way for the CCP to legitimize containment of an area inside another country that can eventually be turned into a special administrative region, like Hong Kong, or a ward area (electoral subdivision) that is ultimately controlled by the CCP behind the scenes.[26]

China is well on its way to achieving all of this, with the help of people serving the party in Canada, and via a complex matrix of interlocking facilitators and strategies.[27] That includes liberal use of the carrot and stick method, often as a method of training elected officials in Canada. Comply and you'll be assured of special favours, votes, and donations to political campaigns; don't comply—or worse, resist— and you will be targeted.

Conservative MP Michael Chong drew the stick. An outspoken critic of Beijing's treatment of Uyghur Muslims, Chong and his family in Hong Kong became targets of alleged intimidation plot. As of May, 2023, the fallout from this confrontation included two consular expulsions— one Chinese, one Canadian—some heated rhetoric from the Chinese Ambassador to Canada, and an agreement by the House of Commons that a committee should be struck to study the alleged targeting of Chong and his family.[28] [29]

The Canadian government responded cautiously, and with some trepidation, to calls that the Chinese diplomats involved in the plot to intimidate Chong and his family be expelled from Canada. Minister of Foreign Affairs Mélanie Joly reacted by saying, "It's about [Chong], but it's also about the interests of the country, and as foreign minister I have to make sure that it is the right decision. And it will be the right decision," she told CBC chief political correspondent Rosemary Barton.[30]

China was acting like a bully again. This time it was the Chinese Ambassador to Canada, H.E. Cong Peiwu, who issued a harsh rebuke against the allegations, warning Canada, via China's official website in this country, to "immediately stop this self-directed political farce, not go further down the wrong and dangerous path." Using ominous language, the ambassador warned that, "Should the Canadian side continue to make provocations, China will play along every step of the way until the very end.[31]

This same May 4 statement was still the main message displayed on the embassy's website on May 17, more than a week after Canada's May 8, 2023 decision to expel Chinese consular official Wei Zhao and declare him "persona non grata." Joly announced that she took the decision to expel Wei Zhao "after careful consideration of all factors at play," and warned that Canada "will not tolerate any form of foreign interference in our internal affairs. Diplomats in Canada have been warned that if they engage in this type of behaviour, they will be sent home."[32]

## TIPPING POINT

If you are a politician in Canada, you are either for or against China. There is no middle ground. If you support China, you can count on votes and financial support; if you take a stand against China, at best you might be the subject of a smear campaign.

Former CSIS director Richard Fadden never revealed who the compromised politicians were back in 2010, but rumours were rife within the Chinese diaspora.

Over the next decade, as politicians came and went, some observers in the intelligence community were increasingly convinced that the CCP was engaging in foreign interference and that state actors were conducting hostile activities on Canadian soil.

The CCP was consolidating ethnic voting power in large cities in eastern and western Canada. This suited Canadian Prime Minister Justin Trudeau and his Liberal party just fine. All they had to do was rubber stamp the candidates that the CCP chose to run in key ridings, and use United Front proxies that represent these ridings, who are embedded in the party, to rubber stamp the nomination, according to agents who worked for the Sisters (CSIS).

United Front agents, skilled in sharp power tactics designed to manipulate diplomatic policies by influencing and undermining Canada's political system from sea to sea, would do the rest to get them elected by the Overseas Chinese community.

Canada wasn't alone. The same thing was happening in the US, as suggested by the political career of Democratic California Rep. Judy Chu, who was called out for her ties to alleged Chinese intelligence groups. According to a Daily Caller News Foundation report (DCNF), "Chu conferred an honorary position with two organizations linked to the United Front Work Department (UFWD), a Chinese Communist Party (CCP) influence operation agency identified as an 'intelligence agency' in 2016." One of these organizations was the United Front led Overseas Friendship Association (COFA). Chu also attended the Xi Jinping event that David Choi went to, sitting only five seats beside him, as indicated by a photo taken at the event.[33] [34]

As China's wealth and power have expanded globally, its strategy to influence officials on both sides of the border, as well as the Canadian and American elite, has become more sophisticated. This is often done with the help of politicians who are working on behalf of the interests of China under the pretext of trade relations.

According to Bethany Allen-Ebrahimian, author of *Beijing Rules*, "both the Chinese government and Chinese companies, often with close state ties, have retained lobbying and public-relations firms in the U.S. Beltway, in some cases hiring U.S. officials as personal lobbyists."[35]

This book exposes how the CCP has done the same thing in Canada and more, infiltrating the highest offices in the land and reshaping the nation from within. We present real case studies that reveal the nexus between the CCP and all three levels of government in Canada, law enforcement, and key institutions.

This book also looks closely at espionage operations and reveals how the United Front Work Department, through NGOs and hometown associations, installs pro-CCP candidates who are automatically elected in ridings where the party has a concentration of power.

Through careful reporting based on work by a team of researchers, we identify United Front agents and take a deep, hard look into operations they are running, including insight into foreign information manipulation and interference (FIMI), where we look at the "behaviour of an actor."[36]

We also examine how large donations from philanthropists with ties to United Front organizations shape political campaigns, and we expose how Canadian universities and research facilities are being taken over by CCP entities.[37]

We take a hard look at the nexus between the CCP's United Front activity in Canada and their ties to tycoons, and their ties to projects that are covers for a slow infiltration and installation of Xi Jinping's unofficial Belt and Road in Canada. And we investigate those individuals who are working for China inside Canada, helping to recruit the next generation of talent for the motherland.

## THE CASE OF RICHARD LEE

One of the stories that we helped to break and that brings to light the CCP's infiltration and influence in Canada is the strange story of Richard Lee.

Born in Zhongshan, China, Richard Lee immigrated to Canada in 1971 and quickly became a superstar politician in Vancouver. Lee was a well-known, well-liked politician who had a quiet disposition. He was a constant fixture at both pro-Hong Kong and pro-CCP events over the years, but so were a lot of other politicians. Elected to the Legislative Assembly in 2001, he climbed to the rank of deputy speaker, the first MLA of Asian descent to ever serve in that role in BC. He had planned to run federally for Justin Trudeau's Liberal Party in 2019 but decided not to seek the nomination when his wife became ill.[38]

In January 2019, Lee wrote a letter to Chrystia Freeland, then the foreign affairs minister, and cc'd to Justin Trudeau and Jody Wilson-Raybould, the attorney general. The letter described a trip that Lee had made to China with his wife in 2015. When they arrived at the Shanghai airport, Lee told Freeland, they were detained by Chinese authorities. He and his wife were separated, Lee's personal cell phone and his government-issued BlackBerry were confiscated, and he was forced to reveal his password for the BlackBerry. After eight hours, he was told that he was guilty of endangering China's national security, and that he and his wife would have to leave the country immediately. "It could happen to anyone," Lee later told Global News. "If someone in Canada does something not to China's liking, your visa will be cancelled. It's a serious situation."[39]

After Lee returned to Canada, he informed Rich Coleman, the BC minister of public safety and solicitor general and also a former RCMP officer, that he had been improperly detained. Lee felt he had been targeted because every June 4, he would participate in candle-lighting ceremonies outside the Chinese consulate in Vancouver to commemorate Tiananmen Square. But Coleman ignored his complaint, Lee claimed, and he decided not to press the issue. In December 2018, however, when Michael Kovrig and Michael Spavor were jailed in China in retaliation for the arrest of Huawei CFO Meng Wanzhou, he finally felt motivated to tell his story to Canadians.

By this time, three years had passed. Lee claimed that in addition to his letter to Freeland, he'd also written to China's then ambassador to Canada, Lu Shaye, to no avail. When he got nowhere following official channels, he reached out to us to see if we could help him get his story to a wider audience. We contacted journalist Sam Cooper, who ran the story on Global and got it the national attention it deserved.

But still, questions remained. What was on Lee's government-issued BlackBerry, and what happened to it when it was in the hands of the CCP? Did events unfold the way he said they did, or was he being leveraged in some way? And what was to be made of that three-year gap in reporting the incident? After Lee's story went national, the Sisters contacted us through a pre-existing channel of communication and told us we were wrong to portray him as a victim.

Which side of the fence was Richard Lee really on? As is so often the case where China is concerned, each answer just raised more questions. And determining who should be doubted and who can be trusted in a world full of clandestine operations run by sprawling spy agencies is far more challenging than most people realize.

# CHAPTER 2

# UNITED FRONT 101

## THE CCP'S FOOT SOLDIERS IN THE HYBRID WAR AGAINST THE WEST

To understand the impact China's influence and infiltration campaigns are having in Canada, we have to understand the power dynamics among the different CCP-aligned groups in this country and where they fit into the overall structure of the United Front network.

At the top of the pyramid, of course, is the Embassy of the People's Republic of China (PRC) in Ottawa. This is the nerve centre, and all information and directives flow from there to PRC consulates in Vancouver, Calgary, Toronto, and Montreal. They issue orders to provincial United Front commanding-level organizations, who in turn issue directives to subordinate hometown unit associations.

United Front hometown unit associations are generally tied to cities, towns, and provinces back in China, and they're typically run by prominent community leaders who have personal or family connections to the region each association represents.

---

PHOTO: Prime Minister Trudeau attends "Cash for Access" event at Miaofei Pan's house. Pan's home was the target of arson and gun shots at his house.

Some of the Cantonese hometown associations have been around since the 1800s and were at one time legitimate social or cultural organizations, but they have been taken over by pro-CCP factions over the last couple of decades as long-time members have aged out. Co-opting well established organizations gives a veneer of credibility to the pro-CCP activities these organizations are now engaged in. Canadian politicians think they are dealing with local hometown associations from the past, when really they are dealing with groups tied to the powerful United Front Work Department of the CCP. There are also newly formed groups—mainly Mandarin speaking associations—being added on a regular basis.

According to Chen Yonglin, a political affairs officer at China's consulate in Sydney who defected to Australia in 2005, most of these new groups were founded in the aftermath of the Tiananmen Square massacre, when China wanted to break Western sanctions. This confirmed what we'd learned from agents connected with Operation Dragon Lord.

In effect, we can think of the entire network as a sort of spy superhighway. Information and orders travel from the PRC government to its embassy in Ottawa and down through the ranks from there. At the same time, information collected on the ground is going in the opposite direction—up the ranks from the local to the provincial to the national level, and even back overseas to China. It's a kind of secret shadow government operating inside our borders, and it's an arrangement that is replicated in countries all around the world.

So what happens on a consular level? At a glance, the four PRC consulates in Canada, located in Vancouver, BC; Calgary, AB; Toronto, ON; Montreal, QC, are engaged in the same activities as any other consulate: issuing visas, replacing lost or stolen passports, providing information on local laws and regulations, and so on.[1] But they also function as a point of contact for overseas students attending university or conducting research, as well as for businesspeople and investors looking to trade or do deals in Canada. This creates opportunities to collect intelligence or issue orders.

## CANADA'S UNITED FRONT NETWORK SETUP

Canada is the world's second-largest country after Russia, stretching across 3.8 million square miles (9.9 million square kilometres), which, according to Canada FAQ, means that "the UK could fit into Canada over 40 times."

Canada is a top global producer of oil and gas, minerals and metals, forestry and fish. It's so vast that it is surrounded by three oceans—the Pacific, the Atlantic, and the Arctic—and its massive, sprawling coastline stretches 243,772 kilometres (151,473 miles) long [2]

It also has the world's longest undefended border, where trees, mountains, lakes and farmland are the only thing that separates Canada from China's reviled enemy, the USA.

In Canada, practically speaking, the United Front network is largely broken down into two distinct east and west centers that we call hubs. In eastern Canada (which for UFWD purposes consists mainly of the Greater Toronto Area), the hub ranges from Toronto to Markham, which is a diverse city of about 300,000 people, almost half of whom identify as Chinese or Chinese Canadian. Thousands of miles away on the Pacific Coast, the western Canada hub encompasses Vancouver, Richmond, Burnaby, and the Tri-Cities (Coquitlam, Port Coquitlam, and Port Moody). Both hubs have created new media outlets to help support state media and provide a steady stream of local propaganda that is easily communicated across the nation.

Our investigation started with the United Front in the western Canada hub in Vancouver, British Columbia, where we look into two CCP-affiliated organizations that are part of the United Front network in Canada.

On the street, the People's Republic of China consulate is referred to as the Big House. It gives orders to a handful of commanding-level organizations, which, in turn, give orders to hundreds of unit associations under them.

One of the key commanding-level organizations in the western hub is the Canadian Alliance of Chinese Associations (CACA). Established in 2008, CACA is located outside of Vancouver in Richmond, BC. Richmond is home to the largest Chinese diaspora in North America.

CACA isn't just an ex-pat community group. They maintain strong ties with Beijing and municipal governments across China. Its main goal is to build people's loyalty and sense of connection to the Communist Party of China, and its own website has, at times, promoted its involvement in "various activities of the Overseas Chinese Affairs Office (OCAO) and the All-China Federation of Returned Overseas Chinese (ACFROC).[3]

CACA is actually an umbrella group for more than a hundred hometown unit associations catering to immigrants from a variety of regions in mainland China who speak Mandarin. Each unit association is comprised of strong personal or historical ties to provinces, autonomous regions, and cities back in China. The Canada Shandong Chinese Business Association, for example, is made up of members who come from, or have ties to, Shandong, China's second most populous province. If you were born in the city of Hefei, you would likely join the Canadian Anhui Folks Association. Someone who was born in Jinjiang would likely belong to the Quanzhou Friendship Society of Canada. Larger and more prosperous regions in China have hometown associations that have their own chambers of commerce and industry associations attached to them. Such is the case with Quanzhou Friendship Society of Canada and its chamber, the North America Chinese Alliance of Commerce.[4]

The leaders are not your garden variety communists. You have to have money to be a leader and tight connections to the party to even be considered a candidate for leadership. Some even have organized crime connections and then there is the political nexus weaved throughout it all. For example, the double-homicide of a leader with Quanzhou Friendship Society of Canada, Wu Shumin and her partner, soccer pro, Sun Yinging. Wu Shumin was a frequent attendee at Quanzhou Friendship Society events where she hop-knobbed with high-net-worth individuals and the politically connected. In the spring of 2022, Wu and her partner were gunned down inside their white BMW outside their $7 million dollar mansion in the affluent Point Grey neighbourhood of Vancouver. The case is sill open.

The Wenzhou Friendship Society, which operates out of a large club-house, also made national headlines in 2022 for allegedly operating a Chinese police station set up by the China's Wenzhou Public Security Bureau, under the Ministry of Public Security (MPS). A Spanish organization known as Safeguard Defenders said there was evidence of at least 102 "Chinese Overseas Police Service Centres" in fifty-three countries, including the one in Vancouver, operated by the Wenzhou group, and three in Toronto, under the auspices of Nanzhou.[5]

Another important commanding-level organization in the Vancouver area is the Chinese Benevolent Association (CBA).[6] Located in Vancouver's Chinatown, it was established in 1889 by immigrants from rural areas of southern China who'd come to Canada to build the Canadian Pacific Railway. It caters to Cantonese speakers and those speaking other dialects from the region. The CBA is a great example of a legitimate organization that has been co-opted by the United Front. While it once advocated for railway workers who faced discrimination and dangerous working conditions, today the CBA is affiliated with business and trade organizations in Guangdong, Hong Kong, and Macau, and it represents fraternal and secret societies, like the Hongmen, a Freemason-like organization (Tongs and Triads). They also run an Overseas Service Center, community meeting center, and a Chinese police station, independent of the Vancouver police.

On the surface, the CBA may look like any other historical community group, in that it hosts a wide range of benign-seeming cultural events, including the Chinatown parade, and fundraises for issues of concern to members. But these activities are mostly just opportunities for United Front supporters to wine, dine, and influence Canadian elected officials and forge relationships with influential Chinese business tycoons that will ultimately, indirectly, lead to policy change that favours Beijing.

The way to look at these two commanding-level groups is like this: The mainland (Mandarin-speaking) hometown organizations under the Canadian Alliance of Chinese Associations (CACA) are newer and connected directly to the CCP and the PRC police and intelligence agencies, whereas the Cantonese organizations are mainly tied to influential Chinese business tycoons. They are all about building and maintaining vast business empires. But they need the CCP to maintain and manage their empires abroad, which is where the CBA comes in. They function as the government face representing their business interests here in Canada.

## MEMBERSHIP HAS ITS PRIVILEGES . . . AND ITS OPPRESSION

As we said earlier, to become a leader of a hometown unit association you need to have money. Money equals prestige in China, and the more prestigious the leadership, the more attention the embassy and local consulate will pay to the group.

Most leaders of hometown associations are wealthy elites with businesses back in China controlled by the State. We have identified many of these leaders. Many of them are owners of pharmaceutical manufacturing corporations and real estate developers back in China, which rely heavily on government approval.

The purpose of the unit associations, beyond sharing a common bond connected to their hometowns, is to help the motherland influence operations overseas and to collectively wield the CCP's influence and power abroad over political parities and elected officials They are also used to control overseas diaspora and their families and business associates back home in China.

It's a way to herd people into manageable groups that local PRC consulates can control. Control can come by way of state contracts for their businesses back in China or punitive actions against families and friends in China, if they don't do what they are ordered to do.

Unit organizations are also used to build camaraderie among Chinese people living overseas who are marshalled into engaging in community activities, in Canada, on behalf of the motherland, and who are assigned tasks to do for the local Chinese consulate.

We see this often with photo-ops of donations by these groups to causes that bring together local elected officials, prominent business persons, and representatives of the Chinese consulate.

There are plenty of non-elite CCP members in Canada who are not in any visible leadership role within these hometown associations who operate in the shadows as part of a wider network of underground CCP. These are people who work and live in Canada, building and establishing legitimate business operations, who just happen to be active members of The Chinese Communist Party (CCP).

Individuals like Ding Yongqin, also known as Mr. Peanuts Man, purveyor of mixed nuts and member of the Northwest Benevolent Association. An organization founded by Burnaby City councillor, James Wang, along with the grandson of a patriotic People's Liberation Army general.

We spoke with Ding to ask what is expected of a CCP member living overseas in Canada? Ding was evasive, but we could speculate based on his career path and long history with the CCP that started with membership in the Communist Youth League. Ding started his career with an affiliate of the State owned, China Resources Corporation (in the Gansu Province) exporting broad beans, lentils, black melon seeds, fennel seeds, and dried bracken.

Consider this as a possible reason why the CCP might call on Mr. Peanuts Man from time to time—Food Security.

China is the world's second largest economy with a population at around 1.4 billion, a fifth of all humankind. With memories of food scarcity and starvation during the Cultural Revolution, the CCP would have to ensure food security for its people if it was to keep Xi Jinping's great rejuvenation for the nation and Chinese dream alive. To control the population, the CCP would need to deliver to its people so that they would not rebel. Now multiply the thousand of CCP members living in Canada, involved in all walks of life and careers. "It's like a cult—once you are in you can't easily get out," said one of our confidential sources with intimate knowledge of how the CCP operates. "Part of what makes it hard to leave is that CCP membership is very much wrapped up around money," he told us. Our source explained that the party takes a percentage of a member's salary and pay in exchange for prestigious titles and lucrative government contracts. In return for this, CCP Members are also expected to be loyal to the party and to answer it's call which could include anything from the illegal to legitimate business or engaging in propaganda related to donating to hometown causes, disasters, and overseas missions.

## CASE STUDY—OPPORTUNITY IN CRISIS

Lorna Fandrich is a long-term resident of Lytton—a village of about 250 residents, located in the Fraser Canyon in southern British Columbia—and the founder and curator of the Lytton Chinese History Museum, started in 2017.

Despite its tiny population and relative remoteness, Lytton has played a noteworthy role in BC's history, as home to Indigenous settlements, gold rush miners, a trading post, European settlers, and Chinese railway workers. In the 1880s, Chinese railway workers were brought by ship from both California and China to start building the Canadian Pacific Railway (CPR) from the West Coast at the same time that European laborers began building the eastern section from the East Coast. More than 17,000 Chinese railway workers arrived to build the railway through the Fraser Canyon.[7][8]

Despite the remote location, China's top diplomat made the trek up the windy road through the scenic Fraser Canyon to visit Lorna Fandrich's Chinese History Museum in 2020.

The following year, a wildfire destroyed much of the town, including the Chinese History Museum and all 1,600 artifacts housed within it.[9]

Officials concluded that the fire was likely caused by human activity.[10]

This tragedy and the events that followed bring to mind the quote by Chinese General and strategist Sun Tzu, who famously said, "In the midst of chaos, there is also opportunity."

In the aftermath of the fire, the United Front came to town, by way of the newly formed Canada Chinese Loving Volunteer Association and Foundation (CCLVAF)—an organization set up by Wei Renmin, a big-time tycoon real estate developer in China who lives in Canada. Wei started both the Canada Chinese Loving Volunteer Association and Snow Goose Media, two entities that share the same address in Richmond, BC. The CCLAP donated $50,000 to the rebuilding of the museum, with Snow Goose Media on hand to capture the cheque handing ceremony. But it wasn't Wei or the CCLAF who donated the hefty sum to rebuild Lytton's Chinese History Museum. According to Lorna Fandrich, the money came from the members of the commanding-level United Front organization, CACA.[11] [12]

Lorna confirmed that she got more than just money to rebuild the museum building. She also received approximately 500 artifacts donated by the members of the Canada Chinese Loving Volunteer Association, some of which included items from Hong Kong and Taiwan. What's more, the Chinese Consulate in BC also donated funds to purchase artifacts.

But these donations appeared to come with strings.

"I wanted to stay out of the politics of Hong Kong and Taiwan," Lorna told us. She believed that any artifact from after 1940 had the potential to cause controversy by triggering discussion of Taiwan. Moreover, she said she was advised that she should keep the time period that the museum covers to between 1858 and 1940. When we asked her why, she said it was to avoid political discussion or recognition of Taiwanese independence, which took place in 1945.[13]

Wittingly or unwittingly, by going along with this advice, Lorna Fandrich was playing directly into the hands of the CCP.

Restricting their collection to items from before 1940 meant that all artifacts, including the donated pieces from Taiwan and Hong Kong, would automatically be Chinese. At first this sounds like a small concession, but such a compromise came with a significant impact. At a minimum, it effectively erases the whole issue of Taiwanese sovereignty from the museum's offerings.

Taiwanese sovereignty is a complex and highly contested matter. Whereas the PRC claims that Taiwan is or should be part of China, history clearly shows that Taiwan is basically the original Republic of China (ROC), and has been since the end of World War II. Technically, the ROC could claim mainland China as its own, since it defeated the Qing Dynasty and controlled the entire region. The People's Republic of China was formed after the ROC, and if not for Japan invading China, the ROC could still be in control of the mainland.

Taiwanese independence is really a matter of the realization of its identity by other nations and not the act of fighting to be independent. It has been independent since the end of World War II, when Japan lost and ceded the land (formerly known as Formosa) back to the ROC (a political party), which became known as Taiwan.

So when the owner of a small museum in Lytton, BC allows a local proxy for the People's Republic of China to determine the dates and focus of its exhibits in a way that treats Taiwanese artifacts as Chinese, it adds to the sense that Taiwanese culture is being coopted, changed, and destroyed by the CCP. The People's Republic of China is doing this with other cultures as well, like the Mongols, who conquered old world China. The PRC forced France to cancel an exhibit of Genghis Khan and forbade them to use the term Khan or face severe penalties. As of this year, France has decided to defy China and will display the exhibit in Nantes in October of 2023.[14]

Back in Lytton, Lorna Fandrich showed no such resistance, or even any real awareness of the ways her Chinese History Museum exhibits were being shaped by the wishes and directives of the CCP. She readily admitted that she was offered interpretation services for free, and did not appear concerned about the fact that accepting this offer would allow the United Front to shape the narrative according to CCP-approved versions of events.

The main purpose behind wanting to control the narrative has a lot to do with Xi Jinping's great rejuvenation of the nation, which entails restoring China's once-great reputation in the world, while also achieving the so-called peaceful reunification of Taiwan.

CACA members were staunch supporters of the party's plan to take over Taiwan—a plan that the CCP cast in terms of reunification, not annexation, despite Taiwan's having been part of the old Republic of China and not the PRC. CACA made its position clear in a press release that said, "We overseas Chinese in Canada resolutely support the position of the Chinese government and fight resolutely against all external forces that try to split and destroy China's unity."[15]

China has also denied historical records regarding Tiananmen, the Hong Kong democracy protests, and the detainment of Uyghur Muslims in internment camps—all topics that could conceivably be aired and analysed in exhibits at Lytton's Chinese Historical Museum, were it free to explore these issues.

For a sense of how these views can trickle down into the narratives that are presented by museums, we turned to Ivy Li, former chief designer at the Royal Ontario Museum in Toronto. Ivy Li thinks there is a huge problem with the CCP funding Canadian Museums—something they are doing at an alarming rate.

"Museums are an important part of public education," she told us. "They are usually seen as trusted sources for historical records. If the CCP can control or influence the contents, presentations, and interpretations of our museums, they can re-write history and whitewash their dictatorial aggression to democracy."

She also believes that the Lytton Museum rebuild is just a small part of a much larger plan by the CCP to rewrite both China's and Canada's history.

Lorna acknowledged that when she retires, in the not too distant future, the artifacts will likely be shipped to Vancouver's new Chinese Canadian Museum. Was this also part of the bigger plan—to install artifacts in a private small-town museum with the CCP's version of facts so that when they are ultimately given to other, more prominent museums, the CCP's version becomes authentic? An ingenious long game could easily involve using small museums, like the Lytton Chinese History Museum, to gain access to larger ones, in order to gradually influence and saturate Western society's museums with CCP-approved narratives.

During the public consultation meetings for the new Chinese Canadian Museum, a timeline of significant historical events was presented to the public for feedback. There was no mention of the Hong Kong 1967 riot, which was directly linked to the CCP's cultural revolution, and which resulted in a large influx of immigrants to Canada. Also missing was the 1984 Sino-British joint declaration, the 1989 Tiananmen Massacre, and the 1997 Hong Kong handover—all events that directly and indirectly impacted Canadian immigration history. In fact, the entire 1990s was missing, even though there was a surge of immigrants from Hong Kong pouring into Canada at that time, driven by fear of the CCP after the Tiananmen Massacre. The only reference made to the wave of immigration from Hong Kong and Taiwan was via a mention of the 1985 Investment Canada Act.

We asked Viviane Gosselin, who, with Denise Fong and Dr. Henry Yu, co-curated *A Seat at the Table: Chinese Immigration and British Columbia*, the inaugural project of the Chinese Canadian Museum, how issues concerning Tiananmen Square and the Goddess of Democracy would be portrayed in future museum exhibitions. The University of British Columbia permitted the installation of a replica of the Goddess of Democracy statue in 1990, based on the same statue created during the 1989 Tiananmen Square protests. At the time, Bill Yee who was president of the CBA, wrote a letter to UBC president David Strangway suggesting that "for anyone else outside [of] China to get involved in those kinds of decisions really gets close to interfering with another country's affairs." Bill later became a director of the museum until allegations that he denied the Uyghur genocide in Xinjiang came to light prompted his removal over concerns that the museum could be politicized by individuals sympathetic or under the influence of the Chinese Communist Party. In response to our question, Viviane said, "history is fluid and can change depending on the views of that particular time."[16] While this may be strictly true, it also smacks of revisionism, and raises the likelihood that the Chinese Canadian Museum is susceptible to influence and rewriting China's past based off of CCP ideology.

Yet another facet of the CCP's strategy to reshape Canadian historical narrative using political clout and by infiltrating museum boards and advisory committees has to do with equating the Chinese Exclusion Act from 100 years ago with the modern-day foreign agent registry that has been proposed in the wake of foreign influence on Canada's electoral process.[17] [18]

Raising money for causes in Canada in order to reshape narratives actually makes sense if you think about it from a hybrid warfare perspective. But why would a hometown association leader raise money for his or her hometown province or city? The answer is simple: In keeping with the great dream of Chinese unification and expansion, the CCP expects all Overseas Chinese to contribute to the safety and prosperity of their home towns back in China.

This is because United Front work is tied to China's social credit system, which we discuss later in the book. If you have money and want to keep it, you have to stay on the right side of China's ruling communist party.

The hometown unit associations are where the real wheeling and dealing goes on. Individual organizations compete with one another for fundraising dollars, political influence, and the attention of people higher up the ranks—all with the encouragement of the Big House.

In some ways, the structure of these groups resembles a military hierarchy, and the camaraderie and competitiveness are similar to what you would find in an army unit.

Only Overseas Chinese join these hometown unit associations, but not everyone joins for the same reasons. There are those who become involved because they feel tied to people with a shared language and life experience. One woman told us that she joined her local unit when she first moved to Canada because she was lonely and didn't speak English. (We later discovered that she is a high-ranking United Front agent.)

Then there are those who join these groups for the social capital, or *guanxi*. They are driven more by the desire to make business connections and build mutually beneficial relationships than by ideology. It's also the responsibility of all Chinese—including those living overseas—to serve the motherland. The penalty for failing to do that is severe.

Finally, there are those who are ideologically driven. William, a source who has gathered a great deal of intelligence from inside these groups, told us that within each group, there is always a cadre of hard-core nationalists who are involved in everything. He suspects these individuals are United Front agents working on behalf of the motherland, but some could simply be amateur patriots. They're often very wealthy and would have a lot to lose if they failed to toe the party line.

Mixing among the regular members are penetration agents—more commonly known as moles or sleeper agents. These people are usually affiliated with the Ministry of State Security (MSS)—basically Chinese intelligence and secret police—or the People's Liberation Army (PLA). We know of at least one member of a unit association who is a former MSS officer—he claims to be retired—but most penetration agents keep any such affiliation to themselves and just blend in with the crowd. It is common for the MSS in Canada to carry out covert influence operations without telling embassies or consulates what its agents are doing, to allow for plausible deniability.

## PROFILE OF A COMMANDING-LEVEL UNITED FRONT LEADER

Miaofei Pan is the former president of CACA and founder of the Wenzhou Friendship Society. A wealthy real estate developer who moved to Canada a decade ago, he is a fascinating case study in what it's like to be the leader of a commanding-level United Front organization and then fall from grace.

Pan owns several multimillion-dollar homes in upscale Vancouver neighbourhoods, and was at one time so well connected that he hosted a fundraiser for Justin Trudeau in one of his homes.[19] But more recently, that home had been targeted by gunfire, and a second home he owned in Shaughnessy was badly damaged in a fire that city inspectors determined was arson.[20] We reached out to Pan after his garage was damaged by a Molotov cocktail in a third strange incident—he insisted all three were warnings.

It is unheard of for a Chinese tycoon to invite Western journalists into his private home, but that's what happened with Pan. We sent our Project Mosaic team to interview him and invited Sam Cooper of Global News, who was, at the time, researching his book, *Wilful Blindness: How a Network of Narcos, Tycoons and CCP Agents Infiltrated the West*. He joined us remotely along with anti-CCP blogger Benson Gao, who called in from China, while Louis Huang was there to translate.

We wanted to ask Pan what had caused his fall from grace and if he believed he was being targeted by the United Front. He surprised us by accusing Benson Gao of masterminding it all. Gao, he said, was using WeChat to paint him as a disreputable businessman with a string of bad dealings and lawsuits back in China, including one involving a man named Qibo Wang. He (Qibo Wang) co-founded the Chinese Canadian Society for Political Engagement (CCSPE), a non-profit whose goal is to elect Chinese Canadians to political office and bring attention to issues affecting Chinese expats.[21]

Pan had apparently concluded that Gao was some kind of social media hired gun who had been engaged by Qibo Wang to discredit Pan after a business deal went sour. Pan claimed that because of Gao, people who had once held him in high regard now treated him as a pariah who attracted bad *feng shui*. He went so far as to file a defamation suit against Gao. He won that suit, but the judge awarded him only a single dollar in damages and noted that many of Gao's most incendiary claims about Pan did seem to be true.[22]

As we looked on, Pan and Gao appeared to want a rematch, with Louis Huang interpreting. The two had a lively discussion in Mandarin that often returned to the fundraiser, or cash-for-access event, with Trudeau. That event became a lightning rod in the debate over foreign influence of high-level politicians in Canada.[23] At the time, the Trudeau government was reviewing a $1 billion bid by China's Anbang Group, a stakeholder in failed HQ Vancouver,[24] to buy a chain of BC retirement homes. Soon after the deal went through, the CCP seized control of Anbang.[25]

Maybe, we thought, the United Front didn't like all the negative media attention that Pan's fundraiser had attracted. Had he agreed to talk to us because he wanted to set the record straight? Or was he trying to use us to send a message to the CCP? We knew that the party sometimes used United Front agents to spread conspiracy theories and even threaten people, all in an attempt to discredit critics and bring Overseas Chinese into line. Maybe this was Pan's way of trying to call off the dogs?

One thing that did seem clear was that Pan appeared to be trying to restore his reputation by going on a spending spree in his hometown by donating millions to upgrade his hometown's infrastructure.[26] It's not uncommon for people who've fallen into disfavour to try to spend their way back into the CCP's good graces. One way is to invest back into their ancestral hometown back in China as part of the Great Rejuvenation of the Nation. In fact, this is what many people feel Guo Wengui was doing by funding the protests in front of Benson Gao's home. On the face of it, these seemed to be anti-CCP protests financed by a man who claimed he was being politically persecuted by China. But in fact, the protests targeted a CCP critic, not a supporter, which is the kind of manoeuvre the party tends to like. Louis Huang even told a syndicated reporter that he believed Guo had targeted Benson Gao to curry favour with the Chinese government. "Other Chinese dissidents in the United States have reported similar attacks on them by [Guo's] group members," the story noted, "whom Huang alleges are paid to protest at all hours of the day."[27][28]

## STRENGTHENING CANADA'S UNITED FRONT NETWORK

In September 2022, Yang Shu took over from Tong Xiaoling as head of the PRC consulate in Vancouver. It was an unusually low-key changing of the guards, with no propaganda-filled goodbye party to send Tong on her way. Instead, she slipped off quietly after almost five years of sometimes contentious service—a tenure that coincided with the Meng Wanzhou case, the COVID outbreak, accusations of election interference, and rising tensions over Taiwan and the plight of the Uyghurs. Veteran China watcher Charles Burton noted that Tong had been "exceptionally effective" in furthering the United Front's campaign to exacerbate social tensions, undermine the media, and influence political figures.[29] "Her departure is probably something that we would welcome, as this kind of United Front work engagement of people, particularly persons of Chinese origin who have Canadian citizenship, is not really consistent with normal diplomatic functions," Burton told a Glacier Media journalist, in an interview before Tong's successor had been named. He said he hoped that she would be replaced by someone "more oriented towards diplomatic activities . . . and not [some]one who has such an explicitly political role in seeking to divert the loyalty of Canadians towards a foreign country."

Burton's hopes turned out to be misplaced. Instead of a non-partisan old-school diplomat, Canadians got Yang Shu, who was very much cut from the same cloth as Tong. One of his first public events as consul general was a ceremony to mark China's National Day, which is the anniversary of the CCP's founding of the People's Republic of China.[30] The event, which was attended by at least one local city councillor, had been organized by CACA, the controlling-level United Front organization.

But even before Yang Shu arrived in Vancouver, the groundwork was being laid for a new United Front strategy that would see the eastern and western hubs and their commanding-level organizations work closer together with unified objectives, to create an even stronger network in Canada.[31] [32] Among other things, this new strategy called for the United Front to mobilize when natural disasters and other wide-scale emergencies struck back in China. We saw some of this in the early days of the Covid-19 pandemic, when many unit associations in Canada co-ordinated to collect personal protective equipment (PPE) and ship it to their sibling regions back home. The United Front is particularly adept at capitalizing on the opportunities that such emergencies can provide, whether those are public relations opportunities meant to burnish China's reputation internationally or something more malign, like attempting to profit off counterfeit PPE.

The new strategy also called for widespread support of Liberal-led policies like gun restrictions and tax relief for pandemic-affected businesses. And there was the usual call to encourage trade and investment exchanges with enterprises in the Asia-Pacific region, as well as a push to promote Canadian multiculturalism. As part of this, the United Front network was also instructed to fight back against discrimination with renewed solidarity between the eastern and western hubs. In reality, this meant propagandizing racist incidents using Chinese state-run media outlets that operate in Canada.

In the eastern hub, CCMEDIA News runs the Confederation of Toronto Chinese Canadian Organizations (CTCCO).[33] [34] The western hub has Richmond-based Snow Goose Media. As we mentioned earlier, Snow Goose is owned by real estate developer Wei Renmin, who is also honorary chairman of the Canadian Alliance of Chinese Associations (CACA), a commanding-level United Front group.[35]

What stood out most for us with the new east-west United Front strategy was that the two hubs were calling for the establishment of a Canada-wide communication system as part of an eight-point consensus agreement between the two hubs. Specifically, point number seven calls for establishing a regular communication system. Once a major incident occurs, online video communication should be launched immediately, with mutual consultation and timely response, so that the Chinese in the east and west can coordinate and act in a unified manner.

Overseeing the signing ceremony for this agreement in Toronto was Conservative Senator Victor Oh, an attendee of many United Front events in Canada. This is the very essence of a shadow government and what the United Front is all about: taking orders from the CCP and acting on them inside Canada's borders.[36]

Meanwhile, Chinese tycoons—the third arm of China's Unholy Trinity—continued investing in key Canadian industries, including energy, real estate, shipping, and mining. But occasionally, they also put their money in some suspiciously strange places. For example, one wealthy businessman named Jin Pingliang spent ¥60 million (about CAD$10 million) to buy the nearly bankrupt Greater Vancouver Zoo, located in Aldergrove, BC. Pingliang had made his fortune bringing bouncy castles to China, but he was also a member of a number of CCP groups, including the Wenzhou Municipal Committee of the Chinese People's Political Consultative Conference, as well as several United Front organizations.[37]

Given the general decline in popularity of zoos throughout North America, this hardly seemed like a shrewd investment. But Jin Pingliang told a CCP diplomacy committee in 2015 that he had made the purchase because of his deep commitment to animal rights, and because "running this zoo is not only an industry, but also a window to show and spread the image of Chinese people and Chinese companies."[38] Maybe that's all this was—a PR gambit designed to tell China's story in a positive light and earn some international goodwill.[39] [40] [41] [42]

But then again, perhaps it was no coincidence that the zoo's neighbour is Naval Radio Section (NRS) Aldergrove, the primary communications relay site for Maritime Forces Pacific.[43] (In other words, it relays data from shore-based facilities to seaborne ships.) NRS Aldergrove is home to all kinds of sensitive communications equipment and is remotely operated, which increases the risk of compromise. [44] The location of the zoo and its sale to a Chinese national and member of the CPPCC should have been of concern to Canadians due to its location next to a key military communications relay site. It is noteworthy that about 440 acres of the Aldergrove site are used for the antenna field, while the remainder is used as an electromagnetic interference (EMI) buffer zone from local development. All that is to say that it might be considered a little concerning given China's espionage and cyber-attacks in North America. It is discomforting to know that this kind of thing occurs and there is no consideration given to the potential risk to national security.

## A MUSHROOMING THREAT

According to the Dragon Lord document, "The marriage between PRC intelligence agencies, triads and influential Chinese business tycoons pose[s] a real, clear, and mushrooming threat to U.S., Canadian and Australian security interests."[45] In this book, we show how the CCP operates in the shadows while the United Front and its huge network of controlling-level organizations and unit associations provide cover.

These smaller groups are nimble and inexpensive to run, and they carry a degree of respectability. Gerry Groot, head of the Department of Asian Studies at the University of Adelaide, made exactly this point on an episode of *The Little Red Podcast*. "These smaller organizations can be invoked to give legitimacy to particular claims, such as endorsing Chinese claims or policy or whatever [the] CCP wants," he explained. "Creating these groups is easy in democracies, and they can create very specific ones . . . A lot of these groups are created by entrepreneurs who try to parlay these so-called community associations into political influence—to curry favour with the UFWD. So if you have something specific on Muslims and there is a discussion in China about Muslims, then the tendency in Western media, when reporting on this, is to balance the claims, giving weight to each side's opinion. So they come to these organizations, who endorse the party line, for comment."[46]

In the next chapter, we'll show exactly how these organizations manipulate the media, confuse the public, target enemies, and use duped or willing politicians to support them along the way.

## CHAPTER 3

# THE TARGETS

## THE CCP'S SILENT INVASION OF CANADA

In the summer of 2019, an angry mob of aggressive pro-Beijing nationalists harassed and taunted a group of people inside Vancouver's Tenth Church. The congregants, a mix of elderly and young ethnic Chinese, were there to pray for peace and justice in Hong Kong. Eventually, the police had to be called to escort them safely from the building.

It was a bizarre scene for a liberal city known for its weekly rallies on behalf of every kind of social justice issue imaginable. Vancouver is, after all, the birthplace of Greenpeace, and has taken a progressive stance on issues like safe injection sites and drug decriminalization. And yet, there was little to no reaction from the public or the media when the church was surrounded and its parishioners were bullied.

In fact, this was the second clash between supporters and opponents of the CCP on this day. The first was at the Chinese consulate on Granville Street, the main artery heading into Vancouver. In that incident, groups of pro-democracy adherents and CCP nationalists faced off on opposite

PHOTO: Edward Hong Tao waves the PRC National Flag. He is frequently seen in the company of Canadian politicians at events.

sides of the street in duelling rallies well-covered by the mainstream media. After they all dispersed, a small contingent from the pro-democracy side went to Tenth Church to pray. This group included Liang Muxian, former CCP member and agent for the United Front.[1] Once there, they were soon surrounded by the nationalist mob—mostly comprised of foreign students studying in BC, with protest leaders, such as Edward Hong Tao, blending into the mob like true Marxist revolutionists. Among those who participated in this mob action are people who adhere to the same ideological views as those who have been systematically replacing crosses in Christian churches in rural China with photos of Xi Jinping, and who support the killings of thousands of Uyghur Muslims.[2]

But the media was conspicuously absent, and the church's senior pastor, Ken Shigematsu, did nothing more than issue an appeasing statement asserting that he "stands, in a non-partisan fashion, with those who advocate for the freedom to worship whatever faith they choose, without fear."[3] It was not quite the reaction one would expect from the pastor of a church that promotes itself as "a community of spiritual transformation that seeks social justice for all."[4]

Where was the moral outrage? Where was the courage to step up and be heard? Why didn't the mayor of Vancouver, NDP-affiliated Kennedy Stewart, speak out or demand answers? Why didn't the Vancouver police investigate the matter as a hate crime? Their own officers saw what happened first-hand when they escorted the mostly elderly parishioners out of the church to protect them from the pro-CCP mob.

That the mayor, the media, the police, and even the church failed to respond with even the mildest criticism suggests one undeniable truth: the CCP controls Vancouver. That's a bold statement, but let's see why it's true.

## ACTIVE MEASURES

Over the past twenty or more years, the CCP has used the United Front to run propaganda and influence campaigns in Canada, infiltrate key institutions, and cultivate relationships with politicians, businesspeople, academics, and religious leaders. In those years, many individuals, companies, and institutions have become dependent on Chinese money. Sometimes that dependency has happened through corruption—people got rich through gambling, prostitution, drug trafficking, and money laundering—but sometimes it has happened in completely open and legal ways. Western police forces and militaries are engaged in training their Chinese counterparts. Our universities have welcomed and become reliant on fees from foreign-exchange students. And our political institutions have signed on to massive infrastructure deals tied to Xi Jinping's Belt and Road Initiative. If these are the carrots dangled by the CCP, the sticks are intimidation and threats of trade sanctions. In the words of British journalist Nick Cohen, "In many countries, criticizing China is the new blasphemy . . . China is now a more active and influential voice at the United Nations because so many countries are benefiting from billions of dollars in Chinese investments through its 'Belt and Road' infrastructure programme. As Norway found in 2010, and Australia found [in 2020] when it asked for an international inquiry into the origins of Covid-19, those who blaspheme against China face cyber-attacks and sanctions. Better to take the rewards and avoid the punishments."[5]

But there's also a more insidious explanation for why people and nations sometimes keep quiet when they should be speaking out—it's a component of hybrid warfare called ideological subversion. This tactic is aimed at the culture, ideology, and mindset of the citizens of enemy countries, which, to Russia and China, means all Western nations.

What exactly is ideological subversion? For the answer to that question, let's turn to Yuri Alexandrovich Bezmenov, a Soviet-era journalist for the Russian state-owned news agency RIA Novosti and a former KGB informant who defected to Canada in the 1970s and ended up working for Canada's state broadcaster, the CBC.[6] Bezmenov was an expert in ideological subversion—or what is sometimes called active measures—and described it as a "slow process" of shaping public opinion using disinformation, propaganda, and other means. The goal of an active measures campaign, Bezmenov explained, is to change people's "perception of reality . . . to such an extent that despite the abundance of information, no one is able to come to sensible conclusions in the interests of defending themselves, their family, their community, and their country."[7]

A successful campaign allows a country to take over a perceived enemy without firing a single shot.

What happened at Tenth Church provides a good example of how a country's culture and institutions can be used against it. Public protests are as Canadian as maple syrup. Freedom of peaceful assembly is so foundational to our society that it's enshrined in the Charter of Rights as one of four fundamental freedoms (the other three are freedom of conscience and religion; freedom of thought, belief, opinion, and expression; and freedom of association). Protests are a way for people to express how they feel about decisions made by governments or other powerful institutions. But here, that bedrock belief was subverted—the CCP supporters surrounding the church were not staging a legitimate protest but engaging in intimidation and harassment dressed up to look like a protest.

And this wasn't the first time that the CCP had tried to influence Canadian public opinion by manufacturing outrage.

## REVELATIONS FROM A DEFECTOR

Chen Yonglin, the former government official who defected to Australia in 2005 and became an outspoken critic of the CCP, came to Canada in 2007. While here, he made a number of astonishing claims about the CCP and the National Congress of Chinese Canadians (NCCC). For example, Chen alleged that the organization was at the top of a pyramid of quasi-governmental NGOs set up by the Chinese embassy to act as an arm of the CCP. He asserted that the goal of these organizations was to control and influence the Chinese Canadian community and the Canadian government. He even alleged that the NCCC executive secretary, David Lim, was the Canadian representative for the overseas edition of the *People's Daily* newspaper, the official mouthpiece of the Chinese Communist Party.[8] Chen also asserted that the situation in Canada was not unique. Organizations like the NCCC had been created in countries around the world, he said, as a reaction to frosty diplomatic responses to the Tiananmen Square massacre.[9]

Chen Yonglin's account was corroborated by Ping-Teng Tan (aka Chen Bingding), the first president of the NCCC, who acknowledged to Chinese state-run media that the Federation of Returned Overseas Chinese—another name for the United Front—was searching for influential Chinese Canadians to serve as consultants for the CCP. Ping-Teng Tan himself was one of just thirty-two overseas members of the National Committee of the Chinese People's Political Consultative Conference, an advisory group and a key part of the United Front. He was also one of the first overseas consultants appointed to an advisory body reserved for close and trusted supporters of the Chinese regime.[10] None of this is very surprising, but it was a surprise when Ping-Teng Tan also admitted to being on the legal advisory committee of the All-China Federation of Returned Overseas Chinese.[11] [12]

The Chinese Overseas Federation Law Commission was founded in 1982, seven years before the Tiananmen Square incident and nine years before the creation of the NCCC.[13] It is a legal advisory body of the Overseas Chinese Federation, and, as of 2015, it had a membership of more than a hundred scholars and lawyers from domestic and foreign legal circles who act on behalf of the CCP in pushing Beijing's policies overseas.[14] The commission also has subcommittees that advise on civil economy, criminal law, intellectual property rights, international trade and arbitration, and administrative labour. The work the members engage in is related to overseas publicity, general law education, and legal advice for Overseas Chinese in countries like Canada and the US.

Guess what was the very first task the law committee gave itself when it was founded in 1982? According to internal and open-source documents, it was to assist Overseas Chinese federations in dealing with "historical legacies around the world," which is largely considered by those who follow United Front activity to be CCP code for revising history to show China in a better light. This was exactly what the NCCC was doing when it plotted to co-opt the head-tax issue from the CCNC.

Since the 18th National Congress of the Communist Party of China in 2012, when Xi Jinping took the reins as general secretary of the CCP, the Overseas Chinese Lawyers Legal Advisory Committee of the China Federation of Returned Overseas Chinese has focused on the smooth implementation of the Belt and Road Initiative around the world, a topic we will examine in more detail later on.[15] The committee is also tasked with helping innovation-driven development—which, depending on your point of view, could mean supporting inventive new ideas for a modern society or skirting patents and stealing technologies by exploiting academic openness in Canada, the US, and other Western nations.[16]

Lastly, the committee provides legal advice to Overseas Chinese, a particularly bitter irony given China's history of brutality and human rights violations. It's preposterous to suggest that China needs to protect the legal rights of its people in Canada—a nation of immigrants safeguarded by a federal system of parliamentary government with strong democratic traditions. But this is just one more example of the CCP's divide-and-conquer approach, which is designed to sow discord and undermine loyalties among Overseas Chinese.

## CONNECTING THE DOTS

Chen Yonglin became an invaluable source in helping us connect the dots as we tried to identify more United Front–aligned groups and place them in the broader hierarchy. He told us that a simple way to identify a political agent is to take note of his public stand on human rights issues. Agents are "those who support [the] CCP's Hong Kong national security law or [the] Uyghurs' genocide," he explained. "[The] National Congress of Chinese Canadians announced their loyalty to the CCP. Canadians should be worried."

We decided to put Chen's theory to the test at a local anti-racism rally hosted by several well-known United Front leaders. We asked speakers who were championing anti-racism initiatives what they thought about the human rights abuses being visited on Uyghur Muslims held in concentration camps in China. We were met with disdain, denial that the camps even existed, and aggressive demands that we prove a genocide is taking place. All the while, these same people were standing on the steps of the Vancouver Art Gallery condemning systemic racism in Canada.

It became clear that the CCP was co-opting more and more legitimate events for its own purposes and amplifying problems rather than working towards solutions. The Chinese government and its supporters also deliberately conflated issues like human rights, racism, and democracy, then used those issues to pump up their reunification mandate (bringing Taiwan back into the fold, using military force if necessary). And all these initiatives were being managed by a large United Front network made up of hundreds of NGOs.

Chen confirmed that the CCP is very skilled at using NGOs to shape narratives. "They formed a good number of United Front controlling organizations like [the] NCCC and also [the] Canada Chinese Peaceful and Unification Association," he explained. As a higher-level organization, the NCCC was made up of members from other subordinate organizations. David Choi had been the chairperson of the NCCC since 2010. He is also the CEO of Royal Pacific Realty, one of Vancouver's largest real estate companies. His firm has more than 11,000 agents and boasts of having sold billions of dollars in Vancouver real estate. Despite enjoying the freedoms and benefits of living in Canada, Choi publicly supported the CCP's controversial extradition bill, which sparked the 2019 pro-democracy Hong Kong protests. He then organized a full-page advertisement in Vancouver's *Sing Tao* and *Ming Pao* newspapers to denounce the protesters as radicals. The ad listed hundreds of United Front subordinate organizations as backers.[17] "The affairs of Hong Kong are the internal matters of China," it read. "We oppose any intervention by any foreign forces."

On Western social media platforms, Choi also posted a video alleging that the majority of Chinese Canadians support the national security law in Hong Kong and insisting that the legislation would provide protection for the public and solidify Hong Kong's status as an international financial centre. He took the video down after pushback from the local Hong Kong community. But his views in support of China's reunification were amplified in the state-run *China Daily* newspaper, where he appeared to condone the brutality of Hong Kong police in the name of national security. "The Western countries, without exception, have their own national security laws and should not have a double standard with Hong Kong's legislation," he told the paper, which identified him as the executive chair of the NCCC.[18] In the same article, Ping-Teng Tan was quoted as saying, "Hong Kong's government should have had such legislation for a long time . . . Burning the flag, hitting government departments, overt violence against the police, destruction of property in public facilities; no country can allow such behavior to endanger national security. It is absurd to say that the central government has no right to legislate."

We knew that the NCCC and its affiliate groups were considered "top brass" in the United Front, but just how high up were they? There were signs that the power was shifting from the nationally run NCCC in the west to the eastern branch in Markham, Ontario, just a four-hour drive from Canada's capital. Chen all but confirmed this when he told us that he suspected the NCCC was no longer the top dog of the United Front network in Canada. He explained that with new NGOs being formed all the time, the success of any one group and its position in the hierarchy would depend on its willingness to spend money and make greater efforts to promote the CCP in Canada. Loyalties between the party and these organizations can shift and are usually tied to funding and special privileges from overseas Chinese missions. "This is quite common," said Chen. "The richest control it all."

Chen said there were indications that the NCCC had been forced to relinquish its role as a commanding-level organization, and that now the China Council for the Promotion of Peaceful National Reunification was playing a leading role in Canada, through proxy organizations set up in Canada, including one called the Canada Chinese Peaceful and Unification Association. The CCP's highest-priority United Front work involves taking over Taiwan.

"All of these groups have similar names and are part of the Beijing branch," Chen told us. "They play a leading role now." But even if the NCCC was no longer a high-ranking organization, its members were still working hand in glove with CCP officials, given that all of these groups, from the most to the least influential ones at any given time, exist in Canada under the authority of the CCP. The China Council for the Promotion of Peaceful National Reunification, for example, is an umbrella organization of the United Front Work Department of the Chinese Communist Party (CCP), tasked with promoting unification between mainland China and Taiwan. Its proxy organization, the similarly named Canada Chinese Peaceful and Unification Association, carries on the same work within Canada. Ultimately, all these United Front groups are engaged in the same activity: shaping the narrative for the CCP inside Canada's borders, and attempting to win Canadians over to CCP-approved ideas. This hybrid war tactic includes multiple overseas reunification organizations set up to promote what China calls the reunification of the motherland, and to challenge any pushback towards what they call the anti-independence movement. Taiwan has sought help from the US to fight back. What happens if China succeeds in taking over Taiwan? Is the Arctic next?

## CHAPTER 4

# THE MYSTERIOUS LIST

### EXPOSING THE AGENTS ACTING FOR THE CCP IN CANADA

In 2018, the All-China Federation of Returned Overseas Chinese (ACFROC) issued a list of twenty-four United Front agents designated as Overseas Committee Members. We call them agents. ACFROC is a United Front CCP-led organization that liaises with ethnic Chinese people living outside of mainland China. Every 5 years they hold a national congress where they review the work done by overseas compatriots around the world, nominate candidates for the CPPCC, plan work for the next 5 years, and decide on leadership.

These agents are ideological soldiers for the CCP United Front who work on behalf of the motherland overseas They are deputised by the party to help China win the hybrid war against the West, and many had dual roles as leaders of hometown associations and business and industry organizations, through which they gained access to high-level politicians. Most had their own businesses in China that have been propped up by the

---

PHOTO: Some of the All-China Federation of Returned Overseas Chinese (ACFROC) agents assigned in Canada.

CCP in order to ensure their financial success, which is then turned into a tool for influence overseas in Canada. By this we mean that Chinese business tycoons are expected to use their own money, if it was made with the help of lucrative government contracts, to sponsor overseas politicians and political parties or donate to social services, such as hospitals. In some cases, the CCP has even custom-created businesses, including large real estate development companies, as cover for clandestine activity. This is one of the main ways that the CCP has been able to hide how they buy influence in Canada, which they frame publicly as a matter of building bridges between China and Canada. How can you tell if the CCP is behind a huge project or sponsorship gift in Canada? Usually a representative from the local PRC Consulate is holding one corner of an oversized cheque along with the developer and local politicians at a propaganda-style photo op ceremony.

A quick look at the individual agents on the list provided a hint at the various roles they may have played on Canadian soil, and the tasks assigned.

One of the agents listed was Fujian native Xu Jianlun. He is a textile industry tycoon and proprietor of a high-end amber jewelry brand, and serves as honorary president of the North American Chinese Entrepreneurs Association in Canada. He is also a member of the Fujian Provincial Committee of the Chinese People's Political Consultative Conference. His patriotic bona fides were established when he reportedly told a state-run media organization that "No force can stop the progress of the Chinese people and the Chinese nation."[1] [2]

Montreal-based Jia Ming, president of Shandong Chamber of Commerce in Canada, was also on the list. One of the tasks assigned to him (and by extension to the Shandong Chamber) by the CCP was to help build the Jinan High-tech Zone, as part of the great rejuvenation of the motherland. This involved recruiting talent, including scholars teaching at Canadian universities and scientific research institutions.[3] [4]

Toronto-area businessman Xiao Chuqiang (Eric Xiao), president of CPAC (formerly known as the Chinese Professionals Association of Canada), was also on the list. CPAC was co-founded by Bai Ning, vice chairman of the Zhejiang Federation of Returned Overseas Chinese and brother to Burnaby City Councillor, James Wang. CPAC runs a number of programs designed to train future leaders, including a leadership training program with Toronto-Dominion (TD) Bank.[5] [6]

Another ideological worker for the CCP United Front political warfare effort is Fujian native Lin Xingyong, chairman of the Hualian Association and director of the One Belt and One Road Canada Promotion General Association and the Confederation of Toronto Chinese Canadian Organizations (CTCCO), until he was allegedly expelled for unknown reasons.[7][8][9]

Lin Xingyong was given many important tasks to accomplish on behalf of the motherland while in Canada, but what stood out for us most was his work organizing the first Memorial Day for victims of the Nanjing Massacre.[10] A propaganda tool that contorts one actual historical massacre among many in order to deflect criticism from the CPP's current political agenda, the Nanjing Memorial Day project is the CCP's rejoinder—and its attempt at an ideological antidote—to the Tiananmen Square massacre and other human rights abuses by the Chinese government, under the administration of Chinese Communist Party (CCP), such as the unjust incarceration of Uyghur Muslims and other ethnic and religious minorities in Xinjiang.

Authors Fengqi Qian and Guo-Qiang Liu aptly summarized the motives behind the CCP's global push to create Nanjing memorials in an abstract of their research paper, "Remembrance of the Nanjing Massacre in the Globalised Era: The Memory of Victimisation, Emotions and the Rise of China," saying "The Nanjing Massacre Memorial showcases the way in which the collective memory of victimisation is shaped and disseminated under the Communist Party to promote China's national aspirations and legitimise China's claims in the contemporary world."[11]

Those were just a sampling of the United Front agents on the list and some of what they were assigned to do in Canada. Our research would lead us to dig deeper into the lives and activities of others on the list, to find out more about what they were tasked with doing inside Canada by the CCP. We investigated six listed agents: Wang Dianqi, Grant Lin, Hilbert Yiu, Franco Feng, Guo Taicheng, and Wang Wenkang.[12] While it would take an entire book to report on our research into these agents, we do mention several of them in the context of the issues and stories that we chose to focus on in this book.

What we discovered was one more data point in the larger mosaic that would ultimately reveal more than has been known to date about the reach and the extent of CCP operations in Canada.

We asked Chen Yonglin, the former CCP member and Australian consular defector, what China wanted from the West.

Chen told us that China viewed Canada as a small power, much like Australia. But at the same time, it was considered an attractive target because of its social and economic ties with and proximity to the US. China saw Canada as a way of gaining access to the States, just as the Dragon Lord report had said.

Chen explained that whatever China couldn't get from the US through technology theft, corporate espionage, and other covert means, it could get indirectly from Canada and Australia, by means of the close relationships these countries have with the States. "Australian laboratories and universities share their knowledge and technology with their US counterparts," Chen told us. "There are no restrictions."

Sometimes that knowledge sharing even happens directly with China. In 2017, the *Sydney Morning Herald* reported that scientists at some of Australia's top universities were collaborating with Chinese institutions that had ties to the People's Liberation Army.[13] "The scientists' work," the paper reported, "includes sophisticated computing seen as essential to China's ambition to eclipse the United States in advanced military technology." The article goes on to describe partnerships between the head of China's foremost military research centre and several expat Chinese scientists who specialize in fields like artificial intelligence and surveillance technology.

In mid-2020, the US expelled more than a thousand Chinese graduate students and researchers in an attempt to counteract what the State Department described as China's "wide-ranging and heavily resourced campaign to acquire sensitive United States technologies and intellectual property, in part to bolster the modernization and capability of its military."[14] In Canada, a House of Commons committee heard a claim that some components of China's surveillance network had been developed at Canadian universities. Former CSIS director Richard Fadden told the CBC that he thought it was "a bit bonkers" not to close off some fields of study to Chinese researchers. "There are some areas where we should simply say, 'You can't study in those areas . . . And for the life of me I don't understand why, with the Five Eyes or the United States or NATO, . . . [we] couldn't come up with [a] commonly accepted list of areas and say, 'We, as NATO, are not going to allow work in this area.'" Fadden said that because Canada doesn't have the preoccupation with national security that the US does, it's viewed by China as "an easier target."

None of this is news to Chen Yonglin. He told us that since 2008, China has been recruiting overseas academics and entrepreneurs through its Thousand Talents Plan (TTP). This initiative—which encourages Chinese experts living and working in countries like Australia, Canada, and the US to share not just their skills but also the results of their research—has alarmed Western intelligence agencies enough that they have made their concerns public. On July 7, 2020, FBI director Christopher Wray gave a speech in which he said, "The greatest long-term threat to our nation's information and intellectual property, and to our economic vitality, is the counterintelligence and economic espionage threat from China. It's a threat to our economic security—and by extension, to our national security . . . China is engaged in a whole-of-state effort to become the world's only superpower by any means necessary."[15] In Canada, CSIS also warned that the TTP was a way to steal Canadian technology and intellectual property for both military and economic gain. In the agency's annual report for 2020, director David Vigneault wrote, "The fluid and rapidly evolving environment caused by COVID-19 has created a situation ripe for exploitation by threat actors seeking to advance their own interests . . . In 2020, CSIS observed espionage and foreign interference activity at levels not seen since the Cold War."[16]

Chen noted that the threats from Beijing are multifaceted. Yes, China wants to build its own wealth and military might, but it also wants to destabilize targeted nations by draining them of their natural resources, subverting their political and social institutions, and eroding their relationships with other countries. "In 2004, when I was in the PRC consulate [in Sydney], China held an ambassadorial conference; we were instructed to see Australia as a neighbouring country. China wanted to turn Australia into a dependent country like France after its strategic bid for the South China Sea, which is a resource rich in oil, natural gas, rare earth minerals, and fish."[17]

Chen said that China was interested in making Canada a stable supplier of natural resources—a tactic Beijing had also employed with Australia. "Internally, the PRC ambassador talked openly with us that China wanted to see Australia as a resource supply base," Chen told us. "[The CCP] need[ed] to make a stable supply, so it's important to make friends—special friends! We called it all-around diplomacy [because it] included all levels of contacts—politically, culturally, economically, militarily." He pointed out that today, Australia is the largest exporter of liquefied natural gas (LNG) to China. That may sound like a good deal, but it also creates ties between Australia and China that can be hard to break—the proverbial golden handcuffs.

Chen said that China had a similar agenda for Canada because of its abundant natural resources, including metals like nickel and copper, minerals like potash (used to make fertilizer), fish, wood and paper products, and oilseeds like canola. Nuclear power technology is another big want for China, which has plans to build a hundred or more new reactors in the coming decades.[18]

With its huge resource-rich territory and small population, mostly strung out along the undefended border with the US, Canada was truly ripe for the picking.

It made sense that the CCP would set its sights on Canada and use agents of influence, including politicians and policy makers, to achieve its goals.

## AGENT DIANQI AND THE CCPIT

The China Council for the Promotion of International Trade (CCPIT) is an organ of the CCP founded in 1952. Its mandate is to develop trade and economic relationships between China and other countries and regions globally. The CCPIT has long been associated with the Chinese Communist Party's United Front strategy and is tasked with organizing trade fairs and events in promotion of the Belt and Road Initiative. As far back as 1957, in a report titled *The United Front in Communist China*, the CIA called it a "front organization" and warned that one of its main objectives was "to persuade businessmen in non-Communist countries that strategic embargoes on trade with the Soviet bloc and China are detrimental to their own best interests."[19]

The Zhejiang Council for the Promotion of International Trade (CCPIT Zhejiang) awarded a license to the liaison office of the three countries in Thailand, Canada and Mexico and signed cooperation agreements with them.

Wang Dianqi was appointed Chief Representative of the CCPIT Zheijiang Province Liaison Office in Canada at an elaborate dinner and ceremony held in Vancouver on Sept. 9, 2018. Attendees included many high-level consular officials, as well as several CCP representatives who had travelled from China for the occasion. In another sign that the CCP is in the shadows running these trade offices, is that the centre seat at the head table was given not to Wang Dianqi but to Gao Xingfu, who is a CCP member and the vice-governor of Zhejiang Province. Dianqi sat to Gao Xingfu's side. Next to Wang Dianqi sat a local politician, MLA Teresa Wat. (Seating arrangements at CCP functions always reveal who is most important, and in this case, they showed, once again, just how intertwined Canadian politicians had become with the Chinese government.)[20][21][22][23]

A CCPIT press release reported on Wang Dianqi's speech, in which he said that it is necessary to seriously assume the responsibility of the liaison office, live up to the expectations of the leaders of Zhejiang Province and the Provincial Council for the Promotion of International Trade, and support its role in promoting economic and trade exchanges between Zhejiang and Canada.[24]

Since 2016, according to *China Daily*, CCPIT has opened more than one hundred trade information offices in export-oriented areas of China, such as Zhejiang, Jiangsu, and Shanghai.[25] It also has dozens of offices in countries around the world, including Germany, the UK, the US, and Canada.[26] Whenever you see a high-level trade forum between superpowers or trade symposiums involving many countries, you can be sure that CCPIT had a hand in putting it together.

What makes the examination of Wang Dianqi so fascinating is that we can trace his rise to power in Canada as a local overseas United Front leader back to 1989, when he was just a small restaurant owner giving handouts to local PLA troops as an entrepreneur. From there he immigrated to Canada to set up shop here but there is little to no online track record in Canada to show he had made a success of himself as a new immigrant to Canada. He was then appointed to his various roles as head of different United Front organizations, which inevitably brought him closer to elected officials. This was a familiar pattern—rags to riches stories of hustlers who put the motherland ahead of their own personal needs, then magically over a short period of time became wealthy business owners in transit while immigrating to Canada. By the time they get to Canada they are immediately assigned various roles in their respective United Front hometown associations. From there they gain a foothold in local government through the support of elected officials.

The CCP is strategically sending its citizens to Canada to help prose-lytize the cause of the motherland's reunification, chase the Chinese dream and push for Xi Jinping's pet project—the Belt and Road. To describe the Belt and Road Initiative (BRI) in the simplest way is to call it a modern-day silk road that is designed to shift the global economy away from the USA to China, with all the belts and roads going to and from China, which is at the center. It consists of two main components: the land-based Silk Road Economic Belt and the oceangoing Maritime Silk Road, also known as the Polar Silk Road (PSR).[27]

The return is often money and business favours for their business back in the motherland. This, of course, is on a micro level. The bigger pic-ture—the macro level—is revealed through CSIS's Sidewinder report and once again highligted in the Dragon Lord Appendix document revealed in this book. Operation Dragon Lord and its examination of China's Unholy Trinity, the marriage between PRC intelligence agencies, triads, and influential Chinese business tycoons.[28]

The Operation Dragon Lord document talked of "triads, working in concert with high-profile Chinese expatriate businessmen, have assumed control of dominant media and financial institutions in the U.S. and Canada" The report went on to say that this, in turn, has permitted "Beijing to exercise some control over the assets and revenue of Chinese institutions in return for immunity from prosecution for triad leaders, who are deeply involved in the multi-billion dollar drug and people smuggling trade."

While there are more prominent pro-CCP figures like Wang Dianqi who show outward displays of loyalty to the regime, you can be sure that there is much more going on behind the scenes with them and others hidden behind layers of interconnecting Chinese elite business people, pol-iticians, and well-established organizations like CCPIT. All are working to advance Beijing's interests overseas, in particular Xi Jinping's Belt and Road.

Australia has long been wary of Xi's signature project, which it views as a potential national security threat. "We saw very little in additional economic benefit for signing up [to the Belt and Road Initiative]," one unnamed senior government official told ABC News in 2017, "but a lot of negative strategic consequences if we accepted Beijing's offer."[29] In Australia, where the CCPIT is also active, it became very clear that the organization was attempting to bypass the federal government by signing Belt and Road deals directly with individual states and cities.[30]

The same thing happened in British Columbia when then-Premier Christy Clark met with a delegation of high-ranking government officials from the Guangdong province of China to ink the deal. The delegation included 200 business and government officials led by Hu Chunhua, Member of the Politburo of the Communist Party of China (CPC) Central Committee and Party Secretary of the Guangdong Provincial Committee.

A Memorandum of Understanding said that "British Columbia and Guangdong will work co-operatively to leverage new and existing transportation partnerships to strengthen the trade capacity of their respective gateway and corridor networks, expand cooperation in the natural gas sector and enhance cooperation in marine scientific research and environmental practices, maritime transportation, shipbuilding and repair, and fisheries and seafood."[31]

Here's where things become muddy, though. It's normal to trade with other countries, but it's not normal to use trade relationships to manipulate or extort those countries into doing your bidding. Trade agreements that were being sold to Canadians as a win-win were, in fact, slowly chipping away at our sovereignty. How many companies need to be sold and how many research agreements need to be signed before we're at the point of owning nothing? What happens once we've handed everything over to China? When we've caved to its every demand? When will China start asking for things we can't afford to give? In our view, this has already started to happen. China owns so many of our politicians and is tied to so many companies in the West that its officials are practically on speed-dial with the highest offices in the land.

In 2021, the mayor of Vancouver, Kennedy Stewart, announced to a local news outlet that he had suspended contact with Chinese government officials and declined an invitation to meet with the country's ambassador to Canada after federal MP Michael Chong was sanctioned by China for denouncing its treatment of Uyghur Muslims.[32] "I really do think relations between Canada and China have taken a turn for the worst," Kennedy was quoted as saying. "Until I get advice differently or requests from the federal government to take those meetings, I'm just not taking those anymore." What caught our attention wasn't that the mayor was taking a stand on something, but that he was admitting to having been in close communication with a foreign state under communist rule. Stewart had earlier acknowledged getting a "dressing-down" from the Chinese consul general after Huawei's Meng Wanzhou was arrested at the Vancouver airport. American officials had accused her of committing fraud to circumvent US sanctions against Iran. We reached out to Kennedy to ask him about his decision to abruptly suspend contact with local PRC diplomats since we thought this was an odd thing to admit to. Kennedy didn't respond to us. He later admitted to other media that he had a two-hour meeting with agents from Canada's spy agency, which advised him that their briefing reports went up the chain but that nobody is paying any attention. While he didn't outright say that he lost his bid at re-election to Ken Sim because of China's interference, he implied as much to local media.[33]

*The Globe and Mail* reported that China's Vancouver consulate interfered in the 2022 municipal election, according to a report by Canada's spy agency, CSIS. The PRC Consulate in Vancouver fought back, posting this response: "Recently, some Canadian politicians and media repeated the so-called 'China's interference in Canadian elections,' smearing and discrediting the Consulate General of China and the consular officers. The Consulate General expresses strong dissatisfaction and firm opposition to it."[34] [35]

The consulate was known for lashing out when it came to bad news reports on China. In the past, they've released statements condemning the government, including for its response to the Uyghur genocide, calling allegations of human rights abuses "the most outrageous lies of the century" and imploring Canadian politicians to "take off their tinted glasses [and] respect the truth."[36]

They were even using politicians soft on the regime to help by serving as mouthpieces, often conflating criticism of China with racism and calling for scrutiny of Canadian media who put the regime under a microscope. We saw this federally and locally when MLA Teresa Wat advocated for tighter media and editorial control in a letter she sent to then BC Premier John Horgan.[37] [38]

In the letter, Wat requested that the BC Government "apply to the National News Media Council for a review of media coverage to determine the extent, if any, to which language, visual depictions and editorial content may have conditioned people to accept racial stereotyping and racial intolerance."

## CHAPTER 5

# GROUND ZERO

### WHERE AND HOW THE CCP LAUNCHED A
### COMPLEX HYBRID WAR AGAINST THE WEST

Herbert and Marion Pritchard lived in ground-zero Vancouver their entire lives. Bert, as he liked to be called, worked for the Vancouver Fire Department, while Marion worked for Eaton's department store. In 1970, the year they married, the Pritchards scraped together enough money for a down payment on a $34,000 basic starter home known as the Vancouver Special, in the least expensive area of the city, East Vancouver. It was the perfect postwar home, both large enough and affordable enough for the average family. The Pritchards spent the next forty years in their home, leading a comfortable life up until their twilight years when they sold it in 2016 for a staggering $1.7 million. That's an increase of 5,000 percent.

For the Pritchards, this was, of course, a great thing. And they were not alone in their windfall. According to Credit Suisse's annual Global Wealth Report, which analyzes household wealth of people around the world, Canada is creating more millionaires at a faster rate than the USA, with

---

PHOTO: The China Minsheng Investment Group (CMIG) has invested in BC. They have a strong presence in countries participating in the "Belt and Road" initiative.

1,681,969 millionaires out of a population of 36,991,981, which translates to 4.5 percent of the population. One driver of this is real estate.[1] Those who already owned homes and sold them for hundreds or thousands of times what they originally paid for them obviously made out nicely. But for the next generation of Vancouverites and in other metropolitan cities in Canada, home ownership is now an impossible dream. Even renting is beyond the reach of many people in a city that routinely ranks among the world's least affordable when it comes to housing prices.[2] The obscene wealth gap in ground zero Vancouver was the first clue that something wasn't quite right. It had become an open question: Who or what was to blame? Was this a natural phenomenon or was it all by design?

Some have tried to explain away Vancouver's wealth discrepancy as a natural, or at least expected, result of the economic impact of hosting the 2010 Olympics. This theory seemed to lend credence to headlines at the time about Lamborghinis and Maserati suddenly appearing on the streets of Vancouver—vehicles that were routinely impounded from street-racing teenagers with N (novice) driver's licences.[3] But no one seemed to be asking where the money came from that allowed these kids to afford half-million-dollar supercars.

It wasn't until around 2016 that the media started to question the role of unexplained wealth and real estate. The turning point came with a series of articles on outrageously expensive homes owned by individuals with no source of income. *The Globe and Mail* broke a story about nine students "with no apparent source of income" buying $57-million worth of single-family homes in Vancouver's affluent Point Grey neighbourhood."[4] At the time, Canadian banks had a policy of not verifying sources of income for foreign buyers with no credit history—meaning, non-Canadians faced less scrutiny than domestic borrowers wanting to buy homes. Four of the students in the *Globe* story had received mortgages from major banks like BMO and CIBC.

What was even more troubling is that "student" and "homemaker" were among the most common occupations listed on land-title documents, according to David Eby of the NDP. The government opposition housing critic held a press conference on student-owned housing and the housing bubble in Vancouver,[5] and explained his concerns, saying, "It's incredibly strange that a student would be able to afford such a luxurious and multi-million-dollar property."[6]

Headline after headline seemed to point to an increase in foreign own-ership of BC homes, primarily by citizens of China, with little to no source of income. The *Vancouver Sun* revealed that one of the majority owners of a luxurious Point Grey mansion on billionaire row was a "student" named Tian Yu Zhou.[7] Tian Yu had a 99-percent interest in the five-bedroom mansion, which was purchased from Canadian entrepreneur Peter Brown, the founder of the Canaccord financial services company (now Canaccord Genuity Group), which has become the largest independent investment dealer in Canada.[8] And if students being able to buy mansions for mil-lions of dollars isn't enough to blow your mind, the Brown residence was bought for well above the asking price. Tian Yu Zhou put down a cool CAD $31.1 million, only $5.5 million over the home's assessed value of $25.6 million. Of that, Canadian Imperial Bank of Commerce (CIBC) provided a $9.9 million mortgage, with biweekly payments of more than $17,000.[9] It would seem that money was no object for the student from China, and no concern for the bank.

There is even more to this puzzling story. The *Vancouver Sun* noted that in the previous two years, Brown had donated $62,500 to the BC Liberal Party, which was in power at the time, and which had deep con-nections to the CCP. Brown also happened to be a longtime BC Liberal Party fundraiser. Eby, the NDP housing critic, was quoted as saying, "I think we shouldn't underestimate the connection between the government saying there is no issue with the real estate market in Vancouver at the same time one of their major fundraisers is selling his home to a student for . . . significantly over the assessed value." He added, "The government's donors are directly profiting from this crazy real estate market while a lot of hard-working families are suffering."[10]

This issue was so significant that it was even picked up by news outlets south of the border. In 2019, National Public Radio (NPR) published a report titled "Vancouver Has Been Transformed by Chinese Immigrants."[11] The article noted that Vancouver had a larger share of Chinese residents than other big North American cities, including New York, San Francisco, and Toronto. It said that many people in China perceive Vancouver as safe and politically and economically stable. But the piece also noted that money-laundering operations at government-run BC casinos had raised questions about the legitimacy of the funds flowing in from China and pointed to those funds as a driver of the real estate boom in the region.

"This has driven up prices," NPR said, "and added to a run on the city's housing stock." This view was supported by an independent review of money laundering conducted by a former deputy commissioner of the RCMP for the BC attorney general. The review showed that of the CAD$7 billion laundered in British Columbia in 2018, CAD$5 billion flowed through real estate deals.[12] Operation Dragon Lord noted that "Triad organizations have established operations in large Canadian cities, which border on the U.S. and offer these criminal gangs easy access to major U.S. Cities and financial institutions, to promote their illicit activities."

While the surge in prices was good news for sellers like the Pritchards, it was terrible news for locals wanting to buy in. NPR profiled one young couple who felt they had no hope of becoming homeowners one day. And they noted the negative effect on the city of foreign buyers who snap up homes they have no intention of living in.

Stories were proliferating about unlit condo units and entire neighbourhoods sitting empty, and the situation was getting under everyone's skin. Many of these properties were found to be owned by wealthy foreign investors, including those with ties to the CCP who were land-banking their wealth. We toured a British Properties neighbourhood where entire streets were abandoned. In front of one mansion—thought to be owned by a high-ranking CCP member living in China—weeds grew so high that they obstructed the million-dollar view of the Pacific Ocean.[13]

In contrast to this, the *fuerdai*—meaning "rich second generation"—were seen by many, including those within the overseas Chinese diaspora, as "flaunting what they haven't earned" and appearing to rub it in the faces of locals.[14]

Global News reported that in 2016, there were at least two thousand vehicles worth more than $150,000 registered in Vancouver.[15] Perhaps not surprisingly, the hotspot for Ferrari- and Lamborghini-watching wasn't the local beach or some fancy club, either. It was at the local university, the University of British Columbia (UBC), where so many of those attending were wealthy foreign students from China that the school was jokingly referred to as the University of Beautiful Cars.

Vancouver's wealth disparity even had the supercar dealers questioning the source of funds from buyers so young that they appeared jobless. . "As a dealership operator, I see these young kids driving these super cars and super luxury cars, and no one has looked at the source of income and audited this. Some of these cars are [worth] a half million dollars. It's so blatant. It seems like it's a norm here now. As a citizen I see a young person bringing funds in from China and driving cars like that as a norm[,] and someone should be doing something about it," said a dealer confidentially to one of the provincial investigators looking into what role money laundering has had in the real estate and luxury car markets in the region.[16] The same dealer also admitted to investigators that his dealership accepted WeChat Pay and UnionPay, which are China-based direct debit cards. "They're not buying on Canadian Visa cards and paying bills here," he said, noting that there isn't a dealership in the city that doesn't take payment that way.

"About 10 times a month we'll get a foreign student with zero credit, zero job income, but proof of income through incoming wire transfers[,] and the bank [is] . . . accepting the wire transfers and bank statements as proof of income," said another dealer. "It's unequivocally money launder-ing. People who are not employed . . . showing bank statements with large sums being wired frequently into their accounts . . . These are people who aren't paying income tax, who don't work, but can buy expensive cars with money coming from out of the country."[17]

While Vancouver may a playground for some, it has also served as a base of operations for CCP elite because it is part of the Asia-Pacific region. Make no mistake about it, the perks are the expensive mansions, private schools, and a fleet of luxury vehicles the goal is to create outpost for operations overseas.

Chinese Business Tycoon, Mailin Chen, who supposedly made his fortune as a duck farmer. A venture that apparently enabled him to buy over 13 properties in Vancouver area including a $51.8 million dollar mansion on billionaire row facing the entirety of Vancouver's skyline. Just a stone's throw from where Wu Shumin and her partner met their tragic fate.

Mailin rose in the ranks of the upper echelon of the CCP to become a member of China's top political advisory body, the Chinese Political Conference (CPPCC).

He reportedly flies his Bombardier jet from Vancouver's South Airport to Papua New Guinea (PNG) according to reports from the island country that is part of the Australasian realm. Chen was possibly sent as a back-up after the government refused to extend a special mining Lease to Zijin - China's largest mining company and its Canadian joint-venture partner

Barrick Gold Corp in 2020 over the Porgera Joint Venture gold mine in Papua New Guinea.

Residential real estate and supercars weren't the only things China's wealthy elite had their sights set on in lotus land. Commercial real estate and corporate takeovers were also on the menu.

In early 2016, the Bentall Centre, a downtown Vancouver office complex and underground shopping plaza, was bought by China's Anbang Group for more than CAD$1 billion.[18] That single sale made Chinese buyers the largest group of foreign investors in Canadian commercial real estate—they represented 65.4 percent of more than CAD$2 billion in total deals across the country in the first six months of that year.

In 2018, the Chinese government temporarily seized control of the Anbang Group, which was accused of violating laws and regulations and thus threatening the company's solvency.[19] "The Chinese government doesn't want to have a company default on foreign debt," one China-watcher explained, "and it also wants to teach a lesson to other Chinese business people that the [Communist] party is in charge." This move gave the CCP control over Anbang's huge portfolio of foreign assets, making for some crazy headlines back in Canada. "How the Chinese Government Took Control of BC Seniors' Homes," read one.[20] Suddenly, grandma and grandpa in Vancouver were living in a retirement home owned by the Chinese government.

Even Vancouver's landmark Grouse Mountain ski resort, the mountain directly behind Vancouver's cityscape, was affected. In July 2017, *The Globe and Mail* reported that the Chinese state-created investment company, China Minsheng Investment Group (CMIG), bought the resort.

CMIG was initiated by the All-China Federation of Industry and Commerce, which is run by Chinese industrialists and businesspeople under the leadership of the United Front Work Department of the Chinese Communist Party (CCP). CMIG is said to follow a "Go Out" strategy of actively cultivating and developing in China and countries along the Belt and Road Initiative, with a goal of promoting China's economic transformation.[21]

What excuse was given to justify effectively allowing the CCP to buy up a local landmark? Tourism experts tried to explain that interest in the province's resorts had jumped sharply in the past few years. "Chinese investors have purchased other places around the province, from restaurants to pubs to resorts," the CEO of the Tourism Industry Association of BC told the *Globe*. Canadians were also part of the problem behind allowing the CCP to buy up Canadian real estate and businesses.[22][23]

Why are the kids of wealthy elites from China, with ties to the CCP, flaunting their wares so blatantly? Why are wealthy elites from China, with ties to the CCP, buying up residential and commercial property? Is this all part of a larger plan?

Looking at Operation Dragon Lord, it's clear that, as a result of Beijing "exploiting Canada's lax immigration laws, border patrols, and generous social welfare system, triad leaders and their associates have been able to establish a well-nourished base of operations in Canada."

The economic blitzkrieg that started in ground zero Vancouver and has migrated to other metropolitan cities in Canada and the USA is a part of the CCP's hybrid war on the West. This, in turn, has created an affordable housing crisis and myriad social issues, exacerbating mental health challenges, drug dependency, and homelessness. And these things can, in turn, lead to rising crime rates and costly interventions by Canada's already strained socialized medical system. The result is social chaos.

## ECONOMIC BLITZKRIEG

In 2020, in a speech at the Gerald R. Ford Presidential Museum, then US attorney general William Barr said that China is engaged in an economic blitzkrieg—"an aggressive, orchestrated, whole-of-government (indeed, whole-of-society) campaign to seize the commanding heights of the global economy and surpass the United States as the world's pre-eminent superpower."[24] China, he said, was "no longer hiding its strength nor biding its time."

To understand what Barr meant by an economic blitzkrieg, let's take this out of the China vs. the West arena for a moment.

It's not uncommon for countries to use their economic muscle to bend other nations to their will. This is what's happening when democratic countries impose economic sanctions on other nations, for example—the purpose is to provoke change. And change is supposed to come because economic sanctions can cause far-reaching problems by stirring up social, political, and cultural unrest. That's the whole-of-society effect.

Case in point: the US has maintained a trade embargo against Cuba since the early 1960s. The aim of the embargo, according to the Cuban Democracy Act of 1992, is "to seek a peaceful transition to democracy . . . and greater respect for human rights."[25] Continued resistance, the US warned, could result in "a collapse of the Cuban economy, social upheaval, or widespread suffering."

If you've ever travelled to Cuba, you will have seen for yourself the whole-of-society effect of sixty years of sanctions. Havana's streets are filled with vintage cars, for example, because the embargo ended the importation of both American-made vehicles and their parts. But the impacts go well beyond that. In 2018, the UN calculated that the embargo had cost the impoverished island at least $130 billion.[26] Some estimates are many times higher than that. And ongoing travel restrictions make it challenging for Cuban Americans to visit relatives who still live on the island. All of this in a wholly unsuccessful effort to motivate Cubans to free themselves from communist rule.

What China is doing is slightly different in form but not too dissimilar in terms of its desired effect. The government is engaging in deliberate economic subversion directed at Western Canada. It's covert and without justification, and its aim is to create economic instability in order to provoke catastrophic social chaos. The endgame has everything to do with Canada's proximity to the US and China's stated goal of becoming the world's only superpower by 2050.

China's economic blitzkrieg against Western Canada started in the 1980s with foreign investors like Hong Kong's richest man, Li Ka-shing, who was a regular on the Forbes list of the world's wealthiest, and who bought up a huge amount of commercial real estate in the nerve centres of Canada, including Vancouver's Expo 86 lands in 1988 for $320 million.[27]

Urban planner Andy Yan is the director of Simon Fraser University's City Program, and has conducted a number of studies on foreign ownership of residential homes in Vancouver. Yan estimated that non-Canadians own around $75 billion in residential property in the city.[28]

Often, capital flight, the large-scale exodus of financial assets from a nation, is driven by political or economic instability, currency devaluation, or the imposition of capital controls. But in China's case, it was sparked by the UK's 1997 handover of Hong Kong to the PRC and the uncertainty that caused. Wealthy Chinese saw Vancouver as a stable place for their money. "It's actually the desire for safe haven . . . where you are looking for a hedge against political, economic, social insecurity, and I think, increasingly, climate change," Yan told NPR.[29][30] An added issue is that the PRC doesn't allow people to own the land their homes are built on, even though the idea of property ownership is firmly embedded in Chinese culture.[31] This makes Canada extremely appealing. Its permanent resident status allows Chinese expats to live in the country even though China still considers them citizens.

But China doesn't want its people to transfer assets out of the country, so it has put in place a capital barrier limiting how much money can be taken out to US$50,000 a year. How, then, is it possible to buy homes in Vancouver worth millions of dollars, and why would banks loan money to students and homemakers from China with no income source?

Moreover, what role, if any, do the PRC consulate, United Front hometown associations, United Front agents, and overseas liaison offices set up by the CCP have to do with the buying up of Canada?

## WHALE GAMBLERS AND LOAN SHARKS

We stood together in a stuffy, cubicle-lined office in Shady Pines, a nickname for the RCMP's E Division HQ in Surrey, BC. A liaison officer from one of the American three-letter agencies passed on a list of more than two dozen individuals who had travelled between Vancouver and Las Vegas in private casino jets. These high fliers seemed to be arousing the suspicions of the Financial Crimes Enforcement Network (FinCEN)—the US equivalent to Canada's FINTRAC, but with more teeth. The people listed were so-called "whale gamblers" associated with Asian organized crime, a couple of pseudo-celebs, and individuals known to affiliate with the CCP, including several of the names from the United Front list we covered earlier.

Calvin "Cal" Chrustie, a veteran RCMP officer who headed up a group inside the Federal Serious and Organized Crime (FSOC) unit inside the RCMP E-division in BC, had provided the Americans a spot at Shady Pines to better coordinate with the US consulate and collaborate with the RCMP on cross-border issues mostly concerning transnational organized crime (TNOC). Chrustie's group was focused on identifying strategic level threats and mitigating the danger that TNOC posed to Canadian national security.

In many cases, what there was to work with was just raw data collection, which is not intelligence in itself. Before it can be used, any data has to be collated, analyzed, assessed, and correlated to additional relevant data. Useful information has to be identified and extraneous material removed. But raw data is a solid starting point, and in this case, it might have been the beginning of a covert intelligence effort to dig into the steamy underworld centred on BC's government-run casinos.

An investigation into money-laundering was suggested to the RCMP by Len Meilleur, executive director of the Gaming Policy and Enforcement Branch (GPEB), which regulates the province's casinos. Meilleur wanted law enforcement to work with his gaming compliance and enforcement investigators to determine whether gamblers were laundering money made from drug trafficking, sex trafficking, and other illegal activities through BC's casinos. This led to the creation, in 2016, of the Joint Illegal Gaming Investigation Team (JIGIT),[32] a task force that brought together GPEB and the RCMP's E Division Combined Forces Special Enforcement Unit (CFSEU). JIGIT's was to provide investigative and enforcement response to the insight they gleaned from the data collected by the BC Lottery Corporation (BCLC) and other sources.

Brad Desmarais—a veteran crime fighter who had stints with the Vancouver Police Department before joining BCLC in 2013 as vice-president of corporate security and compliance—was responsible for all anti-money-laundering initiatives in BC casinos at the time. In 2015, Desmarais decided to reach out to Chrustie, who took the initiative when it came to thwarting TNOC and wasn't shy about telling decision makers what was happening. If people within the casinos, the government, and enforcement agencies were looking the other way while mobsters laundered the proceeds of crime, he was going to speak up about it. We were definitely on the same wavelength when it came to exposing the CCP's infiltration of Canada and making threats known to government and other agencies.

Desmarais asked Chrustie to look into a guy named Paul King Jin, a loan shark who provided dirty money to whale gamblers at government casinos. These are high rollers who consistently wager large amounts—as much as $100,000 a hand in baccarat, their preferred game. They could be VIPs or business tycoons, or they could be politically exposed persons (PEPs), those in prominent positions who have the ability to influence decisions and control resources.

Paul King Jin (PKJ) was a self-proclaimed junket operator for the 14K and Sun Yee On triads out of Macau. A junket operator—or what we call a facilitator—is able to provide the whales with anything they want, including prostitutes, drugs, and exotic foods. They rent space in a casino and pay a percentage of any money spent to the operator. The casino makes money when the gambler loses, and the junket is paid a commission from the casino for bringing in VIP gamblers. They also make extra money off of the services they offer to VIP gamblers.

Money launderers were also moving dirty funds through casino bank accounts and high-roller rooms, and they were known to work with organized crime syndicates and foreign spies, which Paul King Jin was also wrapped up in.

PKJ ran his operations through multiple locations, including the River Rock Casino. He was as tough as they come—a former member of the Chinese national boxing team, which is modelled on the Russian Red Army team, a hint that he had connections to the People's Liberation Army (PLA). More PLA connections would reveal themselves through his links to high-roller ex-PLA hero Rongxiang "Tiger" Yuan.[33]

PKJ was born in China but lives in Richmond, BC. He has been a Canadian citizen for over twenty-five years, after moving to Canada just as China's Unholy Trinity was beginning to take root. Before settling on the West Coast, he lived in Montreal and then Toronto, where he is believed to have connected with the Sun Yee On triad.

PKJ is the antithesis of the low-key criminal who flies under the radar. Insiders know that he is not at all careful, and is known to routinely beat people up and deliver bags of money between various casinos and the offices of an underground bank called Silver International. In court filings, PKJ acknowledged delivering more than $2 million in cash to a client in a Richmond coffee shop.[34] Several times, he was caught on surveillance video in the River Rock Casino parking lot, supplying high rollers with hockey bags stuffed full of cash. In his spare time, he operated a massage parlour with known links to prostitution and an assortment of illegal gambling dens run out of private mega-mansions in Richmond. It was these illegal gambling dens that put PKJ in the spotlight. He was overexposed and became a problem—for everyone.

In 2015, the RCMP launched what ended up being the largest money-laundering investigation in Canadian history. Dubbed E-Pirate, the operation targeted Silver International and its owner, Jian Jun Zhu, and determined that more than $200 million per year was laundered through Silver's Richmond offices.[35] PJK was a key figure in the probe, which involved more than two hundred police officers and went on for over two years until it collapsed in the fall of 2017.

E-Pirate revealed links between BC government casinos, casinos in Macau and Las Vegas, and international drug traffickers, organized crime figures, and loan sharks. It also showed how money moved between Canada, Latin America, and Asia via Chinese underground banks. Yet it still collapsed. E-Pirate had the charges stayed because the legal team for the prosecution disclosed the name of a source to the defence. This put that person's life in danger, resulting in a stay of proceedings.

Insiders are divided over whether it was sloppy work or a deliberate move to sabotage the investigation. The "sloppy work" theory was not entirely implausible, given that 200-plus cops had their hands on the files, and given changes in crown lawyers over several years. With the vast amount of data that had to be cataloged and translated during the investigation, it's not hard to imagine mistakes being made.

We also can't dismiss that Operation Dragon Lord talked of clandestine interference by pro-CCP allies and powerful relationships working to help the CCP in Canada. Could these power brokers have derailed E-Pirate?

According to the report, "A detailed examination of contributions to established federal and state political parties in the U.S., Canada and Australia, found that triad-controlled firms have repeatedly made generous donations, and to often-successful political candidates." The report also went on to say that PRC Intelligence exploited their triad ties to successfully recruit foreign Chinese nationals in Canada who are employed in sensitive military-related industries.

While E-Pirate was a BC RCMP "E" Division file, we can't overlook that Cameron Ortis, a senior intelligence official who served as director general of the RCMP's national intelligence coordination centre in Ottawa, may have been involved with the investigation. Ortis was charged in connection to another "E" Division file relating to a company called Phantom Secure,[36] which was selling encrypted cell phones that were the focus of US law enforcement[37] for their use in cartel, Iranian, and Chinese organized crime. Phantom Secure happened to be located a few doors down from the exposed underground bank Silver International.[38]

These questions provide a compelling case that PRC intelligence had infiltrated and influenced Canada's political, military, and law enforcement circles. It is not out of the realm of possibility that E-Pirate was deliberately derailed by agents of the CCP intelligence apparatus.

## A CHANGING OF THE GUARD

In 2017, BC voters went to the polls, and after a closely contested election, the NDP was able to form a minority government with the support of the Green Party. With the new government came new hope that action would finally be taken to stamp out money laundering in BC's casinos.

Much of that hope resided with David Eby, a fresh-faced, hard-working young lawyer who was named the new attorney general. Eby was the former executive director of the BC Civil Liberties Association and had a reputation for being principled but firm. One of his first orders of business was to appoint Peter German, a former deputy commissioner with the RCMP, to independently investigate the intelligence provided to the attorney general. It seemed like the time was right for the tide to turn and for the corruption that was seen or suspected by so many of us who were a part of the investigation process to be exposed. But would he actually call out China for being the source of the money laundering problem in BC?

On March 31, 2018, German's first report was released. Called *Dirty Money*, it confirmed what we, as contributors to the intelligence that was gathered and given to Eby and German, expected—that hundreds of millions of dollars in illegal cash linked to organized crime and the drug trade had flowed through BC casinos, causing widespread economic and social chaos.

But while *Dirty Money* mentioned Chinese Triads and Tongs and Asian organized crime's role in money laundering, it failed to directly connect this activity to the real facilitators of the problem—the Chinese Communist Party (CCP), and specifically the relationship between the triads and influential Chinese business tycoons to China's intelligence agencies—China's Unholy Trinity.

A year later, in 2019, German released his second report, *Dirty Money 2*, which looked at the impact of money laundering in BC on real estate, luxury vehicle sales and horse racing. In this report, money from China was mentioned as being a primary source, but in the context of capital fleeing

China. "In the past few years, Greater Vancouver has been at the confluence of the proceeds of criminal activity, large amounts of capital fleeing China and other countries, and a robust underground economy seeking to evade taxes. These three rivers of money coalesce in Vancouver's property market and in consumer goods," the report said, under the subheading Real Estate. Again, nothing was mentioned about the CCP or China's Unholy Trinity.[39]

## CHAPTER 6

# THE CCP'S WAR CHEST IN THE WEST

## FUNDING OPERATIONS THROUGH TRANSNATIONAL ORGANIZED CRIME

Hundreds of millions in funds were washed through major casinos in BC, and much can be associated to illicit fentanyl sales. Of an estimated $7.4 billion that is believed to have been laundered in BC in 2018, $5 billion is said to have passed through the real estate market.[1] According to BC Minister of Finance Carole James, "The amount of money being laundered in B.C. and through real estate is much more than anyone predicted."[2]

We could sense that Attorney General Eby was becoming increasingly frustrated with the state of play in BC. He wanted to do more to stop the flow of dirty money from China, but it seemed as if he was getting blocked. Peter German's reports had identified the PRC as the main source of

---

PHOTO: David Eby, the Attorney General in BC (2017–2022), tackled the problem of organized crime and the laundering of hundreds of millions of dollars in BC casinos.

illicit money coming into Canada, but stopped short of tying it to China's Unholy Trinity or analyzing its overall impact on real estate in the region.[3]

In an attempt to do more, Attorney General Eby appointed former provincial Supreme Court justice Austin Cullen to head up a wide-ranging commission of inquiry into money laundering. Commonly known as the Cullen Commission, the Commission of Inquiry into Money Laundering in British Columbia was tasked with digging into the problem and proposing solutions.

The presser announcing the commission was a well-rehearsed public relations event, complete with grainy closed-circuit footage showing bags of money being brought into the River Rock Casino and clandestine meetings taking place in the parking lot. It was clearly meant to convince the public that the new government was serious about addressing crime and corruption.

The public heard virtual testimony from 199 witnesses over 143 hearing sessions. What was happening in Vancouver was more than just money laundering, more than just one threat stream. One of the Cullen Commission's sub-categories was Transnational Organized Crime (TNOC), which also includes drug trafficking, human smuggling, extortion, and a host of other illicit activities that are perpetrated across international borders by air, land, and sea. We knew the key threat actor was the Communist Party of China and China's Unholy Trinity, not just organized crime. Their target was not just BC and Canada, either, but also the US, meaning that the United States also had a stake in how the BC government addressed what was going on. China's hybrid war with the West reaches well beyond the Canada-US border and makes use of not just criminal enterprises but also rogue states like Russia and Iran.

The problem, as we saw it, was that the government was telling the public its version of the problem—which was that what was happening in Vancouver was a localized white-collar crime problem, isolated to the region. It was presented to the public as if it were something that could be fixed with a few new laws, the creation of a sin commission, and some policy changes.

What's worse is that many of the participants who were given status to speak at the hearings equated calling out criminal activity originating in China under the control of the CCP regime with being racist. This despite the fact that these same participants appeared to have no similar concerns with calling out Mexican drug cartels or Middle Eastern organized crime networks, who, German pointed out, also have "a strong foothold in Vancouver."[4]

The view that calling out China for its role in money laundering is automatically racist was bolstered by lawyer Jessica Magonet of the BC Civil Liberties Association (BCCLA). Magonet chastised Eby for making "broad statements about Chinese investment" in Vancouver real estate, which she said "may help perpetuate a harmful narrative that conflates Chinese money with dirty money in British Columbia."[5] In an article later posted to the BCCLA website, Magonet wrote about the organization's efforts to challenge alleged anti-Asian racism at the commission, and asserted that "contrary to popular belief, foreign investment is not driving BC's skyrocketing housing prices."[6] She also lauded Professor Henry Yu, who had appeared before the committee several months earlier, for his "critical insight into how anti-Asian racism, white supremacy, and Canada's immigration laws have shaped our conversations about 'dirty money.'"

Dr. Henry Yu is a professor of history at the University of British Columbia (UBC) who first came to wider public attention in 2018, when he testified in a class action lawsuit challenging the foreign-buyer property tax brought in by David Eby to help cool the Lower Mainland's overheated real estate market. A Chinese student tried to certify the class action by arguing that the tax discriminated against Asian buyers like her.[7] Dr. Yu provided expert testimony on BC's history of discrimination and submitted a written report to the court, but the judge ultimately excluded the document, saying Dr. Yu "fail[ed] to support some statements with identifiable sources." It was "more like a position paper in the form of an argument rather than an expert report," the judge wrote. He also noted that Dr. Yu "was often non-responsive to questions and argumentative[,] acting more like an advocate than an independent expert."[8]

At the Cullen Commission, Dr. Yu once again appeared as an expert witness, and again offered testimony based largely on personal opinion held up as fact. For example, he said that in Vancouver's Shaughnessy neighbourhood, "there is a fairly de facto or in practice idea that you don't sell to Chinese."[9] He also implied that the BC government had no standing to question modern-day real estate transactions because the province occupies traditional Indigenous lands.[10]

When we asked the commission's legal team why they would have allowed Dr. Yu to testify as an expert after his work was deemed deficient in the previous high-profile case, they issued a statement that said, in part, "The Commission team is aware of the reality of racialized discussion in the public realm regarding real estate in Vancouver and wanted to provide the Commissioner with context and insight on this important topic. The Commission team called multiple subject matter experts in a range of areas . . . and felt that it would be beneficial to hear from Dr. Yu because of his extensive work in this important topic."

Just to be clear: there is no question that British Columbia has a history of shameful attitudes towards and discriminatory laws targeting Chinese people, and that prejudicial attitudes exist to this day. In fact, anti-Asian racism rose exponentially during the pandemic, as has been well documented in the media.[11] But this situation has also been amplified by the CCP. This is a textbook United Front stratagem, whereby legitimate issues like heightened racism are co-opted in ways that magnify the problem, create discord, and incite further social chaos.

We had also heard from some of our sources that the premier's office, at the behest of influential United Front agents, had pulled strings to get Dr. Yu standing at the Cullen Commission, specifically to redirect the political narrative away from China as the main source of dirty money and as the cause for the real estate crisis. This seemed plausible, given what we knew about the deep connections between Yu and an advisory group that he co-chaired with David Choi from the United Front led National Congress of Chinese Canadians. The advisory group, known as the Legacy Initiatives Advisory Council (LIAC), was set up to advise the premier and the government and to implement the recommendations from the Chinese Historical Wrongs Consultation Final Report, authored by Teresa Wat.[12] This council includes several members who have been appointed consultants for the Chinese community by United Front organizations.[13]

Numerous members of the advisory committee have strong ties to the BC government and/or the Communist Party of China. One of those is Don Bain, who was also special advisor to the premier, and now serves as deputy chief of staff for both Horgan and the new premier, David Eby. Also on the committee is William Ma, who was instrumental in organizing the 2019 Ninth Conference of the World Guangdong Community Federation event in Vancouver for the United Front's Overseas Chinese Affairs Office of China's Guangdong Province. Ma was also involved in designating Vancouver Chinatown as a National Heritage Site, another United Front led project, that we discuss in more detail in a later chapter.[14] [15]

Other council members include Thomas Chan, head of the Chinese Consolidated Benevolent Association, and Queenie Choo, the previously mentioned CEO of the United Front organization, S.U.C.C.E.S.S.

The Chinese Historical Wrongs Consultation report-grew out of a series of public forums and was produced by Wat's office, which recommended that the government provide $1 million to fund "initiatives that celebrate the contributions of both Chinese Canadians and others who suffered discrimination."[16] Although it was only meant to be a temporary committee, the LIAC carried on its work for several years, until the NDP government created the Chinese-Canadian Community Advisory Committee in 2018.[17] [18]

LIAC was a perfect example of how the CCP can legitimately influence change and push for Beijing friendly policies at a provincial level by supporting a pro-China politician who gets voted in. They in turn create or amplify a problem, back it up with a study or testimony from an expert, recommend the creation of a committee, then stack it with pro-China appointees who have connections to media outlets, universities, political parties, and other influential entities. From there the propaganda spreads. In effect, the United Front is creating a legitimate platform to influence and strong-arm senior government officials to steer public sentiment in a pro-China direction. The return is political support from the United Front network of hometown associations whose membership and influence represents a large portion of the diaspora.

Influencing politicians isn't even something that the United Front hides anymore. They put it on full display. Not only is the United Front coordinating activities between the East and West hubs, but multiple Canadian Teochew associations have also consolidated into one powerful organization. Those giving speeches at the grand inauguration ceremony were representatives from all three levels of government, including Canadian MP Wilson Miao (Liberal), Members of the Legislative Assembly of BC (MLAs) George Chow (NDP) and Michael Lee (BC United), and various municipal mayors and councillors, including Vancouver Mayor Ken Sim, who used the opportunity to thank the Teochew members for supporting his candidacy.[19]

Consider also what the commanding-level United Front organization, the Canadian Alliance of Chinese Associations (CACA), has admitted to. In 2017, prior to the money laundering inquiry, a statement was issued. Wang Dianqi, who was the Chairperson of CACA at the time, along with sixteen representatives of the Chinese community held a roundtable meeting at a hotel in Richmond with then Minister of Finance, Michael de Jong. The meeting was called to discuss the 2017 provincial budget introduced by the BC provincial government of the day. The press release states that they (the United Front) put forward their opinions and suggestions to the provincial government on topics such as regional budget details, elderly services, and policy stability. United Front agent Wang Dianqi also made specific requests, including that the provincial government attach importance to the contribution of Chinese people, especially new immigrants, to British Columbia, and allocate funds to build monuments on twenty-one Chinese historical sites. The reason given for the demand was "so that the next generation of Chinese can increase their love and dedication to Canada on the basis of understanding history." What they really mean is to dictate history according to CCP-approved narratives.

Speaking about Wang Dianqi's other demands of the provincial government, the press release said that, "He also hopes that the provincial government can truly enrich the people with the fiscal surplus, such as increasing investment in Richmond law and order issues."

Other sources of information revealed teams that were scheduled to visit election candidates led by Wang Dianqi, and election support tips and clinics set up by the United Front in the Vancouver region.[20][21]

Returning to the burning question of why the government would not want the truth to come out about the CCP being the backbone of money laundering's impact on housing and the fentanyl crisis, we can see a twofold answer.

First, politicians were more interested in looking like they were taking action to combat money laundering than in actually doing something. They wanted to appease the public with reports and inquiries that go nowhere, and in doing so, hopefully pick up some votes, knowing that nothing would change. They were playing politics with our national security.

The second reason is even more terrifying than the first. Simply put, Canada couldn't put the cork back in the bottle. As the author of the report on Operation Dragon Lord astutely surmised, China's Unholy Trinity had infiltrated Canada from as far back as the 1990s and was now fully embedded in politics, business, and government.

Imagine the fallout if every level of the Canadian government decoupled from China financially. The Cullen Commission couldn't let the public know that dirty money from China was flooding BC and causing social chaos, including a housing crisis and a fentanyl epidemic.

## DERAILING THE INQUIRY

As the Cullen Commission progressed, it became clear that many parties were using it as a platform to promote their own narratives to the general public. Lawyers representing employees of the province's casinos and the regulatory agencies meant to be overseeing them portrayed their clients as whistleblowers who tried to sound the alarm but were stymied at every turn. Meanwhile, the provincial government of the day, the NDP, didn't want to cause a panic and jeopardize the votes that the United Front would bring in. They also seemed to use the commission as a way of tarnishing the Liberals, their main political rivals. The RCMP, for their part, didn't want the public to be left with the impression that they were not capable of stopping transnational organized crime.[22]

There was also another elephant in the room that no one really wanted to talk about. That is the simple, sad, and undeniable truth that the province of BC generated $25 billion in gambling revenue over the past thirty-five years, and no one wanted to kill the golden goose. In 2021–22 alone, BC's casinos took in $1.3 billion in net income, and $11.2 million of that went into the COVID-strapped coffers of the federal government.[23] And here's another harsh truth: Even if Canada really wanted to stop the flow of dirty money from China, it would be almost impossible to do it because the country is too corrupt and the sources of funds too well hidden.

All of this explains why there was no appetite for pursuing money laundering at the provincial or federal level. The province of BC had huge business agreements with Chinese companies, politicians didn't want to burn votes, the RCMP wanted to look like they were on top of crime, and the public purse depended on casino money.

If that's not bad enough, between 2021–22, $147.2 million was allocated to a special health account, at least in part to fight the fentanyl epidemic that was the source of much of the dirty money in the first place.

Ironically, BC needed the financial proceeds from money laundering in order to pay for its fentanyl crisis.

BC's problem with money laundering is that it is part of a self-perpetuating system that has no purpose other than to sustain itself—a self-licking ice cream cone.

What we had hoped to see was a commission that looked at the whole-of-society aspect of money laundering, and especially at connections between the PRC and transnational organized crime. Multi-agency intelligence reporting indicated that the United Front was facilitating the movement of people and money into and out of Canada. We also hoped the commission would consider the use of criminal agents with ties to the CCP in both illegal and government casinos, not only in BC but across Canada. The problem, we knew, was not just low-level money-laundering gangs but multinational criminal enterprises connected to nation states operating in Canada.

You may be wondering where the Sisters are in all of this. Isn't it their raison d'être to collect and analyze intelligence in order to expose threats to our national security? Yes! But unlike the CIA or other three-letter agencies within the Five Eyes intelligence community, CSIS is a sub-ministry that takes its orders from Public Safety Canada, which, in turn, falls under authority of the Prime Minister's Office. Lacking support, it has been unable to counter the increased threat from China.

There are also limitations within the Canadian legal system, including a lack of financial and human resources, that seriously impact the ability of law enforcement to tackle transnational organized crime. In his reports, Peter German concluded that lack of law enforcement was the real obstacle to addressing the money-laundering problems in BC. For example, in an investigation that ran from 2010 to 2012, the RCMP failed to find a single predicate crime or identify the source of any of the money being used in the casinos. From then until 2015, German noted, there was no policing in the casinos whatsoever.[24] When the RCMP finally started looking seriously at the casinos in 2015, the money launderers were already entrenched, and had forged connections to people and organizations that presented serious national security threats.

Canada is the only country in the Five Eyes alliance that does not have a national strategy on transnational organized crime. In 2011, the Obama White House officially acknowledged the threat these criminal enterprises posed to US national security, warning that "TOC networks are proliferating, striking new and powerful alliances, and engaging in a range of illicit activities as never before . . . [resulting in] a convergence of threats that have evolved to become more complex, volatile, and destabilizing."[25] This acknowledgement opened the door for information to be shared among Five Eyes defence, security, intelligence, and law enforcement agencies at the classified level. It has made it possible for the US, the UK, and Australia to combat cartels and terrorist organizations like Hezbollah. It seems obvious that Canada would want to be part of that team, but the rules here are not set up to stop high-level bad actors.

In Canada, we have legal protocols that make it difficult for law enforcement agencies to track suspicious financial transactions or untangle organizations that are made up of layers of numbered companies. And even when we get that information, we don't have a way to share it among agencies that handle classified data. We just don't have the same processes as the rest of the Five Eyes members.

Let's say you have a gangster who commits crimes and also has ties to Russia or China. In Canada, each piece of evidence or intelligence gathered against this person will be held in a separate file by a different agency. No one is able to fit the pieces together to see the bigger picture—or what's sometimes referred to as the common operating picture (COP). There's no one looking at this person's foreign ties and trying to understand who is doing what with whom. The culture is to lock up information to keep it from being disclosed, but the unintended effect of that is to limit people's ability to see the COP. This makes it impossible to maintain an awareness of the full spectrum of threats to Canada. Information is power, and law enforcement agencies don't want to lose control of their data.

Another problem is that Canada is reactive, not proactive. We aren't good at anticipating crimes and stopping them before they can happen. This reactive posture allows bad actors to grow their networks without fear that a national law enforcement agency is actively trying to stop them. Instead, law enforcement waits until a crime is committed, or reported, and then collects evidence related only to that crime.

To collaborate effectively with our Five Eyes partners, we have to understand the threat streams and entities operating within Canada. Patterns, trends, and associations will help us forecast future criminal activity and can guide intelligence collection. When the entire picture is available, it's easier to make connections. There is a world of difference between investigating a murder, which has an obvious starting point, and identifying a terrorist who is believed to be planning an attack. The latter has no predicate offence. Do we wait for the bomb to go off? Or do we do everything within the law to try to stop it? That could mean checking to see if this individual has unpaid taxes or an unregistered firearm or money coming in from a suspicious source. But if there's no plan to maintain some level of awareness across the threat environment, we're at the mercy of the criminal networks and have nothing of worth to offer to our partners in other countries.

This is why it was such a problem that BC's NDP government was doing an about-face on its own inquiry by downplaying China's role as the main source of dirty money coming into the province. In 2020, the BC NDP platform didn't mention money laundering once.[26] Nothing to see here, folks!

And the Cullen Commission continued on down this path as well. In an interview, senior commission lawyer Brock Martland fell just short of admitting that the commission was deliberately steering clear of criticizing China. "I don't want to sound too defensive," he said, "but I don't see that there is a basis to say that we have . . . come down on one side or the other in terms of either making this about China or Asia . . . or on the other hand avoiding the topic. I think we tried to follow the evidence where it takes us."[27]

Even the City of Vancouver got in on the act by trying to co-opt the term "Vancouver Model" in a way that took the focus off of China. Coined by Professor John Langdale, transnational crime and financial crime expert in Macquarie University's Department of Security Studies and Criminology, the term "Vancouver Model" was widely adopted by Canadian media during the Cullen Commission hearings, as a way of describing how wealthy elites looking to move large amounts of money out of China make deals with Asian criminal syndicates with links to Vancouver.[28] As if to reorient the public from anything that could be used to criticize China, then-Vancouver Mayor Kennedy Stewart pointedly co-opted the term in 2021, transferring it from money laundering to the decriminalization of drugs. Mayor Stewart's office showed off the term's new meaning in a one-page announcement that mentions the "Vancouver Model" four times in five paragraphs. Promising to address "substance use as a health issue, rather

than a criminal justice issue," the mayor says that, "City staff, expert consultants, and members of my own team have worked overtime to develop
a Vancouver Model that fully embraces a health-focussed approach to save
lives." Detached from its original context in discussions of transnational
crime, the Vancouver Model becomes a way for the City of Vancouver to
"work with community organizations and people with lived experience to
divert drug users away from the criminal justice system, connect them with
health care, and support them on a path towards healing."[29]

In addition to forcing law enforcement agencies to adopt new language,
this rebranding also takes a page right out of the United Front Work
Department playbook. In an era when news stories last hours instead of
days or weeks, this was actually a textbook disinformation trap that would
ensure the Vancouver Model was lost to everyone except those who were
completely immersed in the story.

## IN CANADA, TRIADS ARE IN CHARGE

There is a justifiable fear that gangsters who are given access to testimony
and court documents could seek retribution. There is also a very real
concern for the safety and security of government employees and law
enforcement officers who testify in court.

These fears became a reality when Justice Cullen decided to grant
standing to Paul King Jin (PKJ), a known criminal and the key subject of
the RCMP's E-Pirate probe into Silver International, a Richmond-based
underground bank that allegedly laundered as much as $220 million a year.

Once granted standing at the Cullen Commission, PKJ had the ability
to make submissions and otherwise exercise the rights of a participant—
including by questioning witnesses.

Shockingly, that decision was made even though PKJ had recently
been the victim of an attempted assassination. While sitting at a window
seat in a Japanese restaurant in the heart of Richmond, Jin and his Silver
International business partner, Jian Jun Zhu, a fellow gangster who had just
returned to Canada from China, were shot at point-blank range. Zhu was
killed and PKJ was wounded. The RCMP quickly concluded that it was a
targeted shooting, with Sergeant Frank Zang telling the media, "There is
nothing so far to suggest this incident is connected to the ongoing Lower

Mainland gang conflict or any of the other recent acts of violence."[30] Two men were later arrested in connection with the crime.[31]

In 2015, the police warned PKJ after they got a tip that his life was in danger. This time, there was no warning. Why not? How good are police informants if they don't know about one of the most brazen targeted hits in Vancouver history? The shooter was a small-time hood, but that doesn't mean the hit wasn't ordered at a very high level. Maybe it was the cartels, or the Iranians, or someone higher than PKJ who had issues with Zhu. So many possibilities. But one thing was certain: this was no low-level gang conflict. And a target of an attempted hit like that has no business standing in front of a provincial commission of inquiry, questioning witnesses. The whole thing conjured images of John Gotti, the Teflon Don, smirking in court and thinking that he would never go to jail because no one would ever testify against him.

Granting PKJ standing at the Cullen Commission was just the latest in a string of shocking missteps that allowed PKJ to operate his CCP-connected criminal enterprise with impunity. There was also the failure of the E-Pirate investigation, which collapsed when the prosecution released unredacted files to the defence, putting the lives of confidential informants in jeopardy.[32] And then there was the government-issued licence given to PKJ's son to operate a security company out of his father's martial arts gym. We helped break that story when one of our intel sources told us that PKJ was starting a security company and had created a promotional video using a doppelgänger for Huawei CFO Meng Wanzhou.

Perhaps Justice Cullen naively believed that by giving PKJ standing, he was giving equal say to the criminal underworld, whose members rarely speak out. He suggested as much in his opening statement: "It is important to note that because of [their] secretive nature, money laundering activities do not leave behind much clear evidence of their existence," Justice Cullen said, "nor do they generally produce witnesses who are motivated to publicly speak about it."[33]

At any rate, the Cullen Commission carried on, calling witnesses and examining evidence before releasing its final report in June 2022. That report concluded unequivocally that "extensive money laundering occurred in the casinos of the Lower Mainland over the course of a decade, from approximately 2008 to 2018."[34] Justice Cullen estimated that in that period, casinos accepted hundreds of millions of dollars from VIP patrons, a practice that "ensured continued demand for illicit cash." This demand, he said, "was exploited by criminal organizations, who used it as a means of converting bulky and highly suspicious cash into more convenient and discreet forms while also transferring it to other jurisdictions."[35]

Cullen also examined the effectiveness of law enforcement and other efforts to stop money laundering. That examination, he wrote, showed that "there is a real need in British Columbia for a dedicated provincial money laundering intelligence and investigation unit."[36] He also urged the province to make "significantly stronger use of asset forfeiture—both criminal and civil," and create "an unexplained wealth order regime."

Cullen's recommendations were fine as far as they went, but over the course of the eighteen-month inquiry, it became obvious to us that there was little interest in uncovering the full spectrum of threats in the province. To do that, the commission would have had to bring in the Five Eyes agencies, secure a classified area to hold proceedings, and give commission members the highest levels of security clearance so they could question intelligence agents. Without getting to the root causes of money laundering—which is a component of TNOC, which, in turn, is a component of hybrid warfare—the commission was never going to address the full spectrum of illicit CCP operations. David Eby had attempted to elevate the provincial inquiry to a federal level, but his efforts were swept away. We can only conclude that Ottawa didn't want to be exposed to full legal scrutiny. Even as we write this, Ottawa is fighting against calls for a public inquiry into Chinese political interference as presented in Spring 2023.[37]

Nor was the provincial NDP government blameless. A week after the Cullen Commission wrapped up its witness testimony, Finance Minister Selina Robinson named Greg Moore the new head of the British Columbia Lottery Corporation (BCLC). Moore was previously the CEO of Icona Properties, a real estate development firm founded by Tony Cai, who was a member of the municipal arm of the Chinese People's Political Consultative Conference (CPPCC), an advisory body of the CCP.[38] In 2017, Moore had travelled to China as part of a trade delegation coordinated by the Chinese consulate in Vancouver and sponsored by businessman James Wu of the Canada China City and Town Friendship Association, which the *Toronto Star* described as working to "promote closer ties with Beijing and collaborate with government-affiliated associations in China."[39]

The simple truth is that Canada is soft on criminals and has not even attempted to understand the nexus between immigration and TNOC. This is a sentiment that even PKJ agrees with.[40]

We interviewed PKJ at his gym on the outskirts of Richmond, beside the banks of the Fraser River. Ironically, the gym is just a few blocks from the Richmond RCMP detachment. When we went there, the government was pursuing Jin and his wife, Apple Wei, with a civil forfeiture claim on the grounds that the building, valued at more than $7.7 million, was bought with the proceeds of crime.[41] Months later, PKJ converted part of it into an auto body shop for high-end cars and a private restaurant.[42] It wasn't lost on us that body shops are often linked to car-theft rings as part of a broader organized crime enterprise. Meanwhile, creating a private restaurant inside his gym would offer PJK a greater degree of protection for VIPs from China, including visitors from the CCP.

Paul King Jin started the interview by declaring his love for his adopted home. "I love the country," he said. "Canada is a better country."[43] As we began to press him on topics like the aborted E-Pirate investigation, he immediately became defensive. "Nobody who charged me, nothing, four years already," he said.[44]

When the gym wasn't being used for boxing tournaments or as a chop shop, Jin's gym often played host to high-profile events where Canadian politicians rubbed elbows with gangsters and Chinese state officials.[45] MPs Joe Peschisolido, Raymond Chan, and Carla Qualtrough were among those who showed up for photo opportunities with Jin at various events like the Canada-China-US-Mexico Elite Friendship Boxing Tournament, an exhibition-style prep tournament for the Chinese national boxing team ahead of the Tokyo Olympics.[46]

The Chinese boxing team event was especially noteworthy because it brought together all three entities of China's Unholy Trinity: government officials, gangsters, and business tycoons. In fact, PKJ's connection to the 14K triad, one of the most active in Canada and the second-largest triad in the world, was a significant piece tying together TNOC and the CCP in British Columbia.

It's an understatement to say that we were shocked when BC's minister of tourism, arts, and culture, Lisa Beare, held a press conference with PKJ inside his gym in 2019, even as the federal government was trying to foreclose on the property.[47] When we tried to ask her if she realized she'd been rubbing elbows with a known triad member, she said, "I'll have to get back to you on that." Of course, we never heard from her again.

Politicians go to these events to shake hands and pose for pictures because they are shilling for votes, and they know votes are available in the Chinese Canadian community. Plus, they get treated like celebrities, in keeping with the CCP's influence operations playbook. But these events are a two-way street, and the politicians are not the only ones benefiting. All too often, they end up as props in CCP propaganda campaigns.

Vancouver City Councillor Pete Fry told the *Toronto Star* that he didn't initially realize he was being used in this way. "I've attended events organized by Chinese government officials," he explained, "and see how they later manipulate the messaging to go hard on a nationalistic framing of the people attending their event and implying things that weren't perhaps expressed by the attendees."[48] Fry eventually had his eyes opened, but too many politicians still fail to see what's going on right in front of them.

## BIG CAT AND THE CONSULATE

But for all that, PKJ was not the fat cat at the top. That honour goes to Rongxiang "Tiger" Yuan, a former PLA war hero with a distinctive tiger-stripe scar on his face. We started to look at Tiger after someone from the RCMP National Weapons Enforcement Support Team (NWEST) mentioned that he had amassed the largest private gun collection in Canada.[49] While doing some social network analysis using open-source intelligence techniques, we came across images that we believed Jin's bodyguard had taken at Tiger Yuan's compound outside of Vancouver. The compound, known as the Tiger's Lair, was on eleven acres of prime agricultural land, surrounded by fifteen-foot cedar hedges and a chain-link fence, and guarded by more than thirty security cameras. It was also a great place to entertain VIPs from China, including CCP heavyweights.

Although the photos taken by the bodyguard didn't confirm the existence of a rumoured underground shooting range and fortified bunker, they did show that the compound housed a large cache of weapons and ammunition, as well as an impressive collection of military vehicles.

Tiger Yuan's facial scar was a memento of his days as a platoon leader for the Fourth Reconnaissance Company, fighting the Vietnamese army in the Xinhai region in the late 1980s. We know from historical propaganda articles published in China that Chairman Deng Xiaoping granted Tiger and his comrades hero status for a mission in which they covertly infiltrate enemy ranks, apparently by donning Vietnamese army uniforms.

Thirty years into the future, Tiger is a billionaire who purportedly made his money in aluminum before branching out into other industries in China, the US, and Canada. He wasn't some reclusive Howard Hughes–type billionaire. He made his presence known around Vancouver and ran the Canada-China Friendship Association, a recognized United Front group. But he wasn't as conspicuous as some United Front comrades, who loved to be a part of CCP propaganda efforts built around sports, entertainment, and cultural events. Still, Tiger did like a good party, and he once gave a speech at a large concert by famed opera singer Li Yugang, which was attended by CCP elite and Chinese consulate members.

Our team also found private video of Tiger and Beijing-born Chinese singer and actor Sha Bao Liang singing karaoke, and we gave a copy to Global News investigative journalist Sam Cooper and others to publish on social media to help expose relationships between Chinese citizens in Canada and CCP members.

It's easy to understand why PRC consular officials in Vancouver would be drawn to Tiger. He has a commanding presence and a noticeable military posture when he stands. In fact, CCP officials appeared to hold him in such high regard that in 2019, China's top diplomat in Vancouver, Consul General Tong Xiaoling, invited him to sit with her at a major CCP-led event called the Chinese Cultural Heritage Festival. Tiger was even invited to give a speech to a stadium filled with several thousand pro-CCP attendees. "Don't forget who brought you here to Canada—the motherland," he said, to thundering applause.

We still had many questions about Tiger, though. News reports described him as a "whale gambler," and we knew he had connections to suspected money launderers and organized crime. We also knew he was connected to CCP officials, industrialists, and influential Canadian politicians like MP Joe Peschisolido. But there was a lot we didn't know. For instance, was he still in the PLA, or had he perhaps transferred to the Ministry of State Security (MSS)? And if the latter, had he been sent to Canada on some kind of mission? Was the Tiger's Lair compound really just a hedonistic hideaway for members of the CCP? And if so, what was the purpose of all those guns and ammo and the rumoured fortified bunker?

Perhaps he was more than just a businessman. Could Tiger be the head of United Front operations in BC?

Whatever his role for the motherland is, it was important. We could see that from the deference paid to him by the consular officials and other CCP VIPs. He was obviously much more than simply a whale gambler. We know that China's Unholy Trinity works with junket operators and gamblers and even wealthy tycoons who make their money legitimately. Tiger was involved in many business endeavours—some legitimate and some likely not. We focused our attention on one: a digital currency that our research suggested was part of Xi Jinping's Belt and Road Initiative.

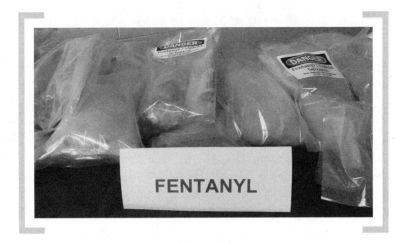

## CHAPTER 7

# THE CCP'S BLUEPRINT FOR THE WEST

## THE AIMS AND OBJECTIVES FOR THE PARTY

The CCP regime has gargantuan ambitions to become the dominant world superpower by 2049—it's a vision of the future that Xi Jinping calls the Chinese Dream. In his very first address to his people as president, in March 2013, Xi said, "We must make persistent efforts, press ahead with indomitable will, continue to push forward the great cause of socialism with Chinese characteristics, and strive to achieve the Chinese dream of great rejuvenation of the Chinese nation."[1] He upheld patriotism, reform, and innovation as the core of this mission. "To realize the Chinese road," he asserted, "we must spread the Chinese spirit."

On the way to that great rejuvenation, the government has, for decades, been rolling out policy statements known as Five-Year Plans. These plans, which tackle everything from corporate finance to information infrastruc-

---

PHOTO: China is deliberately fueling the illicit fentanyl epidemic in the West to destabilize civil society.

ture to green technology, are strategic blueprints for how the government intends to drive the Chinese economy. The 14th Five-Year Plan, released in 2021, focused largely on the digital transformation of Chinese society and called for the creation and implementation of a new currency known as the digital yuan or the digital renminbi. It's an idea that has the potential to become the single biggest threat to the free world.

To grasp the danger this poses, we first have to understand how the Chinese economy works. The world tends to think of China as an economic powerhouse, but it's still a socialist market economy with a significant degree of government intervention and a large number of state-owned enterprises. It's a system that has served the country well as it transformed itself into a more advanced modern society. But, as numerous economists have pointed out, it's also a system replete with contradictions. How can an economy operate in the public good and serve private interests at the same time? In reality, the "socialist" part massively outweighs the "market" part—meaning, corporations are always expected to put ideology ahead of profit.

This mix of public and private enterprise may look like a type of capitalism to some, but ultimately the economy, like everything else in the country, is tightly controlled by the Chinese Communist Party and reflects the CCP's authoritarian impulses. One recent example is China's social credit system, which was launched in 2014 and has been variously described as a tool for promoting social stability and an "Orwellian creation" designed for social control.[2]

The social credit system monitors people's behaviour and deducts or adds credit based on things they do or fail to do. On its face, this might sound like a conventional credit score, the kind we all have with companies like Equifax and Transunion, which collect information about us to determine our credit-worthiness. But the Chinese credit system is much, much more far-reaching than that. It logs not just financial behaviour but also social and what might be called moral behaviour. You could, for example, lose points for jaywalking or playing too many video games and gain them for donating to charity or having children.[3] As your score rises, you may be rewarded with benefits such as better schools for your children or shorter wait times at hospitals. But if your score falls, you could end up on the positively Orwellian-sounding List of Dishonest Persons Subject to Enforcement—more commonly known as the blacklist.

This is exactly what happened to Liu Hu, a journalist who often wrote about official corruption and misconduct in China. He was charged with and found guilty of defamation, according to a story in *The Globe and Mail*, and in 2017, he discovered that he had been placed on the blacklist. People on the list are deprived of many fundamental rights—in Liu's case, he was unable to get loans, buy property, or book plane tickets. And he was just one of the seven million people on the list at that time.

As the social credit system grows in reach and influence, the list will only get longer. The goal is to have a country-wide system that assigns every business and citizen a code or identity number linked to a permanent record. "If you go to a credit China website, and you have an entity's credit code, you can type that in and pull up credit records," Samantha Hoffman, of the Australian Strategic Policy Institute, explained to *Wired UK*. "Individuals will have ID-linked codes."[4] It's not hard to imagine how this level of surveillance and data collection could go wrong. "Put in the hands of the Chinese government the ability to determine your level of honesty and you have a perfect storm of human-rights abuses," said Maya Wang, a researcher for Human Rights Watch.[5]

Maybe it seems like this is China's problem and we really shouldn't care if they turn their country into a dystopian surveillance state. But in an increasingly globalized world, territorial borders mean less and less. This is where we come back to the digital yuan.

## CONTROLLABLY ANONYMOUS

Unlike bitcoin and Ethereum, the digital yuan is not a cryptocurrency but a central bank digital currency (CBDC). That means it's issued by the People's Bank of China (PBOC) and then distributed to individual branches, which, in turn, puts the currency into consumers' hands (via an app, for instance). In an article in a state-backed publication, Fan Yifei, deputy governor of the PBOC, said that there was a "pressing need to digitalize cash and coin" because these traditional currencies are expensive to produce and store.[6] He noted, too, that paper currency is particularly vulnerable to counterfeiting. Proponents of the digital yuan also argue that it will allow authorities to better track and curtail illegal activities like money laundering, tax evasion, and terrorist financing because transactions will be reported to the central bank on what Fan called "a controllably anonymous basis."

It's this last element that gives critics pause. Journalist Frederick Kempe, writing for CNBC, noted, "China's different approach to privacy provides it a competitive advantage. The U.S. and European need to satisfy privacy concerns will complicate CBDC development. Conversely, Beijing sees the digital yuan as a way to further strengthen its already formidable surveillance state."[7] This becomes more concerning when you understand that China's ambition is to create a global digital currency. "Chinese officials have made no secret," wrote Kempe, "that their greatly accelerated efforts at introducing and distributing the digital yuan are an opening move in their long-term strategy to undermine the dollar's global supremacy and expand their influence." A partnership with SWIFT, which facilitates international financial transactions, Kempe noted, was a sure sign of Beijing's plans for its digital currency.

Some commentators see even greater threats. Kyle Bass, a financial expert and hedge fund manager, described the CCP's foray into digital currency as a Trojan Horse—a way for Beijing to gain influence and control around the world, particularly in the West.[8] This is a view shared widely by our contacts in the defence and intelligence communities. And sources have told us that the ultimate plan is to integrate the digital yuan and the corporate social credit program to create a sophisticated and comprehensive surveillance system with a global reach.

At its heart, the digital yuan is really about monitoring and control. If you know who is buying what, why, and when, that gives you leverage you can use in all kinds of ways. "You're giving them the ability to export their digital authoritarianism to you," Bass explained. "The Chinese government could bribe you directly without being under the watchful eye of regulators or law enforcement. Imagine if the Chinese government has the ability to bribe, cajole, coerce anyone anywhere in the world if you're holding on to their money. Imagine that world. That world would be a much worse place to live in."

This view was echoed by Sir Jeremy Fleming, one of the UK's top spy chiefs, who warned that the digital yuan could be used for nefarious ends. "If wrongly implemented, it gives a hostile state actor the ability to surveil transactions," he said in a 2021 interview with the *Financial Times*. "It gives them the ability . . . to exercise control over what is conducted on those digital currencies."[9] Fleming noted that when foreign states have the potential to collect data on another country's citizens, it could erode that country's sovereignty. China, he said, was the "biggest strategic issue" facing the UK and was "starting to exercise real influence on the way in which the rules of the road are going to operate in a technology and digital context."

That influence is a concern for both individuals and corporations. Potentially, the Communist Party could rewrite the rules for any Western company that does business in China. They could say, for instance, that if you export goods to the country, you must accept payment in digital yuan, without exception. Now imagine that you get into a dispute or say something about China that the CCP doesn't like. With a few keystrokes, they could cut you off from your funds—they'd have your goods *and* the money they were supposed to pay you for them. If you think that sounds far-fetched, remember what happened to H&M when the clothing giant decided to stop using cotton from Xinjiang over concerns about forced labour. In response, a CCP youth group spearheaded an extensive boycott and brutal social media campaign that all but erased the company from China's retail landscape.[10] In other words, there already exists a punishment-based system for corporations that don't comply with the regime—and that will only intensify once the government has more punitive tools at its disposal.

## GETTING THE WORD OUT

We were so disturbed by China's social credit system and how it might intersect with the digital yuan that we published an article about it in the April 17, 2021, edition of the *Sunday Guardian* in India.[11] Our attempts to sound the alarm in Canada had mostly been stonewalled, and this seemed to be the only way to get the message out. Even though India is on the other side of the globe, it faces many of the same issues as Canada when it comes to the CCP. The Indian government has a vested interest in working with Western intelligence agencies and investigative journalists because the country is perpetually on the cusp of war with China.

In part, our article told the story of a seemingly innocuous Vancouver hot pot restaurant to show how the Chinese government might collect data on another country's citizens, all in plain sight. The manager of the Haidilao Hot Pot in Kitsilano confirmed to us that sixty surveillance cameras had been installed in the thirty-table restaurant at the behest of corporate headquarters as part of the social credit system. When we asked why so many cameras were needed, the manager said they were there to "punish" employees who failed to uphold corporate standards and to "people track."

The Kitsilano restaurant is one of more than a thousand Haidilao Hot Pots, mostly in mainland China but also in places like London, New York, and Toronto. But this particular franchise happened to be close to the PRC consulate and within walking distance of the mansion where Meng Wanzhou spent her house arrest. It's easy to imagine who some of the other patrons may be. "Customers at a popular ethnic Chinese restaurant, especially in an upscale area, could be diplomats and politicians entertaining their guests, CEOs discussing their business strategies, professionals talking about company projects, journalists conducting interviews," said Ivy Li, a writer and activist with Canadian Friends of Hong Kong. "Diners discuss a wide range of subjects, especially after a couple of glasses of wine. The dining table in a popular restaurant is one of the best places to eavesdrop on someone."[12]

In our visits to the restaurant, we surmised that the cameras were networked—meaning, they could conceivably be sending live video footage directly back to China. This raised all kinds of red flags for us about the data being collected and whether the restaurant was in violation of British Columbia's privacy laws, which regulate how organizations can collect, use, and disclose information on individuals. You would think the government would be furious to learn that a foreign-based business was seemingly spying on Canadian citizens, but when we reached out to the Office of the Information and Privacy Commissioner and the Ministry of Labour in BC, we mostly got back meek statements about how the province expects corporations to follow the law.

For our part, we couldn't help wondering what would happen if the Haidilao Hot Pot began using facial-recognition cameras, listening in on cell phone calls, and tracking e-commerce purchases. Were these sixty cameras in this one restaurant a penetration test? Were they intended to see what response this level of surveillance would provoke in Canadian law enforcement, not to mention the public at large? If so, the passive replies we received from the various government ministries were worrisome. If no one cared about the cameras, why wouldn't Haidilao try something even more invasive? Think of this as espionage by trial balloon.

All we could do was keep trying to sound the alarm, and, fortunately, our bet with the *Sunday Guardian* paid off. Our article was picked up by *Apple Daily*, an anti-CCP newspaper in Taiwan, and went viral in several countries, as well as in Hong Kong. This led to a lively debate in Taiwan's parliament over the use of cameras in government buildings. Radio and TV commentary shows also picked up the story, and the mayor of Taipei held a news conference.

Of course, given this level of exposure, we knew the CCP wouldn't sit back and do nothing in response. In June 2021, Hong Kong authorities used the controversial new national security law to raid the offices of *Apple Daily* and freeze its assets, forcing the paper to cease operations. While the CCP claimed publicly that it was acting in response to *Apple Daily*'s coverage of the Hong Kong protests, we heard from our intelligence sources overseas that our story was the final straw.

Soon after, we were hit with pro-CCP disinformation videos by China's keyboard army, known as the "50 Cent Army," who are active on Chinese social media platforms and tasked with defending and protecting China's image overseas.[13] Our story was then co-opted by right-wing conspiracy websites that looked like they were from the southern US. Stories that are associated with or boosted by right-wing or conspiracy sites are often de-platformed from mainstream social media. It's one of the many tools in the CCP's disinformation toolbox. The closer we got to the truth, the worse the pushback from the CCP.

There was, however, one silver lining to all this: immediately following the publication of our article, the Haidilao Hot Pot in Kitsilano got a sudden urge to renovate, and removed most of its cameras.

## CHINA'S CHEMICAL WARFARE AGENT

Let's kick this up a notch and talk about fentanyl and how it might fit into China's global plans, alongside the social credit system and the digital yuan. We all know the devastation the fentanyl epidemic has brought to North America in the past decade. In the US, overdose deaths topped ninety thousand in 2020, a new record, and almost two-thirds of those were due to synthetic opioids (primarily fentanyl).[14] In Canada, there was a spike in overdoses in the first two years of the pandemic, with more than 15,000 deaths between April 2020 and March 2022.[15] Of those, the vast majority (more than 80 percent in 2022) involved fentanyl, with BC, Alberta, and Ontario the most severely impacted provinces. In both countries, males accounted for three-quarters of deaths, and young men between twenty and thirty-nine were especially hard hit.

Some intelligence and law enforcement professionals view fentanyl as a chemical warfare agent that has been deliberately spread by the CCP as part of its hybrid war against the West. They say there is a compelling argument that young people of military age have been specifically targeted. Even if you find that unconvincing, it's hard to dispute that the effects of the illicit drug trade have been catastrophic. Even if they don't overdose, people who use synthetic opioids are often stripped of their ability to function as productive members of society. In addition to devastating the lives of those who become addicted, the burden of caring for their health and welfare frequently rests with the government and society at large. Social chaos can result when public healthcare systems are stretched to their limits and crime rates rise.

Vancouver is the epicentre for North America's illicit fentanyl trade—a stream of precursors and powdered opioids flows from manufacturing plants in China into BC and from there to the rest of Canada and south of the border. All of this traffic is aided by powerful transnational gangs that work in unison with legitimate businesses and the Chinese state—aka the Unholy Trinity. As we saw in earlier chapters, the cash transactions tied to these deals are snow-washed through British Columbia's government-run casinos and the overheated real estate market in key United Front hub cities like Richmond, BC, and Markham and Richmond Hill, Ontario. Provincial and federal governments take their cut at the casino tables and from the taxes generated by the real estate market. And they need it, too—these governments are desperate to find ways to pay for the costs associated with the deadly fentanyl epidemic. Meanwhile, the laundered funds get transferred back to China, where the vicious cycle repeats.

Fentanyl arrives here in all kinds of ways. People don't realize, for example, that a huge percentage is simply sent through the mail. A lot is sent in commercial shipping containers and even smuggled aboard legitimate fishing vessels. Fun fact: only 3 percent of cargo containers are searched, and for the most part, customs officials are looking for chemical, biological, and nuclear threats, not drugs. Despite some wins by customs and law enforcement, it's impossible to control the flow of drugs without the cooperation of the Chinese government.

There are two undeniable truths about fentanyl: one, it is easy to turn into currency, and two, as a chemical agent, it's more effective than the chemical weapons used in the two world wars. In the US alone, more than nine hundred thousand people have died of overdoses since 1999,[16] far exceeding gas casualties among all allied nations in both wars. The only real difference is the battlefield—and the escalating fentanyl epidemic is being fought on every street in North America.

Couldn't China simply crack down? Yes and no. In 2019, the country did succumb to international pressure and ban the production of fentanyl and several of its variants.[17] But many manufacturers simply switched to producing the precursor chemicals used to make fentanyl, and these can be harder to track and regulate. Also, they can be produced in small spaces with fairly simple equipment. In fact, many legitimate pharmaceutical factories also manufacture chemical components for illicit distribution using criminal syndicates.[18] These same factories supply ingredients for essential drugs to Big Pharma corporations in Canada and the US. It's just one more example of the connectivity between the CCP, criminal enterprises, and business tycoons—China's Unholy Trinity—and how they operate in both legitimate and illicit arenas.

Imagine a scenario where a drug manufacturer in China cuts off the supply of key ingredients required for critical medicines, or uses those ingredients as leverage to force Big Pharma giants to engage in outright espionage against their own country. This doomsday scenario is not beyond the realm of possibility. If we have learned anything from the COVID-19 pandemic, it's that we have to be prepared and start working on countermeasures.

# CHAPTER 8

# THE GAME

## HOW THE CCP INFILTRATES AND INFLUENCES GOVERNMENTS

On February 12, 2019, Justin Trudeau kicked off the Vancouver Chinatown Spring Festival parade with the eye-dotting ceremony known as Hoi Gong. This ancient Chinese tradition symbolizes waking the dragon up from his slumber and kick-starting the festivities.

That evening, the party moved inside for a banquet hosted by the Chinese Benevolent Association (CBA). The fête was held at Floata, a local restaurant popular with the Vancouver PRC consulate when hosting large celebrations. The atmosphere was festive. Red faux-silk lanterns dangled from the ceiling, and on the main stage, a display of lucky flowers sat before a row of alternating Canadian and Chinese flags, all set against a red velvet curtain. The sound of party chatter and clanking dishes provided the soundtrack as VIP guests worked the room dressed in a colourful array of Tang suits. This was to be an especially auspicious occasion; the prime

PHOTO: Canadian politicians Don Davies, Jenny Kwan, and Senator Yuen Pau Woo attend a PRC National Day celebration.

minister and his defence minister, Harjit Sajjan, would be at the banquet to welcome the new PRC consul general, Tong Xiaoling.

Despite the inviting atmosphere, however, there were underlying tensions. Only two months earlier, Huawei CFO Meng Wanzhou had been arrested at the Vancouver airport. This, in turn, had sparked the retaliatory arrest of the Two Michaels—Michael Spavor and Michael Kovrig—Canadian citizens living and working in China.

As the banquet room started to fill, RCMP bomb-sniffing dogs swept the room ahead of the prime minister's arrival. Members of Trudeau's RCMP security detail took up their posts around the room. But then something unusual happened.

All at once, a contingent of Mao-suited guards entered the room and positioned themselves in a similar fashion to the Mounties. One stood directly in front of a media platform that was cordoned off with a rope. Instead of clearing the room, the prime minister's detail allowed the men to stay.

Later, we asked RCMP spokesperson Sgt. Chris-Manseau, the district advisory NCO of media relations, if this second team was there to provide security for the Chinese consulate. The answer we received was puzzling. Sgt. Manseau told us that he "spoke with our protective detail and they said they couldn't identify the other agency as they aren't aware of their identities and weren't sure if having them identified could compromise their employment." As for the name of the company, Sgt. Manseau said, "...it was suggested that you reach out to the venue as they will have a list of who was employed that day. I just don't have that info . . ."

All of this happened despite the fact that the main goal of any situation is "deconfliction"—military speak for reducing the risk of actual conflict. The prime minister's protection detail does not control the movement or access of other dignitaries—especially those with diplomatic passports. This seemed to suggest that Trudeau's own security detail didn't have a clue about who was in the room with them while they were "protecting" the prime minister.[1]

At any rate, the festivities carried on as scheduled. Soon, Trudeau himself entered the room, standing front and centre with Harjit Sajjan on one side and Hilbert Yiu, a known United Front member, on the other. As the "March of the Volunteers," the national anthem of the People's Republic of China, began to play, this chummy mix of Canadian politicians, Chinese consular officials, and United Front operatives stood solemnly at attention. A large screen displayed a propaganda video that included images of the People's Liberation Army and clips of Chairman Mao's portrait hanging above the Gate of Heavenly Peace in Tiananmen Square as white doves of peace flew past in slow motion.

When the video ended, Hilbert Yiu took to the stage, flanked by Terry Yung, an off-duty staff sergeant with the Vancouver Police Department and frequent attendee at United Front events, and his wife, city council member Sarah Kirby-Yung. Looking down from a raised platform, Yiu proceeded to remind—some might say threaten—the Canadian prime minister of what China expected of him and where his loyalty and duty should reside.

"Despite recent challenges," Yiu intoned, "we hope that both governments maintain the relationship. We praise Prime Minister Pierre Elliott Trudeau for his pioneering work on the diplomatic front. We have great expectations on his son, Prime Minister Justin Trudeau, to grow this relationship to a new level."

As the night came to a close, politicians and United Front agents— their names called out one by one, in order of importance—joined members of the Chinese consulate on stage. Together they let out a collective cheer as cannons released colourful streamers into the air.

To most Canadians, this event might have looked like nothing more than a festive cultural occasion. But to anyone willing to peer just beneath the surface, it underscored how entrenched CCP and United Front activity had become in Canada. It's not every day that the prime minister and the minister of defence stand at attention for CCP propaganda videos and smile through a barely disguised dressing-down delivered by a known United Front agent. It also showed us that the CCP had a firm grip on Canadian institutions, and that wolf warrior diplomacy was being used to send a public message to Justin Trudeau. The dragon had most definitely awakened from its slumber.

How did we let things get this bad?

## FRIENDLY, HARDLINE, OR AMBIGUOUS

The CCP has deep, behind-the-scenes control over many Canadian government institutions through the installation of pro-CCP advisors and aides to premiers, ministers and mayors.

These advisors and aides have been known to block freedom-of-information (FOI) requests relating to China by deliberately creating excessive delays and inadequate searches. They are also known to encourage politicians to attend events co-hosted by hometown associations with the support of the Chinese consulate. They also separate Chinese media from English speaking media.

These events are often framed as festivals and cultural events, but are really part of CCP influence campaigns. Since these advisors and aides hold the key to publicizing these events, they can and will block Canadian media from having the opportunity to report on them to the wider public—while at the same time granting special access to state-run media, always with a propaganda message that shows the CCP in charge of the Canadian politicians. Then these reports are propagated on Chinese social media.

These same advisors and aides have essentially created a dual government system—one for Chinese diaspora and one for the rest of the public. Very often these two worlds collide when a reporter starts to dig because a source has revealed a CCP event that a politician is attending or they were seen engaging in mask diplomacy or at a propaganda photo ceremony accepting a donation for a public hospital.

This happened to investigative journalist, Sam Cooper when he reported that "United Front groups in Canada helped Beijing stockpile coronavirus safety supplies." The response from the united front was to start yet another new NGO which they claimed on their website was formed on behalf of people who felt they were unfairly portrayed in the report. They also started a fund to pursue a lawfare claim against Cooper as a way to silence him. Those who contributed to the fund included the same criminals that Cooper reported on in other investigations. The astounding part of this is that we uncovered elected officials who actively participated in the strategy sessions on how to go after Cooper. So much for protecting the 4th pilar of democracy in Canada.[2]

This doesn't happen only in Canada—it's a problem all over the world. And it happens not just on the national level, in Washington or Ottawa or London, but on the provincial, state, and local levels, too. US Secretary of State Mike Pompeo made this point in a speech he gave to the National Governors Association (NGA) in February 2020. To show how United Front agents target and then ingratiate themselves with elected officials, Pompeo described an invitation he received to an event called the US-

China Governors Collaboration Summit, co-hosted by the NGA and the Chinese People's Association for Friendship and Foreign Countries.[3] It sounded, as he put it, "pretty harmless." But then he went on:

> *What the invitation did not say is that the group . . . is the public face of the Chinese Communist Party's official foreign influence agency, the United Front Work Department. Now, I was lucky. I was familiar with that organization from my time as the director of the Central Intelligence Agency. But it got me thinking. How many of you made the link between that group and Chinese Communist Party officials? What if you made a new friend while you were at that event? What if your new friend asked you for introductions to other politically connected and powerful people? What if your new friend offered to invest big money in your state, perhaps in your pension, in industries sensitive to our national security? These aren't hypotheticals. These scenarios are all too true, and they impact American foreign policy significantly.*

Pompeo went on to note that in 2019, a think tank in Beijing generated a report that categorized all fifty American governors on their views about China. "They labeled each of you 'friendly,' 'hardline,' or 'ambiguous,'" he told the group. "I'll let you decide where you think you belong. Someone in China already has. Many of you, indeed, in that report are referenced by name."[4]

Pompeo's speech was a warning to governors not to assume that they had somehow escaped China's attention. He told them to verify business inquiries and "not to make separate individual deals" with China that could "undermine national policy."

"And, in fact, whether you are viewed by the [Communist Party of China] as friendly or hardline, know that it's working you, know that it's working the team around you," Pompeo warned. "Competition with China is happening inside of your state, and it affects our capacity to perform America's vital national security functions."[5]

His message should also have been heeded here in Canada, where politicians sometimes seem naive about the Communist Party's goals and the way it operates. Take, for example, the case of Don Davies, a BC MP for the NDP.

In 2015, Davies told the *China Daily*, a newspaper owned by the CCP's propaganda department, that his Vancouver riding included a large proportion of people of Chinese heritage. "I take it as a special privilege and obligation for me to try to learn as much as I can about the political, economic, cultural and social issues between the [two] countries," Davies said, "and to strengthen those relations."[6]

What he failed to mention was that many of his constituents came from Asian countries not under communist control. Like many politicians in Canada, Davies appeared to think that all people of Asian heritage are supporters of the communist regime. Was he unaware that there was a worldwide anti-CCP movement brewing, with many Canadians at the forefront?

Perhaps the most puzzling aspect of Davies's comment, though, is that permanent residents living in Canada would be the only ones considered Chinese citizens under Chinese law. So who was he really working for? It would seem it was mostly Chinese citizens who live part-time in both Canada and China.

All of this was very concerning, given that Davies is a member of the National Security and Intelligence Committee of Parliamentarians (NSICOP), where he holds top-secret clearance and has sworn an oath to obey and uphold the laws of Canada, and not communicate or inappropriately use information obtained in confidence as part of his work on the committee.[7]

NSICOP was established by Justin Trudeau in 2017. Some opposition MPs say it is a sham committee designed to protect the prime minister from accountability and oversight in his dealings with China.[8] Unlike similar bodies in other Five Eyes countries, NSICOP is neither a standing committee nor a special committee of Parliament. Rather, it is an agency of the executive branch, overseen by the Prime Minister's Office. In June 2021, the Tories pulled their MPs from the committee to protest the Liberal government's refusal to hand over unredacted documents related to the firing of two Chinese scientists from Canada's highest-security National Microbiology Laboratory.[9]

For many years, Don Davies has had a cozy relationship with the Chinese consulate in Vancouver. He frequently attends PRC soirées, including one event where he told Chinese state-run media (the only media invited) that he wanted Canada to repair its relationship with China, which he said had been on a positive trajectory before the arrest of Meng Wanzhou. Davies, a lawyer by trade, hinted that the minister of justice could just make that problem go away, like magic, then blamed the US and Donald Trump for precipitating the crisis.[10]

Just by speaking to *China Daily* about Chinese constituents in his riding, Davies tends to reinforce the idea that all ethnic Chinese in Canada automatically fall under the authority of the CCP. It's a short step from that to saying that the CCP is in charge of the Chinese diaspora in Canada. This view is distressingly common among Canadian politicians. And why is that? People like Davies don't seem to realize that many, if not most, Chinese immigrants likely came to Canada to get away from the CCP. Or perhaps he does realize that, but just doesn't care.

The United Front has been masterful at handpicking "friendly" politicians who will then work to represent the CCP's interests over those of their own countries. We saw a prominent example of this in the wake of the Meng Wanzhou arrest, when John McCallum, then the Canadian ambassador to China and previously the country's defence minister, gave a press conference to Chinese-language media in which he offered Meng advice on how to defend against extradition.[11] It was such an egregious breach that Prime Minister Trudeau had to force him to resign.

What happened with McCallum was an example of one form of CCP leverage and manipulation. As Clive Hamilton and Mareike Ohlberg described it in their book *Hidden Hand*, targets like McCallum "are wooed not by inducements, but by playing to their vanity and their desire to be agreeable."[12] But there is another, more insidious type of manipulation. When China's Ministry of State Security (MSS) identifies a target, that triggers the intelligence-gathering process. MSS operatives start to collect private information to build dossiers on Canadian citizens—more often than not elected officials, but also sometimes VIPs and even the children of prominent people. Those dossiers are then used to leverage those people in ways that advance the interests of the CCP in Canada.

In our experience, information in a dossier is collected from many potential sources, including social media, corporate records, English- and Chinese-language newspapers, and government documents acquired through freedom-of-information requests. A dossier could include innocuous details like personal schedules, lifestyle habits, and social networks, but it also typically covers things like political leanings, educational background, religious views, sexual proclivities, financial situation, and family and professional spheres. Even rumours form part of the dossier. The end result is a psychological profile that can be used to create leverage.

Once a dossier is complete, a plan to influence is initiated. This can be as simple as making a politician feel special by offering VIP invites to consular events and facilitating introductions to high-ranking CCP officials. Or it can be more sinister and involve money and the promise of votes. In the end, it's all a form of political subversion.

In August 2021, Matthew Pottinger, the former US deputy national security adviser, warned the Senate Intelligence Committee of the dangers of the CCP's intelligence-gathering activities. "The party compiles dossiers on millions of foreign citizens around the world," Pottinger explained, "using the material it gathers to influence and intimidate, reward and blackmail, flatter and humiliate, divide and conquer."[13] He said that this type of intelligence gathering had "always been a feature of Leninist regimes, but Beijing's penetration of digital networks worldwide has taken this to a new level." He told the committee members that China had stolen enough data to be able to build a dossier on every American adult.

Pottinger said that the United Front's intelligence-gathering efforts were active and ongoing. "United Front work is an immense range of activities with no analog in China's democracies," he told the committee. "China's leaders call it a 'magic weapon.' The CCP's ninety-five million members are all required to participate in the system, which has many branches. The United Front Work Department alone has three times as many cadres as the U.S. State Department has foreign service officers. Instead of practicing diplomacy, however, the United Front gathers intelligence about and works to influence private citizens and government officials overseas, with a focus on foreign elites and the organizations they run."

Once again, we must stress that this isn't only a US problem. In Canada, we believe these intelligence dossiers are being used to strategically target elected officials so as to advance Beijing's interests and ambitions—a war without a single shot being fired. Later in the book, we will describe possible cases of political subversion and let you decide just how leveraged a politician is. But first, we'll tell the story of one of our own team members to show just how the CCP plants a single seed of influence and then nurtures it until it grows into something much more insidious.

## MAGIC WEAPON

Doug (not his real name) is the father of a Project Mosaic team member. He was a Canadian intelligence agent at the height of the Cold War. Doug had had a difficult childhood—he lived in an orphanage for the first two years of his life—and was a risk taker with little empathy and no capacity to forge strong emotional bonds.

Doug's whole life was a lie. His day job (the nature of which we can't reveal) provided cover for espionage activities that took him to the far reaches of the globe. He was a real-life James Bond, meeting arms dealers and MI5 agents in a world characterized by sexpionage and dead drops. Doug used his wife and children as props, turning family vacations into cover for secret missions. While other families went camping or caught cheap flights to Florida, Doug's went to East Germany, then a rigidly controlled communist state, to make a coordinated handoff of documents. Afterwards, they spent a harrowing thirty minutes racing back to Checkpoint Charlie in a Soviet-made Lada sedan.

Doug's daughter remembers an incident in the early 1980s that shaped her views about China. Her father, she said, was playing host to a group of Chinese aviation maintenance engineers on a government exchange trip to Canada. These exchange trips were quite common in the aviation industry in the 1970s and 1980s. Doug told his daughter that it would look good if she joined him, but he also warned her to be careful. He had noticed that one member of the group was always watching the others, evaluating their actions and keeping them in line. This man, he told his daughter, was likely a CCP political officer.

A source who spent a lot of time in China during the Cultural Revolution told us that political officers are often from the United Front and will usually present themselves as the coordinator of whatever delegation they're travelling with or perhaps as an interpreter. They want to blend in and avoid scrutiny, but at the same time, they set themselves apart and are always watching for any hint of espionage or any potential defections. Several of the engineers in the group Doug was hosting had already spent time in jail on false charges, including the head engineer, who had been in prison for over twenty-five years. So tensions were high.

One afternoon, Doug took the group to Vancouver's Chinatown to show them around. The political officer took the opportunity to make contact with Doug's daughter. Getting down to her level, he smiled and gently placed his hand on her shoulder—a paternalistic gesture we have seen CCP operatives use again and again. "Never forget how much China loves you," the man told her. "You are so special, and the motherland loves you. We will always be here for you." Then he went on to ask her something that to this day she doesn't want to reveal, but she says that he was looking for specific information about her father. Remember that when the United Front targets someone in order to influence them or turn them, they are already armed with knowledge of that person's weaknesses, strengths, needs, etc., from the dossier. Did the political officer know that Doug was an emotionally distant father and sense in his daughter a need for affirmation and love? Perhaps that's what the dossier on Doug and his family said.

## THE CCP AND THE TRUDEAUS

As a young man fresh off studies at Harvard and the London School of Economics, Pierre Trudeau embarked on a year-long tour through Eastern Europe, the Middle East, and Asia in 1948–49. It was his first trip to China, and he returned again in 1960 with his friend Jacques Hébert, a labour lawyer and journalist from Montreal. On the CBC Radio program *The New Matinée*, Hébert later described how he and Trudeau would slip out the back door of their hotel late at night to escape the surveillance of their "commissar," and he also talked about their fruitless efforts to have private conversations with Chinese journalists and economists.[14] But somehow the two did manage to snag an interview with Mao Zedong for the influential Quebec political journal *Cité Libre*.

At that time, China was in the midst of withdrawing from the Great Leap Forward, a program of rapid industrialization that also involved organizing citizens into large-scale self-sufficient communes. The Great Leap Forward had been championed as a way to accelerate the industrialization process in a country with an enormous population and a huge landmass, but today, it's widely seen as an economic failure that led to the starvation deaths of as many as thirty million people.

Trudeau and Hébert later wrote a book about their experience called *Two Innocents in Red China*. Published in English in 1968, the year Trudeau became prime minister, the book was a whimsical and sometimes insightful look at a country that had been largely closed to Westerners for decades. (In 1972, Nixon became the first US president to visit China.)

In today's China, no two Canadians are held in higher esteem than Pierre Trudeau and Norman Bethune, the battlefield surgeon who pioneered the practice of mobile blood transfusions and served with Mao's Red Army in the Second Sino-Japanese War, from early 1938 until his death from blood poisoning in November 1939. So respected was Bethune that Mao himself wrote a eulogy, "In Memory of Norman Bethune," which was required reading in elementary schools in China during the Cultural Revolution.[15]

When Pierre Trudeau became prime minister, he immediately set about reviewing Canada's foreign policy. His top priority was to formally recognize Mao's government. He even told the *Ottawa Citizen* in December 1968 that he wanted "a new China policy," and that years of alienation "should not bind us forever."[16] By 1970, Trudeau had achieved his goal— Canada officially recognized the Communist Party of China as the sole legitimate government of the original Republic of China, severing diplomatic ties with Taiwan in the process.

The wheels were greased for the CCP to infiltrate Canada, and things were starting to move fast.

In 1972, the federal government acquiesced to Mao again by recognizing his friend Bethune as a Person of National Historic Significance. The house where Bethune was born was turned into a museum, and a slew of lectures, films, and books were produced. It didn't matter that Bethune was virtually unknown in Canada at the time and had done nothing to advance Canadian medicine.

A year later, Prime Minister Trudeau went on another tour of China and received a last-minute invitation to visit with the frail, eighty-year-old Chairman Mao. And, in 1975, when the People's Republic of China applied to the International Olympic Committee to be allowed to compete once more in the Olympic Games, Canada supported its newfound friend. This dispute carried over into the Montreal Olympics (even though China was excluded), when Canada told Taiwan that it couldn't compete under the name the Republic of China. The United States was on Taiwan's side and even threatened to back out of the games at one point. A compromise floated by Trudeau to Taiwan was ultimately rejected, and Taiwan pulled out of the games the day before they opened.[17]

On its face, this looked like a diplomatic disaster, but in fact, it was a clear message to the CCP that Canada was onside and would even challenge the US at times. This was also one of the first times that Trudeau's loyalty to the CCP was on full display and was possibly a sign that Beijing had the ability to make demands of him—leverage, if you will.

Four decades after these dramatic events, *Two Innocents in Red China* was republished by the CCP with the permission of the Trudeau family. In a 2016 interview with CPAC, the public affairs channel, Alexandre 'Sacha' Trudeau said that he had been approached by Chinese officials about reprinting his father's book.[18] After making a trip back to China to prepare to write the preface to the new edition, Sacha Trudeau said, he was encouraged by the Chinese to write a book of his own. That book was eventually published as *Barbarian Lost: Travels in the New China*, an admiring travelogue that occasionally argues the merits of one-party rule and includes quotes defending the CCP.

While Sacha Trudeau was travelling the country meeting with artists and farmers and migrant workers. Xi was already consolidating power, Uyghurs in Xinjiang and Chinese dissidents living abroad were being targeted, and the CCP was refining its plans to turn China into the world's only superpower.[19]

Back in Canada, Justin Trudeau was making plans of his own. In 2006, he was recruited to chair the Liberal Party's elite Red Ribbon Renewal Task Force, which was looking at the party's governance structure, fundraising practices, and election readiness. The task force was also intended to be a springboard to bigger things for Trudeau. The following year, he successfully ran for office. By 2012, Trudeau was preparing to step into the role of Liberal leader and candidate for prime minister. As he made his case to voters, he released what could be described as a manifesto of sorts, in which he suggested that the centre of gravity for global wealth was shifting from the US to China, and that the rise of emerging markets in Asia was a wealth-generating opportunity for middle-class Canadians.[20] Trudeau noted that Canada had a lot of the natural resources that China would need. "China," he wrote, "is scanning the world for acquisitions like a shopper in a grocery store . . . Canada has perhaps more potential to capitalize on this . . . than any other country. From minerals to energy, from education expertise to construction, we have a lot of what China needs."

He wasn't wrong. The centre of gravity was indeed shifting to Asia, thanks in large part to legwork from Liberal Party leaders going back to his father decades earlier. And there's no question that the CCP was shopping for natural resources and wanting to invest in industries like oil and forestry. But Trudeau downplayed the national security implications of encouraging Chinese companies to invest in Canada and vice versa. "In certain sectors, national security concerns will be real," he acknowledged, before adding flippantly that a Chinese company's ownership of 3 percent of oil sands leases "hardly constitutes a national security issue."

The company in question was the China National Offshore Oil Corporation, or CNOOC, which is a state-owned enterprise and one of the largest oil and gas companies in China. It has invested heavily in oil products, liquefied natural gas, pipelines, and other facilities. And together with COSCO, one of the world's largest shipping companies, CNOOC has made a fortune transporting crude oil and liquefied natural gas around the globe.[21] But US counterintelligence officials have also accused COSCO of using its legitimate shipping activities as a front for intelligence gathering.[22] "Cosco operates a fleet of ELINT [electronic intelligence] trawlers for the PRC government that can sit in Long Beach harbor and eavesdrop on communications throughout the Los Angeles area," one official said.[23] And, in 1996, COSCO was involved in transporting two thousand AK-47 assault rifles into California with the help of Poly Technologies, the biggest arms exporter in China.[24] The guns were believed to be destined for militant gangs in the United States.[25] At the time, the US had an assault weapons ban in place.

This is the heart of the problem that we face in North America. Despite the framing Justin Trudeau tried to offer Canadians, it is never just about trade growth or ownership percentages. When dealing with China, everything is about leverage and opportunities for espionage, and there is a human cost hidden behind every venture.

## PAY-TO-PLAY POLITICS

By April 2013, Justin Trudeau had won the Liberal leadership in a landslide. Seven months later, when asked during a public appearance which country he most admired, he said, "There's a level of admiration I actually have for China. Their basic dictatorship is actually allowing them to turn their economy around on a dime."[26] Was this bizarre statement a trial balloon meant to test the tolerance of the Canadian public? Or was Trudeau attempting to send a message to the CCP?

It's not beyond the realm of possibility that the heir to the Trudeau political dynasty could have been conditioned as a child for his role as prime minister as an adult. This is just one of the working theories that intelligence analysts we know have batted about to explain the rise of Justin Trudeau and his apparent loyalty to the CCP regime.

When he was elected prime minister in November 2015, concerns were already being raised in the intelligence community about the apparent ease with which the CCP had been able to infiltrate Canada. Members from our research team that are part of law enforcement and intelligence circles started to ask questions. Who was helping the CCP advance their agenda? And, more importantly, what shape did that agenda take?

As we showed earlier in the book, the United Front often operates behind interconnected layers of NGOs, business associations, and companies like law firms. On the face of it, these entities stand alone as real services, but when linked together, they form a complex web providing cover for the CCP to conduct operations in Canada. They're also a way for pro-CCP candidates to run for office and hide big-money donations used to influence policy—so-called cash-for-access or pay-to-play schemes. We untangled one of these intricate webs to show how the CCP has been able to infiltrate and influence the highest levels of Canadian government.

The Pierre Elliott Trudeau Foundation is an independent charity established in 2001, thanks in part to a $125 million contribution from the federal government. Justin Trudeau was a member but withdrew from the foundation's affairs in 2014 under the pressure of an ethics probe. Alexandre 'Sacha' Trudeau remained on the board, as the designate of the Pierre Trudeau estate.

In 2016, two Chinese billionaires, Zhang Bin and Niu Gensheng, donated $1 million to the Trudeau Foundation and the Université de Montréal. While the bulk of the donation—$750,000—went to the university's law school, the remaining $250,000 was for the foundation and included funds to build a statue honouring Pierre Elliott Trudeau.[27]

This donation raised eyebrows because it came less than two weeks after Zhang and Niu met Justin Trudeau at a private $1,500-a-plate Liberal fundraiser. "The fact that a significant portion of the funding is going to a statue of the Prime Minister's father does raise some concerns," China expert Charles Burton told *The Globe and Mail*.[28] "I'm sure, on an emotional level, Mr. Trudeau would be pleased to see a statue of his father, and [that] would incline him to feel well-disposed to those who arranged it."

Zhang Bin is not just a billionaire businessman but also a member of the Chinese People's Political Consultative Conference, an advisory body to the CCP. The *Globe* article also called him "a force for the spread of Chinese influence" through his work with the China Cultural Industry Association, a group that includes "senior figures in the People's Liberation Army, and navy and Communist Party bosses." Niu is a milk tycoon who was implicated in the 2008 tainted milk scandal, which resulted in the deaths of six Chinese babies. He also heads the China Charity Alliance, which reports to China's Civil Affairs Ministry, according to *The Globe*.

Also present at the fundraising dinner were several Communist government officials and banking and insurance magnate Shenglin Xian. At the time, he was waiting on Ottawa's approval to open a bank, called Wealth One, for Chinese Canadian clients. That approval was given just two months later. "Certainly, there is an overall strategy on the part of the government of China to try to gain influence [with] critical Canadian decision-makers," Charles Burton noted. "It's part of an overall co-ordinated strategy to try to enhance influence here."[29]

This part of the story was well covered in the Canadian press, but we kept digging and unearthed even more concerning connections. One thread led us to Ouyang Yuansen, honorary president of the Huazhu Overseas Chinese Service Centre, a Toronto-based United Front organization, and also a founding shareholder of Wealth One Bank of Canada. One of his partners there is Morris Chen, the president of The China Council for the Promotion of International Trade (CCPIT). CCPIT is a global organization that develops business relationships and exchanges with foreign countries, and it has long been associated with the United Front network.[30]

What was in front of us were data points that showed multiple overlapping connections between billionaire tycoons, people associated with the CCP, and Canada's highest-ranking politician. The prime minister either doesn't realize or doesn't care that the people he's accepting money from—for the Liberal Party or his own family foundation—are connected to the Communist Party at the highest levels, and some are even known United Front members. He has made decisions as PM that suggest a too-cozy relationship with China—abstaining from the Uyghur genocide vote in 2021 is just one obvious example of that. While the world watched on

February 1, 2023, the PM was part of a historic vote of 322–0 in favour of Liberal MP Sameer Zuberi, a private member's bill to resettle up to 10,000 Uyghur refugees in Canada. An initiative spearheaded by the World Uyghur Congress headed in Canada by Mehmet Tohti. Worth noting is the only MP who did not vote for the resolution was MP Han Dong who slipped out just before the vote. What else might he be doing to curry favour? This is an open question with all Canadian politicians, but so far there have been no clear answers. Meanwhile, Canadians had another pressing question in mind when the entire board of directors and the president and CEO of the Pierre Elliott Trudeau Foundation resigned, citing "politicization" of the scholarship organization. Was a $200,000 deal that Sacha signed with Chinese billionaire Zhang Bin years ago a backdoor attempt to influence his brother, Prime Minister Justin Trudeau? Or is there more to the story?

Sacha stood his ground, reportedly telling the committee, "We're wasting our time on the notion of interference. I have seen no trace of it."[31] [32] [33]

## FORCED COMPLIANCE

What the Operation Dragon Lord document did for Canada is provide us with the inflection point when the ground under Canada shifted. The point when the Chinese Communist Party (CCP) invaded Canada, albeit silently, and launched a hybrid war against the West.

Canadians now had the benefit of hindsight and could see signs that Canada's political establishment and civil society has been infiltrated. Canadians were now starting to take notice, ask questions, and demand answers.

The CCP would fight back aggressively, using backchannels aimed at censorship, propaganda, and disinformation meant to control narratives.

Ottawa's push to regulate online content with Bill-11, an Act to amend the Broadcasting Act, was just one response to this.[34] [35]

Another was the 2023 Federal Liberal Party policy resolution, sponsored by the BC wing of the party, that would call on the government to combat disinformation in Canada. The policy stated that disinformation is an "existential risk to humanity" that required government censorship when it came to "material published on (media) platforms and to limit publication only to material whose sources can be traced."[36]

The policy sounded like it was straight from the usual talking points that spokespersons for the Chinese Communist Party have made against Canadian media many times over.

Responding to allegations of election interference, the Embassy of the People's Republic of China in Ottawa remarked, on its website, that "... some Canadian politicians and media patched up false reports and spread all kinds of disinformation," and that "These actions seriously deceived and misled the public, poisoning the atmosphere of China-Canada relations."[37]

Was it a coincidence that the new east-west United Front strategy in Canada was calling for the establishment of a nationwide communication system? We know for certain that the leveraging of media to influence information and alter public sentiment in Canada is part of hybrid warfare. We could already see signs of efforts being made to alter public sentiment in Sacha Trudeau's book, *Barbarian Lost*, where he writes, "Yes, I still occasionally defend the CCP; for one I don't think China could've come so far so quickly without the unity and organizational power it has provided."

Indeed, one has to hand it to the CCP. Through ingenious methods and remarkable feats of social control, the CCP has pursued a system of broad outreach and constant surveillance, keeping its citizens and the global community of Overseas Chinese feeling connected or beholden to the motherland, or both. Like a strict parent that has cultivated an air of benevolence, the CCP instills fear and loyalty in its citizens and maintains control over its diasporic communities around the globe, while also buying silence or support from politicians in countries where it establishes itself as a secondary cultural presence, always striving to become primary. Canada is only one site among many in this hybrid war against the West. But it is an important one, for reasons that will become clear in the next several chapters.

# CHAPTER 9

# UNDERCOVER NGO

## HOW THE CCP CO-OPTED A NON-PROFIT AND USED IT AS A BASE OF OPERATION

Qiu Yuanping made her magnificent entrance into the banquet celebrating the grand opening of the Active Engagement and Integration Project (AEIP)'s new offices in Beijing. Clad in a black-and-white pinstriped dress, with her hair in a neat bouffant, she exuded a Hillary-Clintonesque power vibe that was rarely on display in the male-dominated world of the CCP.

At the time of the AEIP event, in 2015, Qui was in charge of the Overseas Chinese Affairs Office (OCAO), which is part of the United Front Work Department (UFWD) of the Chinese Communist Party (CCP). Her attendance at the event signified that the AEIP—a then-new program, run by S.U.C.C.E.S.S., the Canadian NGO that provides immigration services to Chinese nationals moving to Canada—was a big deal to the CCP.

To mark the occasion, Canada sent a high-level delegation that included the Canadian ambassador to China, Guy Saint-Jacques; S.U.C.C.E.S.S.

PHOTO: The Overseas Chinese Affairs Office (OCAO) of the State Council partnered with Canadian funded NGO, S.U.C.C.E.S.S.

CEO Queenie Choo (known for wearing an honourary Canadian naval uniform bestowed on her by Liberal MP Harjit Sajjan when he was Canada's defence minister); and two of the NGO'S board members, Grant Lin and Doug Purdie.

A real estate developer, Grant Lin was also the vice-chair of S.U.C.C.E.S.S. at the time, and is listed as a United Front agent on the official state website of the All–China Federation of Returned Overseas Chinese (ACFROC), one of five units of the United Front Work Department.[1] Doug Purdie is an accountant who has worked with most of the Big Four firms and is also on the board of directors of the Hong Kong-Canada Business Association, a role he shares with Catherine Yuen, who works with the Hong Kong Economic & Trade Office in Canada. This organization is closely aligned with the local PRC consulate in BC and the Chinese embassy in Canada.[2][3]

At the AEIP celebration, Canadian and Chinese VIPs sipped champagne and sported purple corsages—a shade often used to symbolize royalty and/or peace and harmony. These sartorial touches could have been meant to add panache to the event, or they could have been intended to soften criticism of a joint program between Canada and the CCP. Either way, some Canadian officials, including Harjit Sajjan, came in for criticism for attending the event.[4]

The AEIP was promoted as a chance for would-be immigrants from China to receive one-on-one pre-departure counselling courtesy of the Canadian government. In Chinese state media, it was referred to as the Transit Station, and the Canadian NGO S.U.C.C.E.S.S. was put in charge of running the new Beijing station.[5]

Is it a good thing or a bad thing for a Canadian NGO to be on the ground in Beijing, directly involved in bringing Chinese nationals to Canada? According to a 2021 report in *The Globe and Mail*, it might be bad. A Chinese company owned by the Beijing Public Security Bureau—a branch of the municipal police—had been subcontracted to run the city's Canadian visa application centre on behalf of IRCC.[6] "China police own a company that collects details of people applying for visas to Canada . . . giving Beijing security services a direct stake in the processing of private information provided by people planning travel outside China," the paper reported. The company, called the Beijing Shuangxiong Foreign Service Company, also has "close ties with China's ruling party," including through the Beijing Youth Politics College, which, the *Globe* noted, "played a foundational role in training new generations of Communist Party leadership."

Among those interviewed for the article was former Ambassador Guy Saint-Jacques, who attended the AEIP Transit Station opening. He told the paper, "You can bet the Chinese government is interested in knowing who is going to study where abroad, who is going as a tourist and who wants to leave and immigrate." Robert Potter, an Australian cybersecurity expert, pointed to even greater concerns, noting that inside knowledge of another country's visa application process was valuable intelligence. "If you can see who is getting declined and who is getting approved," he was quoted as saying, "it gives you a better chance of getting your agent through."[7]

Given the connections between the Beijing Shuangxiong Foreign Service Company and China's ruling elite, it is probable that the CCP has full access to the information getting processed through Canada's Beijing visa centre. This could create many compromising situations and even endanger people applying for refugee status on humanitarian grounds, like Uyghurs, for example.

Now consider how the S.U.C.C.E.S.S. Transit Station, which offers pre-arrival counselling under the guise of immigration support, plays into all this. Could it be that the CCP is using the Transit Station as a stop-and-control point for refugees and immigrants wanting to go to Canada? Is it gaining access to their information in order to threaten and leverage them, or worse? Are they being screened as part of a process to catch dissidents who might be flight risks? We were told by a source that the CCP allowed him to keep his social media accounts and immigrate to the US on the understanding that he could be called upon in the future to work for the party. One of his parents, he said, is also always held back in China as human insurance.

For the Chinese government, this arrangement not only provided potential access to sensitive immigration documentation, but opportunities to leverage immigrants.

Another concern is that the S.U.C.C.E.S.S. Transit Station could be being used to funnel sleeper agents into Canada without S.U.C.C.E.S.S. even knowing. In 2021, government sources in the UK confirmed that they knew of sleeper agents applying for British visas under the pretence of seeking refuge from the Chinese state.[8] Spies could be entering Canada the same way, with help from the Transit Station inside China. Remember how China's Unholy Trinity, cited in the DOJ document regarding Operation Dragon Lord, entered into Canada in the early 1990s.

The intrigue around what the Transit Stations are all about increases when we look at Canada's S.U.C.C.E.S.S-run Chinatown Service Centre. The centre has been designated as an "Overseas Chinese Service Centre" branch (OCSC) by the Overseas Chinese Affairs Office of the State Council (OCAO). Another project run by Qiu Yuanping, it is one of forty centres around the world, in over sixty countries.

The Vancouver S.U.C.C.E.S.S. Chinatown service centre and the other centres around the world are part of a global plan called the Overseas Chinese Benefit Project, sometimes referred to as the Global Harmony Project. It's a massive world-wide project that is broken down into an eight-point plan that includes (not in order of importance): (1) The construction of overseas Chinese organizations; (2) the development of Chinese education; (3) cultural exchanges; (4) promotion of Chinese food[9]; (5) Traditional Chinese medical care; (6) career support; (7) information services; and (8) the service centres.[10] [11] [12] [13]

The CCP's United Front Work Department (UFWD) runs the "Overseas Chinese Service Centre" (OCSC) branches that operate out of Canadian-based non-profits in Toronto, Montreal, and Vancouver. They also operate branches out of non-profits in seven US cities.

We asked Philip Lenczycki, an investigative reporter with the US based Daily Caller News Foundation (DCFN), to break down the motivation for China installing these service stations around the globe. We often consulted with Lenczycki because of his experience as a former professor of Mandarin and East Asian civilizations and his investigative series on the service centres in the US.

"There are logistical obstacles for China when it comes to their ambitions for global dominance and key projects such as the BRI. Exporting the BRI system is going to be very challenging for the Chinese government if it can't even control the Overseas Chinese population. Their solution has been to implement a global governance system that . . . satisfies Chinese already living abroad, while also continuing to make it attractive and easy for new immigrants to move overseas.[14]

He went on to analyse the transactional relationship between the CCP and Overseas Chinese, saying, "Help is provided for issues concerning international trade, security, law, government services like passport renewal, medical care and more in exchange for what is near and dear to the Chinese Communist party's heart: retaining loyalty and cultivating patriotism among Overseas Chinese. All of this is done as a way to instill a sense of obligation for the motherland . . . which, in practical terms, means Overseas Chinese reinvesting in China—whether it be with money sent to financially support family members left behind in China, financial support sent back for hometown projects, or the transfer of knowledge or skills to China—all of which contributes to achieving the dream of the great rejuvenation of the Chinese nation."

For Lenczycki, it's significant that the CCP wants to draw as much knowledge from Overseas Chinese as possible, while also preventing brain drain to other countries. "The party . . . wants to ensure that what is learned overseas, such as technologic know-how, ultimately benefits the motherland by seeing to it that overseas talent who acquire degrees at North American universities or take up prestigious posts in Western companies are made to transfer this knowledge or wealth back to the motherland."

On another level, Lenczycki told us, the CCP's approach to Overseas Chinese is all about social control. "The CCP . . . wants to control Overseas Chinese, such as pro-democracy dissidents, to prevent them from influencing others in the diaspora to turn against the party. The eight great plans, that includes the overseas service stations, is an answer to all of this."

It makes sense that the Overseas Chinese Benefit Project and its eight-point plan, while seeming like a way to retain culture and help immigrants, are actually more about social control. Foreign countries don't typically create expensive programs inside other countries purely for the purpose of retaining culture and helping immigrants.

Make no mistake—the CCP is using this plan to maintain a tight hold on Overseas Chinese, for the benefit of the motherland. While ostensibly setting up centres to provide immigration services like issuing passports and licenses and offering translation services for police matters, they are, in fact, operating a shadow government for the CCP.

The overarching goal is to separate Overseas Chinese living in Canada from Canadians. The effect and intent of this is to create a dual system, inside Canada, for Canadians and Overseas Chinese. Simple plans, like creating a robust traditional Chinese medical care system for Overseas Chinese, might seem innocuous enough, but every move in the direction of a dual system tends to dilute the aims of the Canadian health care system, while giving the CCP another avenue for monitoring Overseas Chinese. It would not surprise us if the longer-term goal was to create a separate medical system that would allow the CCP to directly control patient care for its citizens living in Canada. The CCP is tapping into legitimate concerns and issues affecting Overseas Chinese, as a way to control them and eventually take away their freedoms—from inside Canada.

## CCP POLITICAL ACTION ORGANIZATIONS

From its modest beginnings in 1973, S.U.C.C.E.S.S. had grown into one of Canada's largest social service agencies, with experience providing language training, employment counselling, and other services to newly arrived immigrants. It was a genuine success story—and a perennial favourite with Canadian politicians. According to publicly available information from the Canada Revenue Agency, the government gave S.U.C.C.E.S.S. close to $40 million in 2021–22—or more than 82 percent of its total budget.[15] Not a bad day's work for a known United Front organization.

Funding for the AEIP Transit Station in Beijing, on the other hand, was shrouded in secrecy, and the program's true purpose was hidden behind carefully crafted explanations, vague accounting descriptions, and glossy brochures that talked the good talk about multiculturalism. But that was all sufficient for the politicians who signed the massive $22.4 million cheque. That this was a special financial arrangement between the CCP and the Canadian government wouldn't become apparent until 2019, when Immigration, Refugees and Citizenship Canada (IRCC) issued a press release saying they were giving millions in funding to S.U.C.C.E.S.S. to deliver settlement services to newcomers *before* they arrive in Canada, under a contract that would run until 2023.[16]

In many ways, S.U.C.C.E.S.S. is a quasi-governmental organization, with characteristics of both public- and private-sector agencies. In democratic countries like Canada and the US, governments rely more and more on these types of groups to help them implement public policy. While there are some benefits to quasi-governmental organizations, they have the potential to weaken a government's obligation to represent its citizens fairly and impartially, and they most definitely erode public accountability—a crucial component in democratic governance.

From a national security perspective, they are also vulnerable to infiltration. More than a decade ago, analysts were warning the US government about the dangers of these hybrid organizations. "The relationship of this burgeoning quasi government to elected and appointed officials is a subject of growing concern," one report noted, "as it touches the very heart of democratic governance: to whom are these hybrids accountable and how is the public interest being protected over and against the interest of private parties?"[17]

So, on another level these NGOs can also function as political action organizations for political parties—a backdoor way to gain votes with ethnic blocs. No one would dare risk questioning a non-profit organization, even though they could very well be tied to foreign entities that are masquerading behind the façade of museums, educational events, arts, dance troupes, human rights organizations, and multicultural groups designed to influence.

Not only has China used non-profits in Canada to reshape Canada's national identity and influence the masses, but since the Canadian government provides generous financial support of arts, multicultural programming and heritage, some of these foreign influence campaigns are being funded by the Canadian taxpayer.

Take, for example, David Choi's National Congress of Chinese Canadians. They received $5,000 from Canadian Heritage for a Canada Day event called Celebrate Canada Together 2023. They appeared to use the money to host a private BBQ, then later a press conference called "I Love Canada, Canada is My Home." The message, however, was less about celebrating Canada Day and more about commemorating the anniversary of the Chinese Exclusion Act.[18] [19] [20]

This message was in line with the United Front's overall strategy across Canada to use the Chinese Exclusion Act from 100 years ago to justify the claim that any attempt to create a foreign agent registry would be racist. This message was being promoted by sitting Liberal Senator Yuen Pau Woo. [21] [22] [23]

Senator Woo started the non-profit ACCT Foundation (Action Chinese Canadians Together) with his wife, Teresa Woo-Paw, and a couple of well-known Canadians, including Dr. Henry Yu, who we talked about earlier for his role with the Cullen Commission.[24] [25] [26]

The ACCT Foundation received $157,000 in seed funding when it started in 2017, thanks to Liberal Mélanie Joly, minister of Canadian Heritage and minister responsible for multiculturalism.[27] Since then, the foundation has consistently received large donations from the federal

Liberal government, including over $700,000 from Immigration, Refugees and Citizenship Canada. What did they do with this money?[28] [29]

While the ACCT Foundation claims to be a non-partisan group dedicated to creating a more equitable society in Canada for Chinese Canadians, its founder, Sen. Yuen Pau Woo, actively engages with CCP party officials. In 2018, for example, he met with China's Consul General, Tong Xiaoling, in Vancouver, so that she could brief him on a report by the 19th National Congress of the Communist Party of China.[30]

The senator has also supported Beijing policy by opposing the motion to label China's treatment of Uyghur Muslims as genocide. Canada, he argued, should avoid criticizing other countries, given its own mistreatment of Indigenous peoples.[31]

Not long before, the United Front tried to turn Canada Day into Multicultural Day, but the attempt foundered. Now they were campaigning to turn Canada's birthday into something called "Humiliation Day," a term used at the turn of the century when the Exclusion Act was repealed. On July 1, 2017, Canada's birthday card was a series of headlines in almost all of the national newspapers, referencing 'Humiliation Day.' ACCT Foundation's PR firm, paid for by grants from the Liberal government, acknowledged that they were behind the coverage.[32]

In the lead up to Canada's muted birthday, ACCT held a National Remembrance ceremony in the Senate of Canada Chamber to mark the 100th anniversary of the enactment of the Chinese Exclusion Act in Canada.[33] The speakers included Canadian politicians known for supporting the CCP and the global policy campaign strategies director at Meta (Facebook) platforms.

All of these campaigns share a goal of further fragmenting the Canadian nation and subsuming it within multiculturalism. This idea, which can only assist the CCP in its drive for global dominance, had already received support from the Liberal government as early as 2015, in a now infamous *New York Times Magazine* interview with then newly elected Prime Minister Justin Trudeau, who cheerfully summed up Canada's lack of a cohesive identity by telling the paper, "There is no core identity, no mainstream in Canada." The *Times* article pointed to what it called Trudeau's "most radical argument," that "Canada is becoming a new kind of country, defined not by its European history but by the multiplicity of its identities from all over the world." Trudeau described Canada as "the first postnational state," a country that privileges "shared values—openness, respect, compassion, willingness to work hard, to be there for each other, to search for equality and justice" instead of nationalism per se.[34]

Organizations like S.U.C.C.E.S.S. fit neatly into this model, contributing to the erosion of Canadian institutions and identity by exporting important parts of the immigration process to far-flung places, beyond the oversight of elected Canadian officials. In the case of S.U.C.C.E.S.S., they have built a solid reputation, much of it deserved, as an NGO providing contracted immigrant services on behalf of Canada. This foundation has allowed them to operate with little to no oversight and with the backing and blessing of the Canadian government and broad support from all political parties, whose members love the photo opportunities that come with the NGOs fundraising events.

Despite the fact that S.U.C.C.E.S.S.'s Chinatown Service Centre looks like a typical government service agency, with rows of inexpensive chairs arrayed around the room, there are signs of opulence that reflect the NGOs relationship to the CCP. Its walls are adorned with gold-plated tributes to major corporate donors, and visitors are invited to flip through glossy coffee table brochures, featuring photos from celebrity galas hosted by its fundraising arm, the S.U.C.C.E.S.S Foundation.

Today, more than 40 percent of S.U.C.C.E.S.S.'s clients come from mainland China—a big change from the 1970s, when the organization was founded and mostly served people from Hong Kong. Journalist Douglas Quan took note of this shift in a 2019 *National Post* article about how S.U.C.C.E.S.S. had originally condemned the violence in Tiananmen Square but did nothing to mark the thirtieth anniversary.[35] One former S.U.C.C.E.S.S. board member told Quan that members of the current board were likely reluctant to court controversy with respect to China. "It is important to be aware and vigilant that the PRC consulate is very skilful [at] exerting its influence," he was quoted as saying. "Sometimes it's not in the best interest of the local community and sometimes it's not in the best interest of Canada." China watchers have warned that Beijing likes to cultivate relationships with community organizations, Quan wrote, and then use those relationships to suppress criticism.

It is common for the Chinese government to target organizations that are well established and have a solid reputation, like S.U.C.C.E.S.S., then slowly take them over. While S.U.C.C.E.S.S. clearly started off with good intentions and a genuine desire to help recent Chinese immigrants to Canada, the organization was co-opted by the CCP's United Front. Despite this, however, money keeps flowing from the Canadian federal government to help support the organization, with few questions asked.

S.U.C.C.E.S.S. has attracted and continues to attract many fine people who still embody those good intentions on which the organization was founded. But over the years, it has also drawn support from some people with strong CCP ties.[36] One of these is–former board member David Choi, who heads the National Congress of Chinese Canadians, a United Front organization. Walter Soo, also a former board member, was the vice-president of player development for Great Canadian Gaming and was reported to have coordinated the whale gamblers at the River Rock Casino, a major component of Vancouver's money-laundering problem.[37] Christine Brodie, a key figure on the board of S.U.C.C.E.S.S. for many years, is married to Malcolm Brodie, the mayor of Richmond, home to the largest Chinese diaspora in North America, and a frequent attendee at United Front organization events. Finally, there is the current chair of the S.U.C.C.E.S.S Chinatown Service Centre, Inspector Terry Yung, who leads the diversity, inclusion, and Indigenous relations section of the Vancouver Police Department. Married to Vancouver city councillor Sarah Kirby-Yung, Terry Yung is a frequent VIP guest at PRC consulate propaganda events around town and has come under scrutiny for his role in helping to train Chinese police recruits.[38] [39]

S.U.C.C.E.S.S. has denied being an official Overseas Chinese Service Centre (OCSC), much less having any affiliations with the Chinese Communist Party. This, despite the fact that the organization is an affiliate of the United Front led Chinese Benevolent Association (CBA), opened the Active Engagement and Integration Project (AEIP) in Beijing, and is listed in Vancouver as an official Chinatown Service Centre Overseas Chinese Affairs Office (OCAO).[40]

We reached out to S.U.C.C.E.S.S. board members multiple times and received no response—that is, until corporate matriarch Queenie Choo sent us an email that was evidently intended for the organization's accountant. In it, she referred to a member of our investigative team as a problem that needed to be dealt with. Using initials, she recommended that board members Donnie Wing and Terry Yung take care of the problem, but didn't say what she meant by that.

Was the email sent in error, or was it a thinly veiled threat to get us to back off? Whatever the cryptic message was meant to convey, it told us that we were hitting a nerve with our investigation.

S.U.C.C.E.S.S. has cultivated an image of itself as a 100% Canadian, non-partisan, non-profit, multi-cultural social service agency serving newcomers, seniors and families. But as we continued to unravel the details of what was behind the Beijing Transit Station and what role it might play in the United Front's plan to achieve its core objectives, we hit a nerve with the NGO and uncovered an even bigger plan—one that reached around the globe and had direct implications for each and every Canadian.[41]

## S.U.C.C.E.S.S. AND THE CCP'S GLOBAL OVERSEAS COMMUNITY PROJECT

In hybrid warfare, governments use soft power to co-opt rather than coerce. This involves using propaganda, money, and other tools to shape people's perceptions. The Marshall Plan for rebuilding postwar Europe is a successful American example of soft power in action. China's Belt and Road Initiative is another such example—the government builds much-needed infrastructure, both inside and outside China, and that boosts trade, creates jobs, raises the standard of living, and generally improves people's lives. But it also fosters dependence and gives China economic leverage. This is why it's sometimes referred to as neo-colonialism or debt-trap diplomacy, especially in the context of developing countries accepting loans from China to build much-needed bridges and roads At some point, we can be reasonably assured, the debt will be leveraged for political ends.

Chinese Service Centers are a crucial part of the CCP's use of soft power. The real goal of these centres is to allow the CCP is to compel Overseas Chinese to serve in place by further advancing the reunification of the motherland, and help China achieve the Chinese dream of becoming the world's dominant superpower. The deputy director of the Overseas Chinese Affairs Office (OCAO), which manages overseas issues including oversight of Chinese Service Centres, confirmed as much—that the centres exist not only to solve problems, strengthen skills, protect rights and interests, and develop careers, but also to help "realize the great rejuvenation of the Chinese nation."[42]

It was clear from this statement that the aid centres were involved in a lot more than providing social services and general settlement support for new Overseas Chinese. Perhaps a better question is, why would China even need to provide social services for Chinese living in Canada, when those services were provided to all residents, including Chinese nationals who live in Canada?

The CCP wants all its people—in China and around the world—to serve the motherland first and foremost. Through the Consulate of the People's Republic of China in Vancouver, the CPP aims to "widely contact and serve overseas Chinese, actively popularize education of Mandarin, unite with overseas Chinese and push forward the cause of peaceful reunification of the motherland."[43] If that's not plain enough, Article 55 of the Constitution of the People's Republic of China states that "It is the sacred duty of every citizen of the People's Republic of China to defend the motherland and resist aggression."[44]

A way to achieve these goals is by keeping Overseas Chinese connected to each other and to the motherland, through food, art, culture, and, most importantly, family. Family is crucial, because the people we love and/or to whom we owe our lives can be leveraged.

## AN EIGHT-POINT PLAN TO WARM OVERSEAS HEARTS

The Chinese government estimates that over 90 percent of overseas Chinese are engaged in catering and related industries overseas, and the CCP sees the promotion of Chinese food overseas to enhance soft power.[45]

An investigative report by Philip Lenczycki quoted co-author McGregor, who said that the "Communist Party (CCP) intelligence arm have hosted cultural events featuring pro-CCP propaganda and performers tied to China's government and military." Activities like this, McGregor added, offer "a perfect platform for the CCP to invite elected officials, whom they can then influence into endorsing the CCP's narrative, and, in turn, influence broad masses of people."[46] [47]

Factoring into this is Canada's real or perceived identity crisis, which the CCP has used to its advantage—a crisis fuelled, as we've already seen, by descriptions, from on high, of Canada as a "postnational state."

Meanwhile, Canadian tax dollars are being used to fund activities hosted by United Front-controlled organizations in Canada as a way to *shape* Canada's identity. Unfortunately, such activities have worked to further erode Canadian identity and have exposed Canadians to CCP propaganda.

Dance troupes are in every country where the Overseas Community Project and Overseas Community Service Centres are found. They are an effective propaganda tool because they can curate their own performances that includes propaganda and incorporate elected officials who are there under the misguided belief that they are attending a cultural celebration.

In 2015, the Toronto Huaxing Troupe/Chinese Star Art Troupe became one of four in the world to be named, by the Overseas Chinese Affairs Office of China, as part of the Overseas Community Project.[48] By 2017, the troupe was already preforming at a large-scale gala to celebrate Canada's 150th National Day. Called "Ode to Canada, Chinese Love," this two-and-a-half-hour evening opened with a review of Canadian history, as told by the Chinese government over three chapters, with one of them emphasizing multiculturalism.[49]

Philip Lenczycki points to an agenda underlying these kinds of events that may not be immediately apparent. Uninformed audiences "will see extremely talented people and think that China can't be that bad," he said, but such events typically involve propaganda departments and military performers who served in the People's Liberation Army and attended the People's Liberation Army's Academy of Art.

Given all of this, it makes sense that clips from video recordings of performances by the Toronto Huaxing Art Troupe are being used in story vignettes that also contain custom messages to UFWD hometown associations. These same videos are combined with messages from CCP members and party officials, set to background music that includes CCP Propaganda Department approved patriotic tunes.[50] Moreover, Canada is more vulnerable than other countries to these kinds of soft power moves, given its embrace of multiculturalism and its inclusive, fragmented approach to national identity.

We've only just scratched the service by exposing the service centres that are listed by the Overseas Chinese Affairs Office (OCAO). Many of these Chinese service centres also have police centres attached to them, in keeping with one part of the eight-point plan. As Philip Lenczycki said to us, these overseas Chinese service centres allow the Chinese government to get a foot in the door across the entire world.

"They're trying to standardize the United Front system for how they do these type of influence operations, both on the Overseas Chinese community [and] the locals," he said. "It provides them with opportunities to make inroads with business and get into government."

Moreover, the policing aspect, "while obviously concerning," Lenczyski said, "is also a distraction from the more profound takeaway, which is that the CCP is setting up shop on sovereign soil." As "truly horrible as it is that the CCP tracks dissidents," he added, "it's arguably far more insidious that they've essentially crafted an entire playbook on how to roll into towns, bamboozle the locals, win over police and politicians, and silently infiltrate the existing power structure in order to acquire our technology and whatnot."

In the upcoming chapter called "The Rise of the Puppet Mayor at Ground Zero," we'll see that the combined service centre/police station model has been replicated elsewhere and has taken on myriad forms within other covert sites not listed by the OCAO, across Canada and the US. By creating public overseas centres, the CCP is only letting us know what they want us to know. They are willing to expose some of their own activity as a penetration test, to see where Canada's tolerance level is at. They have framed this activity as a way of helping foreign nationals with consular protection services like translation for crimes, licence and passport renewal, but there is plenty going on in the shadows that we may never know about until it is too late. One area of concern has to do with the way law enforcement has helped China capture human assets and used S.U.C.C.E.S.S. and other Overseas Chinese Service Centres as an outpost for the complementary global Chinese programs Operation Fox Hunt and Operation Sky Net.

When Operation Fox Hunt was launched in 2014, it saw the repatriation of hundreds of alleged criminals. Operation Sky Net was initiated a year later, in 2015. Sky Net provided enhanced intelligence capabilities that included examining underground banks, offshore companies, and documents such as forged driver's licences—anything that would help the fox hunters track their targets. This meant China's Ministry of Public Security would have to have special access to bank records and driver's licences. Citizen status in other countries was also a key collection tool for tracking financial fugitives, so the PRC initiated a household registration system to investigate dual citizenship. Programs like this work hand in hand with the service centres and their in-house police stations to facilitate monitoring and tracking.

Chillingly, this allows the CCP to maintain control over its citizens, wherever they might live.

# CHAPTER 10

# CHINA'S HUMAN HUNTERS IN CANADA

## THE CLANDESTINE CAMPAIGN TO CAPTURE CHINESE CANADIANS

It wasn't entirely shocking to those who knew ex-RCMP William (Bill) Majcher when he was arrested at Vancouver International Airport (YVR) on July 20, 2023.

Majcher was involved in asset recovery—a polite term for bounty hunting humans and finding assets like real estate and currency. According to a statement by the RCMP, the Integrated National Security Enforcement Team (INSET) launched an investigation in Fall 2021, looking into William Majcher's suspicious activities, alleging that he contributed to the Chinese government's efforts to identify and intimidate an individual outside the scope of Canadian law. Just who this individual was remained a mystery at the point of publishing.[1]

---

PHOTO: China has recruited ex-police for asset recovery of Chinese Nationals living in Canada.

Majcher was said to have two co-conspirators: ex-RCMP officer Kenneth (Kim) Marsh, who is based in Vancouver, BC, and former supervisory special agent for the FBI, Ross Gaffney, who is based in Pompano Beach, Florida. Gaffney is the principal and co-founder of Gaffney, Gallagher & Philip, LLC, a forensic consulting firm specializing in complex international economic crime investigations, anti-money laundering training, asset tracing, due diligence, special events and crisis and consequence management.[2]

We started looking into Majcher's and Marsh's activities ourselves after we discovered some information during our investigation into S.U.C.C.E.S.S. and its possible ties to operations Fox Hunt and Sky Net.

The information related to an anti-corruption program launched in 2014 by President Xi Jinping, purportedly targeting wealthy citizens and corrupt Communist Party members who have fled overseas with large sums of money.

In 2015, Canadian Ambassador Guy Saint-Jacques, who served in the People's Republic of China from 2012 to 2016 and who attended the S.U.C.C.E.S.S. Beijing transit station ceremony with key United Front figures, gave an exclusive interview to *China Daily* on Canada's partnership with China over Operation Fox Hunt.

"Canada has had very close collaboration with the Chinese government to address such issues," he reportedly said, then went on to affirm that in Canada, "we have no desire to harbor fugitives, and we don't want to be known as welcoming fugitives."[3]

Knowing how well this view would have been received by the CCP, we decided to reach out to Ambassador Saint-Jacques for confirmation. We asked his office whether he indeed made these statements that seemed to be in support of Operation Fox Hunt, or whether his words were taken out of context by the state-run newspaper.

The ambassador did not grant us an interview—a representative from Global Affairs passed us off to the RCMP, which gave us a generic non-answer—but signs point to Saint-Jacques' statement having been accurately reported by *China Daily*. In the same article, the director of the Chinese Ministry of Public Security International Cooperation Bureau, Liao Jinrong, praised Canada for "attach[ing] great importance to the intelligence the Chinese police give them and cooperat[ing] closely with us over the investigation of cases, arrests of suspects and repatriation work."

The same *China Daily* article also revealed, through Saint-Jacques, that China and Canada planned to sign an agreement to share the assets that

Chinese fugitives transfer illegally to Canada. Saint-Jacques was quoted as saying that the agreement would "provide a legal basis for Canada to share the proceeds of forfeited assets with China, once we identify the transferred illegal money belongs to criminals or criminal organizations."[4]

Recent news reports appear to reflect a change in Saint-Jacques' former stance on China. In a 2023 interview with CTV's Vassy Kapelos, the former ambassador spoke pointedly about China's alleged targeting of Michael Chong and his family, and said he was "not surprised at all" to hear of China running an intimidation campaign against the Canadian MP.

"This is part of typical Chinese behaviour, and they have become bolder over time with the actions they're taking," he said. "They do this with members of the Chinese diaspora, they do this with students, and they keep watch on everyone."[5] In a *Globe and Mail* opinion piece he wrote the same year, Saint-Jacques pointed to a "growing deterioration in the relationship between Canada and China" following the expulsion of Toronto-based Chinese diplomat Zhao Wei and the removal of Canadian consul Jennifer Lynn Lalonde in Shanghai.[6] Saint-Jacques wrote that he hopes for "a new beginning with China—one where Canada can better protect its interests and values, as well as its citizens from foreign interference."

This represents a distinct change in tone and messaging between 2015 and 2023. Before any pushback began to appear in response to pressure from China, Canada was poised to make a lot of money off an agreement to facilitate the return of Chinese nationals accused by the Chinese government of being criminals.

This collaborative and transactional approach to helping China with its repatriation goals started with an MOU (Memorandum of Understanding) on an agreement to combat crime, drawn up between China's Ministry of Public Security and the RCMP under Prime Minister Harper and Chinese President Hu Jintao. The MOU was drawn up in 2012, one year before Xi Jinping came to power.[7]

As summarized in a Joint Communiqué from the Prime Minister of Canada's Office (PMO) on Sept. 13, 2016, "The two sides determined that the short-term objectives for Canada-China cooperation on security and rule of law are to: start discussions on an Extradition Treaty and a Transfer of Offenders Treaty as well as other related matters; pursue discussions on cyber security and cybercrime cooperation; complete work related to the signing of the Agreement Between Canada and the People's Republic of China on Sharing and Return of Forfeited Assets; renew the Canada–China MOU Concerning Cooperation in Combatting Crime between the Royal Canadian Mounted Police and the Ministry of Public Security of China; and finalize negotiation of a one-year MOU on the Pilot Project between the Canada Border Services Agency and the Bureau of Exit and Entry Administration where Chinese experts will be invited to assist in the verification of the identity of inadmissible persons from mainland China in order to facilitate their return from Canada to China."[8] [9]

In 2021, a senior spokesperson for the Canada Border Services Agency (CBSA) dispelled any notion that there was an active agreement in place. The CBSA "does not have a Memorandum of Understanding or agreement as described," the source said, adding that "dialogue was to occur," but "no document was finalized or signed."[10] Also in 2021, a spokesperson for Global Affairs Canada confirmed that "Canada and China negotiated and signed an agreement on the sharing and return of forfeited assets" that "would come into force" once it was ratified by both countries. "As the agreement has not come into force," they added, "no sharing nor return of forfeited assets has occurred under the terms of the agreement."[11]

The RCMP has not confirmed whether they have a revenue-sharing agreement with China, but when asked about their role in Operation Fox Hunt, they said, "The RCMP is aware of these reports and we take reports of criminal activity seriously. While we cannot comment on individual cases or investigations, Canadians and all individuals living in Canada, regardless of their nationality, should feel safe and free from criminal activity."[12]

Despite the absence of an official (ratified) agreement between China and Canada, a spokesperson with RCMP HQ acknowledged that there was indeed an MOU for combatting crime between the RCMP and the Ministry of Public Security of the People's Republic of China, but that the RCMP did not have the authorization to release a copy of it. We know that the RCMP is still involved in international policing and contract work leading to repatriations, and that it has received revenue under the RCMP's International Operations program.[13] In a 2017–18 report, the RCMP said it has worked "to address gaps in Canada's anti-money laundering regime . . . by leading a Canada-wide effort to create a coordinated model between criminal asset recovery and civil asset recovery." This model, the report said, "will help ensure that all options are explored to disrupt the ability of criminals to profit from their crimes."[14]

In 2018, thirty-nine RCMP liaison officers, four regional manager liaison officers, and twelve criminal intelligence analysts were posted to twenty-six strategic international locations, including China, specifically Beijing and Hong Kong. One of their mandates is to maintain the exchange of criminal intelligence between the RCMP and foreign authorities.[15]

The unfortunate problem here is that the CCP manufactures files on people they want to arrest, with contents that are often "fake" or based on witness testimony that is coerced and/or otherwise leveraged by the CCP to corroborate allegations that may or may not be factual.[16] Moreover, if Liao Jinrong, director of the international cooperation bureau under the Ministry of Public Security, is to be believed, Canada has "welcomed Chinese witnesses to testify in Canadian courts to help charge those Chinese criminals" whom the CCP seeks to repatriate.[17] This can set in motion a complex matrix involving private intelligence firms, ex-cops, lawyers, accountants, banks, airport security and others whose testimony can easily be made to fit China's plans to repatriate whoever they wish to bring home. With the facts of each case laying open to manipulation by state actors, truth becomes no more than a variable, and justice can too easily become an elusive goal.

Canada has tried to offset these dangers. By 2019, the Avoiding Complicity in Mistreatment by Foreign Entities Act (ACMFEA) was enacted to safeguard against profiling alleged criminals who could be at "a substantial risk of mistreatment" by a foreign entity. The RCMP said in later reports that were applying ACMFEA to at least one other program, and "modernizing our approach to profiling foreign law enforcement entities with whom we share information."[18]

But the question remains: who was making money off repatriations, and how? Although Canada had a framework in place for sharing forfeited property with foreign nations under the Seized Property Management Act, and although we know that the RCMP receives revenue for international policing,[19] we had little success uncovering who was paying whom, or tracking down how much money Canada made, if any, from repatriating Chinese nationals under Fox Hunt. Even the Department of Justice provided a less-than-satisfactory response to our question, saying, "It turns out Global Affairs Canada is better placed to answer your initial questions. You should hear from them shortly."[20]

By 2020, it became obvious that Fox Hunt wasn't just about repatriating criminals. The director of the Federal Bureau of Investigation (FBI), Christopher A. Wray, gave an impassioned speech at the Hudson Institute in New York, claiming that the purpose of Fox Hunt was political repression, not anti-corruption. Canada's spy agency has since followed suit, acknowledging that Fox Hunt wasn't all that it was portrayed to be, and that it was also being used to repatriate citizens who are dissidents, not criminals.

Despite these shifting winds of public support, however, certain Canadian professionals continued to support Fox Hunt. One of those is Vincent Yang, a senior associate at the International Centre for Criminal Law Reform and Criminal Justice (ICCLR) at the University of British Columbia. When asked about his role in repatriation cases, Yang told us, "Yes, I served CBSA as its expert witness in some fugitive cases. And I was called as a witness for some real refugees from China too."[21]

Yang described his role as an expert for the Canadian government on Fox Hunt cases: "Like the other expert witnesses called by the Government of Canada in that case, my job was to provide concrete and updated information and opinions about the relevant Chinese laws and practices that may help the Members to assess the specific kind of risks that the claimant may face when he returns to China, such as the risks of the death penalty, torture, etc." Herein lies the problem, Yang admitted, while he also admitted to being a trusted ally of the United Front: "Yes, I attended the 11th CPPCC conference as an 'invited overseas Chinese representative' in 2008 when I was based in Macau as a law professor. In fact, during 2001-2018, I was based in Macau and attended numerous events that could be considered the so-call 'United Front' activities.'" Yang described the CPPCC as an organization of the United Front, saying, "The CPPCC is indeed defined by the CCP as an organization of 'the United Front,' but I happily accepted its invitation to attend the 2008 conference and I am still glad to have that chance to share the good Canadian values and practices at that high-level platform of 'political consultation.'"[22] Yang appeared to see his role as one of 'paradiplomacy,' working from within to bring best practices to China's anti-corruption efforts as a Canadian. We see his role as one of aiding political repression by a dictatorial state.[23]

Repatriation efforts have become an even thornier issue for the Canadian government than they were when Saint-Jacques first loaned his support to Operation Fox Hunt in 2015. Although the climate has changed and Canada seems less willing now to go to bat for China on every extradition case, China continues to be able to rely on networks of investigators, and professionals, like Yang, who continue to participate in the 'cottage industry' that allows the Chinese government to pursue political opponents around the world.

## HUMAN HUNTING

Public Safety Canada says, "The PRC and other foreign states attempt to threaten and intimidate individuals around the world through various state entities and non-state proxies. These states may use a combination of their intelligence and security services as well as trusted agents to assist them in foreign interference activity on Canadian soil. While some states may attempt to threaten and intimidate individuals in the name of fighting corruption or to bring criminals to justice, these tactics can also be used as cover for silencing dissent, pressuring political opponents and instilling a general fear of state power no matter where a person is located. The PRC's Operation Fox Hunt is one such example. The PRC uses this program as a means to identify and try to repatriate to China individuals who they allege are corrupt."

The Public Safety report went on to say that China has conducted Operation Fox Hunt in Canada since 2014, and that Canada initially worked with Chinese officials to support their (China's) investigations. They noted that increasingly stringent criteria on the PRC investigators involved in this program have been added, beginning in 2015, but didn't say if Canada had officially stopped all cooperation with China when it came to repatriating Chinese nationals.[24]

You would think that would be the end of it. No more cooperation with China. Think again. Canada has a protocol on foreign criminal investigators working in Canada on behalf of countries like China. So, when a foreign criminal investigator from China that is part of their mobile Operation Fox Hunt police team enters Canada, they are supposedly chaperoned by the police with jurisdiction.[25]

The RCMP claims on their website that they play a significant role in coordinating and communicating foreign requests with the Interpol Office at the RCMP when it comes to pursuing criminal investigations in Canada by other states.

We can think of a few problems with China being allowed to conduct investigations on Canadian soil.

First, Chinese operatives would act as police inside Canadian borders. This is a nonstarter, since no democratic country can afford to allow a communist nation's police to function independently within its borders.

Second, Interpol was increasingly coming under scrutiny for its relationship with China ever since Meng Hongwei, a high-ranking Chinese Communist Party member who was selected to serve as the president of

Interpol in 2016, disappeared while on a visit back to China from his post in France. Meng was subsequently accused of accepting over $2 million in bribes and was eventually sentenced to thirteen years and six months in prison.[26] This made us wonder how much Canadian authorities can rely on partnering with Interpol, given that Interpol is increasingly allowing autocratic regimes to use the agency's red notices—requests for international help with police investigations—to catch exiled dissidents.

Third, there are ex-police working with active law enforcement officers, often making large sums of money to assist with bounty hunting operations. This opens the possibility of police being influenced into making decisions that might impact the legal rights of others or being compromised into obtaining intelligence or services as part of the exchange of information that benefits China.

Yet another problem with allowing China's operatives to roam Canada armed with dossiers on Chinese Canadians that may be entirely fake, aided by the RCMP, is that China is using these human hunting expeditions as propaganda. Videos of their exploits around the world have been turned into propaganda with TV shows displaying exhausted hunters passed out in the hospital from the sheer effort of being in a perpetual state of hot pursuit. The hunters were portrayed as heroes to the Chinese people and as a warning that you can't hide from the CCP.

Deputy Captain Zhai Zexuan, who goes by the code name 'Boss,' is billed as a Hunter for the Party and People. He is said to be most proud of his Operation Fox Hunt medal, earned for two continuous years of fox hunting around the world. Boss was one of twenty bounty hunters who belonged to a mobile police team assigned to scour the globe in search of China's most wanted. Newspaper accounts said Boss performed over thirty-five overseas missions in twenty-one countries. By the end, he was said to have been so exhausted by the work of pursuing and capturing humans that he passed out in trains and at one point required hospitalization.

Naturally, in true CCP propaganda fashion, a camera was there to capture these multiple dramatic moments. Images of handcuffed and hooded criminals being escorted back to China are designed to not only publicly humiliate those being repatriated but also to send a message to other Chinese nationals that there will be no refuge for them, even in the West.[27]

In a case covered by CTV television network's award-winning broadcast journalist Judy Trinh, there were shades of Operation Fox Hunt as

Edward Gong (Xiao Hua Gong), a wealthy Chinese-Canadian business-man and politician, was said to have been paraded in handcuffs through a shopping mall in Toronto.[28]

Gong would eventually sue the Ontario Security Exchange Commission, accusing Canadian investigators of relying on coerced confessions after a joint probe by the Ontario Securities Commission (OSC) and the Royal Canadian Mounted Police in collaboration with China's Ministry of Public Security and authorities in New Zealand. Gong's statement of claim alleges the OSC invited Chinese government agents to Canada to investigate him and were wined and dined by Canadian officials. "The [Chinese government] delegation was treated to expensive meals and other hospitality by the OSC," the statement reads. "The OSC knew or ought to have known that the invited [Chinese government] operatives would act as police on Canadian soil."

All of this just scratches the surface of how Operation Fox Hunt has been able to successfully repatriate Chinese nationals on Canadian soil. China's hunters were armed with dossiers filled with information that was gleaned from ex-cops, private investigators, private military contractors, accountants, lawyers, police, airport security, immigration firms, global security firms, financial service companies, global banks and more.[29]

By the time Chinese operatives landed on Canada's doorstep, they already knew where to look and they came prepared with both real and manufactured evidence to justify the repatriation of Chinese Canadians.

Who are the people gathering the evidence for China? To answer that question, we need to circle back to RCMP Inspector William (Bill) Majcher.

## SHADOW JUSTICE

In 2000, the joint sting operation known as RCMP-FBI Operation Bermuda Short led to the arrest of more than fifty individuals accused of wire and securities fraud. At the time, RCMP Inspector William (Bill) Majcher was working in Miami, Florida, as an undercover on the case. The time period for this was during the 1990s to early 2000s.

Kenneth (Kim) Ingram Marsh, who goes by the name Kim Marsh, travelled to Miami to meet with Majcher near the end of Majcher's posting. Together they would travel to Costa Rica on a private case that Kim Marsh was working on. The case was so successful that it would cement their pro-fessional relationship and lead them to work together again many times.[30]

In 2003, after Operation Bermuda Short wrapped up, the RCMP started a new unit called the Integrated Market Enforcement Teams (IMET). Created as part of the Government of Canada's strategy for enhanced protection of Canadian capital markets,[31] the IMET team is made up of police officers, lawyers, and other investigative experts, according to the RCMP website. On the strength of his work on Operation Bermuda Short, Bill Majcher was promoted to become the head of the first Vancouver branch of IMET, the same team that would later investigate him for suspicious activities.

Detective Inspector Craig Hannaford, who led the Toronto branch of IMET, would later investigate allegations of wrongdoing by Canadian officials in the case of Ed Gong, an Operation Fox Hunt case from Canada.

Marsh, meanwhile, became commander of the International Organized Crime Investigation Unit, a unit responsible for large-scale, covert operations in Europe, Asia, and North America.

Both Mounties—Majcher and Marsh—would eventually retire from the force and start private investigation firms. Majcher ended up working in Hong Kong, for EMIDR Limited, a company he co-founded, and that claims to have considerable expertise in national state kleptocracy, state sponsored espionage, intelligence gathering, sanction violations, bribery and corruption, money laundering, asset tracing, and covert investigative operations.[32] [33] [34]

Marsh ended up in Vancouver, where he founded a firm called West Coast Investigations & Consulting, which operated in a shared space with forensic accountants who had been working with large, global accounting firms.

In 2002, an organization called IPSA International (later becoming Exiger) made an offer to acquire Marsh's company and bring it into the IPSA fold, through the creation of a Vancouver subsidiary. IPSA was an offshoot of a security guard company located in San Francisco that turned into a global anti-money laundering and international due-diligence firm.

Marsh would work for IPSA for fifteen years. During this time, IPSA was fined $259,200 by the Office of Foreign Assets Control (OFAC) for violating US sanctions on Iran in 2012, in relation to contracts IPSA had with two countries in assisting with their citizenship investment programmes.

The next time the two ex-Mounties would meet was as private investigators in Hong Kong, in 2010, when they worked cases together for the Chinese government. Their deep connections with law enforcement agencies made them invaluable to the CCP in its quest to hunt down missing assets from around the world.[35] In his book *The Cunning Edge*, Marsh describes their "overlap[ping] skills sets" and said he considered Majcher to be his second set of eyes and ears.[36]

A charismatic fixture on the global investigations scene, Majcher would sometimes drop hints about his work in China. At a foreign correspondent's club banquet in Hong Kong, Majcher devoted part of his keynote address to an anecdote about a conversation he'd had with an official of China's Ministry of Public Security (MPS).[37] Speaking to the crowd of mostly journalists and diplomats, he said the official told him, "Bill, you have something that's unique." Majcher implied that MPS had something on him, but he declined to provide specifics, saying only, "It's a long story why Chinese government officials know me. They knew my professional life before, and [my] background."[38]

Majcher, who mentions in his keynote that he has worked for Chinese state-owned enterprises (SOEs), then gave the reason why the Chinese government really wanted to work with him. "They said, Bill, you have informal relationships with police and intelligence services that will allow us to save a lot of time."

Majcher was known for speaking his mind and for using backchannels to cut through red tape, rather than going through treaty requests that can take years and not net any meaningful results.

"To have informal channels and relationships that can tell us we are moving in the right direction to go after money, to go after assets . . . that's what we do in the West . . . to get around the difficulties of sometimes going the formal route," Majcher told the correspondents' club crowd. Moreover, he shared that the CCP was more than willing to use information gleaned through back channels. "So will they [the CCP] go after it? Are they going after it? One hundred and ten percent," he said.[39]

A person on the right side of the law might ask, where's the harm in not following protocol when it comes to catching big bad guys, right? The problem is that Majcher was working for the CCP and elite business tycoons, using his police and intelligence contacts inside Canada and the US to hunt down individuals inside Canada accused by the CCP of crimes that they may or may not have committed.

When Project Mosaic interviewed Kim Marsh in 2017, he reflected on China's large wealthy class and on President Xi's drive to stamp out corruption. Marsh told co-author Mitchell, "It's been estimated that there [are] thirty-six million high-net worth people in China, and that is the population of Canada. There has also been a push in China by President Xi on corruption bribery. The way the system worked in China, and has worked for centuries, is that the individual at the higher end of the pyramid in politics are referred to as politically exposed people who have to be looked after before deals/contracts are executed. It's well-known that this is the norm and has been the norm in getting business done in the Chinese market. There has been a push by President Xi to stop that," Marsh said. It would appear that Marsh was describing Operation Fox Hunt / Sky Net.[40]

## ASSET TRACING AND RECOVERY INVESTIGATIONS

At the time of publication, the case against Majcher had not yet begun, and no one really knew the details of what led to his arrest. All that most people knew was that he was alleged to have used his knowledge and extensive network of contacts in Canada to obtain intelligence or services to benefit the People's Republic of China, and that Marsh was alleged to be a co-conspirator, along with a former FBI officer. The case had all the markings of Operation Fox Hunt, with allegations that Majcher contributed to the Chinese government's efforts to identify and intimidate an individual outside the scope of Canadian law.

We actually started looking into Majcher two years prior to his shocking arrest, and at the time we found a surprising connection to the CCP's United Front Work Department (UFWD) Overseas Chinese Service Centre (OCSC) branch in Vancouver inside the immigrant NGO, S.U.C.C.E.S.S.

This is where Robert (Beau) Hunter IV enters the picture. In 2008, Beau was a director of IPSA International, working under Kim Marsh. We traced Beau's early career back to the US Navy, when he was stationed in Florida as a foreign relations analyst.

Also, in 2008, Beau started Global Intellectual Property Securities (GIPS), a consulting firm that provided a vague description of the services they offered.

GIPS's head office was registered to a law office with a mailing address inside a UPS post office box. The firm had little to no online presence, beyond a website, and no social media. The only way to contact the company was through generic email.

Global Intellectual Property Securities (GIPS) is in partnership with the Hong Kong investigation firm SUZZESS, but Beau's role within the organization remains murky at best. Even his bio features no more than a stock photo of a headless body holding a pen to accompany a short description of his work history.[41]

SUZZESS, not to be confused with S.U.C.C.E.S.S., is a global detective agency that specializes in international private investigation.[42] The company is managed by Yosh Wong, an international private investigator who also sits on the board of the Council of International Investigators and belongs to the World Association of Detectives. According to his bio, he has handled many cross-border fraud investigations, including assets tracing on a multi-billion-dollar scam.[43] [44]

SUZZESS and Global Intellectual Property Securities Inc. (GIPS) "regularly [handle] cross-border investigations and other inquiries in the Asia Pacific region." Prior to staring SUZZESS, Yosh Wong worked for the Florida-based Ackerman Group LLC, a big-name security-intelligence firm whose principal management team includes former personnel with the CIA, FBI, and military special-operations units.

You may be thinking, what does all this add up to? It sounds like just another private investigation firm. The difference here is that Beau also worked for the immigration settlement service NGO, S.U.C.C.E.S.S., and did so at the same time that he worked for a private investigator in Hong Kong that specialized in asset-tracing and recovery investigations.[45]

Our investigative research on Beau turned up very little. His name appears on only a few press releases related to S.U.C.C.E.S.S., and there is no photo of Beau and little to no biographical information about him on the organization's website. This is in contrast to the rest of S.U.C.CE.S.S.'s management.

We know from first-hand experience that Beau didn't attend the organization's annual feature fundraising events that were aimed at Vancouver's well-heeled set. And to our knowledge, Beau has never held a single press conference. All of this can be considered highly unusual for the director of communications of one of Canada's largest NGOs.[46]

When we started making inquiries with S.U.C.C.E.S.S., we actually managed to talk with someone who identified himself as Beau, but he abruptly hung up when we asked him about his role asset-tracing and recovery investigations inside the NGO. After this, Beau's name disappeared from the S.U.C.C.E.S.S. website.[47]

Our intelligence sources confirmed with us that Beau's real job is to perform asset-tracing and recovery investigations on behalf of the Chinese government, through his partnership with private detective Yosh Wong and his Hong Kong based company SUZZESS.

Whether Beau's work with SUZZESS was sanctioned by the S.U.C.C.E.S.S. board whose chair at the time was Terry Yung, a well known Vancouver police officer, was an open question that we could not answer.

Yung was also on the board of the Justice Institute of BC and was cited for his involvement in the institute's police-training program set up for China's Public Security agency, the same agency that launched Operation Fox Hunt. Moreover, the FBI arrested JIBC-trained Chen Zhichen for her role for targeting Chinese nationals in America.[48] [49] [50]

We know from Ambassador Guy Saint-Jacques, who attended the red-ribbon cutting soirée in Beijing hosted by S.U.C.C.E.S.S. together with United Front elite in 2015, that Canada would "help China to repatriate corrupt officials who have fled there and confiscate their assets," and that "Canada has had very close collaboration with the Chinese government to address such issues."[51]

While Canada appears to have changed its tone officially when it comes to Operation Fox Hunt, repatriations are still happening, and the system itself hasn't changed much. Vancouver's S.U.C.C.E.S.S. Chinatown Service Centre and its subsidiary, the Chinese Police Centre, for example, are controlled by CCP's Overseas Chinese Affairs Office (OCAO), and both organizations are set up to offer vulnerable Chinese immigrants help settling in Canada. Sadly, it would appear that S.U.C.C.E.S.S. is willingly or unwittingly helping to identify and hand back those whom the Chinese government has targeted as corrupt, possibly for a share in asset recovery.

# CHAPTER 11

# CHINA'S INFLUENCE ARMY

## DIGGING DEEP INTO CCP PROXIES AND THEIR POLITICAL FRIENDS

For his meeting with BC premier John Horgan in 2018, long-time CCP member Xu Minghua donned a Chekist Soviet leather jacket, the very pinnacle of 1920s communist chic. It was the perfect fashion statement for a high-level CCP bureaucrat and a member of many Orwellian-sounding government committees, including the Zhejiang Provincial Commission for Discipline Inspection and the Provincial Party Committee Inspection Leading Group. Sources had told us that he was probably also a Ministry of State Security agent. He was certainly an operative of Operation Fox Hunt, a kind of China's Most Wanted program that travels the world chasing down businesspeople and public officials the CCP has accused of corruption.[1]

And now he was getting face time with British Columbia Premier John Horgan. But first he had a stop to make. Before setting off to see the premier, Xu took members of the Zhejiang Provincial Supervision Commission to meet with Hu Qiquan, a top PRC consul and political

---

PHOTO: United Front agent of influence, Frank Zhou, admits to being an advisor of Prime Minister Trudeau.

attaché in charge of United Front activities in BC.[2] Among those accompanying the Zhejiang delegation were a pro-CCP news outlet and Michael Lee, a Liberal member of the BC legislature and one of the new favourite politicians targeted by the CCP in the volatile BC political arena.

What was the purpose of these meetings? And who had arranged for a high-level CCP official to meet with the head of government in British Columbia?

When we set out to answer these questions, we had no idea our investigation would take us to the other side of the country and an acclaimed theatre director in bucolic Prince Edward Island.

## THE CCP THREE

Duncan McIntosh has had a career in theatre that would be the envy of most thespians. He's been the artistic director of the Charlottetown Festival, the Citadel Theatre in Edmonton, and the Shaw Festival in Niagara-on-the-Lake, and in 2008, he founded the well-regarded Watermark Theatre in North Rustico, PEI. He's also the partner of Wade MacLauchlan, the former president of the University of Prince Edward Island and a Liberal MLA who became the provincial premier in 2015 after the sudden resignation of Robert Ghiz. MacLauchlan served as premier until 2019, when the Liberals lost the election after a dozen years in power.

In addition to being life partners, Duncan McIntosh and Wade MacLauchlan are partners in many business ventures. In 2008, for example, they started Anne in China Inc., which calls itself the exclusive authorized agent for Anne of Green Gables books and merchandise in China.[3] In 2012, Anne in China Inc. published a Chinese edition of *Anne of Green Gables* with Tsinghua University Press. The book included forewords by Laureen Harper, wife of Prime Minister Stephen Harper, and Li Zhaoxing, a former Chinese minister of foreign affairs. Robert Ghiz contributed an afterword.

McIntosh and MacLauchlan had another partner in Anne in China Inc.—a man named Xuan "Frank" Zhou. Zhou came to Canada from China in the early 2000s, when he was just twenty years old. He studied mathematics at Simon Fraser University in Vancouver and while there met Sherry Huang, who became his wife and business partner.[4] They returned to China for a brief period before settling in PEI in the mid-2000s. Eventually, they started a consulting company called Sunrise Group with offices in PEI and China.

Over the years, Sunrise Group has grown into a sprawling operation with interests in many different business sectors, including transportation (Sunrise Logistics), finance (Sunrise Capital), and education (Study Abroad Canada). It's also a big booster of some venerable PEI cultural institutions—in addition to its Anne Shirley connection, Sunrise is the authorized agent for Charlottetown's Cows ice cream in China and was at one time a principal sponsor of Duncan McIntosh's Watermark Theatre.

But we were interested in a different arm of the business, called Sunrise Immigration. According to the company website, Sunrise is the only "authorized immigration intermediary" for both PEI and New Brunswick.[5] It provides immigration consulting services to a variety of clients, including "provincial and federal governments, investors, and general skilled immigration candidates," and specializes in "recruiting high-quality talent from all over the world for local enterprises through the AIP [Atlantic Immigration Program]." The AIP helps designated businesses recruit skilled foreign employees, who in turn get a pathway to permanent residency.

When Wade MacLauchlan became premier, he made immigration the centerpiece of his economic plan, dubbed "The Mighty Island."[6] The province roughly doubled its annual immigration targets and focused its efforts on attracting skilled workers and entrepreneurs. With the help of the AIP and the related Provincial Nominee Program (PNP), the premier said he hoped to reverse "a demographic trend that wouldn't turn out very well," according to *The Globe and Mail*.[7]

But here's where things start to get a bit murky. Until it was overhauled in 2018, PEI's version of the PNP granted approved candidates immediate permanent residency if they put $200,000 in escrow and agreed to live on the island and operate a business there for one year. If they met these requirements, they would get their $200,000 back, but many wealthy immigrants—now legally permanent residents—simply forfeited the money and moved to other provinces right away. It was for them a small price to pay to buy their way into Canada.

For some islanders, this was an unpleasant reminder of one of the biggest scandals of Robert Ghiz's time as premier. In 2011, three whistleblowers accused senior officials who ran the previous iteration of the PNP of fraud and bribery. That version of the program brought more than $400 million into PEI from immigrant investors, but according to *The Globe and Mail*, "much of the money never made it past middlemen who worked with both prospective immigrants and companies looking to capitalize on the program."[8] The officials, the whistleblowers alleged, funnelled the money to businesses run by friends and family members, and also fast-tracked immigration applications that didn't meet the program's criteria. The RCMP investigated the allegations, but ultimately no charges were laid.[9] The whistleblowers later sued the government, and Ghiz himself, for giving their personal information to the Liberal Party, which then leaked it to the press.[10]

All of this brought us back to Frank Zhou, business partner of the PEI premier and the man who facilitated the immigration relocation of a Tibetan Buddhist group to PEI called Bliss and Wisdom. A group that has come under intense scrutiny for facilitating the immigration of monastic students from China to Canada and the exploitation of loopholes to purchase vast quantities of land on the island. Facilitator is a good description for Zhou because in addition to helping people navigate the province's immigration system,[11] he also arranges junkets to and from China, sets up meetings with Canadian and Chinese government officials, and introduces Canadian businesspeople to their Chinese counterparts. He even offers his services as translator on occasion.

Zhou has been involved with many trade missions to China. In 2016, he was part of New Brunswick premier Brian Gallant's nine-day trip to the country, and the following year, he joined Justin Trudeau's second official state visit to China. In a particularly busy 2018, he facilitated trips for Nova Scotia premier Stephen McNeill, Newfoundland premier Dwight Ball, and his good friend Wade MacLauchlan, the premier of PEI. On Sunrise Group's website, the company describes itself as "the mission service provider" for these trade junkets.[12] It seems Frank Zhou is the go-to guy for anyone in Atlantic Canada who wants to do business with China or immigrate to Canada.

But according to Lei's Real Talk, a vodcast on U.S.-China relations, Zhou was more than just a wheeler dealer with a keen knack for bringing people together. Zhou is a 3rd generation red princeling. A term applied to the descendants of prominent and influential senior communist officials. Zhou's paternal grandfather was Comrade Zhou Zhigao, a Red-army hero from the early days of the communist revolution.[13]

Zhou's pedigree opened doors in China but it's his non-profit organization, the Canada-China Friendship and Goodwill Association (CCFGA), that has opened political doors in Canada under the pretext of encouraging educational and cultural exchanges between the two countries.[14] CCFGA's president is none other than Duncan McIntosh. The organization was incorporated in January 2015, a month before Wade MacLauchlan was sworn in as premier.

As the person at the helm of the Canada-China Friendship and Goodwill Association, McIntosh is ostensibly tasked with encouraging educational and cultural exchanges between Canada and China, through the CCFGA's close association with the Chinese People's Association for Friendship with Foreign countries (CPAFFC).[15]

And what could be wrong with friendship or goodwill?

The problem with this is that the CPAFFC is a CCP-funded organization that the US State Department has designated as a foreign mission of the PRC, under the control of the United Front Work Department. The designation was made in a State Department press release that said the CPAFFC is "a Beijing-based organization tasked with co-opting subnational governments," that "has sought to directly and malignly influence state and local leaders to promote the PRC's global agenda."[16]

The Canadian government has not made any similar designations concerning the CPAFFC, but Canada's spy agency, CSIS, has reported that foreign interference techniques used by foreign state actors includes cultivation, such as "building a strong friendship or relationship with someone to manipulate them into providing favours and valuable information."[17]

Lynette Ong, associate professor of political science for the Munk School of Global Affairs & Public Policy at the University of Toronto, spoke to a special House of Common committee on Canada-China relations about the strategies used by United Front affiliated groups to gain influence in Canada. Ong advised the committee on key organizations under the United Front umbrella, such as the Chinese People's Political Consultative Conference, which "brings together non-CCP social elites domestically," and she mentioned the work of "peak" UFWD organizations such as the China Overseas Friendship Association, the All-China Federation of Returned Overseas Chinese, Chinese students and scholars associations, and numerous Overseas Chinese friendship and hometown associations.

"By co-opting these organizations under the umbrella of the United Front work," Ong told the committee, "the party seeks to shape the narrative and extend its influence overseas. This raises the question of whether activities of these organizations are instances of 'foreign influence,' such as attempts to project China's soft power overseas, or they amount to 'foreign interference.'" Ong added that the covert nature of some of these groups and activities "makes a fair and impartial assessment more challenging."[18]

Authentic people-to-people exchanges are absolutely critical in helping to understand other cultures for engaging in trade relations. But the UFWD and associated friendship organizations are funded directly or indirectly by the Chinese Communist Party and are not really about people-to-people exchange; it is more accurate to call them vehicles for foreign influence.

The CCP will use people, especially family, who are in close proximity to high-priority targets, as a means to gain access and ultimately influence powerful people by enabling them to set up an NGO in association with a CCP friendship organization or even help them secure a position within a foreign lobbying firm.

People like Duncan McIntosh might be in a position to be used as conduits of the CCP solely because of their close and intimate connections to people in positions of power.

The more powerful the target, the more likely there is to be a substantial payoff. Hunter Biden, son of the president of the United States, is a prime example of this. As a foreign lobbyist, he was paid millions of dollars by Chinese elite for access to his father, President Joe Biden.

The CCFGA falls under the auspices of the Chinese People's Association for Friendship with Foreign Countries (CPAFFC), which is a Beijing-based NGO created by the Chinese government. The CPAFFC is part of the CCP's foreign affairs apparatus, and it "claims to have established 46 friendship associations abroad and developed cooperative relationships with nearly 500 groups in 157 countries."[19] Its stated goals are to enhance people's friendship, further international cooperation, promote common development, and safeguard world peace, and it does this, it says, by organizing visits to China, hosting cultural groups, and sponsoring performances and exhibitions abroad.[20] In practice, though, the CPAFFC is an organ of the United Front Work Department, and like other friendship organizations, its real aim is to promote the interests of the CCP.

According to a study by the Center for Strategic and Budgetary Assessments (CSBA), a Washington think tank, the CPAFFC is active in a wide variety of fields, including politics, science and technology, environmental protection, and sports. It sometimes downplays its connection to the CCP, but its leadership is drawn from the upper ranks of the party. Its current president, Lin Songtian, was once China's ambassador to South Africa.[21] Lin has said publicly that he believes the US Army was responsible for the COVID-19 outbreak in mainland China.[22]

Like other friendship societies, the CPAFFC targets those who are connected to powerful people or influential groups with the goal of effecting policy change or shaping public opinion. Typically, the targets have some influence of their own but are not as well-known as the people or groups they're connected to. For example, the CPAFFC works with Neil Bush, the third son of George H.W. Bush and the founder of the George H.W. Bush Foundation for U.S.-China Relations, a Houston-based nonprofit that pushes for closer ties with China.

In their book *Hidden Hand: Exposing How the Chinese Communist Party Is Reshaping the World*, Clive Hamilton and Mareike Ohlberg examined Bush's many links to and comments about China. They showed, for instance, that he was a nonexecutive chairman of a real estate company owned by Gordon Tang and Huaiden Chen, who in 2016 made an illegal $1.3 million donation to the presidential campaign of Neil's brother Jeb.[23] In 2019, Axios reported, Neil Bush told a forum in Hong Kong that "American-style democracy 'would not work for China' and would be 'destabilizing.'"[24] On other occasions, he has complimented the country's system of governance and parroted CCP talking points.

On January 10, 2019, the CPAFFC invited Neil Bush and two other scions of American political dynasties—Chip Carter, son of Jimmy Carter, and Chris Cox, grandson of Richard Nixon—to attend a reception commemorating the fortieth anniversary of the establishment of diplomatic relations between China and the United States at the Great Hall of the People in Beijing. At the reception, Chip Carter read a congratulatory letter from his father. Later that year, the Bush Foundation awarded former president Carter its inaugural George H.W. Bush Award for Statesmanship in U.S.-China Relations.[25] In presenting the award, Neil Bush chided people for their "anti-China rhetoric" and declared that "China is not the enemy of our nation, but rather, an indispensable partner and vital stakeholder in America's future." Music to the CCP's ears.

We had to wonder if, given his connections to the United Front through his Canada-China Friendship and Goodwill Association, Frank Zhou had targeted Duncan McIntosh, partner to the premier, in exactly this same way. And if he had, what was his endgame?

## ALL IN THE FAMILY

On May 6, 2016, Zhou travelled to Jinhua, a city of seven million people in Zhejiang province on China's east coast. While there, Zhou reported to the foreign affairs office about the work his CCFGA had been doing to promote people-to-people exchanges; to further collaboration in education, business, tourism, and other fields; and to "normalize" cooperation between the two countries.[26] [27]

A little over five months after Zhou's trip to Jinhua, Duncan McIntosh met with Xie Yuan, the vice president of the CPAFFC.[28] The two were working out a plan for new avenues of cooperation between PEI and the federal government. While they met, Xie expressed his appreciation for Frank Zhou's friendship society and how it had improved relations between Canada and China. McIntosh—a proxy for the CCP whether he knew it or not—echoed Xie's sentiments and promised to continue working with the CPAFFC to facilitate leadership exchanges and other new initiatives.[29]

According to the conservative think tank, the Heritage Foundation, the United Front lead CPAFFC does not hesitate to apply pressure once a relationship with an official has been established, engaging in a strategy that often includes offering trips to China and discussing possible investments in industries that relate to national security.[30] Pointing to an example of this process, Lee Edwards relayed the case of a Chinese official who, according to Secretary of State Pompeo, "threatened to cancel a Chinese investment if a certain governor traveled to Taiwan, whose democratically elected president is deemed by Beijing to be too independent." Edwards noted that "No one is unimportant in CPAFFC's calculations—its people cultivate county school boards and local politicians through so-called sister city programs."[31]

According to a source with close ties to the Province of BC's premier's office, in 2018, Duncan McIntosh organized a meeting for a delegation from the Foreign Affairs Department for Oceania and the Americas from the Province of Zhejiang, ostensibly under Zhou's Canada-China Friendship and Goodwill Association (CCFGA) who answer to CPAFFC, of which he is the president.

Captions under provincial publicity photos taken at the event reveal that BC's Premier John Horgan met with Mr. Wen Zhang, director of the Zhejiang-based Foreign Affairs Department for Oceania and the Americas, to discuss common priorities and bi-lateral cooperation.[32] What is not revealed is that the person standing in the photo with Premier Horgan is not Wen Zhang but Xu Minghua, a top-ranking CCP member assigned to travel with the delegation, who was in charge of the Zhejiang Provincial Committee of the Communist Party of China.[33]

Just two years later, McIntosh set up that meeting between Xu Minghua and John Horgan. We may never know what was discussed, what kind of coercion was attempted, or what was agreed to behind closed doors. But we do know that the government of British Columbia has signed dozens or maybe even hundreds of memorandums of understanding with China, state-run organizations, and companies tied to military that compromise our national security, and that the details of these MOUs are often kept out of the public sphere.[34]

As a case in point, James Wang, a municipal councillor for Burnaby, signed an MOU in 2016 at the Chinese Cultural Centre in Vancouver's Chinatown, with the Henan Acrobatic Group Chinese.[35] According to state media reports, the strategic cooperation agreement included a plan to promote Chinese culture in Vancouver and other Canadian provinces.[36] The ceremony was also attended by PRC consulate representatives and several high-ranking CCP party officials.

Wang did the same thing again in December 2019 at another signing ceremony held in the Trump Tower in downtown Vancouver, where he put his signature to an MOU with a foreign company from China, as a Burnaby councillor. We asked Mike Hurley, mayor of the City of Burnaby, about these MOUs. He promised to get back to us but never did. We also asked the city about the meeting, through a Freedom of Information request, but there was no record of the event.

James Wang was no stranger to the United Front. As mentioned earlier, his brother, Bai Ning, is the vice chairman of the Zhejiang Federation of Returned Overseas Chinese. In Feb 2021, he took part in a general meeting dedicated to planning and mobilizing overseas Chinese to realize Xi Jinping's 5-year plan.

He (James Wang) served as an overseas consultant for the Weinan Federation of Returned Overseas Chinese (United Front) prior to becoming a city councillor.[37]

"MOUs are vitally important to trade and investment in B.C. as they often lead to firm investment commitments," according to Teresa Wat, who was the Minister of International Trade and Minister Responsible for Asia Pacific Strategy and Multiculturalism at the time. What was Wang doing signing an MOU for Vancouver as an elected official from another city, and why the lack of transparency?

## CHAPTER 12

# TALENT RECRUITMENT

### THE CCP'S INFILTRATION OF ACADEMIA

On January 28, 2020, the chair of Harvard's chemistry department was ushered out of his Ivy League office in handcuffs and charged with lying to federal investigators.[1] Charles Lieber, an esteemed nanoscientist and head of the eponymous Lieber Research Group at America's most illustrious university, was eventually convicted of misleading investigators about his affiliation with the Wuhan University of Technology (WUT), among other offences. Lieber concealed from Harvard the fact that, beginning in 2011, he was a so-called strategic scientist for WUT and a participant in China's Thousand Talents Plan (TTP). Under the terms of his TTP contract, the Chinese government gave him a $50,000 monthly stipend, about $150,000 in living expenses, and more than $1.5 million to establish a laboratory in China. Because he was also the recipient of millions of dollars in grant money from the US National Institutes of Health and the Department of Defense, Lieber was obligated to disclose "any significant foreign financial conflicts of interest, including funding from foreign governments." He

PHOTO: Chinese talent recruitment programs recruit elite foreign-trained scientists as well as steal technology.

failed to do that. On December 21, 2021, Lieber was found guilty on two counts of making false statements to the U.S. government, two counts of filing a false income tax return, and two counts of failing to report foreign bank accounts. As of early 2023, he was awaiting sentencing and facing up to twenty-six years in prison and $1.2 million in fines. On April 26, 2023, he was sentenced to six months of house arrest.[2]

Lieber's high-profile arrest was a result of the heightened attention being paid to the Thousand Talents Plan during the Trump administration. In 2019, a Senate subcommittee had concluded that the plan "incentivizes individuals engaged in research and development in the United States to transmit the knowledge and research they gain here to China in exchange for salaries, research funding, lab space, and other incentives. China unfairly uses the American research and expertise it obtains for its own economic and military gain."[3] The FBI agent in charge of the Boston field office that arrested Lieber put it more bluntly: "The Chinese government's goal . . . is to replace the United States as the world superpower and it's breaking the law to get there."[4]

## REVERSING THE BRAIN DRAIN

The Thousand Talents Plan—one of more than two hundred CCP talent recruitment programs—is a pillar of China's strategic goals and has set off alarm bells among Western nations. In its rush to modernize its society (especially its military) and ratchet up its innovation-driven economic growth, China has increased the pressure on academics and entrepreneurs to share not just what they know but the research and technology at the heart of that knowledge. While much of the focus of the TTP has been on Chinese expats who were educated or are working at prestigious universities overseas, many Westerners with elite skills have also been recruited for the program, as the Charles Lieber case showed. To attract top-level talent with knowledge about or access to cutting-edge scientific research and technology, China offers huge salaries and generous research grants, among other inducements.

You might think this sounds like the type of thing Western countries routinely do as well. In Canada, for instance, the government spends $300 million a year to recruit and retain world-class researchers in engineering, health sciences, humanities, and social sciences through its Canada

Research Chairs Program.[5] Also, China historically has been plagued by a brain drain—most Chinese who go to the West to study opt to stay there. Is it really surprising that the government would devise a program to reverse that trend and encourage its own citizens to come back and build up their country of birth?

Talent recruitment isn't a problem in and of itself. In fact, Western countries have for decades been the beneficiaries of China's brain drain. But the goal of the TTP isn't for China to catch up to the West—it's to surpass it. And to achieve that goal, the Chinese government is willing to encourage participants to engage in misconduct and even illegal activity, including industrial espionage and intellectual property theft. The scale of China's efforts is also unlike anything seen in the West. A 2020 study by the Australian Strategic Policy Institute (ASPI) noted that according to official statistics, the country's talent-recruitment programs attracted almost sixty thousand participants between 2008 and 2016.[6] The ASPI report said that China had been assisted in its efforts by hundreds of talent-recruitment stations operating in countries like the US, the UK, Australia, and Canada.[7] We'll talk more about these stations later in this chapter.

Most concerning of all, of course, is the type of people China is targeting and what it expects them to do once back at home. While the Canada Research Chair program spreads the wealth (39 percent to natural sciences and engineering, 39 percent to health sciences, and 22 percent to humanities and social sciences), the TTP focuses on scientists and engineers, especially those working on what is sometimes referred to as dual-use technologies—meaning those that have both civilian and military applications. In September 2022, NBC News reported that many scientists enticed back to China through the program put their skills to use making "advances in such technologies as deep-earth-penetrating warheads, hypersonic missiles, quiet submarines and drones."[8] NBC's report was based on a private intelligence study prepared by Strider Technologies.

One person profiled by NBC was Zhao Yusheng, who had received nearly $20 million in taxpayer-funded grant money over the eighteen years he spent working at the Los Alamos National Laboratory (site of the Manhattan Project), where he led a project developing bombs capable of digging deep underground. In 2016, Zhao joined a talent-recruitment program and returned home to China. He eventually became the vice president of Shenzhen's Southern University of Science and Technology, which, NBC noted, conducts defence research. Coincidence? It seems unlikely. As FBI director Christopher Wray put it in a 2020 speech, "American taxpayers are effectively footing the bill for China's own technological developments."[9]

Zhao, it should be noted, has never been charged with or convicted of a crime. But plenty of other people in comparable positions have. In 2019, for example, an agricultural scientist named Xiang Haitao was arrested for stealing trade secrets belonging to his former employer, Monsanto. He was charged with economic espionage and eventually pleaded guilty to that crime.[10] In 2013, Zhao Huajun was also charged with economic espionage after he stole patented cancer research material from the Medical College of Wisconsin, apparently to provide to Zhejiang University in Hangzhou. He eventually pleaded guilty to a reduced charge.[11] And then there was the case of Noshir Gowadia, an Indian-born US national who was arrested on espionage-related charges in 2005. He had shared classified information when helping China design an exhaust system that would make its cruise missiles less susceptible to detection and interception.[12] In 2010, Gowadia was found guilty and sentenced to thirty-two years in prison.

It might be tempting to dismiss these cases as a few bad apples easily led astray by the promise of a big payday. But that ignores the role played by the CCP in all this. Zhao Huajun was given a prestigious position at the Zhejiang Chinese Medical University just one month after admitting guilt in his case, and Noshir Gowadia was abetted in his efforts by an official from China's State Administration of Foreign Experts Affairs.[13] Far from punishing these people for their wrongdoing, China appears to encourage and even reward them.

## THE GREAT DISAPPEARING ACT

As these instances of misconduct piled up, governments in the US, Canada, and elsewhere finally started to pay more attention to the Thousand Talents Plan. China's response to this increased scrutiny was to scrub references to the program from the internet and make its recruitment activities even more covert. In 2018, the plan's official website deleted all articles about the program and eventually went offline entirely. The ASPI, in its 2020 study, described seeing leaked internal documents that told recruiters not to use email to communicate with potential TTP candidates. "[They] should be notified under the name of inviting them to return to China to participate in an academic conference or forum," one document advised. "Written notices should not contain the words 'Thousand Talents Plan.'"[14]

Despite going underground, the program still seemed to be operational and continued to use talent-recruitment stations to identify and engage with potential candidates. The ASPI reported that it had uncovered six hundred of these stations in the world's most technologically advanced countries (and the actual number may be much higher).[15] The country with the most stations, not surprisingly, was the US; Germany, Australia, the UK, and Canada rounded out the top five. These stations are often run by overseas organizations that have connections to or are part of the United Front network. The organizations receive a small annual fee for managing the stations, as well as bonuses—or bounties, if you will—for each person they recruit. They also perform other tasks, such as arranging trips to China for candidates and collecting data on research projects.

In Canada, there are at least forty-seven talent-recruiting stations, according to the ASPI report.[16] Four of these were established by the Fujian Provincial Overseas Chinese Affairs Office, a known United Front organization, in 2016. John McCallum, then the immigration minister and soon after the Canadian ambassador to China, appeared at the opening of one station and was pictured alongside a member of several organizations run by the United Front Work Department.

In December 2020, Global News also reported on a collaboration between the National Research Council and a Chinese company called CanSino Biologics.[17] They were supposed work together to produce a vaccine for COVID, with CanSino developing the vaccine and the NRC mass-producing it in Canadian labs. But the deal collapsed when China failed to release the vaccine candidate for testing in Canada.

Several intelligence agents told Global that the CanSino deal should have raised red flags for the Canadian government. In 2016, the company had started a Chinese-American talent-recruiting program with the help of a United Front organization, and the company's co-founders were both members of the Thousand Talents Plan. Former CSIS director Ward Elcock called the TTP "a vacuum cleaner collection strategy," hoovering up vital information and technologies and giving nothing in return. With no real explanation for why China had failed to release the vaccine candidate, some intelligence analysts speculated that the country had got what it wanted from Canada—potentially including proprietary technology—and had no more to gain from proceeding. "It looks like what China did is they got what they needed and they stopped the vaccine shipment," said Michel Juneau-Katsuya, author of the Sidewinder report. He noted that the NRC had previously lost valuable intellectual property to China, including in a 2014 cyber attack.

Through our own research, we uncovered several additional examples of TTP members working in Canada or with Canadian organizations and potentially recruiting others to the cause. Take, for instance, the case of Dr. Zu-hua Gao, chair of the Department of Pathology at McGill University's Faculty of Medicine. In 2018, Dr. Gao was invited to attend the 13th Chinese People's Political Consultative Conference (CPPCC) in Beijing, a great honour for Overseas Chinese. This experience inspired him, he said, to rethink how he could be more effective in his job at McGill. "During this meeting, I gained a better understanding of the political system in China, which is very different than what we have in North America," he said. "Knowing how they run a country the size of China definitely inspired me to rethink how I could be more effective in doing my job as the chair of a department."

It's a strange takeaway about a political system that's a brutal communist regime that surveys its own citizens, violently represses opposition, censors speech, and engages in large-scale human rights abuses. We couldn't help wondering which of these Dr. Gao wanted to bring to McGill.

This is the other prong of the TTP—Overseas Chinese who remain in the West but are still encouraged to promote the interests of the CCP as a matter of patriotic duty to the motherland. In 2013, Xi Jinping told a meeting of the Western Returned Scholars Program (another United Front organization), "The party and the state respect the choices of those studying abroad . . . If you stay abroad, we will support you serving the country through various means."[18] Those who choose to live and work in other countries, he stressed, can still "write their names on the glorious history of the great rejuvenation of the Chinese nation."

The TTP also offers short-term contracts that require only two months a year in China. Some people set up partnerships between their employer in the West and an institution back home—a joint lab, for instance—to conceal potential conflicts of interest. "This may mean that they're effectively using time, resources and facilities paid for by their home institutions to benefit Chinese institutions," the ASPI noted.[19]

For China, the obvious advantage to leaving people in place is that they interact with Western scientists and researchers, giving them access to valuable information and technologies. In fact, the ASPI report noted that the CCP "treats talent recruitment as a form of technology transfer."[20] In this way, China is able to take advantage of the Western tradition of academic openness and the free exchange of ideas. The country acquires advanced research without having to fund that research itself—instead, as Christopher Wray noted, Western taxpayers are footing the bill.

Our team researched the extent of the CCP's infiltration of academia in Canada over several months and could see the party's footprint everywhere, from scholarships to scholarly exchanges. We even came across job postings and scholarships for students from China wishing to work and study at Canadian universities where one of the requirements is that they support the leadership of the Communist Party of China and the socialist system with Chinese characteristics, love and serve the motherland.[21] [22]

We also discovered all kinds of recruitment events held at various Canadian universities. When Lanzhou University, for example, sent a delegation, that included party officials, to tour colleges and other institutions on the West Coast, the visitors were welcomed with a recruitment event at UBC. Later they were given a private tour of TRIUMF, Canada's particle accelerator centre, before moving on to visit the College of Chemistry at UC Berkeley.

## DOSSIER: FRANCO FENG

Franco Feng (also known as Feng Rujie) was one of twenty-Four United Front agents assigned in Canada by the All-China Federation of Returned Overseas Chinese (ACFROC) mentioned in "the List" that we discussed in an earlier chapter. He is the chairman of the Chaozhou Association of Vancouver, a hometown association whose aim is to provide finances and talent back to their region.[23]

Reports from inside China show Franco on patriotic Red Tourism, a term to describe ex-patriots from current or former 'red' countries, such as China and Russia, visiting locations with historical significance to their red past. We've seen images of Franco dressing up in blue vintage Chinese military soldier attire while he engaged in patriotic exercises at the Yan'an Spiritual Research Center (Training Center) of the Party School of Yan'an Municipal Party Committee (Yan'an is considered the spiritual homeland of the Communist Party of China).[24] And Franco's contributions to the motherland don't stop there; he also owns a large pharmaceutical manufacturing company in China and is one of the leaders of an influential United Front organization.

In 2017, Franco and the Chaozhou Association of Vancouver held a ceremony for the Shantou Overseas Talent Work Liaison Station. In attendance were fellow United Front agent Hilbert Yiu, United Front ally Fred Kwok, and Canadian MP George Chow, Minister of State for Trade in BC at the time.

The focus of the Overseas Talent Liaison Station was to recruit talent in the fields of medical technology, elder care, computing, and finance such as experts who would return as entrepreneurs to set up business in Shantou City as part of the great rejuvenation of the nation. It is one thing for patriotic Chinese nationalists to want to send Canadians back to China to build the nation up, but why was Canadian MP George Chow helping the PRC recruit talent in Canada on behalf of China?

Recruitment of talent was no small effort, either. Shantou launched the construction of 161 key projects with a total investment of 196.6 billion yuan (CAD$38,658,239,810.40), all with the help of overseas Chinese.

According to translated news reports by the Shantou Overseas Chinese Federation, Franco participated in the National Congress of Returned Overseas Chinese and Dependents of Overseas Chinese. He said of the event: "Our hometown is a famous hometown of overseas Chinese. We hope that through this conference, we will further promote the friendship between overseas Chinese and help Shantou further build the Hometown of Overseas Chinese." Franco went on to say that he will continue to boost investment in Shantou and promote technology, research, and development in pharmaceutical and pharmaceutical companies in his hometown.

This is where everything comes into view. Franco, while living in Canada, made it clear that his priority was to continuously work to advance technology and cultivate more overseas talent for the purpose of helping build Shantou's infrastructure.[25] The Thousand Talents Plan was one of Franco Feng's commitments as a United Front agent to the motherland.

## COME ON DOWN!

All these events took place *after* the TTP had supposedly been suspended by the Chinese government. But our team found plenty of evidence that the TTP program was still actively recruiting new candidates, though not necessarily under the same name.

One particularly odd initiative was a real-world pitch competition in the style of *Dragon's Den* or *Shark Tank*. Organized by the Western Returned Scholars Association (WRSA)—a UFWD program for participants in the Thousand Talents Plan, and the primary forum for interacting with Chinese scholars and scientists—these competitions featured scientists hyping their own ideas to try to gain funding from China or appointments at Chinese businesses and universities. These contests carry out the work of the TTP, but with more glitz and glamour.[26]

The main event is the Innovation & Entrepreneurship International Competition, commonly known as the Olympics of innovation and entrepreneurship, in Shenzhen, China. Before reaching that summit, participants compete in division-level competitions in ten major cities around the world: London, Berlin, Sydney, Tokyo, Tel Aviv, Eindhoven, Madrid, Paris, San Francisco, and Toronto.[27] The Toronto event is hosted by the Sino-Canada International Innovation Centre, which was established in 2017 to encourage collaboration between China and Canada in fields like biotechnology and clean technology. The winners of the Sci Innovation Centre event go on to compete against the other division winners in the final round in Shenzhen.

It all sounds quite legitimate, and yet it's really just the Thousand Talents Plan dressed up in different clothes. The purpose is not so much to find worthy start-ups in need of seed money but to identify leading-edge scientists and entrepreneurs who might have valuable intel they're willing to share if the price is right. And as always, the United Front is lurking in the background, pulling the strings.

Proving that the UFWD is wrapped up in all of this wasn't hard. One of the founding organizations of the Sci Innovation Centre is the Canada Confederation of Shenzhen Associations (CCSA), which is connected to the Shenzhen Overseas Chinese Affairs Office and the Shenzhen Overseas Chinese Federation, which in turn are connected to the United Front Work Department. The honourary chair of the CCSA's board of directors is Victor Oh, who is a member of the Canadian Senate. In 2018, the senator hosted a ceremony between the Shenzhen Municipal People's Government and the City of Toronto.[28] Toronto Mayor John Tory and Wang Gang, the deputy-secretary general of Shenzhen Municipal Government, placed letters to the future and holograms of themselves into a time capsule to be unsealed in 2058. The event was meant to symbolize the forty years since China's reform, and to mark the opening of communication with the West.

Senator Oh is no stranger to controversy. In 2020, he was recommended for censure in the Senate for ethics violations after he accepted an all-expenses-paid trip to China in 2017.[29] Among those accompanying Oh on the trip was Toronto developer Ted Jiancheng Zhou, who *The Globe and Mail* noted has close ties to the CCP.

When the ethics officer began investigating the trip, the senator reportedly tried to mislead him. "Your committee is of the view that Senator Oh's conduct during the inquiry, particularly in relation to his attempt to mislead the Senate ethics officer and withholding information, does not uphold the standards of responsibility and accountability inherent to the position of senator," said the ethics committee's final report.[30]

Although the censure recommendation was largely for show, it does underscore the importance of establishing—and then enforcing—guidelines for all academics, researchers, politicians, and others who have access to sensitive information or who may be in a position to be leveraged in some way. We also need to increase awareness of programs like the TTP and make sure that everyone engaging with these programs understands their true purpose, which includes buying and otherwise acquiring foreign expertise and intellectual property for the benefit of China and to advance China's stated goal to be the world's dominant superpower by 2049.

Fortunately, at least some decision makers have started taking the threat from China more seriously. In Alberta, for example, the provincial government ordered a freeze on partnerships between its public universities and Chinese state entities in mid-2021. And in October 2022, the government announced that it had hired Gordon Houlden, the executive director of the China Institute think tank, to craft new rules for foreign collaborations.[31] We see this increased scrutiny beyond Canada's borders as well. Texas A&M, for example, halted a climate research project with China over concerns about espionage and intellectual property theft.[32]

In the words of Greg Levesque, the lead author of the Strider report mentioned earlier in the chapter, "China is playing a game that we are not prepared for, and we need to really begin to mobilize."[33]

## THREAT TARGET: SOFT POWER ASSAULT ON CANADA'S EDUCATION SYSTEM

Canada's spy agency issued a 'Threat Overview' brief in 2022 that confirmed our worst fears. "The greatest threat to Canada's prosperity and national interest is foreign interference and espionage," the report stated. "Hostile state actors seek covert access to Canada's sensitive proprietary information and cutting-edge research in an array of advanced scientific fields and across public sector, private sector, and *academic institutions*, with the goal of acquiring economic, commercial, scientific, military, or security advantages. For example, China is increasingly using non-traditional collectors, such as those in academic and research settings, to acquire sensitive, protected, or proprietary technologies that can be militarized or are dual use."[34]

Canadian universities have signed dozens if not hundreds of MOU's for research, joint degrees and student exchange programs with Chinese universities. Many of those are affiliated with the University of British Columbia, which has proudly publicized signing an unprecedented number of partnerships with leading Chinese universities.[35] UBC signed its first MOU with a Chinese university—Peking—in 1980, and by 2016, the school had ninety-five agreements with fifty-two universities in sixteen provinces from mainland China. In addition to collaborations with universities, UBC has also developed research and training collaborations with governments, corporations, research institutions and hospitals in China.[36][37]

By 2023, awareness of these and other concerns had trickled down to Canadian media, which reported on the findings of US strategic Intelligence Company Strider Technologies Inc. that dozens of Canadian universities collaborated with scientists connected to China's military between 2005 and 2022.[38]

As concern grew around China's foothold in Canada, the federal government announced that it intended to stop funding research with connections to the Chinese military and urged Canadian universities to do the same. But would Canadian universities actually heed the government's warning? There are some signs that universities are waking up to the need to be more careful in their dealings with China. The University of Waterloo, one of Canada's top research institutions, ended its research partnership that started in 2016 with Chinese tech giant Huawei, in 2023.[39] But the reality is that not every post-secondary institution may be willing or able to follow Waterloo's example. Many universities are so enmeshed with and dependant on China, through shared partnerships and the money that foreign students bring in, that it is likely not possible to decouple.

An even bigger looming threat is China's creation of private school education for K to 12 and private school post-secondary education. This has fast become a way for the CCP to groom a new generation of Canadian home-grown talent. It is all part of China's bold new education reform plan, called China Education Modernization 2035.[40] [41] [42] [43]

This plan calls for China's active participation in global educational governance, including the accelerated construction of overseas international schools with Chinese characteristics. The plan also includes the promotion of Belt and Road education action; training of international talents; improving policies for overseas students to return to hometowns to work; improving the quality of Chinese-foreign cooperatively run schools; optimizing Confucius Institutes; and strengthening international education in Chinese.[44]

China wants, in essence, to create a 'one-world school.' And there was no better place to kickstart China's plan than Canada.[45] [46] [47] [48] Making inroads into Canada's education system serves China's larger goals of completely infiltrating Canadian critical infrastructure and leveraging key entities in positions of authority across public and private sectors. One major goal has been to offer the children of Overseas Chinese Canadians education that has Chinese characteristics dictated by the CCP. Part of this centres around teaching Chinese language and culture through China's global Confucius Institutes, founded in 2004. Millions of students have been enrolled in hundreds of Confucius Institutes worldwide. But since the US State Department has designated the Confucius Institute as "a Foreign Mission partially funded by the PRC government under guidance from the CCP's United Front Work Department,"[49] its popularity has waned.

Going back to the eight-point plan to benefit Overseas Chinese, we can see a strong emphasis on education. The plan calls for a wide array of enhancements to Chinese education around the world, including programs to encourage Overseas Chinese to learn national languages and inherit Chinese culture, increased support for Chinese schools in other countries, and improvements in the quality of educational resources for millions of students. In addition, the plan calls for schools and their programs to be transformed, upgraded, and standardized, all towards the goal of improving the overall level of education for Overseas Chinese.[50]

The intent behind this plan is to raise the next generation of communists to serve in place and eventually push the pendulum towards Mandarin as the international language of business, commerce, science and medicine.

## CHINA'S POWERFUL ELITE ARE FINANCIALLY BACKING FUTURE GLOBAL LEADERS

Milk magnate Niu Gengsheng is known for three things: the 2008 Chinese tainted milk and baby formula scandal involving his company, China Mengniu Dairy Company; a large donation to the Trudeau Foundation and the Montreal Faculty of Law together with Zhang Bin, a member of the 12th National Committee of the Chinese People Political Consultative Conference (CPPCC); and his (Niu Gengsheng's) active support for joint Canadian and Chinese business endeavours.[51]

With help from a Vancouver-based business called the New Occidental Education & Technology Ltd (NOET), which he operates with co-founder and principal, Ms. Hong Xu, Niu's charity, the Lao Niu Foundation, plans to facilitate business partnerships between China and Canada by eliminating the language barrier between the two countries.[52]

Other educational joint ventures tied to the charity include arranging the hiring of Mandarin teachers for an exclusive private school in Vancouver, where Niu now lives. Tuition at the school runs between $24,000 and $27,000 per year.

Niu is so committed to teaching the world Mandarin that his foundation has contributed to over sixty-four educational projects, including early childhood education, school construction, educational training, the establishment of scholarships, and so on.

In a related venture, Niu Gengsheng is also connected to the Global Chinese Philanthropy Initiative (GCPI), an organization he co-founded with Bill Gates and three other individuals. The initiative receives funds from several foundations, including the Bill & Melinda Gates Foundation and the Lao Niu Foundation.

The GCPI was founded for the purpose of establishing an education system committed to building a knowledge system supporting the development of philanthropy in China and the world.

As an organization, they engage in bilateral research that examines the contributions of Chinese and Chinese American philanthropists in the US and Greater China. Oddly, this endeavour was funded by Gengsheng himself, and includes the study of his own philanthropic efforts.[53]

The results, according to GCPI, show that among donations by wealthy Chinese business elites, education ranks first above all other sectors. The reason, according to GCPI, is that philanthropists have "identified a need to support the global education of Chinese students. As China becomes more economically and socially developed, it influences and is influenced by global forces. Developing the country's youth to become future leaders who can operate in a global context is an unavoidable imperative."[54]

## IS THE CCP BEHIND PRIVATE ELEMENTARY SCHOOLS IN CANADA?

James Beeke has held high-ranking positions in the Ministry of Education in BC, first as deputy inspector for the province, and later as an inspector of independent schools. His duties included administering the Independent School Act, inspecting and certifying schools, and issuing provincial funding to eligible schools. After he retired from government, he went to China to work as the superintendent of Maple Leaf schools, an international school owned by Chinese billionaire Sherman Jen. Sherman moved to Canada in 1990 before returning to China in 1995 to start Maple Leaf, a prep school for China's wealthy elite, and then moving back to Canada. He now owns and operates dozens of schools in China, including two with locations that teach the BC-based curriculum—one in Xi'an, Shaanxi province, and another in Richmond, BC, on the campus of Kwantlen Polytechnic University (KPU).[55]

As it happens, Xi'an is the start of the ancient Silk Road and a key junction city in today's Belt and Road Initiative. Meanwhile, Richmond, BC, is widely thought to be the start of China's 'unofficial' North American Belt and Road.[56][57]

Sherman was once quoted as saying that one of his long-term goals is to "build the world's largest global school system" in Belt and Road countries. This goal may not apply seamlessly to Canada because Canada isn't officially a Belt and Road country, but that hasn't stopped it from sliding into the role of an unofficial BRI site when it comes to education. Maple

Leaf Schools was part of China's Education Modernization 2035 plan, and its Canadian connections are longstanding and significant.

As explained in a certification inspection report for the British Columbia program of Maple Leaf International School, their BC program follows an educational philosophy that is "based on the belief that through blending the best of the innovations and higher level thinking [in the] Western educational model with the cultural richness and discipline of the traditional Chinese educational model, students will be best prepared to meet the challenges of living and working in a more global society."[58]

It doesn't hurt China, either, that accessing Western teaching allows it to educate its people so that they can more easily adapt and integrate into Western society. This is particularly helpful when sending spies and other agents to conduct covert work.

James Beeke also lives in the Vancouver area, where he manages Maple Leaf Education Systems and is Maple Leaf's superintendent of global education.[59] He is a prime example of a well-connected expert hired by the CCP which could, in theory, serve to serve as a conduit between the party and a foreign government. A skillful person who commands respect, Beeke is precisely the kind of quasi-public figure who can provide a layer of protection for the CCP, allowing it to operate behind a Western façade.

Such a trusted advisor could even explain away questions around the CCP's role in a project in Canada.

Questions related to Sherman Jen's donations of millions of dollars to educational institutions, including Canada's Royal Roads University, which historically provides educational training to members of the Canadian Armed Forces and the Department of National Defence, can be conveniently swept aside.

With a respected Canadian involved, it's easy to look past Maple Leaf's deep connections to the CCP, and Sherman Jen's numerous awards from the Chinese government, including honours bestowed upon him by the Overseas Chinese Affairs Office of the State Council (OCAO)—the external name of the United Front Work Department. It's also easy to forget that Sherman has been an active participant in the Chinese People's Political Consultative Conference (CPPCC), which is a political advisory body in the People's Republic of China and a central part of the CCP's United Front system. Sherman, it's worth noting, has also received numerous accolades in Canada, including an award by Governor General David Johnson, who was assigned by Prime Minister Trudeau as special rapporteur in charge of responding to allegations by unnamed national security sources that China meddled in the 2019 and 2021 elections. Johnson's May 23, 2023 "First Report" focused on broader questions of foreign meddling in Canadian elections, removing the spotlight from China, and ruled out the need for an inquiry, instead recommending a series of public hearings.[60 61 62 63]

The fact that Sherman Jen was lauded by the Canadian government, and that the award was given to him by the same person who the prime minister of Canada put in charge of Chinese political interference, is very significant, especially in terms of optics.

Johnson was acting in conflict of interest, given his ties to both the prime minister and Chinese nationals. The fact that he presented a person like Jen Sherman an award undermines the ability of law enforcement and intelligence to highlight the nature of the threats facing Canada.

We are at war. It is a hybrid war and only the military, federal law enforcement and intelligence agencies seem to recognize it.

When we asked Beeke about these connections, he downplayed the importance of Sherman's involvement in the CPPCC, telling us, in a phone call, that it was all just business as usual.[64] He explained "[t]he process in China, when a nomination is brought forward and people are appointed to key positions, such as a governor of a province," and said it's common for "people who are successful in a variety of businesses [to be] consulted. That is called a consultative committee [CPPCC]. Sherman, in Liaoning province, has served on that committee."[65 66 67 68]

Beeke also countered suggestions that Maple Leaf might be a conduit for any deep state-run foreign interference campaigns, telling us that the BC-connected schools were likely all about, "students in [grades] 10, 11, and 12 being exposed to the full curriculum of British Columbia, all with Western-trained teachers."

The disinformation in this statement runs deep. Beeke seems to want to promote the fiction that Western ideology is influencing China in the Maple Leaf schools, when really it may well be the other way around. Through these and other educational endeavours, China is gaining a foothold from which to further influence the West. Indeed, Maple Leaf clearly states on their website that they promote a curriculum that offers a mix of Western and Chinese education and culture, but the Chinese government was particularly adept at encompassing the philosophical thought and work of the Western world and folding it in with communist ideology as a way to gain trust and influence. This was no more obvious than when we saw photos of students in British-style traditional private school uniforms holding a sign of Mao while raising their fists in the communist salute.

Even more concerning, Maple Leaf is not the only private school headed by a billionaire with ties to the CCP. There are dozens of similar educational institutional partnerships between China in Canada.

Chaoyin International School (CIS) is another private school that also opened in Richmond, BC, in 2021, with financial assistance from the Bank of China. The school caters to international students from China.

Students at the China branch of the Chaoyin School receive CCP ideological and military training, while students at its sister location in Canada are taught Mandarin and Chinese culture and history, according to dictates by the CCP.

Headmaster Gregory Corry, who boasts of having coordinated Canadian Prime Minister Justin Trudeau's visit to a high school he taught at in Shanghai, China, also told Richmond News reporter Maria Rantanen that teachers won't censor sensitive topics, such as Tibet, Tiananmen Square, and the Chinese Communist Party, and would instead "redirect" the conversation.[69][70]

## DOSSIER: GRANT LIN

Huaqiao University (HQU) is a joint endeavor by the United Front Work Department of the Central Committee, the Ministry of Education, and the Fujian Provincial People's Government, an institute directly under the control of the United Front Work Department. It is China's United Front university.[71][72]

*Claws of the Panda* author Jonathan Manthorpe describes HQU as an institution that "emphasizes technical disciplines and has all the hallmarks of a place where CCP security officials can identify and recruit young agents of influence and spies before they return to their home countries."

HQU's connection to Canada is through Grant Lin, a multimillionaire tycoon from China living in Vancouver. Grant owns a large real estate development company in the Vancouver area called Yuanheng and is vice chairman of HQU. He is also the president of the Canadian Fujianese

Friendship Association, and is on the list of United Front agents assigned by the CCP to do work on behalf of the United Front in Canada.

We mentioned Grant Lin in an earlier chapter in relation to his role on the board of directors for the United Front NGO known as S.U.C.C.E.S.S. He served on the board at a time when the organization ushered in the S.U.C.C.E.S.S. Beijing transit station under the direction of United Front leader Qiu Yuanping.

What is Grant tasked with doing in Canada on behalf of the UFWD? And how is his role at Huaqiao University, an institute directly under the control of the United Front Work Department of the Central Committee, tied to that mandate?

We asked Jonathan Manthorpe about the relevance of Grant Lin's role as a director with the institute. The *Claws of the Panda* author was emphatic that the role ties Grant Lin directly to the UFWD. "[T]he mere fact that Grant Lin is a director of Huaqiao University is absolute confirmation that he is associated with the United Front Work Department, which has direct control over the university," he told us. "The university's very name states that it is for overseas people of Chinese heritage, and its promotional statements suggest it is a recruitment centre for agents of influence and to gain access to foreign technology. That purpose is underlined by the emphasis the university's promotional material puts on providing facilities for students working on 'innovation.'"[73]

To find out what exactly Grant Lin has been tasked with doing in Canada, we looked at his meteoric rise as an entrepreneur in China. Grant weaves a powerful 'rags-to-riches' story, with a career that took off at Olympian-level speeds after he joined a company that promoted him within three months to the position of vice president. Another two months later, Grant was president—two promotions within six months, all while he was under the age of twenty-five. At that time, he was considered the youngest head of a state-owned enterprise in the country.

Huaqiao University even described Grant as having "grown from an ordinary poor boy to business elite in just 10 years." They weren't wrong.

His career dramatically shifts gears in 1997, when Grant is said to have gone to Beijing for 'development' training, followed by a period of time in the Australian office of CITIC Group, a company we identified as being connected to China's Unholy Trinity.

Grant returned to China and founded Beijing Yuanheng Real Estate Development Co., with financial backing by the CCP.

Then, inexplicably, he left the management of the state-owned-enterprise (SOE) to his younger siblings before heading off to Canada in or around 1997. Once there, he reportedly started buying and flipping homes in the wealthy Shaughnessy area of Vancouver, going from success to success with each venture. This eventually led to him starting a real estate development company in Canada that was an offshoot of Beijing Yuanheng Real Estate Development Co. This new Canadian-run company was known simply as Yuanheng.

Yuanheng has grown into one of Vancouver's largest real estate development companies, with a portfolio that includes a behemoth development project in Richmond that spans 350,000 square feet of land and that includes twelve buildings and roughly 1,868 units, not including commercial spaces.[74]

Grant's empire in Canada has funnelled money into his United Front work in that country. Among other ventures, he has collaborated with the Overseas Chinese Affairs Office of the State Council of the People's Republic of China on a new scholarship designed to bring ten to twenty young people to visit various parts of the motherland. These trips include meet and greets with the heads of relevant government departments in Beijing. Motherland tours are one way that the United Front seeks to expand its influence.[75]

Hosting youth-oriented trips to the motherland has become commonplace. At the other end of the country, the same thing was happening with the Federation of Canadian Chinese Associations—Council of Newcomer Organizations (CONCO), a commanding level United Front organization that is also involved in "roots-seeking" programs aimed at cultivating the next generation of pro-nationalist Chinese-Canadian youth. All of this takes place with help from the United Front Work Department.[76] [77]

Grant answered to the Communist Party member and director of the Party Committee of the Overseas Chinese Affairs Office of the People's Government of Fujian Province, Yang Hui.

Yang Hui was in charge of the overall work of the Overseas Chinese Affairs Office in Fujian Province. He came to Canada to conduct an inspection of grants work, during which his group discussed national strategies for Huaqiao University in Canada. As mentioned, Huaqiao University's mandate is serving Overseas Chinese and spreading Chinese culture. To that end, the university has implemented a school-wide philosophy of "connecting with China and foreign countries, and cultivating morality and talents." The goal of the institution, according to its website, is to serve the country's overseas Chinese affairs and public diplomacy work to help with the construction of the Belt and Road. Even the word *huaqiao* means citizens of China living abroad—a point Grant Lin reiterated on the Huaqiao University website, where he said that expanding enrollment of Overseas Chinese at universities abroad, especially in Canada, is a key aspect of his role in Canada.[78][79]

## CHINA'S SHADOW GOVERNMENT IN CANADA

Grant Lin's hometown association, the Canadian Fujian Fellowship Association, is prominent enough to have drawn the North American Overseas Chinese Affairs Mission of Fujian Province to Vancouver for the handover ceremony of the Canadian Fujian Fellowship Association to Grant. The ceremony was held inside China's Vancouver consulate, and was attended by local politician John Yap, who was born in Fujian province.

As far back as 2012, Grant met with Comrade Li, who, in addition to having been a member of the Communist Party of China since 1979, is also secretary of the party committee of Huaqiao University and deputy director of the Culture, History and Learning Committee of the Fujian Chinese People's Political Consultative Conference (CPPCC). Officially and ostensibly, the purpose of Comrade Li's visit was to further promote the school's Chinese language education in North America and lend support to alumni and school board members. However, the real purpose for the delegation to visit the education counselor of the Chinese Consulate General in Vancouver was to inspect the work of Grant Lin, who is tasked with helping the Fujian province do its part in the great rejuvenation of the nation and to ultimately achieve the Chinese Dream of global superpower status.

How do Canadian politicians justify going to Chinese Communist Party ceremonies in Canada? They often say that they are attending as a private member of a non-profit hometown association and not as a politician. This excuse has even been used by politicians visiting China to meet with CCP officials there. BC's Minister of State for Trade, George

Chow, travelled to China on a personal trip, but once there, met with the Overseas Chinese Affairs Office of the People's Government of Guangzhou Municipality.[80] In other cases, it is all too easy for Canadian politicians to attend CCP events in Canada under the guise of supporting the Canadian Multiculturalism Act, which enshrined into law the federal government's commitment to promoting and maintaining a diverse, multicultural society.

With Canadian politicians engaging in conduct detrimental to the interests of Canada by lending credibility to the CCP, there isn't much standing in the way of the CCP stealing Canada's talent, research and resources from universities. It isn't just a case of leveraging politicians, poaching talent, and stealing R&D either. The CCP is after much more than that.

Like many universities, UBC engages in two main types of research: basic, which is funded mainly by grants, and applied, which often happens in cooperation with outside companies and organizations. UBC's sponsored research relationships fall into the second category. The university routinely partners with Canadian and global companies for the purpose of providing BC graduate students with experience working in industry and provides researchers with funding to help advance their science. Companies like Huawei, which had a large research relationship with UBC, totalling CAD$7.6 million over three years. These projects fell into the latter category of applied research.[81]

Media reports have focused mainly on theft of research and discovery, but the CCP is also big on targeting industry-sponsored research at universities and using it to generate marketable products through partnerships with companies. These are partnerships with private sector corporations whose aims are to advance research projects for the purpose of product development and commercialization in key industries for which China needs raw material.[82]

Consider the UBC Forestry faculty—Canada's largest forestry school and the largest forestry teaching institution in North America.[83] China, meanwhile, is one of the world's largest consumers of wood products and the second-largest export market for BC forest products.[84]

It makes sense that China would use UBC's Forestry faculty as a gateway into a market that not only allows them access to research but also positions them to encroach on Canadas' forestry sector. Education has been a conduit for China to infiltrate Canada and other Western nations. While there is an aspect of this that is purely trade-based, China never has a single intent on any agreements or projects in Canada. The CCP uses legitimate projects and partnerships to also disguise operations that are part of the hybrid war it is conducting here.[85]

One example of these uncomfortably close relationships can be found in the Asia Forest Research Centre. This UBC program, which says it "works to promote quality education and research capacity by enhancing relationships between UBC Faculty of Forestry and our Asia partners," has the largest forestry transfer program in the world and features eleven partner agreements with universities across China.[86] One of those is a partnership between the Henan Capital Construction Science Experiment Research Institute Co. (CCSE)[87] and the UBC Faculty of Forestry, on the design and construction of modern wood structures. CCSE is an organization that is tasked with capital construction of Henan Province as part of the great rejuvenation of the motherland.[88] [89]

They were given the responsibility by Henan Province to draft two standards on modern timber construction, with a focus on design and quality assurance. UBC agreed to review and comment on the draft standards. The intent of the agreement was to set out a collaborative framework for research and technology transfer in an area of modern timber engineering that can benefit building projects in Henan.[90]

Other forestry-related agreements with murky ties to the Chinese government include Beijing Forestry University, which is considered to be one of the most important global partners of the University of British Columbia, according to Robert Kozak, Dean of the Faculty of Forestry.[91 92 93 94]

Beijing Forestry University has compulsory military training for students, adding a whole other element to foreign students' training in Canada. Military training is often framed as a rite of passage for Chinese students, and while it is generally about learning discipline, some foreign exchange students are, in effect, being trained to be battle ready. They can and will be called upon by the Chinese consulate to serve in place, as we saw when the Tenth Street Church was surrounded by students.[95 96 97]

The Government of China is banking on these foreign exchange students immigrating to Canada, building their networks, and eventually gaining influence within the Canadian forestry industry. This is a long game, designed to forge access to the kind of building supplies that are required to build an empire. What can Canada expect, in terms of loyalty to their adopted country, from students who have People's Liberation Army training and propaganda indoctrination, and whose very success was aided by huge scholarships tied to Sino-foreign cooperative education agreements that hold them to agreements to support the CCP and to volunteer for the motherland in the host country?

Some of those scholarships came from Grant Lin, through the Canadian Fujian Hometown Association and Yuanheng Holding Enterprise. These incentives were given out under the watchful eye of the PRC consulate and the immigration settlement service, S.U.C.C.E.S.S., whose members have attended United Front scholarship ceremonies.[98] With money constantly flowing toward strategic investments in human resources, the CCP has created a well-oiled machine for spreading talent to other countries, where Overseas Chinese can, over time, exert influence on behalf of the motherland.

## PROFESSORS, THINK-TANKS, AND THE SCHOLARLY PILLAGING OF CANADIAN RESOURCES

Dr. Guangyu Wang is the associate dean and director of Asia Forest Research Centre, in UBC's Faculty of Forestry. He is also the president of the Grizzly Bear Institute (GBIC), a think tank created by local Chinese academics and entrepreneurs whose stated mission is to commission and publish research and policy analysis in economics, natural resources, political science, public administration and international affairs.

GBIC members also engage in activities in support of their beliefs and perspectives, which, coincidentally, almost always line up with those of the Chinese government. One of the GBIC's core aims is to promote China's Belt and Road Initiative. As simple as it sounds, the Belt and Road Initiative involves building, and building involves timber, which is something China needs.

Other team members include UBC Professor John Innes, former vice-chairman of the International Federation of Forestry (IUFRO), and Yves Tiberghien, honorary director of the Asia Institute of the University of British Columbia, an Asia-focused research institute and think tank. Tiberghien also serves as executive director of the UBC China Council, an organization that advises the university's leadership on strategy for UBC's engagement with China.[99]

One of the Grizzly Institute's pet concerns is the foreign owner's tax. In an article titled, "The Trudeau Government and China's Billionaires," written by Kwantlen Polytechnic University Professor Guoren Zhang for the Grizzly Institute, Guoren talks about how the China Entrepreneur Club met with Prime Minister Trudeau to raise their demands concerning the foreign owner's tax.

According to Guoren, members of the club, including Hu Baosen, chairman of China Construction Industry Group, listed by Forbes as one of China's 400 richest individuals, expressed frustration with the tax on behalf of foreign investors from China who were planning to buy a home in Vancouver.

Guoren's article points out that Hu Baosen plans to raise the issue with the prime minister, but added that the tax issue would change his investment plans. That is to say, he intended on investing $100 million US in Canada over a three-year period to build new houses, most of which will be sold to Chinese buyers, Guoren Zhang wrote.

Zhang reported that Chinese entrepreneurs have needs for immigration and overseas workers and that he believes that the federal government and the provincial government will likely give them preferential treatment.[100]

## A NUMBERS GAME PROPPED UP BY INFLUENCERS, INDUSTRY, AND ACADEMIA

When we first heard about a plan by a company called GBN Health Technology (Global Balance Nutritionist) to sponsor 200,000 students from China to study in Canada—we weren't terribly surprised.

GBN's plan was to set up a fund to privately sponsor the children of their employees back in Nanjing and Chengdu to come to Canada to get educated. They would start by bringing over 2,000 students, then increase that number to 20,000, then reach their goal of bringing in 200,000 students.

This spectacular announcement was organized by ex-federal Liberal candidate (who, at the time of this writing, was running as a Richmond-Centre candidate under BC United) and former S.U.C.C.E.S.S. board member Wendy Yuan, together with Leah Ding of D&J Education Consulting, with support from NDP MP Jenny Kwan.

GBN is affiliated with two companies in Canada and a start-up called UPWELL, a company involved in running over ten pharmaceutical companies back in mainland China.[101] The company (GBN) is owned by Dr. Yaoming Chen, Dr. Frank Seela, and Xingyuan Cheng. Xingyuan Cheng is the chairperson of the China Women's Development Foundation, which falls under the All-China Women's Federation, a part of the Central Committee of the Communist Party of China.

With those kinds of numbers, GBN had better have a plan for where the 200,000 students will learn and live. Enter CIBT Education Group, Inc., a private post-secondary school in the Vancouver area that says it teaches over 11,000 students annually. Global Education City (GEC), the school's real estate division, is building "mega centres" for student housing.[102]

On the board of directors for CIBT Education Group is Morris Chen, who we have mentioned several times. Morris Chen, you may recall, is involved in Wealth One Bank Canada, the online bank given the thumbs up by Trudeau's Liberals following a major cash-for-access event. He is also the chair of the China Council for the Promotion of International Trade (CCPIT), a well-established CCP trade organization that develops business cooperation and trade events promoting China's Belt and Road Initiative. The CCPIT has long been linked with the People's Republic of China's United Front strategy.[103] [104]

Why would a health and wellness company with a handful of employees in Canada want to bring thousands of students to Canada to go to school? What is the incentive for a Chinese tycoon to build student housing in Canada? The answer once again lies with China's Education Modernization 2035 plan.

China, as part of a plan to export language and culture along the 'unofficial' Belt and Road in North America, wants to revitalize their own country, and to do that, they need talent. They also want to create a single global standard in education that seeks to control how the CCP is portrayed. They plan to achieve this through, among other things, the integration of Mandarin language and Chinese culture in elite private schools that cater to the children of Overseas Chinese living in Canada as permanent residents.

Canada almost seems to be helping the CCP achieve these goals. Immigration, Refugees and Citizenship Canada (IRCC), the same Ministry that helped fund the Active Engagement and Integration Project (AEIP) in Beijing, operated by the United Front NGO S.U.C.C.E.S.S., launched six new immigration streams in 2021. One of them invites 40,000 candidates to apply for Permanent Residence status under a special new program aimed at foreign students.[105] [106]

More than 460,000 international students have entered British Columbia since 2015, with many of them remaining in Canada as permanent residents.[107] *Vancouver Sun* columnist Daphne Bramham summed up China's global education plans succinctly in an article on Maple Leaf schools, writing that, "The Chinese Communist Party government aims to encircle the globe with roads, ports and other transportation infrastructure as part of its 'Belt and Road Initiative' that may soon include the export of language and culture."[108]

According to DCNF investigative reporter Philip Lenczycki, there are "Chinese police camps for kids born overseas, [at] which they wear military uniforms and may even train with practice weapons as we've seen occur in China's kindergarten boot camps. It's extremely alarming knowing there are thousands of children that attend these so-called 'root-seeking' trips each year—yet another concerning aspect of the Overseas Chinese service center program."

As we've shown, the inroads that China has already made into Canadian life traverse all of the key areas that define us as a people and as a nation. From social services to policing, industry, politics, and education, China has established a presence in Canada that should be deeply alarming to anyone who wants Canada to remain an independent country, free of foreign control or interference.

## CHAPTER 13

# THE FINAL MOSAIC

## CANADA'S UNOFFICIAL BELT AND ROAD

Logistics tycoon Guo Taicheng sat at the end of a long conference table in a sparsely furnished room in Surrey, BC, at the other end of the table from his wife and a co-worker, who had made the trip with him.

Behind this small group , a large-screen virtual TV played a continuous loop of triumphant scenes from China's great ascent—a glossy propaganda reel featuring images of Xi Jinping and the People's Liberation Army conquering the world, not only by force but also with the help of a network of roads, bridges, and other infrastructure projects.

As an image track for the famous Belt and Road Initiative (BRI—also known as One Belt, One Road, or OBOR), these scenes highlighted China's ambitious plan to dominate international trade and emerge as the world's superpower by 2049.

Guo, a tycoon who splits his time between China and Canada as chairman of the Hong Kong logistics giant Shing Kee Godown Group (SKG Group), was there to speak to Glacier Media's syndicated reporter

PHOTO: Syndicated reporter Graeme Wood Glacier interviews Guo Taicheng about his "Belt and Road" project in Surrey, BC.

Graeme Wood and *Mosaic Effect* co-author Ina Mitchell about his latest project—a mega-complex that would function as the North American supply chain base for the BRI.[1]

Located in Surrey's former World Commodity Trade Center (now called the Vancouver Logistics Park), the planned complex was to have spanned more than 470,000 sq. ft., or 11 acres (4.5 hectares), and was estimated to cost CAD$190 million.

As of July 2022, when it opened, the park was only about 80,000 square feet, or 1.8 acres, in size. Architectural renderings showing a lineup of China's national flags on the boulevard out front made for a stark contrast to the British-inspired, post-war era concrete brutalist architecture building that served as the backdrop for Guo's meeting with Wood and Mitchell.[2]

As the interview got underway, Graeme slid a piece of paper over to Guo and drew his finger down a list of names corresponding to countries around the world, written in both Chinese characters and English, until he reached a name under the heading of Canada.

Guo could likely see right away that this was not just any list. It was a copy of a list of United Front agents who had been dispatched around the world to work on behalf of the CCP.

"Is this you?" he asked Guo, pointing to the man's name.

Guo hesitated nervously, then nodded, smiled, and said, "Yes."

From the other end of the table, where Guo's wife and co-worker sat, there were audible gasps.

Guo had every reason to fudge the answer to this question. Not only was he a tycoon, but he was also the executive vice president of the China Federation of Overseas Chinese Entrepreneurs, a Communist Party-led trade organization made up of ethnic Chinese business people under the direction of the All-China Federation of Returned Overseas Chinese (ACFROC), which was supporting the Surrey project.

Guo had just taken the unprecedented step of admitting to a Western journalist that he was a United Front agent. China's United Front was, at this point, virtually unknown to most Canadians.[3]

Very few people outside of the intelligence community understood that the United Front was the overseas arm of the Communist Party of China, or that it was tasked with expanding China's influence around the world through a complex and ever-expanding network of espionage, business partnerships, cultural and entrepreneurial ventures, philanthropic gestures, infrastructural investments, and political interference.[4] According to intelligence sources, the United Front also works with Chinese organized crime and Chinese state actors, including the Ministry of State Security (MSS) and the People's Liberation Army (PLA).

Guo wasn't assigned any ordinary task within the United Front. He was not on some minor propaganda mission to shake hands with local politicians and donate to a local hospital in front of state-run media. He had been given the monumental task of building what was, for all intents and purposes, the first Belt and Road project in North America—a vast import-export facility where goods and products destined for North America would be shipped from a hub-and-spoke network. Everything would flow from a mother base in China called the Yanjiao International Trade City–World Commerce Valley, using the most efficient transportation routes along the Belt and Road.

Why would Guo admit to being a United Front agent? According to New Zealand political scientist Anne-Marie Brady, who has written about the the corrosion of democracy under China's global influence, "United Front work" is considered "the duty of all party members—who now include a majority of Chinese corporate CEOs—not just the department itself."[5]

Earlier chapters of this book have shown that the BRI is being brought to Canada without widespread knowledge of, or approval by, Canadians. Neither Canada nor the USA officially signed on to China's Belt and Road Initiative, yet Canada has become an unofficial site of BRI activity, through corporate projects, improvements to Chinatowns, and other forms of economic development and investments that are clearly designed to increase China's influence in Canada.

The World Commodity Trade Center was more than just a building project. It was a mission to covertly bring the BRI to North America through Canada's Pacific Gateway—British Columbia. Ever mindful of efficiency, China wasn't going to create a new BRI, but would instead use Western Canada's already established transportation networks to set up an unofficial Canadian BRI that could then be expanded to other parts of the continent.[6]

A project of this size required approvals, policy changes, agreements with the government, and public acceptance. Such a large-scale construction project, with a massive geospatial footprint, was sure to raise eyebrows. Moreover, Guo's World Commodity Trade Center, with all of its national flags and the backing of the CCP, was strategically positioned less than a few kilometres from two US border crossings in Washington State. China watchers had to ask: Was this another penetration test, like the Haidilao Hot Pot social credit scheme?

The project's location was particularly suspicious. The World Commodity Trade Center was situated on multiple expressways linking to Canada's main railway routes, deep-water harbours, and Western Canada's largest port. All this is in sync with what we know about the BRI in terms of access and efficiency to transportation routes but from a hybrid warfare perspective. China could be using the project to establish a logistics empire that would give it a distinct advantage, including the possibility of creating strangleholds in the supply chain during potential future conflicts with the West.

Consider which state-controlled enterprises were at the opening ceremony of the World Commodity Trade Center. Representatives from state-owned conglomerate COSCO Shipping, China Eastern Airlines, China Southern Airlines, Xiamen Airlines, Sichuan Airlines, Hainan Airlines and other state-supported transportation companies, were all present at the unveiling.[7]

China's COSCO Shipping reported in 2018 that since 2013, COSCO has been exploring Russian Arctic routes for the Maritime Silk Road, signalling a possible threat to Canada's Arctic sovereignty.[8][9]

China is good at using legitimate projects, state-run corporations, and business people as cover in the hybrid war on the West. Still, China's incursion into Canada could not have happened without the aid of Canadian officials—a core issue allowing the CCP to operate in Canada with relative impunity.

While they may think that they are doing the work to build bridges and create joint economic wins, Canadian officials who participate in ventures like the World Commodity Trade Center are working on behalf of the Chinese government, whose representatives may have ulterior motives for pursuing these projects.

We have traced the roots of this particular project back to 2012, when then-Prime Minister Stephen Harper and Hu Jintao, then-president of China, signed the Canada-China Foreign Investment Promotion and Protection Agreement (FIPA).[10] The agreement was signed by Ed Fast, minister of International Trade and minister for the Asia-Pacific Gateway.

The agreement was viewed by many at the time as being a threat to Canadian sovereignty, and Harper was criticized for the lack of transparency around the agreement which ultimately lead to the World Commodity Trade Centre project in Surrey. Two years later, the Canada China Chamber of Industry and Commerce Association (CCCICA), a Canada-China trade organization with close ties to the United Front Work Department, co-hosted the 2nd Canada China Investment Summit in 2014 and signed an MOU that set the framework for the World Commodity Trade Centre.[11] The agreement was inked in the presence of Guo Taicheng, Richard Lee, Canadian Senator Victor Oh, Minister of Seniors (State) Alice Wong, and Yu Shanjun, consul of commerce of the China consulate in Vancouver, along with members of the All-China Federation of Returned Overseas Chinese.

By 2018, the groundbreaking ceremony of the World Commodity Trade Centre took place in Surrey, BC, celebrated by Alice Wong, who gave a keynote speech at the trade centre event. Alice frequently wears two hats; she was not only a federal elected official in Canada but also an honourary consultant of the Canadian Chaozhou Chamber of Commerce and the permanent honourary president of the Vancouver Chaozhou Association. Their leadership also includes Franco Feng, who is on the same United Front list as Guo Taicheng.

Also in attendance were high ranking consular officials and overseas party officials, including Zhu Yilong, vice chairman of the All-China Federation of Returned Overseas Chinese and a member of the National Committee of the Chinese People's Political Consultative.[12]

Given the status of those on the guest list, there could be little doubt that this project was important to the CCP, and that there was more to it than just building a logistics base.


## THE PROJECT OF THE CENTURY

You might be asking, how is it possible that the BRI has been brought to Canada, when Canada hasn't officially signed up for the project?

The answer is simple. China's economic activities, including its infrastructure investments and trade partnerships, are not limited to countries that are officially part of the BRI. China engages in trade and investment globally, including with countries outside the BRI framework, such as

Canada. Both countries have bilateral trade relations, and Chinese investments have been made in various sectors of the Canadian economy, and Canada often cooperates with China through other economic channels and agreements. China can easily hide BRI projects under the umbrella of trade projects with other names.

Everything we have covered in this book, from the United Front's efforts to establish a shadow government in Canada to its practice of buying up key industries and installing Chinese police stations in major metropolitan cities and more, culminates in this chapter's exploration of China's ambitious plan to create global trade routes, and therefore global dominance, through its official and unofficial Belt and Road projects.

The Chinese Dream is also part of the inspiration for the Belt and Road Initiative and Made in China 2025, a state-led industrial policy that seeks to make China dominant in the global high-tech manufacturing sector.[13] This—the Chinese Dream—is one of the core motivators behind the work that the United Front is doing in the West.

## THE WEAKEST LINK

Canada wavered over the years when it came to officially signing onto the BRI, but this hasn't stopped provincial officials in Canada from entering into quasi-BRI arrangements with China. In 2016, BC Premier and BC Liberal leader (now BC United) Christy Clark, and her minister of international trade, and minister responsible for the Asia Pacific strategy and multiculturalism, MLA Teresa Wat, met with a delegation of high-ranking CCP government officials to discuss joint projects.[14] That meeting resulted in a Memorandum of Understanding (MOU) between the province of British Columbia and the Chinese province of Guangdong on areas related to transportation, infrastructure, and resource management. The MOU set out terms for the provinces to leverage new and existing transportation partnerships in order to strengthen the trade capacity of their respective gateway and corridor networks, expand cooperation in the natural gas sector, and enhance cooperation in marine scientific research and environmental practices, maritime transportation, shipbuilding and repair, and fisheries and seafood. All of these areas fall under the umbrella of China's One Belt, One Road Initiative and BC's Pacific Gateway Strategy.[15]

In 2018, Premier Clark addressed a packed conference room filled with BC and Chinese officials, including high-ranking CCP Politburo member Hu Chunhua, who is now the vice premier of the People's Republic of China.[16] Clark said she looked forward to working with the CCP towards "building a One Road, One Belt policy between our two countries, our two provinces . . ."[17]

Clark pointed to two consular officials in Canada whom China had officially tasked with bringing the BRI to Canada through British Columbia. "We are working together on the One Belt, One Road Initiative, led by Ambassador Luo in Canada very ably and also by Consul General LIU Fei," she told the room. With a hint of excitement, she added, "We are working together to establish Vancouver and British Columbia as the gateway to North America for Asia."[18]

The two provinces will build on the "existing fruitful cooperation in the areas of trade, investment, liquefied natural gas (LNG), green technology and education to advance all-round cooperation under the framework of the Belt and Road initiative and the Pacific Gateway Strategy and enhance their position as the gateway to the Pacific and the outside world," Clark said.

During his interview with Guo Taicheng and in the subsequent article, Graeme Wood raised the obvious question: "How could an MOU [that falls under the scope of the BRI] have been done without a free trade agreement between China and Canada?"

Canada invested in the Asian Infrastructure Investment Bank (AIIB) in 2017, which is considered a core component in the funding of the BRI, contributing close to 1.3 billion Canadian dollars (US$995 million) for a 1 percent stake—but this still wasn't a trade agreement.[19]

Simply put, the Clark government didn't care about the lack of a trade agreement with China, or about the implications of getting into bed with the Chinese Communist Party. In fact, internal memos revealed that BC government staff showed great enthusiasm for Xi Jinping's Belt and Road project.

Hu Chunhua of the Communist Party of China described the mood from the BC government at the time as a "China craze."

Donald Haney, who was the executive director for economic policy and Asia Pacific relations at the time, corresponded with Li Ming, head of the political section at the Embassy of the People's Republic of China in Canada, telling her, "We very much like the 'Belt and Road' theme, and look forward to working with you."[20] He went on to imply that he was seeking more ways to benefit the BRI in Canada, saying, "there are many other initiatives that BC, Guangdong and China are involved in that are complementary to the Belt and Road . . ."[21]

The ease with which the unofficial BRI was ushered into Canada seemed to take China's diplomats by surprise. Even they questioned if the MOU would be approved in the absence of federal government support. Donald Haney reassured them that he had "already notified our Justice department that we are working on the MOU,"[22] and went so far as to suggest to Chinese Embassy staff that the BRI agreement would be rubber-stamped by government. "We do not need approval from the federal government for the MOU or the Joint Declaration. We simply need our BC Ministry of Justice to review and approve the documents," he said.[23]

Lindsay Kislock was the assistant deputy minister of the Partnerships Division of British Columbia's Ministry of Transportation and Infrastructure in 2016.

In her welcoming remarks at the BRI MOU conference, Kislock confirmed that the BRI was already in Canada when she said, "At the heart of [Xi Jinping's] One Belt, One Road Initiative lies the creation of economic cooperation corridors over land with countries on the original Silk Road through Central Asia, West Asia, the Middle East and Europe, as well as by sea by linking China's ports with the African coast, pushing up through the Suez Canal into the Mediterranean."

She added that "Since its unveiling, the One Belt One Road strategy has expanded to include Canada," and that "As Canada's only Pacific province and home to Canada's Pacific Gateway transportation network, BC is well placed to help advance China's One Belt and One Road [sic] Initiative."[24]

Kislock now works for the Western Transportation Advisory Council (WESTAK), a nonprofit transportation advisory organization whose board members comprise the federal minister of transport and provincial ministers from across western and northern Canada, along with executives from the Port of Vancouver and Port of Prince Rupert. When asked about her role in bringing the BRI to Canada, she declined to comment.[25]

This is the new world of politics, where politicians and public administrators who also operate in intergovernmental networks, political alliances, and business collaborations make decisions that serve special interest groups and their own political leanings while potentially harming national security and sovereignty.

The CCP knows this is Canada's weak spot. Political appointments and government administration jobs given to party members are always temporary and easily exploited by the CCP via promises of lucrative contracts to these administrators after they leave office.

After Christy Clark's minority government was defeated in 2017, she resigned as Liberal Party leader and went on to become an advisor on infrastructure and Asia trade and natural resources to law firm Bennett Jones. Among other things, Bennett Jones was the only Canadian law firm to advise China's Ministry of Commerce (MOFCOM), one of the ministries involved in overseeing the BRI.[26][27]

Although Christy Clark was no longer at the helm in BC, the absence of any statement declaring an end to the BRI partnerships by the province's new NDP premier, John Horgan, suggests that it's business as usual, but with BRI initiatives now being pursued in secret.[28]

All of this raises important questions about Canada's ongoing and unofficial involvement in the Belt and Road Initiative in Canada. Where is it, who is involved, and who is driving it?

To answer these questions, we followed the BRI route from the mother hub, the World Commerce Valley in Hebei (the strategic starting point of the BRI in the Beijing, Tianjin, and Hebei region of China) to the Qinhuangdao Economic & Technology Development Zone (QETDZ) and the Qinhuangdao Port to northern BC and down to the World Commodity Trade Center in British Columbia.[29][30][31][32][33]

Qinhuangdao Port in China is on a similar latitude to the Port of Prince Rupert in Canada, located in the remote northern region of British Columbia. According to the Prince Rupert Port Authority, many of the cargo ships from China are destined for this port because it is the closest North American port to Asia.

CBC News reported that "in just 10 years, the small B.C. city has remade itself as a key link between Asia and the United States."[34] A major driver of the port's success is "Project Silk," whose aim was also to create a large container port on Prince Rupert's waterfront, intended for Canadian and American consumers.

The Qinhuangdao Port provides many of the core products and services that North America depends on. And since wider berths equals more containers, it was notable when the port received an upgrade to its berths courtesy of Lin Shaoyi, who resides in Vancouver. Why would he do this? Because, despite living in Canada, he considers it his patriotic duty to aid the motherland. Lin calls himself a patriotic Overseas Chinese leader.[35] In an earlier chapter, we mentioned his role in co-chairing the United Front conference where 200 visas were denied to delegates from China.[36] Lin leads several organizations, including the Vancouver Chaozhou Association, and has signed off on political donations to both main political parties in BC—the BC NDP and BC United—under this organization.[37] [38] [39] [40]

Why does this matter? As a single data point, it doesn't. However, when we start to connect the dots between these port upgrades, the exploration of a Maritime Silk route by COSCO, funding and support by the CCP, the discovery of a Chinese spy balloon drifting through Canadian and US airspace, and unconfirmed sightings of an unidentified similar object flying over central Yukon around the same time, a more complete picture starts to take shape.

The unofficial BRI in Canada is not just about streamlining transportation routes to and from China. It's about creating infrastructure that provides an advantage for China in any future conflict with the West. China's goal for a Maritime Silk Road can and very likely will be used to extend the People's Liberation Army's (PLA) power, the least of which will be to choke off supply chains.[41]

A more complete picture of the North American Belt and Road starts to take shape when you take a short drive from the Port of Prince Rupert to the City of Terrace.

In 2015, The City of Terrace and the City of Qinhuangdao signed a Friendly Exchange Agreement in a closed-door meeting.[42]

City council relied on a section of the Community Charter that allows closed sessions if there are matters "that, in the view of council, could reasonably be expected to harm the interest of the municipality if they were held in public." One of the reasons why the United Front installs allies and agents in municipalities is because they can greenlight projects like this with even less accountability and oversight than the federal government.

Terrace is where the Qinhuangdao Economic & Technology Development Zone (QETDZ), in the Skeena Industrial Development Park (SIDP), is located.[43] It is owned by Taisheng International Investment Services Inc., a Metro-Vancouver-based Chinese manufacturing subsidiary of State-Owned Assets Management Ltd., which is wholly owned by QETDZ.[44]

This proves once again that there are only a few layers between projects like this in Canada and the Chinese government.

The CEO of Taisheng International Investment Services Inc. is Clark Roberts, the former BC Deputy Minister of International Trade in charge of the Pacific Gateway Branch under the Christy Clark government. Roberts was involved in the Belt and Road MOU event with Premier Clark and high-ranking CCP officials. He jointly chaired a breakaway Belt and Road workshop with Huang Mingzhong, director of the One Belt, One Road Initiative Office of NDRC Guangdong Province.[45][46]

At the time, the stated goal of the Belt and Road workshop was to "leverage BC's expertise in infrastructure services in China's Belt and Road Initiative" and form partnerships under the BRI under the umbrella of Canada's Pacific Gateway Alliance.

Canada's Pacific Gateway Alliance is a term that originated with the British Columbia government but which is "widely recognized and used in BC and across Canada to describe the east-west trade-supporting transportation system in Western Canada that connects Metro Vancouver, Prince Rupert and Vancouver International Airport on the Pacific Coast and stretches east thought the Prairie provinces and down into the United States."[47][48]

Continuing on the same route, from the QETDZ in Terrace, we arrive in Prince George, home to the largest airport in Northern BC—where another partnership is discovered. Terrace was officially designated by the federal Canadian government in 2018 as British Columbia's first Foreign Trade Zone (FTZ), allowing products from China to be eligible for tariff and tax exemptions on imports of raw materials, components, or finished goods.[49][50][51][52]

Pro-China politician George Chow was again on hand for the official ceremony to offer his congratulations on the awarding of the Foreign Trade Zone status.[53][54]

China's state-run media reported shortly thereafter that the new CEO of Prince George Airport Authority, Gordon Duke, was invited in November 2019 to Hong Kong to meet with representatives of the Shing Kee Group to discuss investment and cooperation opportunities and learn about the Belt and Road Initiative. One month later, in December 2019, Gordon visited the World Commodity Trade Center in Surrey, BC.[55]

When asked why the United Front intended to build another World Trade Center in the Prince George Duty-Free Zone, the Airport Authority responded that, "they knew we had lots of land up here."[56] [57]


## WHERE THE RUBBER HITS THE ROAD

A scarier prospect than China potentially choking supply chains is that China is also trying to control the products that travel on the BRI and the laws that govern these products as they travel by sea and air en route to North America's Belt and Road.

Canada's former ambassador to China, Guy Saint-Jacques, met with Guo Taicheng in 2015 for a roundtable meeting and signing ceremony to set up a Canadian agriculture commodity pavilion inside the Yanjiao International Trade City—World Commerce Valley.

According to state-run media, the two sides discussed China's import policy, Chinese market facilities, internet e-commerce and industrial chain construction, as well as agricultural products, and the Belt and Road in Canada.[58]

They said that since a new generation of leaders led by General Secretary Xi Jinping came to power, they have successively put forward major strategies, such as deepening reform, the Belt and Road and the integrated development of Beijing-Tianjin-Hebei.

Guo Taicheng was quoted as saying that "the exchange of Canada's import and export, agricultural products, food policies and relevant regulations, as well as the signing of the cooperation framework agreement on the establishment of the Canadian (Agriculture) Pavilion in the World Commerce Valley, will surely bring benefits to the people of China and Canada and become a new milestone in the development of trade between China and Canada!"[59]

BC MLA Teresa Wat, who was on hand to sign the BRI MOU with Christy Clark and the CCP, proudly reported to the BC Legislature that she had attended another BRI-themed event, this time related to food.[60] She then fondly reminisced about the BRI MOU that she signed in 2016 with the CCP. "I took great pride in signing the MOU on behalf of B.C. with China's Guangdong province in 2016 to mutually support and participate in this Belt and Road Initiative and the BC Pacific Gateway strategy. This memorandum meant much more than just another agreement between the two provincial governments. It was a pivotal step in extending the Belt and Road Initiative to North America, which was not originally covered."[61] No one questioned that she was acknowledging that Xi Jinping's prized initiative was active in North America with the help of BC's legislators.

But Wat was there to point out the new MOU that she signed at a Belt and Road International Food Expo she attended. She made sure to thank a United Front association and lobbyists for their work in organizing the event, saying, "By signing this cooperation scheme, B.C. has not only strengthened its relationship with China, our second-largest trading partner, but also seized new opportunities by joining a framework that unites more than 68 countries, 4.4 billion people and 40 percent of the world's GDP. I'd like to congratulate the organizers of this forum, the North American Investment Association and the Canada-China lobbyists, general chamber of commerce."[62 63]

Wat then confirmed that the organizer, The North American Investment Association (NAIA), whose president is Huang Xu Ruiping (Amy Huang), owner of Huijing Foods, was now solely authorized as the exclusive Canadian representative to organize a Canada pavilion in the first-ever Belt and Road International Food Expo to be held in Hong Kong in 2018.[64]

It sounded benign, but this was so much more than just a trade show booth in Hong Kong.

We found no documentation of Canadian government authorization to represent Canada at the Belt and Road Expo, however, a *Richmond News* article provided more insight into this MOU. "Huang led The Canada Pavilion to the first Belt & Road International Food Expo last summer in Hong Kong and brought home $1.7 billion worth of memorandum of understandings (MOUs)." Amy Huang herself said, "Most of our deal was made with Chinese local governments and Chinese state-owned companies."[65]

Another article, this time in *Business in Vancouver*, included this comment from pro-China MLA George Chow: "We'll look seriously at helping organizations such as NAIA when they are doing work on behalf of the province in promoting trade."[66]

NAIA's website reveals dozens of photos of Amy Huang with Liberal Party ministers and a certificate of appreciation from politician-turned-consultant Raymond Chan that was sent to her on behalf of the Liberal Party of Canada. We talked about Chan and his role in the early stages of helping to build the United Front in Canada. The caption that accompanied the certificate was a warning to conservative politicians to do what China wants. "Tories should understand what Chinese Canadian voters think!"[67]

Another statement on NAIA's website, written by Huang, warned that "Canada should reduce dependence on the U.S. economy, vigorously develop economic and trade relations with Asia, and actively engage China's Belt and Road Initiative, a new platform for international cooperation. This is a new direction and an important development strategy for Canada to expand exports and develop its economy."[68]

## MADE IN CHINA

Sarah Hall, Professor of Economic Geography at University of Nottingham, reminds us that "you can travel two ways on any road—in other words, we need to pay attention both to the origins and to local conditions along the BRI."[69] The BRI is not "a fixed entity that is being imposed in a singular fashion," she adds, but a project that is "being developed, reproduced and altered" across many sites. "Understanding these dynamics will be critical to understanding the wider geographical imaginations of the BRI as it shapes the contours of contemporary economic and political globalization with Chinese characteristics."

China doesn't just want to control roads; they want to own goods and services by making geographical indications claims that they were the true originators. Geographical indication (GI) is the right by a nation to claim a specific geographical location or product (e.g., a town, region, or country) originated with a country.[70] [71] [72]

Cultural projects, heritage designations, and claims of "country of origin" have become powerful instruments in helping the United Front reinforce China's national identity overseas, a key driver of Xi Jinping's governance philosophy—to restore China's image and national pride (National Rejuvenation). China believes it can make a case for a number of products, especially agricultural products, by proving they have an inseparable connection with their place of origin through thousands of years of careful development. And it has been a useful tool to bolster other legal claims based on cultural and historical significance as a way to secure much needed food and natural resources from Canada.[73][74]

## BRI APOSTLES

Nothing is off the table for China when it comes to the BRI—including religion.

BRI apostles have an eight-point strategy that includes following high-speed rail routes as well as economic and trade routes with the suggestion to set-up "civilization practice stations" along the way.

"Civilization practice stations" is the CCP's way of introducing institutional reform within "the Church," essentially replacing churches as part of a nationwide project launched by the CCP in July 2018. No longer resembling the traditional church, mosque or synagogue, these stations are used to organize various activities—from agricultural development to entertainment—to attract villagers and ensure they don't follow religions blindly.

The CCP wants a revival within the Christian church, using a term it knows is used by Christians in particular when referring to spiritual awakening.

Drawing upon links to Israel and its shared Judeo-Christian heritage, BRI apostles suggest that when the Chinese church is revived, the entrepreneurs and professionals among its believers will be able to serve Jerusalem, the core of central Asia and the Middle East, with love through the Belt and Road route.[75][76]

BRI apostles have even co-opted the Biblical story of the birth of Jesus, blending it with Chinese astronomy, claiming the Wise Men who traveled by starlight from the "East," with gold, frankincense, and myrrh, were divine inspiration for today's Belt and Road.[77]

China knows that the Belt and Road travels through countries with different religions, languages, and customs along the way. BRI apostles would like Christians to see that China's move to revitalize its economy and to "obtain more diplomatic space" has both material and spiritual aims and effects: ". . . as Pastor Wang said, Christians should see that this policy is not only driven by the export of funds, commodities, and personnel, but also can export the culture and values of heaven."[78]

## GLOBAL GOVERNANCE

China is well on its way to using the BRI to implement global governance, and the North American Belt and Road is no exception.[79]

On March 3, 2017, Ian G. McKay, former national director of the Liberal Party of Canada and adviser to two Canadian prime ministers, met in Beijing with Wang Chengjie, deputy director and secretary-general of the Chinese International Economic and Trade Arbitration Commission (CIETAC), long associated with the CCP's United Front strategy.[80]

On this occasion, McKay was serving in his role as chief executive officer of the Vancouver Economic Commission, the city's economic development agency.[81]

The two sides signed a memorandum of cooperation that would allow CIETAC to open a North American Arbitration Center in Vancouver, the second branch outside of mainland China.

CIETAC North America was registered by Qikun Zhang to his home on the campus of the University of British Columbia in 2018. He is also the director with the global Venture Capital firm Intel-Maple Capital Inc. and UIBE Alumni Association of Canada.

According to open-source information, Qikun Zhang has moved back to China and is the dean for the School of Economics at the Central University of Finance and Economics at the University of China, a national public research university in Beijing.[82] [83]

The CIETAC North American branch operated out of the Asia Pacific Centre, a department of the Vancouver Economic Commission. A signing ceremony was held at the Four Seasons in Vancouver to mark the occasion, with more than 180 attendees, including Chinese diplomats from the PRC Consulate, along with representatives of the Vancouver Maritime Arbitrators Association, Wei Shao, lawyer with Dentons and director of CCPIT in Vancouver, a handful of United Front agents, and again, politician George Chow.[84]

The law firm Norton Rose Fulbright wrote on its blog that "financial disputes were the most common in CIETAC's 2018 newly administered cases, among which, a large portion were Belt and Road related."[85]

We asked Janet Kelly from the Chamber of Shipping in Vancouver if decisions made by CIETAC North America were public and legally binding. She said, "Arbitration decisions are not available as the decision is private between the parties. It is only in the event of enforcement of an arbitral award in a court where a decision may become public."

She went on to say that CIETAC and the Vancouver Maritime Arbitrators Association (VMAA) are distinct bodies and that "the parties to a contract by agreement may choose how any disputes between them are to be resolved," while often choosing an arbitration process ahead of time, in case it becomes necessary.

Under Chinese law, disputes between Chinese companies outside of China's jurisdiction cannot be heard by arbitrators in other countries. That has ramifications for foreign businesses operating in China under locally registered subsidiaries, because any disputes arising out of local Chinese contracts between those local Chinese subsidiaries and another Chinese company must be submitted to arbitration in China.[86]

Despite the fanfare that accompanied the opening of CIETAC North America, it quietly disappeared. No one seemed to know where CIETAC North America was located, if they were hearing cases or if they closed and are now hearing cases out of Beijing.

Even more puzzling, BC's Attorney General's office claims it had no idea CIETAC was even operational. This despite the presence of 180 guests at the opening ceremony, including one of the AG's party members, George Chow.

"While the Ministry of Attorney General is responsible for both the Arbitration Act and the International Commercial Arbitration Act, the ministry had no involvement or knowledge of CIETAC operations," a Ministry of the Attorney General spokesperson said.[87]

How could an entire tribunal open up without the Attorney General's knowledge and approval?

At the time, the Attorney General was David Eby, who is now the premier of BC. He had long been a thorn in the side of the CCP when he took on the challenge to fight money laundering and its impact on housing—pointing to China as a source of the issues.

Eby took into consideration numerous law enforcement and intelligence reports when he announced a public inquiry into money laundering in the province of BC. What he may not have been prepared for was the scope and depth of information given through testimony that would go beyond the spectrum of money laundering, which is a component of threat finance and a sub-component of transnational organized crime in the hybrid warfare model.

As with so much of what happens with respect to China and the BRI, this magically disappearing tribunal remains shrouded in mystery. With the world gradually being swallowed up by China in its relentless march toward global superpower status, transparency is likely to become less and less common all the time. The constant battle to maintain and grow leverage and influence over decision makers and stakeholders equates to ever-changing tactics by the CCP and its vast array of hybrid war assets. There are times when activity is overt, and when exposed, there are responses designed to ensure that mystery and secrecy are maintained and well hidden. Removing organizations entirely, merging or altering leadership roles and personnel, changing tack and garnering new support from groups that have alternative spheres of influence are just some of the ways the CCP's UFWD keeps everyone guessing.

EDITOR'S NOTE: It is worth noting that the Canadian Government seized activity in the bank AIIB on June 14, 2023, under the direction of the Liberal Finance Minister Chrystia Freeland. This came after a Canadian appointed to the board made serious allegations about the Beijing centric management team. Perhaps this is a sign that some in Ottawa may finally be waking up to Beijing's ambitions.

# CHAPTER 14

# CASE STUDY

## THE CURIOUS CASE OF THE TARGETED TOWN

Getting to Powell River from Vancouver starts with a ferry ride, then a drive along the Sunshine Coast through the heart of BC's coastal hinterland. This gets you to the Sechelt Peninsula, where you take another ferry through Jervis Inlet, which offers some of the most picturesque landscapes in the province.

Eventually you arrive at Saltery Bay on the Malaspina Peninsula, an unincorporated community in the District of Powell River.

After a two-kilometre trek on a gravel road that winds through a temperate rainforest of massive fir trees and moss-covered ground, a fork in the road directs you to a clearing on the edge of the ocean near Mermaid Cove, a place rich in sea life.

Here you will find the Hummingbird Cove Lifestyle Hatchery (HCLH) and its subsidiary, Pacific Aquaculture. HCLH is a subsidiary of Linghai Shenziting Sea Cucumber Hatchery, the leading seafood farmer in China's Liaoning province, owned by Xi Ping "Xixi" Ding and her husband, Zhiyi Chen.[1]

---

PHOTO: Agents working on behalf of the CCP are buying up key industries in Canada.

The two investors from China were looking to get into the fish-farming industry in Canada by buying a company that has been in operation for over thirty-seven years. Their intention was to expand into shellfish aquaculture, to meet what they say is the increasing global demand for seafood.

They would start by building a state-of-the-art, 30,000-square-foot facility that, when completed, would be, in their estimation, the largest shellfish hatchery in Canada, with licensing for over twenty varieties of shellfish.

A main goal of the expansion, according to Xi Ping, is to increase the availability of seed in order to eliminate uncertainties associated with traditional shellfish seed supply in Canada, which is known for shortages.

The venture is set to provide a year-round supply of seed for twenty-three farm shellfish species. The Canadian Department of Fisheries and Oceans (DFO) confirmed that they licensed the facility to produce sea urchins, geoduck, sea cucumbers, scallops, oysters, clams and mussels. There is no doubt that they are a legitimate hatchery.

But there is another side to the business: a research laboratory called Pacific Aquaculture, which formed a partnership with Liaoning Ocean and Fisheries Science Research Institute to create a research centre—Liaoning's first in Canada.[2] The Institute is affiliated to the Liaoning Provincial Department of Oceans and Fisheries, and is considered a key provincial scientific research institution in China.

There is little detailed information on exactly what these Chinese research scientists were researching in Canada's sovereign waters.

But what we know so far leads us to wonder if Powell River has become a gateway for the CCP to establish a scientific and possibly even a military presence along BC's Sunshine Coast.

Here is what is known: A signed cooperation agreement between Pacific Aquaculture and the Liaoning research institute promises to bring high-end seafood farming technologies to the shellfish farming industry in British Columbia.

The deal was marked by a ribbon-cutting ceremony at Pacific Aquaculture. Among those in attendance was Chen Chong, a researcher with China Liaoning Academy of Marine and Fishery Sciences.[3]

In an interview with reporters, he pointed out that the seawater in BC is less polluted than in China, and said he expects breeding time will be shorter in BC than in China, with higher expected success rates of seedlings.

Zhou Zunchun, who is the president and chief researcher of the Liaoning Ocean and Fisheries Science Research Institute, is also a longtime member of the Communist Party of China and recipient of its National Advanced Worker award for his contributions to socialist construction.[4]

He also presided over the CCP's 13th Five-Year Plan, which calls for geographic expansion of China's maritime activities in Liaoning province.[5] Students of China's evolving maritime strategy have interpreted this to mean expansion of China's maritime interests beyond their own sovereign waters.

According to 2015 a paper by the Jamestown Foundation, the 13th Five-Year Plan points to "maritime aspirations that are increasingly global in scale and scope." The report's author, Ryan D. Martinson, a researcher at the China Maritime Studies Institute of the U.S. Naval War College in Newport, Rhode Island, notes that the 'proposed' 13th FYP calls for China to build "a 'system to protect overseas interests,' presumably including overseas military facilities." These objectives are "inherently maritime in nature," Martinson writes, "and yet must take place on foreign soil, where China has no inherent rights. It is reasonable, then, to expect that as these initiatives develop, China's 'maritime power' strategy will evolve to suit the country's expanding interests."[6]

At the forefront of China's expansionist marine industry is the Aquatic Genome Research Center, established on June 17, 2016, a partnership between the Beijing Genomics Institute (BGI) and the Chinese Academy of Fishery Sciences (CAFS).[7]

BGI Marine's mission is to "help with the development of the biological economy with genetic technology, and to contribute to the promotion of China's marine industry." They are involved in marine ranching around the globe, through subsidiaries and partnerships that produce products for retailers like Walmart.[8]

BGI Marine's website reveals that they are using molecular breeding technologies, such as parental gene sequencing, sibling selection, and seedling pool cultivation, and that they have engineered seafoods, such as a new, fast-growing hairy crab.[9]

It's possible that the Canadian Research Center is doing similar work, or even working with BGI. Our research suggests that the Liaoning institute was involved in the Ten Thousand Fish Genome Project (Fish10K) in 2019—a large-scale research project that aimed to sequence the genomes of about 10,000 species. The project was launched by several universities and institutes, including BGI, with a stated goal to "accelerate . . . fish genomics research and . . . improve our overall understanding of fish."[10]

These links to large-scale aquatic research projects, genome sequencing, and expansionist maritime strategies raised some red flags, so we reached out to the former mayor of Powell River, Dave Formosa, to see if he could shed light on this hatchery and other rumours that the CCP was covertly slipping into town.[11]

## THE TOWN MAYOR TALKS

Powell River needed the deep pockets of investors to stay afloat, and Mayor Dave was just the man to bring them in. Born and raised there, Mayor Dave was a well-meaning, multi-term mayor and well-liked local entrepreneur.

He spent an hour with one of our Project Mosaic researchers, fielding questions about how pervasive the problem of foreign influence and infiltration had become.[12] At every point, he staunchly opposed any notion that what we presented as potential incidents of CCP interference added up to anything more than foreign investment.

Mayor Dave acknowledged that he played a large role in helping the hatchery get started, but didn't say exactly how he helped. He also confirmed the presence of research scientists at the hatchery, and acknowledged that information could have been shared between the facility in China and the hatchery in Canada.

We asked the Department of Fisheries if the Liaoning Ocean and Fisheries Science Research Institute has a formal agreement with Canada, since the research was being conducted in Canada by Chinese scientists.

The answer we received is that, "there are no research partnerships between Pacific Aquaculture International and the Department of Fisheries and Oceans."[13]

However, they did confirm that Pacific Aquaculture holds a shellfish aquaculture license to operate a deep-water suspended culture facility. In other words, there was nothing stopping the CCP from conducting research experiments in Canada.

It is important to note that Powell River is 32 kilometers away and directly across the straight from the Canadian Forces Base (CFB) Comox—an air base that conducts maritime surveillance as well as search and rescue operations. It's also close to CFB Nanoose—the testing range for torpedoes and sonar-related technologies used by the US and other allied nations.

Having a Chinese facility this close to operational Canadian military facilities—even one that ostensibly focuses only on shellfish aquaculture—is certainly a cause for concern due to the risk of subsurface monitoring.

When asked about the backgrounds of the individuals behind the hatchery, Mayor Dave suggested that they were "super nice people." But when pressed for more information, he didn't know, or perhaps didn't want to know. From his perspective, due diligence was about getting to know them on a personal level and schmoozing—Guanxi, Canadian style. He was not about to dig into their backgrounds or analyze their motivation for wanting to set up shop in Canada.

And why should he? Mayor Dave admitted that although he went on many investment trips to China, and even met with CCP officials, no one from CSIS ever approached him to talk about China or warn him about what to look for. He was flying solo, like so many small-town officials who have been left to their own devices in dealing with China. With no preparation, it can be challenging for local officials to tell a legitimate investment opportunity from a threat to national security, especially when their primary concern is keep their own communities financially viable.

Formosa was so unaware of the connection between the CCP and the Chinese investors he was bringing to Canada that he didn't know that one of the main investors in the hatchery is Morris Chen and his company, Caishen Group.[14]

Morris is a billionaire investor who owns a slew of companies and has his hand in all kinds of deals, including mammoth student housing ventures. He is a major player in Duck Island development in Richmond, BC, and a key investor and director of Wealth One Bank of Canada, the first and only federal chartered bank in Canada that, Morris says, "specializes in helping the Chinese community to thrive."

We have mentioned his role as chair of the North American Investment and Trade Promotion Association (NAITPA), which, for all intents and purposes, is CCPIT, the China Council for the Promotion of International Trade. The CCPIT falls under China's Ministry of Commerce

(MOFCOM) and has long been associated with the CCP's United Front strategy. CCPIT has been integral in setting up the unofficial Belt and Road in North America.

In a now removed webpage that we retrieved, one of Morris Chen's companies, Caishen, talks about its investment in the hatchery, and reveals what possible interest the CCP might have in Hummingbird Cove. Their stated focus is on global seafood consumption, which they say is estimated to reach 160 million tons by 2030, driving growth in the already lucrative business of marine aquaculture.

"Hummingbird Cove Lifestyle Hatchery (HCLH) is positioned to help provide the potential shortfall of roughly 80 million tons of seafood that will be required by global appetites," the website said. ". . . In China alone, the average person is estimated to consume almost 36kg of seafood annually by 2020; Hong Kong, Japan and the United States will account for most exports and thus will drive the bulk of revenues. Located near Powell River, HCLH is conveniently situated to distribute its products along key routes to both the US and Asia."[15]

Statements like this suggest that the hatchery may be part of a larger plan to achieve food sustainability for China's population. The ground for this move appears to have been prepared over a number of years. As early as 2015, an article on China-Canada agricultural trade in *People's Daily* noted that "Canada has a vast territory, fertile land, superior natural conditions, good water quality and air quality, and abundant natural resources," and stated plainly that, due to its high standards of food safety, quality management, and innovative agricultural food products, "Canadian agricultural food is deeply loved by the Chinese people."[16]

Canadian aquaculture appears to be just as enticing to China as Canadian agriculture, especially when it comes to China's unofficial Belt and Road Initiative. In 2019, the Chinese government issued a Belt and Road Agricultural Cooperation Plan under the guidance of the Ministry of Commerce (MOFCOM). Before that, on March 28, 2015, the MOFCOM released an official outline for the Belt and Road Initiative. Coupled with the fact that the Canadian research facility had an agreement with China, we can start to see the linkages between 'the State' and the hatchery.

The hatchery is yet another link in the unofficial Belt and Road chain that we described in the previous chapter. China's investment in fish farming off the coast of BC makes sense when seen through the lens of the Belt and Road Agricultural Cooperation Plan.

But there's more to the story. The Belt and Road Agricultural Cooperation Plan's ties to the Hummingbird Cove Lifestyle Hatchery appeared to be only one small part of a bigger plan to buy up key industries along the Sunshine Coast. Whether all the people involved—from the mayor to the townsfolk and the investors themselves—knew this, remained to be seen.

## SMALL TOWN CAPTURE

If the hatchery was part of a wider scheme, as we suspected, we would need to widen our investigation.

Powell River is a quaint seaside city 30 km from the hatchery. Originally built around a single business, it was, for a time, the site of the world's largest pulp and paper mill. During the heyday of newspapers, one in every twenty-five newspapers in the world was printed on paper from the Powell River Mill. But the newsprint industry has seen a steep decline, and so too has the town.

Mayor Dave was coming to the end of fourteen years in the job when we spoke to him, and he didn't mince words when it came to the town's dire financial situation when he first took office. Quite simply, the tax revenue generated by the town was not enough to sustain the services it needed to operate. Thirty percent of commercial buildings sat empty, the mill was on the verge of closing, and the town was having trouble attracting new residents.

It needed investors, and, as a local entrepreneur, Formosa believed he was perfectly positioned to bring in the right people to raise much-needed capital. He was unapologetic about doing what he had to do to woo the type of investors who could inject large quantities of cash into Powell River. "We sought them out—mostly," he recalled. "After the mill closed down, I would go after anyone to rebuild the community."

Mayor Dave wasn't saying who approached whom first, but he has proudly revealed that he pursued Chinese investors, sometimes at the urging of the BC government, and sometimes with the government's help.

It wouldn't surprise us to learn that the Chinese consulate in BC was only too happy to oblige. The consulate was (and is) big on schmoozing, and loves to create joint ventures between government and industry, dangling carrots in front of politicians. They have the BC premier on speed dial, and they have the connections to make things happen. The Chinese consulate had a consular official, known as the commercial consul, whose job was to facilitate business deals between BC and China. Vancouver was largely considered to have been bought up, so the CCP looked to resource-rich Northern BC, and remote towns along the provincial coast, which offered access to the ocean, pre-existing mills, and established services, such as small general aviation airports.

Powell River may very well have met China at the 2018 annual PRC consulate cocktail party, hosted by the Union of BC Municipalities (UBCM), before these annual fêtes ended in the wake of the arrest of the "Two Michaels."[17]

The UBCM was where all the municipalities in BC met to vote on issues of common concern, which they would then bring back to the province.

While Mayor Dave didn't attend the last cocktail party, Powell River sent council member George Doubt.

## FROM FISH TO PAPER AND PLANES: STATE-BACKED ACTORS ARE BUYING UP TOWNS, KEY INDUSTRIES, AND INFRASTRUCTURE FOR THE CCP

Although it might seem like a big jump to go from fish to paper to planes, that's where story of Powell River and its dealings with China takes us. And the story of what could really be happening in this part of Canada is one that every Canadian should know.

In 2019, Powell River entered into a ninety-nine-year lease with a numbered company,[18] 1170987 B.C. Ltd., for the sum of $600,000. The numbered company is owned by Gaoshi Holdings (Canada) Ltd.

The deal would see a 4.6-hectare parcel of land within the city-owned Powell River Airport be developed into a mixed-use aviation park.

Victor Gao was the director and vice-president of Gaoshi Holdings. His original goal was to build a facility to manufacture small aircraft. This deal was put forward with Mayor Dave, who even arranged to get a $2-million grant for Gao's company.[19]

Together they had their sights set on Murphy Aircraft Mfg. Ltd., a Canadian-made manufacturer of aircraft kits. The company designed and built experimental light aircraft geared for bush flying.

In 2014, Darryl Murphy, founder and president of Murphy Aircraft, announced he was selling his company. Located in an industrial area of Chilliwack, a small city on the mainland one-and-a-half hours from Vancouver, Murphy Aircraft had strong roots in the local economy, and felt quintessentially Canadian, from the maple leaf logo to the social media photos of bush pilots landing on remote lakes in the wilderness.

Mayor Dave had an eye to move the entire company back to Powell River, but the deal fell through when Murphy Aircraft was bought by Duofu International Holding Group's aviation unit, Duofu Aviation. The Chinese company has revenues of ¥175.3 billion (CAD$33 billion), and is engaged in the whole industry chain of general aviation, from research on industrial strategy, investment, financing and production to R&D of helicopters/ electric vertical take-off and landing aircraft/engines, and the construction and operation of airports.[20]

Duofu's chairman is Hu Xingrou, a Zhejiang businessman who is a member of the 12th CPPCC National. He is also on the committee of the Xinjiang Uyghur Autonomous Region, where you will find Uyghur concentration camps. And he serves as honorary president of the Wenzhou chamber of commerce, which is part of the United Front networks in Richmond, BC.[21]

The company appears to have invested globally in aviation companies, acquiring Italian helicopter company Fama in 2022[22] and partnering with the Australian company that created the Pegasus flying car to create a Chinese version of the same.[23]

Duofu installed a new management team in Chilliwack—but for what purpose? Murphy had only sold around 2,000 aircraft kits between 1985, when it opened, and 2014. The company was on sale for $2.5–$4 million, pennies for a company like Duofu. Murphy Aircraft was hardly a cash cow for a huge multi-billion-dollar company.[24]

But Murphy Aircraft offered more than just a business-to-consumer niche product. It had relationships with suppliers such as Titan Continental Motors, Earth X Lithium batteries, and Catto Propellers. It's one of only five kit manufacturers in Canada to have been evaluated by Transport Canada Civil Aviation and been awarded a Special Certificate of Airworthiness. Murphy also owned the intellectual property to the plans for the do-it-yourself airplane builder. More importantly, buying Murphy came with the knowledge and skills that China wanted to replicate as part of its current Five-Year Plan (2021–2025), including the innovative use of drones and upgrading aviation services in the agricultural and industrial sectors.[25]

But the story doesn't end here. We found a company in China called Murphy Air that is a "kit manufacturer" of industrial UAV. The company behind China's Murphy Air is Shenzhen Murphy Aviation Technology Co., Ltd. founded by college student Chen Mo.[26]

According to online reports in China, Chen got his start in the aviation industry in 2010, when he enrolled in the Department of Mechanical and Electrical Engineering at Northwestern Polytechnical University (NPU),[27] majoring in aircraft manufacturing engineering. NPU is in Xi'an, Shaanxi Province, the heartland of the Belt and Road. So it made sense that the school initiated the Belt and Road Aerospace Innovation Alliance, a cooperative platform for dozens of schools inside and outside China, designed to accelerate the growth of China's aerospace industry.

It was in 2011, while studying at NPU, that Chen Mo started his first homemade aircraft manufacturing project, based on a plan he purchased "abroad." Chen's homemade plan was finished a year later, and in 2015, he joined Guangdong Unmanned Aerial Vehicle Co., Ltd. as deputy general manager. In one report, Chen Mo said it was at this company that he acquired knowledge and management experience in drone manufacturing. He also gave a special nod to the business Chaoshan Merchants for training him in their business methods.

In 2017, Chen Mo founded Shenzhen Murphy Aviation Technology Co., Ltd., a company that develops off-road and other large-scale industrial drones under the brand name Murphy Air.[28] It's likely he received financial backing from Guangdong and/or Chaoshan for this venture.

Most likely, Duofu bought Murphy Aircraft in Canada, in order to support the broader advancement of aviation technology in China, which also includes military advancement, and the strengthening of China's UAV industry.

It's an open question if Murphy Air in China is a copycat company that capitalized on Murphy Air Canada's identity or if Duofu's purchase of Murphy Aircraft somehow made its way into a hybrid UAV version of a "kit plane."

All of this brings us back to Mayor Dave and his failed bid to bring Murphy Aircraft to Powell River in conjunction with Gaoshi Holdings.

Oddly, Gaoshi didn't walk away from its plan to lease part of the Powell River Airport when the Murphy Air deal fell through. According to Mayor Dave, they decided to go ahead with the lease anyway, but with a revised plan to offer aircraft storage, maintenance, transit service, and pilot training workshops. It was clear to us that Gaoshi wanted a slice of the Powell River Airport, no matter what deal was on the table. They would just change their business model to suit whatever would help them secure the lease.[29]

We can't speak to what Gaoshi Holdings has planned. We reached out to Victor Gao several times, but he was mum on specifics.

We can, however, speculate as to the big picture behind this deal and others in the aviation industry, based on what intelligence agencies were telling us.

Here's what we know:

Aviation flight training and maintenance schools have been on the intelligence community's radar for a number of years, since 9/11. Yet little stands in China's way when it comes to buying up Canadian aviation companies and training foreign pilots and mechanics from countries like China, who are under the control of an autocratic regime.

China has many reasons for wanting to buy up Canada's aviation industry, including airports and flight training schools. One of those is to own small, remote airports that are close to areas considered choke points, and that can function as logistic hubs for Canada's unofficial Belt and Road.

## AVIC CADRE FLIGHT TRAINING IN CANADA

Thirty minutes from Murphy Air and the Chilliwack Airport is Abbotsford International Airport, home to another company with deep ties to the People's Republic of China. Coastal Pacific Aviation (CPA) is a Canadian flight-training school that has been around since 1973.

Originally owned by Canadians Alan Holley and Cole Shelby, Coastal Pacific has operated a private aviation training program together with Abbotsford Airport and the University College of the Fraser Valley since

1984.[30] In 2014, Chinese-American businessman Jiang Ning took over as company president.

The school is currently training pilots for China Southern Airlines, a state-owned enterprise, and has applied to the Civil Aviation Administration of China to become the fourth Canadian aviation training school qualified to provide training for AVIC. AVIC stands for the Aviation Industry Corporation of China, a Chinese state-owned aerospace and defence conglomerate headquartered in Beijing. In April 2009, *The Wall Street Journal* reported that cyber spies from China "had penetrated the database of the Joint Strike Fighter program and acquired terabytes of secret information about the fighter, possibly compromising its future effectiveness."[31]

AVIC allegedly "incorporated the stolen know-how into their own fighter jets."[32]

The US prohibits any American company or individual from owning shares in companies that the United States Department of Defense has listed as having links to the People's Liberation Army, which includes AVIC.[33]

## JOINT AGREEMENTS WITH MILITARY COLLEGES IN CHINA

Coastal Pacific has carved out a number of joint education agreements with different flight schools in China, including a 2016 agreement with Binzhou College, whose own flight academy was rated as an advanced grassroots party organization in the country, commended by the CPC Central Committee. Kunming University of Science and Technology was another one. Binzhou offers national defence education.[34]

Coastal Pacific and Binzhou College agreed to cooperate in the construction of aviation schools, instructor training and exchanges, practical training for civil aviation maintenance workers, pilot training, and sharing of educational resources.

We can think of a whole host of problems with this set up, but the most concerning is that the National Defense Education Law of the People's Republic of China stipulates that the Chinese People's Liberation Army and the Chinese People's Armed Police Force shall select military instructors.[35] In theory, at least, this means that an aviation program that is being run out of the Abbotsford Airport could be subject to decisions coming directly from the CCP armed forces.

Then there is the fact that for overseas students seeking funding for international studies in Canada, a basic requirement is that they support the leadership of the Communist Party of China and the path of socialism with Chinese characteristics.

We can assume this means that students applying to study in Canada will have to do what they are told. If an instructor is a People's Liberation Army soldier, these instructions could potentially be out of step with Canadian norms or laws.

Then we have to consider the fact that these schools train pilots for China Southern Airlines.

China Southern Airlines is involved in transporting Uyghur Muslims and other minorities into forced labour camps, where detainees have been subject to documented human rights abuses. According to the US Department of State, "detention in these camps is intended to erase ethnic and religious identities under the pretext of "vocational training." Forced labor is a central tactic used for this repression."[36]

*China Daily* reported that by chartering flights to transport "labour-prisoners" in Xinjiang, Southern Airlines was proudly fulfilling its political and social responsibility to the Chinese government, helping to alleviate poverty and facilitate the governing of Xinjiang.

Meanwhile, back in Canada, the premier of British Columbia at the time, Christy Clark, voiced her support for trade links between China and Canada on the aviation front by saying, "China Eastern's expansion of air services is another sign of increasing travel and trade between BC and China. Expanding air services is another way we can leverage BC's competitive advantages to increase trade, create jobs and support communities."[37]

There's more.

According to Coastal Pacific, it is one of the few private schools in Canada able to guarantee that international students who have obtained a diploma or degree certificate at the college in Canada are then eligible to apply for jobs in Canada. Eligibility lasts for up to three years after graduation.

We also came across information that suggested that Coastal Pacific is part of what's known as the Air Silk Road—the aviation part of the Belt and Road. The idea is to build an "air bridge" connecting China and the world through the promotion of a global aviation infrastructure network, using military-civilian integration.

We know of at least one formal meeting over the building of a logistics centre at the Abbotsford Airport. By description, this project sounded like the Belt and Road warehouse that Project Mosaic helped to expose with Glacier Media's syndicated reporter Graeme Wood. That Belt and Road project was no more than 20–30 kilometres from Abbotsford Airport in Surrey, BC.

This meeting, which was arranged by the Chinese consul general, with Coastal Pacific owner Ning Jiang and the manager of the Abbotsford Airport, offers more anecdotal evidence that China was sketching out a path for an unofficial Belt and Road in Canada.

Mayor Dave deflected all questions about why he met with Ning Jiang. There was little to no information on potential plans for a Coastal Pacific satellite campus or a warehouse stop in Powell River as part of the unofficial Air Silk Road in Canada.

What we did know is that the CCP had big plans for Coastal Pacific.

## FOLLOWING THE AIR SILK ROAD

Triton Aerospace, a manufacturing facility in Zhuhai, China, with offices just across the BC-Washington State border, is the new supplier of Coastal Pacific's fleet of planes.

In 2019, Triton, together with Shanghai Zhengbang Industrial Co., Ltd., struck a deal that would include the purchase of fifty aircraft, to be leased to Coastal Pacific. The deal was made at a conference in Beijing, dubbed an "Air Silk Road" event.

This was no boardroom deal; it was negotiated in public, at a gathering co-sponsored by the Ministry of Commerce and the Beijing Municipal People's Government, amid foreign political dignitaries, staff and politicians from various ministries, and representatives of the Chinese government, along with principals from aviation enterprises along the Belt and Road.

The leasing of a large fleet of planes, training commercial and military pilots for China, and sketching out a path for the Air Silk Road were all worrying signs. It felt like an Air America set-up all over again. Air America was the covertly owned and operated American passenger and cargo airline run by the CIA from 1950 to 1976. Only this time, it was the Chinese government that appeared to be meddling in Canadian aviation, buying up airport space, running flight training programs for its own benefit, supplying the planes for those programs, and using business acquisitions to effectively expand its operations into Canadian airspace.

Mr. Thomas Hsueh is a Chinese-American aerospace engineer and the owner of Triton Aerospace, a manufacturer of light aircraft.[38] The company got its wings, so to speak, when its parent holding company snapped up the assets of Adam Aircraft in 2009, including all intellectual property, after that firm ceased operations in 2008 and filed for bankruptcy.[39]

Triton also acquired the legacy deals that Adam Aircraft had amassed over the years—including a major contract dating from 2005, with a team led by Groen Brothers Aviation, Inc.—from the U.S. Defense Advanced Research Projects Agency.

The contract was to design a proof-of-concept high speed, long range, vertical takeoff and landing (VTOL) aircraft for use in combat search and rescue roles. Adam Aircraft was part of the team because they are known for innovative use of modern composite materials, engineering quality, and rapid prototyping processes. Triton effectively bought up the intellectual property of Adam Aircraft, and overnight it had access to documentation related to the U.S. Defense Advanced Research Project.[40]

This was a pattern we were seeing again and again. CCP was acquiring small-to-medium-sized businesses in key industries, using intermediaries, and putting down roots in small communities in Canada.

On the surface, it looked like these companies were being bought up as part of normal international trade and immigration. But as we kept digging we discovered that the CCP always seemed to be in the background, and not everything was about business.

Case in point: We came across some information pointing to a reception dinner that allegedly took place at the Canadian consul in Guangzhou. During the reception, which was held for the 12th China International Aviation and Aerospace Expo, a signing ceremony took place between Coastal Pacific and the producer of a CCP propaganda film, *Smoke in the Desert*. The Chinese government, through various intermediaries, hired Coastal Pacific to film aerial footage in the Osoyoos area, in British Columbia's Okanagan Desert.

The film would be part of a larger propaganda campaign by the CCP meant to showcase China's achievements in combating desertification, and its commitment to cooperating with regions along the Belt and Road and countries around the world that are affected by desertification problems.

That Canada would play host to a signing ceremony that would use Canada as a prop in a CCP propaganda film was yet more evidence that factions within the Canadian government were granting the CCP special favour.

One ironic and potentially alarming aspect of this event is the fact that while China purports to be cooperating with regions along the Belt and Road affected by desertification, they chose to gather footage for the film in British Columbia. It was becoming more obvious that there was an unofficial Belt and Road in Canada and that small aircraft, small general airports, and remote towns in British Columbia were a part of Xi Jinping's master Belt and Road plan.[41]

## FLYING UNDER THE RADAR

Harbour Air is about as iconic a Canadian brand as you could get.

Their ubiquitous Beaver and Otter aircraft seaplanes are a fixture in the Coal Harbour area of Vancouver, flying passengers to remote islands along the coast of British Columbia.

They developed a bit of a reputation for flying politicians back and forth between Vancouver Island harbour, where the BC Legislature is located, and the BC mainland. Even the UK's Prince William, the heir apparent to the British throne, and Catherine, Princess of Wales, flew into Vancouver Harbour on a Harbour Air seaplane.

Harbour Air was all over the West coast, and adding routes all the time, including service to Powell River in 2022.

There was nothing obviously nefarious about the addition of more air routes, as these were popular destinations.

But in 2015, Harbour Air announced that a major Chinese investor acquired a minority share in the company, with a goal to bring commuter seaplane service to China. That minor Chinese investor, however, was not so minor.

Enter Zongshen Group.

It now had a 49 percent ownership stake in Harbour Air, with 25 percent voting shares—the maximum number of voting shares allowed at the time under the federal act for a foreign company owning an aviation company.[42]

The press release by Harbour Air said Zongshen's investment was viewed as a way to strengthen the general aviation market in China and to integrate overseas technology with local manufacturing. This is no doubt true, and to the Canadian public, it likely sounded reasonable. Why not export a unique Canadian model for seaplane commuter air travel, to the benefit of people living or near major waterways in China?

Even better, the deal came with assurances that the strategic partnership would not impact control of Harbour Air, whose Canadian ownership retains 75 percent of voting shares. "All Canadian regulatory requirements have been satisfied," the press statement read.[91]

Certainly, all of what Harbour Air said was true, as far as helping China develop seaplane markets. But could the Harbour Air deal fit into a wider strategy that is part of China's five-year plan for general aviation? This plan covers the period ending in 2025, and includes the development of unmanned aerial vehicles (UAV), most likely for use in any future Sino-US military confrontation over Taiwan, in particular. More to the point, could the Harbour Air deal tie into the CCP's hybrid war on the West? The simple answer is, yes.[43]

A 2018 report on Chinese trade practices by the Office of the U.S. Trade Representative noted that the strategic purpose behind buying up general aviation companies was about "Obtaining and developing cutting-edge technology in the aviation sector," which was said to have "long been an objective of the Chinese government."[44]

The report also detailed how, "In the aviation industry, China uses its purchasing power to require joint ventures and technology transfer in exchange for two types of business opportunities—the sale of commercial aircraft to China's state-owned airlines and the sale of aircraft components to Chinese-made aircraft."

In many cases, these objectives serve a larger goal of securing knowledge transfers for the benefit of the CCP and China. Gu Huizhong, the vice president of the Aviation Industry Corporation of China, the same Chinese state-owned aerospace and defense conglomerate that Coastal Pacific Aviation is training pilots for, revealed as much when he spoke to the reason behind his company's acquisition of Spain's Aritex in 2016. Aritex is one of the world's leading automobile and aeronautics engineering companies, with a presence in Europe, America and Asia.

Huizhong said, "the experience Aritex brings in engineering and technology will be important to fill the gaps in existing know-how in the Chinese market by improving current assembly technology and helping implement future factory concepts in China."[45]

The same could be said about Harbour Airlines. Apart from the material benefits of the deal, China wanted to replicate Harbour Air's Canadian business model in China and other Belt and Road countries. One has to give credit where credit is due. Chinese companies and the CCP know how to learn from others in order to benefit their country. But these lopsided arrangements haven't always benefited Canada, and in some cases they have done real harm.

## MILITARY-CIVILIAN INTEGRATION

When looking into the links between military and civilian operations in China's expansionary plans, we turned our attention to the founder and current chairman of Zongshen Group, billionaire tycoon Zuo Zongshen.

His company started as a motorcycle business in the early 1980s, and has grown to include fifty-two subsidiary companies, and more than 18,000 employees.[46]

Zuo is a member of the China Democratic League, a political party that is an integral part of the patriotic United Front led by the Communist Party of China. In 2018 he won an award by the United Front Work Department of the Central Committee and the All-China Federation of Industry and Commerce for his work as an outstanding builder of socialism with Chinese characteristics. The Zongshen "communist party committee" hosts some of the most pro-national events that we have seen in our research in relation to companies in China.

Li Yao is the executive vice-president of Zongshen Industrial Group. He offered some telling clues at a Zongshen press conference about the Harbour Air deal, and his comments differed markedly from Harbour Air's account of their business dealings.

It was as if they were working from completely different playbooks. For Li Yao, the Harbour Air deal was all about opening new operations routes in Northern BC, to take advantage of oil and gas development in the region. Harbour Air's statement, meanwhile, suggested that the Zhongshen partnership was all about bringing Canada's seaplane model to China. The statement also suggests that Zongshen would benefit by gaining influence over Harbour Air's corporate decision making in Canada.

Li Yao's statement was supported by another agreement that was signed during a trade mission led by then-Premier Christy Clark in 2013. A Memorandum of Understanding was struck between the Zhongshen

Group and the British Columbia Institute of Technology, a government-funded institution, together with Southwest University. The MOU was to develop partnerships and training opportunities relating to the liquefied natural gas (LNG) industry and alternative energy research in China and BC.

Premier Clark had long championed BC as the supplier of LNG to China. Zhongshen was in the background, laying down tracks, while regulatory hurdles were being overcome by the government that would see BC become a major global LNG super player.[47]

But that wasn't all that Zhongshen was doing in BC.

A press release on the Memorandum of Understanding from the British Columbia Institute of Technology also revealed that Zhongshen had its hands in all sorts of new areas, including high-end manufacturing, automobile dealerships, mining, real estate, energy, and finance.[48][49]

We know that Zongshen had projects underway with its subsidiary, Zongshen (Canada) Envirotech Ltd. These partnerships included a high-end development on Bowen Island, a ten-minute boat ride from Vancouver.[50]

Zhongshen also forged a partnership with ElectraMeccanica, an EV Car Company in Vancouver, whose other big investors are marketing guru Ma Li (aka Megan Martin) and her husband, PLA combat hero, Zhang Yuansheng.[51] Megan is the granddaughter of a Chinese democratic revolutionary who was one of the earliest members of the Tongmenghui, a secret society and underground resistance movement founded by Sun Yat sen.[52] Megan is known for her local dinner parties, some of which she held at the Sidaway Mansion in Richmond, which the Ministry of Justice has alleged was an illegal gambling house.[53]

Taking stock of these actors, their connections to the CCP, and the businesses they are buying up, is invaluable in helping to identify what kind of threats are posed in a specific region.

In a conventional war, threats come in the form of bombs and troop movements. In a hybrid war, threats can fall onto a spectrum of seemingly benign actions, like buying up large swaths of real estate, to more subtle but direct threats like engaging in voter interference.

These and other types of hybrid tactics often form part of a wider, long-term plan for capturing foreign entities or countries. It can also mean that buying a Canadian business by a civilian-run corporation might actually be for another, more sinister purpose, like military use.

# CIVILIAN-MILITARY WORK

In 2014, a year prior to the Harbour Air deal, Zongshen announced the start of a drone engine manufacturing project which it proudly framed as its civilian contribution to China's national defence construction.

Two years later, in 2016, newly established subsidiary Zongshen Hangfa Company began mass producing drone engines, including military (counter-terrorism) drones. These were unmanned aerial vehicles (UAV), used mostly for surveillance.

By December 2018, Zongshen was producing C145 engines and ZP1780 propellers for the Pterodactyl I-D UAV.[54]

Designed for use in surveillance and aerial reconnaissance, the Pterodactyl is easy to identify by its distinctive bulge at the tip of the fuselage, where it houses a satellite antenna. This is the model version most widely publicized and actively marketed for its surveillance capabilities.[55][56]

According to state-run media's analysis of the Japan Broadcasting Corporation (NHK) review of the Pterodactyl, the unmanned aircraft is said to strike fear in the hearts of the Japanese. One can only speculate that this has something to do with the fact that the Pterodactyl I is capable of being fitted with air-to-surface weapons for use in unmanned combat.

By 2020, the Zongshen Hangfa C145HT engine completed its first flight with an AV500C helicopter, used for wide-area surveillance and identification tasks on the sea. This ship-based helicopter-style drone—China's first ever in its class—was developed by the Chinese company China Helicopter Research and Development Institute, which worked under the state-owned Aviation Industry Corporation of China.[57]

The model filled a gap in the field of small and light shipborne unmanned helicopters in China and was expected to be used for maritime surveillance. The drone doesn't appear to support arms, but it could always be modified to carry weapons.

According to the Chinese magazine *Ordnance Industry Science Technology*, the drone could be used to provide coverage for ships in the South China and East China seas.[58]

Did any of this sound like the work of a company that just wanted to import best practices in commuter travel by seaplane? That was likely part of it. But that wasn't the whole story.

In an unexpected development, the motorcycle manufacturing tycoon Zuo Zongshen recommended to the National Committee of the Chinese

People's Political Consultative Conference (CPPCC) that China should add the Diaoyu Islands to the CCTV news network weather forecast program. Also known as the Senkaku Islands, these uninhabited islands, or islets, in the East China Sea, are the focus of a territorial dispute between Japan and China and between Japan and Taiwan.

We found it incredibly odd that a tycoon running a billion-dollar motorcycle and machinery empire would suggest anything to the upper echelons of the Communist Party, much less instruct them on weather forecasting practices in the South China Sea.

This was another data point that supported our theory that Zongshen's acquisition of Harbour Air was about more than just commuter travel. In fact, Chongqing Daily inquired of Chairman Zuo about Zongshen's acquisition of Harbour Air, to which he replied, "It's not a financial investment, but a strategic investment."[59]

China was literally ready to go to war over a sovereignty claim that most believe is really over oil rights, and they are building UAVs to use in their arsenal of weapons.

As troubling as the thought might be, the coastal waters off of Canada are also rich in oil, and could attract the same interest.

A deeper analysis of Chairman Zuo Zongshen's statement to the CPPCC offers more clues. For one, he mentioned the use of satellites, but also said that ground information would be needed for an accurate weather assessment. This tells us that China has this capability, which is important to know, because when conducting any seaborne invasion, it's important to have the most accurate weather information possible.

We know that Fengyun meteorological satellites are stationed over the Diaoyu Islands and surrounding areas, and that these satellites continuously carry out meteorological observations, coupled with real-time exchanges of meteorological observation data with many commercial shipping vessels. This set up is certainly sufficient to meet the needs of weather forecasting in the Diaoyu Islands and surrounding seas.[60]

In order to move anything by sea or air, they will need to have a good grip on weather patterns and topography. Not just for "submarines" to calculate what depth to hide, but also because topography and weather data reveals the best time and place to ingress and egress during an attack or infiltration.

Now consider that China already knows that Canada has poor defensive capabilities. Any control they gain along the seaboard, even if it is covert, will aid in any future attempt at conventional use of force. It's called force projection.

We must also consider that Canada relies on the US for assistance, including military protection, and as such, we allow the Americans to enter our water whenever they want. This most certainly is a huge factor in why China wants to position itself along Canada's coast. They see the US as their biggest adversary and the only impediment to their dream of becoming the world's superpower.

From a geographic standpoint, there is a lot going on in the northern coastal area of BC that the public is not necessarily aware of. These little-known factors include a new range of sonar, with investors and foreign entities involved, tied to universities, with scientists on base.

Canadian Forces Base Esquimalt (CFB Esquimalt) is Canada's Pacific Coast naval base and home port to Maritime Forces Pacific and Joint Task Force Pacific Headquarters, only 176 km (109 miles) or 95 nautical miles from Powell River. Sonar experts will tell you that you can hear underwater sound from Hawaii in Victoria.

Float planes are necessary for access to these remote areas. Factor in espionage and access to remote locations using float planes, and it's obvious that you don't just need a company that has a fleet of planes, you need pilots.

A *Globe and Mail* story revealed that the Royal Canadian Mounted Police (RCMP) are investigating three former Royal Canadian Air Force (RCAF) fighter pilots who are training military and civilian pilots in China under the aegis of the Test Flying Academy of South Africa (TFASA).[61] The same thing was happening here with Canadian pilots training Chinese Nationals in Canadian flight schools.

The mosaic was starting to come together.

## STRINGING DATA POINTS TOGETHER

Our investigation into the City of Powell River has tended to expose how the CCP uses tycoons and companies to establish a powerful presence in small towns. All signs point to the frightening possibility that these inroads into remote communities form part of the CCP's broader espionage plans. Having explored these expansionist aims across the aquaculture and aviation industries, we now shift our focus from fish farms, flight schools, and airports back to what we call the ground troops of private education.

Starium Development's owner, Shih-Tao Lu, had his eye on building a Chinese university in Powell River. Shih-Tao Lu already owns a Vancouver-area private school called Eaton College Canada—no relation to the famed Eton in the UK—and wanted to expand into new educational opportunities.

Eaton College Canada specializes in business management, tourism management and hospitality management, among other areas.

There is also Sino Bright High School, a private high school with campuses in China and Vancouver, where international students pay over $22,000 per year for a Canadian education that then makes it easier to apply for citizenship and/or admission to Canadian universities. Sino Bright High School also explored plans to build a private school in Powell River.

They proposed the building of a school on the agricultural land reserve that they hoped would be rezoned, but the deal fell through after a public outcry over possible backroom deals.

Dirk van der Kley is a research fellow at the Australian National University School of Regulation and Global Governance and a former program director for policy research at China Matters, an independent organization that claims to advance sound China policy. In enthusiastic Twitter posts,[62] he confirmed what we already knew, which is that China had, and has, a global education plan. "The PRC govt is now establishing a global set of vocational colleges (think TAFE meets Confucius Institutes)," he Tweeted, with evident support for the idea. "They are housed in local technical colleges, including one in Indonesia (and a bunch elsewhere in the region). There are already dozens globally and more on the way."

He maintains that the schools are simply filling a local need. "China's companies and policymakers are adapting to local demands," he wrote. "They are proving incredibly flexible. If you think it is simply elite capture, it is not."

But this view makes him sound like a CCP apologist, if not a propagandist. The truth is, there is zero local demand for Chinese Schools in Powell River. According to official Powell River statistics,[63] the population stands at around 13,943. Of those, seventy-five residents identify as Chinese. So if demand wasn't coming from within Powell River, what was driving these plans to build new schools for Chinese students in this small BC town? It's easy to see that the tycoons behind these projects were either going to import thousands of international students from China, or had something else up their sleeve.

Mayor Dave confirmed to us that, "they had planned on shipping in the students from China."[64] [65]

Inexplicably, the schools were on hold—for now.

Next, we turned our attention to the business that is the cornerstone of Powell River—their floundering pulp and paper mill, and the reason Powell River exists.

The mill was purchased in 2005 by Catalyst Paper, a company owned by Paper Excellence, which has been headquartered in Richmond, BC, since it relocated there from Europe.

Catalyst is a family-owned business run by the Widjaja family, a Chinese-Indonesian dynasty that founded Asia Pulp & Paper and one of the largest pulp and paper companies in the world.[66]

According to the company's website, Paper Excellence manufactures pulp for the paper and tissue industry, and printing paper, board and packaging, for export to Asia. Meanwhile, Catalyst manufactures 1.3 million tonnes of pulp and paper products, which include pulp, industrial packaging, food service, coated ground-wood, and newsprint.[67]

Shuttered pulp and paper mills in North America have long been a target of Chinese tycoons.

One such company is Nine Dragons, which has been on a global buying spree. It acquired two of Catalyst's pulp and paper mills in the United States for $175 million and an operations center in Dayton, Ohio.

The *Victoria News* on Vancouver Island reported that Catalyst president and CEO Ned Dwyer said the transaction would allow Catalyst to repay a significant portion of its debt, "and focus on our British Columbia operations," which includes the Powell River Mill.[68] This turned out to be not entirely accurate.

In a *New York Times* article about a New England town whose mill was bought by Nine Dragons, many locals speculated that the purchase was all about wanting fiber. "They don't have any," one resident was quoted as saying. "That's the issue in China. They have to get their trees somewhere else."[69]

A statement on the Nine Dragons Paper (Holdings) website gave the game away—revealing that China's multi-national companies are expected to also follow the dictates of the CCP—when it said, "While actively responding to China's Belt and Road initiative, Nine Dragons Paper persists in pursuing international development, while enhancing our production chain."[70]

The buying and shuttering of mills was at least partially about buying up raw material.

Zhang Yin is matriarch of the Nine Dragons Paper empire. She is nicknamed the "Queen of Trash," because she became wealthy by producing corrugated boards out of recycling scrap.[71]

She is also chair of China Overseas Friendship Association and a member of the 10th National Committee of the Chinese People's Political Consult.[72]

The *New York Times* report claimed that the purchase of the mill by Nine Dragons was necessary because the Chinese government implemented its ban on American recycling imports, which in turn jeopardized the supply lines that fed Nine Dragons' business. According to the *Times*, Nine Dragons needed this mill in order to keep its plants running. This is probably partially true, but it is also about fulfilling their duty to the motherland and its Belt and Road ambitions.

Zhang Yin actually confirmed that Nine Dragons was answering Xi Jinping's call of the Belt and Road initiative in an All Federation of Industry and Commerce (ACFIC) propaganda bulletin.[73]

For context, the ACFIC is a non-governmental chamber of commerce for Chinese industrialists and business people under the leadership of the United Front Work Department of the Chinese Communist Party.

Zhang Yin said Nine Dragons' role in the Belt and Road started with the purchase of a mill in Vietnam, and that in order to strengthen the industrial chain and expand upstream resources, the company continues to promote internationalization. This led to the company acquiring four pulp and paper mills in the US in 2018. Zhang Yin said this move was designed to meet raw material needs for the overall Belt and Road plan.[74]

So while it may be partially true that Nine Dragons needed raw material to keep its business running, it's not necessarily because the Chinese government had put in place regulations forcing Nine Dragons to go abroad to acquire raw material. Rather, it's possible that the regulations became a convenient cover to justify the purchase of American mills without disclosing that doing so was to feed Xi Jinping's Belt and Road ambitions.

We know this much—at the re-opening ceremony of the Maine-based acquisition by Nine Dragons, the usual dignitaries attended, including senators and the commercial consul general in New York, Gu Chunfang.[75] Nine Dragons has already made a point of arguing that government regulations were jeopardizing the company's supply lines. But if this was their main issue, why would a representative of the Chinese government attend the ceremony? If Nine Dragons really wanted to operate independently, without influence from the CCP, they had a funny way of showing it.

## A MILL-LESS TOWN DOESN'T MEAN THE GIG IS UP

Going back a few years to 2015, the then-premier of BC, Christy Clark, took a delegation on a trade mission to Asia that included meeting with Zongshen Industry Group, as well as Paper Excellence executives to discuss additional investment opportunities in BC.

Zongshen bought its share in Harbour Air the next year, at the same time that it was actively working with the Chinese government on military drone manufacturing.

Four years later, in 2019, Powell River's main pulp and paper mill, Catalyst Paper, owned by Paper Excellence, sold its Maine Mill in the US to Nine Dragons, a company that declared its intention to work with the Chinese government in implementing the Belt and Road initiative globally. Catalyst justified the sale as a lifeline for the Powell River Mill to stay afloat, but then put it into indefinite curtailment of operations by 2021.[76]

For over a hundred years, the mill had been Powell River's beating heart, its largest employer, and its *raison d'être*. Now it was about to become a mill town without a mill.

There was little information on what the company would do with the prime waterfront land. Mayor Dave told us that while he didn't like that the town's main employer was effectively closing, the owners would still be paying taxes on the land.

In a town that has been the active target of foreign investors with deep ties to China, who have invested in food production facilities, pulp and paper mills, airports, and schools, it gives us pause to consider what the bigger plan might be.[77]

At least one Powell River resident seemed to agree there was something bigger going on.

Local resident Maureen Mason suggested in the Powell River newspaper, *Peak*, that the activity from foreign investors might be part of China's Belt and Road Initiative.

"In my travels, I heard again and again about community plans for the Belt and Road that began with a 100-year lease for airport development, fish farming, deep sea ports and/or waterfront lands," Maureen told the community newspaper.

We wanted to know what Mayor Dave thought of the possibility that the Belt and Road was being covertly brought to small cities that are strategically located near the water and other resources.

He bypassed the larger question focused instead on the individual investors, saying they were all chosen with care, and are capable of maintaining their independence. "I believe that we have been thoroughly careful in getting to know the individuals we have done business with. I would be surprised, based on what I have experienced with them, if those involved in investing in Powell River would have their buttons pressed to push an agenda forward of the CCP's Belt and Road."

He praised the investors, whom he described as full members of the community. "These are people who are interested in our way of life here. The ocean, trees, a place you can raise kids." But Mayor Dave implied that not everyone he met in China would have been an ideal choice for Powell River. "I may have gotten some indication when I went to China of something . . . and I did have some interaction with the CCP government with certain projects that came up from time to time. I felt there was some racism with Sino Bright. These are just individual families that are coming here, yet we refer to them as 'they,' as if they are part of one company."

When pressed, Mayor Dave confirmed that he did in fact meet with CCP officials in China over the airport deal. In fact, he made no real attempt to deny that he had gone to China often in order to broker deals for Powell River in a desperate attempt to keep the town afloat.

Recalling one of his many trips to China, he told us one of the reasons he had to meet with CCP officials there: "They were looking for real estate to expand and wanted to discuss a port to bring containers."

Mayor Dave's opinion on foreign investment was the opinion of the majority. Well-intentioned and welcoming Canadians who still see Canada through the lens of multiculturalism can easily miss what is really going on: the slow and silent invasion that uses multiculturalism as a cover for its slow, hybrid war of real estate deals and corporate mergers, the gateway for a wholesale capture of the host country.

# CHAPTER 15

# CASE STUDY

## THE RISE OF THE PUPPET MAYOR AT GROUND ZERO

*Note: The authors reached out to Mayor Ken Sim's director of communications, Harrison Fleming, multiple times for a response. At the time of publication, they had received no response.*

Ken Sim had just been elected mayor of Vancouver and was attending one of his first public council meetings when he made a strange statement about Vancouver's Chinatown.

"Make no mistake about it . . . a strong, vibrant Chinatown is in our national strategic interests," he told council, then added, "I don't have time to explain why."

This cryptic statement got us thinking. Why would a city mayor, whose job is to fill potholes, greenlight bike paths, and help to build the local economy, focus so intently on a four-block radius within his munici-

PHOTO: Tiger Yuan is a PLA hero and alleged "whale gambler." He participated in a funding event for Vancouver Police.

pality? And why would he say that the area is in Canada's national strategic interests, then decline to say why?[1]

A public statement like this is concerning for a number of reasons. First, there is the fact that Vancouver's Chinatown falls Chinatown is heavily influenced by or possibly under the control of pro-CCP entities with ties to powerful Guangdong business associations and triads. Then there is what has been reported in the media about the nexus between China's political interference in Canada and Vancouver's troubles with money laundering, the city's fentanyl crisis, and organized crime.

This nexus of concerns begs the question: could there be more to Sim's comments than meets the eye? His election campaign was, after all, supported by members of the same Chinatown groups. How far does their influence go?

We wondered if Sim's main election pledge—to create a satellite city hall office in the heart of Chinatown—had something to do with his comments to that first city council meeting. The city framed the satellite office as a necessary step in helping to revitalize Chinatown, which is plagued by anti-Asian graffiti, drug overdoses, and vandalism. Given how much financial support Sim received from pro-CCP interests, we wondered if the satellite office could be viewed as a form of payback. And if so, we wondered, could it be part of a much bigger plan to advance strategic priorities that align with China's national interests?

After all, why build a satellite city hall office a couple of kilometers away from the actual city hall, and why suggest that it is almost exclusively for use by Chinese citizens? Given Vancouver's historical discrimination against Chinese, why separate Chinese from the rest of the citizenry? Supporters of a revitalized Chinatown invoke the need for safe spaces away from anti-Asian racism, but adding separate governing offices within Chinatowns can also stoke tensions by reinforcing divisions between Chinese and non-Chinese communities. To the experienced ear of an intelligence official, creating a space within Chinatown for a satellite city hall office sounds like a CCP tactic to manufacture antagonisms in order to justify some sort of response.[2]

Added to this, questions are increasingly being raised about China deliberately driving much of the social chaos and the amplification of anti-Asian racism in the post-Covid world. And there is widespread concern around China's role in flooding streets with deadly fentanyl. Some have even expressed the view that the fentanyl crisis could be part of a wider chemical warfare strategy to create the very upheaval overseas that United Front organizations are using to back politicians like Sim.

Our undercover sources caught local United Front organizations staging protests against anti-Asian racism just long enough to take photos with Chinese state-owned media. As soon as the media had their main art and their B-roll images, the placards came down and everyone left. So much for impassioned political discourse.

We also recorded Zoom calls in which participants strategized how to retaliate against investigative journalist Sam Cooper, who was reporting on United Front activity and foreign influence. Many involved in staged activities designed to amplify anti-Asian racism are the same individuals who backed Ken Sim's mayoral bid. There was clearly a larger strategy unfolding behind the scenes that probably even Ken Sim was not aware of.

## THE RISE

Ken Sim is the son of immigrants from mainland China and Hong Kong who came to Canada in 1967. He was born and raised in Vancouver and eventually grew up to become a chartered accountant and co-founder of two successful businesses: Nurse Next Door and Rosemary Rocksalt bagels. These ventures have made him a multi-millionaire. By all accounts, Sim is smart and successful, both personally and professionally, and he clearly brought a lot of desirable qualities to the city's top job.

Sim first ran for mayor in 2018, on a pro-business platform, but he lost to ultra-left-leaning professor and former federal MP Kennedy Stewart. When Sim threw his hat into the ring a second time in 2022, it was under the banner of a new, unknown political party called A Better City (ABC). From the outset, Sim's focus was largely on restoring law and order and revitalizing Chinatown. At the same time, his party announced that they would be the first political party in Canada to accept cryptocurrency—a very CCP-friendly announcement, given how many cryptocurrency ventures have been launched in China in recent years.[3]

## COUSIN BERNIE

Despite Sim's strengths as a candidate, there is more to the story of how he became mayor. Part of his success can be traced to local police, developers, and United Front groups that worked together—we say colluded—to put Sim in the mayor's chair. This support likely also included help from behind the Great Wall of China, via Sim's own cousin, Bernard Charnwut Chan, who served as the key advisor to Hong Kong chief executive Carrie Lam during the Anti-Extradition Law Amendment Bill Movement, also known as the 2019 Hong Kong protests. Chan was Hong Kong's law-and-order man, but he is also is a man with a pedigree, and it's one that he would, in all likelihood, have been able to harness to his cousin's advantage.

Bernard's father, Robin Chan, who is Sim's uncle, holds the esteemed role of vice chairman of the All-China Federation of Returned Overseas Chinese (ACFROC), a top-ranking organization in the Chinese Communist Party (CCP)'s United Front network, according to ACFROC's website.[4] In 2018, the Chinese Communist Party transferred responsibility for maintaining relations with Overseas Chinese from the State Council Overseas Chinese Affairs Office (the organization that installed the service center in Vancouver's Chinatown) to the ACFROC.

Ken Sim's law-and-order strategy was eerily similar to that of his cousin Bernard, who advised Lam on how to handle the pro-democracy protests in Hong Kong.[5] There were also many similarities between Bernard's boss, Carrie Lam, who was supported by CCP bigwigs, including Sun Chunlan, who served as the head of the party's United Front Work Department, and those Sim supporters who were members of the Chinese Benevolent Association of Vancouver (CBA).

Although he has denied being a member of the Communist Party of China, Bernard is a big supporter of the CCP. In fact, he positively gushed over them during a forty-minute conversation we had with him for this book.

He even admitted that he met regularly with Xi Jinping during his time advising Carrie Lam on Hong Kong. When asked what they talked about, Bernard would only say that Xi Jinping would encourage him and tell him that he was doing a good job—an apparent reference to Bernard's advisory role during the 2019–2020 riots in Hong Kong.[6]

Just how much influence and advice flowed from Bernard Chan to Ken Sim, whose campaign centered around Chinatown and bringing law and order to Vancouver? Was it just a bit of friendly advice from one cousin to another, or was his role more substantial? Bernard acknowledged that he met with his cousin in Hong Kong in 2018, after Ken's failed mayoral bid. According to Bernard, he worked with Ken on a postmortem of the campaign, and talked to Ken about his planned second run in 2022.

Sim and an ABC majority council won Vancouver's municipal election by a landslide, with 36,139 more votes than incumbent Kennedy Stewart. Sim was immediately announced as the first ethnic Chinese mayor of Vancouver.

Did the new mayor win fair and square? Yes, he did.

Did China interfere in Vancouver's mayoral election? Yes, they did.

Even Canada's spy agency admitted as much in a report by *The Globe and Mail*, referencing a January 2022 CSIS memo that said China's then-consul general, Tong Xiaoling, sought to cultivate pro-Beijing politicians ahead of the municipal election.[7]

So, what's the problem, if Sim won fair and square, and likely would have won with or without the help of CCP proxies in the diaspora and United Front community organizations?

The problem, as we see it from an intelligence perspective, is that Sim was groomed by CCP proxies who have now become the trusted advisors of the new mayor.

As we unpack this case study, you will see that Sim was molded into trusting certain individuals who helped coach him and shape his campaign in a direction that amplified culture wars, and that this strategy, in turn, was used as a way to divide and conquer. By dividing media and the message separately, these influencers were able to create the perception that the entire Chinese diaspora believed that anti-Asian racism was the core problem affecting Vancouver, and that Sim, who was slated to become the city's first ethnic Chinese mayor, was the only one to solve it. The CCP could hold a master class in using identity politics as a tool to destroy democracy. Sim would now be used as a puppet for the CCP, even if he didn't know it.

## DIVIDE AND CONQUER

At a pre-election Chinese-only media roundtable with Ken Sim, reporters from Chinese state media listened intently to the mayoral candidate talk about his lived experience as a young Chinese boy in Canada. He talked about not going to Chinese school because he didn't want to stand out, and about the deed to his first starter home having a race-based land covenant on the property title from way back.[8] [9]

Unexpectedly, Sim apparently broke from his speech to give an impromptu call-out to Tung Chan, who was in the background. "I get to sit here today because I stand on the shoulders of giants," Sim said of Tung, the former CEO of S.U.C.C.E.S.S. and current board member of the Canada Committee 100 Society (CCS100), an NGO started by pro-Beijing journalist Ding Guo. Other board members of CCS100 included Senator Victor Oh, long associated with pro-CCP organizations and activities in the Ottawa region, and Dr. Vincent Cheng Yang, who we spoke to about his role with Operation Fox Hunt.[10]

As with so many of these NGOs, little was known about CCS100. The Chinese version of their website states that they are funded by the government and are dedicated to "promoting the best interests of Chinese community in Canada through knowledge and strategy."[11]

What we do know about the group comes from the anonymously authored Substack newsletter "Found in Translation," which is dedicated to research materials on the CCP's disinformation campaigns and global interference operations.

In April and August 2023, the newsletter published detailed information that revealed that CCS100 founder Ding Guo authored an article in the Chinese language-only *Rise Magazine*, pointing to "a growing trend of criticism directed towards the Chinese community, which he labeled as racism and 'red-smearing' due to the perceived connections between prominent individuals and Communist China."[12] [13]

Meanwhile, fellow CCS100 board member Tung Chan, who Sim gave a shout-out to as his mentor, chaired an online media training session to coach members of the United Front on how to handle questions around connections with the CCP.

One of Project Mosaic's team members sat in on the session chaired by Tung, who used the analogy of a wife beater avoiding detection by declaring publicly that he loves his wife.[14] He suggested that his listeners do the same thing when asked about their connection to the CCP. In a follow-up email asking for clarification by members of our team, Tung stated that he would "rather have the comments stand on their own" than "[try] to clarify them."[15]

Three of the attendees at Tung's workshop—Li Wang (aka Ally Wang), Ivan Pak, and Daoping Bao—deserve special note for their role in starting a collection of non-profit organizations, linked to the United Front, that were set up to attack journalists and politicians who they perceive as criticizing the CCP.

One on these non-profits, MLARA,[16] started by Ivan Pak, has a membership made up of "Canadians who felt unfairly portrayed in an April 30th 2020 Global News report by Mr. Sam Cooper," according to their website. Cooper's story had reported on how the "United Front groups in Canada helped Beijing stockpile coronavirus safety supplies."[17]

Ally Wang even started a petition against the foreign influence registry, and also founded the Canadians Goto Vote Association (ccgtv.org), a group that is sponsored by the Wenzhou Friendship Society, the same hometown association from Richmond, BC, that was being investigated by the RCMP for operating a Chinese police station inside it.[18]

Meanwhile, at Ken Sim's Chinese-only media roundtable, he urged the reporters to "think about our Chinese heritage," and mentioned that "the Chinese built this country," adding, "If it wasn't for the railway, Vancouver and British Columbia would be part of the United States by now." Sim later went on to say that anti-Asian hate crimes were up by over 500 percent. "There is still a lot of issues that we need to address, but I know together we can unite the city and we can address these issues as a society," he told the reporters, adding, "We want to bring the Chinese lived experience to City Hall so we actually have a voice." This from the multi-millionaire mayoral candidate whose voice was already well-established, thanks to his business success and his backers.

Sim then held some break-away interviews with state-run media, in which he emphasized his party's connection to the Vancouver Police and proposed that the problems Vancouver faced with anti-Asian hate could be solved by creating a satellite City Hall office in Chinatown and hiring 100 more police officers for the VPD. It was an offer designed to get the backing of the VPD, who in turn would support Sim and bolster his law-and-order election platform.[19]

## BUILDING A CASE FOR BIG BROTHER

For the first time in Vancouver's history, the Vancouver Police Department's (VPD) union (VPU) would endorse a political candidate. It didn't seem to matter that there might be foreign entities lurking in the background, moving pieces around on the cityscape checkboard.

The police union's president, Ralph Kaisers, didn't respond to our numerous requests for an interview. But he did issue a statement on the website *Safety is a Right*, an organization that claims to be made up of a coalition of concerned citizens, but which was established by the Vancouver Police Union. "Vancouverites don't feel safe in their city," the statement read. "The VPU board and its members are committed to taking action to change that—and if it means getting political, so be it."[20]

Unlike Keisers, Tom Stamatakis, the former president of the Vancouver Police Union and current president of the Canadian Police Association, did respond to us. In an impromptu interview, he suggested that it was unusual for any police union to endorse a candidate or political party. And while he said he wasn't involved in the decision-making process behind the union backing Sim's political campaign, he hinted at other factors that could have driven the decision, including law-and-order issues in Vancouver.[21]

That Vancouver city council is soft on the China threat is one thing, but to have the VPD endorse a plan that gives the CCP a backdoor way to capture ground inside the city, while knowing that CCP influence activity is being reported almost daily in media, is an affront to democracy.

There are three parties in this relationship, though, and the VPD's endorsement of Sim from their union in exchange for 100 officers would only satisfy the VPD and Sim. The United Front wanted something out of this deal as well. After all, the terrible state that Chinatown was in was used as justification for the 100 new police officers, and helped boost Sim's law-and-order brand. Part of that was totally justified. As Jordan Eng, president of the Chinatown BIA, told it, "the neighbourhood's request for increased police is strictly because of the overflow of negative effects from the DTES [Downtown Eastside]," which he described as "social issues" that included "mental health, social disorder, random attacks (mostly on seniors), mischief and vandalism." Some might think the deal struck was a win-win for everyone, but as with everything that the CCP has their handprint on, the devil is in the details.[22]

The city needed a case study to back up the Chinatown revitalization plan that Sim intended to usher in once he was mayor.

So, in August, 2022, before voters went to the polls, the Vancouver Police Foundation paid for a delegation of police, under the leadership of Deputy Chief Const. Howard Chow of the Vancouver Police Department, to travel to San Francisco for a four-day tour of that city's Chinatown, to learn how it was being revitalized, as a model for Vancouver to use. Joining them was a television crew.[23]

We reached out to the executive director of the VPF, Andrea Wright, for more details, including who provided the VPF with the funds for the trip. Wright, whose salary is paid by the Vancouver Police Department, wouldn't reveal who provided the money to send the delegation on the trip, citing the privacy of donors, but did say that the delegation was led and coordinated by the Vancouver Police Department.

Initially, Wright told us that she was instructed by the VPD to refer all questions directly to the VPD, who did not respond to our repeated requests for an interview. If this was just a simple revitalization project, why wouldn't the VPD speak to us about it? Why all the cloak and dagger around cleaning up graffiti and installing potted plants?

When pressed, Wright later admitted that the foundation received a monetary gift of $5,000 from the Canada-China Cultural Communication Association, yet another NGO spin off from members of the commanding-level, United Front-led, CACA.

Some of the events that were held during this excursion beggar belief. There was a dinner, at which People's Liberation Army (PLA) war hero Tiger Yuan made a speech in front of a banner emblazoned with the Vancouver Police logo, and a cheque-issuing propaganda ceremony was held inside the main VPD precinct.

Xue "Kady" Xiaomei, the new leader of CACA and supporter of Sim's first electoral run, handed over the cheque and gave out gift bags, including to a VPD Officer. The group then posed for a photo, clasping their gifts with one hand and making a "show me the money" gesture with the other.

Kady was an upcoming star in the United Front arena, having won a United Front award for service that included bringing the famed People's Liberation Army (PLA) singer Tan Jing to Vancouver to celebrate National Day, under the pretext of it being an "Arts and Culture" celebration. Incidentally, Kady was also involved in holding up anti-Asian racism signs at the fake protest we spoke of earlier, that took place on Dec. 6, 2021 in Vancouver's Chinatown.

As if the cheque-giving propaganda ceremony inside VPD's main precinct were not enough, the Canada-China Cultural Communication Association also created graphics that resembled playing cards, with photos of Chinese elite shown sitting inside a hand that was sprouting hearts.

Below it was the words Donation Recipient and the Vancouver Police Foundation Logo in front of a voter's box.

That the United Front was involved in donating money to the Vancouver Police, likely for use in sending the delegation to San Francisco Chinatown, and that those same donations were used to create propaganda, is an embarrassment of gargantuan proportions. Wright came back to us after all of this was pointed out to her, and said, "In light of recent allegations, and while details are still emerging, the Foundation has decided to return the donation."[24]

Since revitalization of a single area within a city is not typical of what police are mandated to do, and in light of the activity involving the UFWD as the puppet master behind all of this, we could only conclude that the police involvement in the revitalization project, along with the pledge for a new satellite city hall office, was just window dressing for tougher police measures that would include Chinese police-style law and order.

What might these tougher measures look like? In San Francisco's Chinatown, there are security cameras on every street corner. Indeed, the San Francisco Police Department (SFPD) had real-time access to private security cameras through its safe camera program, which they considered a part of their own revitalization of Chinatown. And not just a few cameras, but a thousand cameras, funded by one donor—cryptocurrency mogul Chris Larsen, who reportedly spent around US$4 million to buy them for San Francisco, for what he described as an effort to combat crime.[25]

## THE CHINATOWN DOSSIER

A month after Sim was elected, at the same meeting where he talked about Chinatown being in the Canada's strategic interest, Councillor Sarah Kirby-Yung, wife of VPD and S.U.C.C.E.S.S. CEO Terry Yung, swiftly shepherded in a motion called "Urgent Measures to Uplift Vancouver's Chinatown.[26] The ‚otion instructed city staff to report back with a draft action plan to support urgent measures to uplift Chinatown, including engaging with the VPD and community leaders regarding the San Francisco experience to inform the action plan.

Individuals who went on the trip and came into chamber to voice their support for the revitalization project based on their experience in San Francisco offered us further insight into additional measures that were being considered. As we expected, these proposed changes went beyond graffiti clean-up and new murals. We learned, for example, that the Chinese community police station in San Francisco used WeChat to communicate, and reported issues back to the city.[27] This is a major security risk, since China's Ministry of Public Security took over WeChat's back-end servers for stronger control in 2014. It also blocked all other international social media, forcing overseas Chinese to communicate with their relatives using the App, which is monitored.[28]

But there was a lone wolf of reason at Vancouver City Hall that day, too. Councillor Pete Fry raised the possibility that the revitalization of Chinatown might be coded language to rid the area of homelessness. He put forth an amendment to protect the interests of the area's homeless, many of whom were First Nations. The move was swiftly voted down by the ABC-majority council. The new millionaire mayor later offered an explanation for why he voted against the motion. Speaking directly at Pete, Sim said, "Chinese live in Chinatown, and you didn't mention Chinese . . . the only reason I didn't support the motion is that the amendment didn't acknowledge that Chinese people live in Chinatown."[29]

We were getting major Trojan horse vibes. Chinatown was Sim's first order of business; the UFWD was involved in funding pre-election trips; and things were moving at breakneck speed. All of this seemed like a primer for some far more worrisome agenda driven by the CCP.

As one unnamed source who works in the BC government and who has been used as an intel source for CSIS told us, "the CCP considers Chinatowns around the world as an important part of the broader national and global network of Chinatowns that they can use to create a mini–People's Republic of China outside of China."

## THE PIECES ARE FALLING INTO PLACE

Six months into his job, Mayor Sim and the mostly ABC Council intro-duced the new City Hall office in Chinatown. It was aptly named Won Alexander Cumyow (溫金有), after the former president of the Chinese Benevolent Association—the same organization that threw its weight behind Sim's election campaign.[30] The name was put forth by Mayor Sim and Councillor Lenny Zhou, who claimed in city documents that they relied on Civic Asset Naming Committee and a reserve list of names—even though the Civic Asset Naming Committee was no longer active and had been replaced by the Street Naming Committee, which had yet to meet once during Mayor Sim's time in office.[31]

This was the same name that ACCT, the NGO that Senator Woo and his wife started, wanted for the new redesign of the $5 Canadian bank note.[32] Liberal MP Han Dong petitioned the Bank of Canada for this name, and it probably would have been selected if not for a February 24, 2023 report by Global News that claimed to have sources with knowledge of CSIS intelligence gathering, that said Dong was an alleged "witting affiliate" in China's election interference networks in Canada. According to the Global report, CSIS even had a code name for him—"Scarecrow." Han Dong denied the allegation and left the Liberal caucus to sit as an independent MP.[33] [34] Once again, readers should note that Han Dong has filed an action against Global News and Sam Cooper for their reporting. Both Global and Cooper stand by their reporting based on their sources.

Confidential sources with intimate knowledge of closed-door meetings and off-book backroom chit-chat have told us that China's consulate is pushing for the adoption of a ward system that would effectively turn Chinatown into a semi-autonomous zone similar to the special administrative region (SAR). This is similar to what Ken's cousin Bernard was in charge of running in Hong Kong.[35]

At face value, a ward system sounds good. Residents vote for their area representative, and those representatives vote on all council motions (mayors are still elected at-large). Local government in action, right? But the ward system is only as good as the people and systems that drive it. Vancouver's Chinatown is controlled by the Chinese consulate in Vancouver, through pro-CCP United Front organizations. Turning Vancouver's Chinatown into a ward would effectively mean giving China a seat on city council and awarding substantial government funding to allow them to do what they want to. China would legitimately be operating a shadow government inside Canada's borders.

A Chinatown ward would be further strengthened by Chinatown's UNESCO (United Nations Educational, Scientific and Cultural Organization) world heritage status application, initiated years earlier during Gregor Robertson's decade-long reign. The pursuit of UNESCO designation came from a recommended in a Historical Discrimination Report (HDC) to Vancouver City Council in 2017. The report also recommended that a public apology be made to Hilbert Yiu, former Chinese Benevolent Association chairman. Coincidentally or not, also in 2017, Hilbert was selected as a delegate to the Chinese People's Political Consultative Conference, a political advisory body in the People's Republic of China and a central part of the Chinese Communist Party (CCP)'s United Front system.

For the public apology, Hilbert stood on a platform in the middle of a crowd while Vancouver City Council apologized to him. The event was live fed back to China via state-owned national television broadcaster, China Central Television (CCTV). For insight into this dramatic set up, we reached out to Baldwin Wong, who is the multicultural social planner for the City of Vancouver, and ultimately the person in charge of this apology. Baldwin didn't really answer our question about why an apology was being made through a live feed back to China, but did say that the city was alive to the possibility of foreign interference with the event, and that the city was surprised by the level of interest from Chinese media.[36]

The UNESCO application piggybacked off of the "Official Apology" to Chinese as one of the recommendations put forward by the Historical Discrimination Against Chinese People in Vancouver Committee's (HDC) final report, which included the commitment to pursue a UNESCO World Heritage Site application for Vancouver's Chinatown.

China is now one of UNESCO's largest governmental funding sources and is using the organization to cultivate soft power. Seeking a UNESCO designation for Vancouver's Chinatown was a bold move that would concentrate power in one area and provide a degree of administrative autonomy apart from the municipality and government. They could grant themselves the freedom to define their own rules, security, and manage their own budget without government interference.

This would be not dissimilar to the National Autonomous University of Mexico (UNAM), which has a portion of its main campus in Mexico City but which is also a UNESCO world heritage site. UNAM obtained administrative autonomy from the Mexican government—creating a mini-autonomous zone within a city that allows them to govern themselves, free of interference.[37] [38] [39]

Even without a special zone of protection around Chinatown, Canada was kowtowing to China at the demands of the same powerful pro-Beijing individuals and groups from Chinatown that backed Sim. This was reminiscent of events from 2020, when Canada's minister of health, Patty Hajdu, along with then-Mayor Kennedy Stewart, and BC's health minister, Adrian Dix, agreed to a roundtable discussion at the start of the COVID-19 pandemic with a group called ICCONBC Business Association and members of the Chinese Benevolent Association of Vancouver (CBA).[40] [41]

Following the roundtable was a press meeting that included Chinese community police center director Alex Wang, who also runs a couple of high-end restaurants under Peninsula Canada Holding Group. The company even boasts of being supported by the Chinese consulate: "Since Its establishment, it has been strongly supported by the Chinese Consulate General in Vancouver, the BC Government, and the Guangdong Provincial Government."[42]

Also at the roundtable and press meeting was S.U.C.C.E.S.S. CEO Queenie Choo, Hilbert Yiu, and his martial arts understudy, Paul Tam, who is the head of ICCONBC. The Liberal Party of Canada was a client of Paul Tam's company, Intelli Group, and Paul was a personal friend of the minister of defense at the time, Harjit Sajjan. Sajjan even attended Tam's wedding. It shouldn't be surprising, then, that ICONN board member Wilson Miao, who was also in attendance that day, later became a federal Liberal MP.

They were all there that day to demand that special tax benefits be granted for Chinese restaurant businesses, exclusively, because COVID-19 had, in their opinion, resulted in misinformation about the origins of the pandemic, which led to a 70 percent drop in business. "The nature of our conversation was about the impact COVID-19, the coronavirus outbreak, is having on their business, their organizations, and the fear and misinformation that is rampant online," said Hajdu to local Vancouver reporters that also included a Project Mosaic team member. For two years we tried to find out from the Ministry of Health if select groups were given special dispensation, but we were blocked every step of the way.

The United Front, on the other hand, had the power to get Canada's health minister to travel from Ottawa to Vancouver for a special private meeting in the middle of a global health crisis. And they had enough influence to convince the government to issue a public statement at a press conference with the mayor of Vancouver and the provincial health minister present, to talk about the impact of Covid-19 on the Chinese business community exclusively. Then they boldly stood there, unified, with a message that essentially admonished Canadians for fearing Covid 19, and demanded special tax breaks based on ethnicity. If the United Front was able to accomplish all of this without possessing any sort of administrative autonomy within Canada, how much further might they go if they do manage to succeed in carving out a little island of administrative autonomy inside Vancouver's Chinatown? Should this ever happen, they could effectively make even greater demands on the Canadian government as the representative of Overseas Chinese—bearing in mind, once again, that China sees permanent residents as Chinese nationals under their authority.

Should Vancouver's Chinatown be granted a semi-autonomous zone, it could be the slippery slope that allows the CCP to wield even greater power and influence over Canadian politics than it does now. Chinatowns are not just places for fruit vendors and trinket shops, restaurants and massage parlours; today, they offer a foothold for a Chinese Communist Party whose official mandate is to become the preeminent world power by 2049. Canadians should be deeply suspicious of any move to establish any version of an autonomous zone inside Vancouver's Chinatown, and should resist all such efforts.

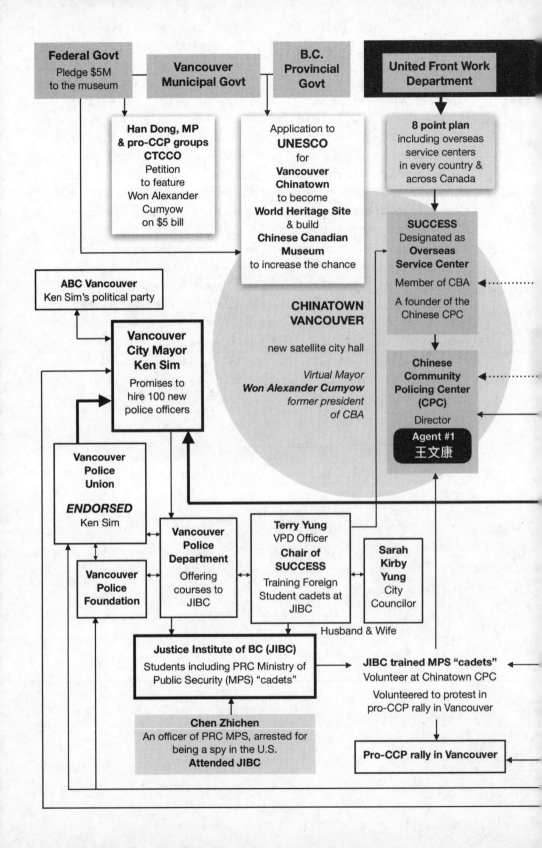

# RISE OF A PUPPET MAYOR
### Data flow diagram of CCP's influence of election to gain control of an area

## PRC CONSULATE (VANCOUVER)

## HKSAR

Commending
level organization

**Chinese
Benevolent
Association of
Vancouver
(CBA)**

Former Chair

**Agent #23**
姚崇英

A founder of the
Chinese CPC

Commending
level organization

**Canadian
Alliance of Chinese
Associations
(CACA)**

**Bernard Chan**
Hong Kong Deputy
to National People's
Congress

**Family of Mayor
Ken Sim & Advisor**

His father
**Robin Chan**
is former
Vice Chairman of
All-China Federation
of Returned
Overseas Chinese
(ACFROC)

**Wenzhou
Friendship
Society**

**Secrete Police
Station**

→ **CPC MPS "cadets"
volunteers**
Volunteer at PRC
Consulate

**Teochew Society
of Vancouver**

**Vote support
for Ken Kim**

Hon. President
for Life

**Agent #20**
馮汝洁

**Canada-China
Cultural
Communications
Association
(CCCA)**

President
**Tiger Yuen**

Financial
sponsorship &
voter support for
police endorsed
candidate

**Tiger Yuan**
People's
Liberation
Army
"Hero"

| 13.加拿大 (24名)： | | | |
|---|---|---|---|
| 1 王文康 | 7 王吉林 | 13 王典奇 | 19 王家明 |
| 2 文伟建 | 8 乐晓春 | 14 邝健民 | 20 冯汝洁 |
| **Agents dispatched to Canada** | 3 许健伦 | 9 孙瑞娟 | 15 李景辉 | 21 肖楚强 |
| 4 余卓文 | 10 沈 毅 | 16 陈德光 | 22 林广场 |
| 5 林性勇 | 11 郑小玲 | 17 段律文 | 23 姚崇英 |
| 6 贾 明 | 12 高如东 | 18 郭泰诚 | 24 薛金生 |

# EPILOGUE

Our goal with *The Mosaic Effect* has been to create awareness around the complexity of the hybrid war that the PRC under the control of the CCP has been waging against the West.

With the CSIS-RCMP probe, code-named Project Sidewinder, and the US led Operation Dragon Lord, as a sort of guide to the collection and research we conducted; We laid out the CCP's strategic battleplan to gain control over Canada and other nations. A master plan that is meant to infiltrate, destabilize and disrupt Canada's neighbour to the south, the United States. This involves a wide range of antidemocratic activities including psyops and the spreading of propaganda, expansive information operations, economic subversion, political influence and leveraging, as well as working with transnational organized crime groups.

The *Project Mosaic* team has been empowered by the countless heart-rending accounts from Chinese Canadians who came to Canada to escape the long reach of the CPP only to have Canada's institutions fail them.

One team member painted a grim picture of her family's sufferings during China's Cultural Revolution. Once persecuted by the Red Guard for being landowners, the plundering tormentors later transitioned into the lap of luxury, working under the CCP's banner. "They were tormented and murdered by the Red Guard for being landowners in China during the Cultural Revolution. These Red Guards and their families ended up working for the CCP government — possibly as a reward. Now they (Red Guard) are living their best lives."

---

PHOTO: Canadian politicians (circled) stand at attention while China's national anthem is sung.

# EPILOGUE

Today, similar maneuvers are being played out across Canada, only instead of Red Guards, it's the United Front Work Department (UFWD) and hometown associations who have been marshalled into action by the CCP, all managed by China's consular officials and China's intelligence, security and secret police apparatus installed in the West.

Here, instead of landowners being tormented and murdered, the CCP is hunting Chinese dissidents in the open with the help of Canadian authorities under China's Operation Fox Hunt. One objective is to stop their activism under the hidden pretext of returning corrupt Chinese nationals to China to face criminal charges. On a more subversive level, they are killing off Canadians with deadly fentanyl and pricing Canadian's out of access to adequate and affordable housing as a way to 'destabilize' peace and stability and undercut Canada's democracy.

Despite warnings from the Canadian Chinese diaspora years ago, the fallout of all this is only now being realized by the West.

Nicholas Eftimiades, a former CIA official and subject matter expert on Chinese espionage tactics, told the CBC's Alexander Panetta, "From my perspective it's like, "Welcome to the party, Canada. You've woken up", "it's amazing it's gone on so long."

We couldn't agree more. But what are Canadian politicos willing to do about it? Especially since many of the same politicos are engaged in quid pro quo arrangements with China's proxies involving donations to local hospital foundations, business improvement associations, and even police foundations. Cash starved small towns and isolated regions rich in resources have been prime targets for the CCP. We have insight into several backroom deals with significant geo-political impact that have escaped scrutiny. And the ultimate shocker that might play into why the Canadian government hasn't addressed our problem with China -- you can run for elected office in Canada and be an active member of the CCP at the same time.

Canadian Prime Minister Justin Trudeau eventually reacted to months of public outcry and called a public inquiry into foreign interference as well launching public consultations for a potential foreign influence registry.

Led by the Honourable Marie-Josée Hogue, puisne judge of the Quebec Court of Appeal. Justice Hogue is mandated to examine and assess interference by China, Russia and other foreign states or non-state actors, including any potential impacts, to confirm the integrity of, and any impacts on the 43rd and 44th federal general elections (2019/2021) at the national and electoral district levels.

By limiting the inquiry to 2019 and 2021 elections the inquiry will miss the opportunity to expose the real corruption that has gone on for decades prior to these elections. What won't be discussed is the free two-hour training class for new Chinese immigrants held by former Liberal MP Raymond Chan prior to 2019. Chan was also the Secretary of State for the Asia-Pacific Region for the Department of Foreign Affairs and International Trade during the time that a former public servant and whistleblower, Brian McAdam, said there was a visas-for-sale cover-up scandal that may have resulted in hundreds of criminals entering Canada illegally.

The same can be said about cash-for-access events predating 2019, where attendees with connections to the Chinese Communist Party (CCP), would pay up to $1,525 per ticket to meet the incumbant Prime Minister, Justin Trudeau.

What's more, the true scope of what the RCMP and CSIS could say in an inquiry will not be available because the inquiry will be in-camera, as it is classified, and nothing substantive will inform the public or be recorded.

Trudeaus rival, law and order candidate, Pierre Poilievre, capitulated to Trudeau's diversion and weak attempt at a single solution to a multi-facetted and extraordinarily complex threat. A sure sign of an equally meager level of understanding of the threat by Poilievre and the Conservatives but a signal that the issue is truly non-partisan.

A foreign influence registry will also be ineffective in fighting foreign interference if the end result only includes listing foreign principals with obvious direct links to the Chinese government. This is because United Front organizations typically register new NGOs in Canada even though they take direction from the Chinese consulate or other CCP entities. Chinese companies also often use nominees and straw people who are Canadian citizens or permanent residents for that extra veneer of trust and to open doors.

If Australia's foreign-influence registry tells us anything, it's that it has been a complete failure for the same reasons. Moreover, the US Foreign Agents Registration Act, or FARA as it is known, is equally toothless with its mandatory compliance and lack of any tangible enforcement.

If Canadians want real change, we need to demand that our policy makers address the internal inadequacies within our institutions and government Ministries. Overlooking the rot at the root of the problem will only amplify China's Canadian footprint and victimize the Chinese, Hong Kong, and Taiwanese diasporas even further.

Jody Chan from the Alliance Canada Hong Kong (ACHK), a national collective of pro-democracy Hong Kong ex-pats in Canada, poignantly captures this sentiment. Underlining the diaspora's longstanding concerns and the urgency for systemic redressal Chan told us, "Foreign influence by the PRC is not new. The diaspora has been raising concerns since the 90's. While it's good that more attention is being paid to this issue, there is a risk that we're chasing after individuals' incidents, partisan interests and breaking news without addressing actual systemic failings in our institutions. Our society remains vulnerable and in need of effective measures to counter foreign interference."

No single government Ministry has failed Canadians as much as *The Ministry of Immigration, Refugees and Citizenship Canada* and its predecessors.

While some may find a fair balance between their allegiance to the Motherland and living in Canada. We can't help but see a correlation between Canada allowing Nazi's to immigrate to Canada after WWII, at the expense of Jewish Canadians, and letting CCP members and allies into Canada at the expense of Canadian Uyghurs and Chinese dissidents who fled to Canada believing it to be a safe haven – unfortunately, it isn't.

We know this because attempts to deal with Canada's growing national security problems have been quietly shutdown. Canada harbours known terrorist entities, like the IRGC and Quds Force. Our justice system can't even put people away for large scale money laundering. Especially after the Supreme Court of Canada ruled that mandatory significant transaction reports that must be sent to FINTRAC, which operates under the Proceeds of Crime, Money Laundering and Terrorist Financing Act, do not apply to law firms owing to Solicitor-client privilege.

The simple fact of the matter is that China is a threat nation, and we need more out of our law makers to restore public trust and protect our sovereignty.

Investigating and writing *The Mosaic Effect* has been a long journey but it only marks the beginning of Project Mosaic's work in exposing the CCP's operations in the West. We have in development, a thrilling spy documentary that exposes the very espionage activity discussed in this book. Only with much more detail and live footage. This book should have made you critically aware of China's hybrid war in Canada, but if it hasn't our accompanying documentary film certainly will.

# AFTERWORD

BY MICHEL JUNEAU-KATSUYA

When we examine the actions of the Government of the People's Republic of China (PRC) and the work of its intelligence services, we arrive at a singular conclusion: they are formidable adversaries. Such an international organization, with its numerous advantages, should not be underestimated. To dismiss or fail to recognize this threat is sheer ignorance, naivety, or deliberate deception. Regrettably, throughout my 40-year career, I've encountered all three of these attitudes from our Canadian political elite.

To ensure success, the PRC's political structure provides it with significant advantages.

China's most significant asset is **TIME**. They have the luxury of time because the dictatorship in China doesn't face elections every four or five years to ensure **continuity in their political life. This, coupled with their CENTRALIZED** PLANNING process, steered by either the Central Committee or the Standing Committees tied to the Communist Party, reinforces a potent centralized chain of command. Furthermore, they have **PEOPLE**. The vast numbers of people employed, willingly or not, to serve their intelligence aims have been challenging the imagination of the Western government and counterintelligence agencies. It's not just intelligence officers but a vast population of travellers, businesspeople, students, academics, and ordinary folks they have coerced or enticed into cooperation.

Their intelligence methodology, known as the "mass collection process," implies that everyone is and will be used as an informant or soldier. This strategy was employed during the Korean War in the early 1950s, using human waves against allied defences. China was not as advanced in terms of technology for its weaponry, but it had a lot of volunteers. So, it used human wave after wave to overcome the Allied lines of defence. Today, the same strategy targets the heart of Western democracies. Their ancient **CULTURAL EDUCATION** shapes the mindset of all Chinese individuals, enabling the Chinese Intelligence Services (CIS) to elevate the concept of "guanxi" into an art. They grasp the essence of **INFLUENCE**, having authored the seminal work, *The Art of War* by Sun Tzu, over 2,000 years ago. No one applies its teachings better than the Chinese Government today.

The authors of the Mosaic Effect have provided invaluable service to Canada and leaders worldwide. The Chinese Government's and the CIS's influence isn't limited to one nation but spreads globally. The book offers a thorough chronology of the CIS's infiltration into Canadian society, detailing their extensive efforts over decades to establish their agents and spread influence across political, economic, academic, and media spheres, thus embodying a ravaging Hybrid War against all democracies.

This book also highlights the Chinese Government's comprehension of the **power of dependency**. They've enslaved generations of political and business leaders by creating an addiction to PRC resources and promises. While it's not surprising to see a nation exert influence over rivals, witnessing major corporations and Prime Ministers succumb is distressing. Some might argue that such actions border on treason.

Presently, Canada, and by extension other Western democracies, face a stark reality: China has been outmaneuvering them for decades. They are poised to exert control, aided by willing domestic and international collaborators.

The world's democracies stand at a crucial juncture. The reach of the PRC and CIS is so extensive that no single nation can resist on its own. China will steadily and effectively expand its control without a united and determined effort to challenge them. Their motto, "Divide and conquer," is executed with remarkable efficacy. While the sentiment "States do not have friends, only interests" has often been true, it has frequently led to undesirable outcomes due to its short-term foresight. The current scenario evokes memories of the revelations by Igor Gouzenko in September 1945. His exposure to the Soviet spy network led to over 50 years of Cold War tensions, proxy conflicts, and political games, costing countless lives. But the Western world was in disbelief when the Gouzenko affair presented its explosive revelations. It took a while before the assessment of this important threat and its implications were fully understood. Have we learned anything from that?

Supported by revelations from Australia, the USA, Great Britain, and now Canada, the authors have unveiled the monumental threat posed by Beijing. If Western allies don't unite against this threat, their sovereignty is at risk.

For Canada, it's time to prioritize national security. Evidence suggests that from Prime Minister Mulroney onwards, all Prime Ministers have been compromised or chosen to be wilfully blind to PRC interference for personal or partisan reasons. This negligence is not only a recent development. Historical decisions have had lasting ramifications for the country's security posture. For instance, the creation of the Canadian Security Intelligence Service (CSIS) has been controversial since its inception, to say the least. Some argue that its establishment was less about bolstering national security and more about deflecting attention from the alleged wrongdoings of Prime Minister Pierre Elliot Trudeau.

CSIS's specific structure and role have come into question over the years. Unlike traditional law enforcement agencies, CSIS was stripped of all its policing power at its inception. Currently, its reporting is limited to the Government, allowing the incumbent Prime Minister to use or misuse the intelligence as they deem fit. This structure hasn't served Canada's best interests. It's alarming that CSIS cannot even adequately warn companies or the general public about the threats the nation confronts. Upon CSIS's creation, there was a strict directive preventing its officers from testifying in any court of law. This has led to the agency consistently refraining from providing essential support and evidence to the RCMP in critical cases. Notable examples include the bombing of Air India, the failed arrest of Ahmed Ressam, the espionage case of Jeffrey Delisle, and the legal debacle involving Adil Charkaoui, to mention a few.

Given these challenges, urgent reforms are needed. A law explicitly addressing foreign interference and its associated penalties must be swiftly introduced. The current legal framework leaves entities like the RCMP ill-equipped to protect the various ethnic groups that are targets of foreign nations. Given CSIS's limitations, it might be prudent to consider returning the mandate and budget for national security back to the RCMP. This would be akin to how the United States relies on the Federal Bureau of Investigation (FBI) for similar responsibilities. The overarching goal should be to enhance Canada's security apparatus, ensuring it can meet the diverse challenges of the modern era. But let's not forget that its success has been directly linked to the help received by the actions or lack thereof by our political elite. Parliamentarians must address the command and reporting structure as well as its mandate for the sake of national security.

This book elucidates the strategies and operations the Chinese Government and CIS have deployed to influence democratic nations. Its insights are crucial in anticipating and countering this formidable foreign influence while guiding democratic leaders around the Globe in safeguarding their countries and citizens.

David Choi from the Canadian led National Congress of Chinese Canadians (NCCC) meets Xi Jinping the "Friendship of Overseas Chinese Associations" COEA and COFA, which merged in 2019, are UFWD front groups. China uses 'friendship associations' to extend influence among overseas elites.

© *Conference for Friendship of Overseas Chinese Associations / Communist Party of China (CPC)*

Ran Wanxiang, Vice Minister of the United Front Work Department of the CPC Central Commitee talks with David Choi of the Canadian led National Congress of Chinese Canadians (NCCC). Many high-ranking CCP officials have visit Canada to inspect operations being conducted in Canada.

© *Lahoo.ca*

**CHINA'S UNHOLY TRINITY:** From left to right: **MP Joe Peschisolido**, Canadian politician; **Tiger Yuan**, Peoples Liberation Army; **Tom Yongpeng** (aka Tom Yang), real estate tycoon; **Paul King Jin**, alleged gangster and money launderer.

Since leaving politics Raymond Chan became a fundraiser for Justin Trudeau and the Federal Liberal Party. Seen here is Raymond Chan and the Chairman of the Zhejiang Overseas Chinese Federation. He also taught classes to new immigrants on how to recruit other new immigrants to vote for the Liberal Party and in particular, Justin Trudeau.

CREDIT: *All-China Federation of Returned Overseas Chinese*

The CBA is a commanding level organization in Canada listed on the United Front Work Department of the Zhongshan Municipal Commitee of the Communist Party of China website.

**RIGHT:** Bill Yee, a retired provincial court judge, member of B.C.'s Chinese-Canadian Advisory Commitee, and past president of the Commanding-level Chinese Benevolent Association (CBA), requested that UBC remove the statue.

*Courtesy of UBC Archives / Erwin Wodarczak*

加拿大溫哥華 **中華會館** 一九〇八年成立
**CHINESE BENEVOLENT ASSOCIATION OF VANCOUVER**
108 E. PENDER ST., VANCOUVER, B.C. CANADA V6A 1T3  TEL. (604) 681-1923  Established 1908

January 23, 1991

Dr. David W. Strangway
President's Office
The University of British Columbia
6328 Memorial Road
Vancouver, B.C.  V6T 2B3

Dear Dr. Strangway,

It has been reported that your University has approved the application by some people who proclaims to support democracy in China to place a Goddess of democracy statue in the Campus.

Our Society has resolved unanimously in the last Board meeting to submit the following for your consideration:

(a)  The Park Board has already rejected a prior similar application made by the group because of the massive opposition in the Vancouver Chinese Canadian community.

(b)  The presence of a statue of this kind in the campus does nothing positive to the viewers who normally see it other than to remind them of an incident in Beijing.  On the other hand, the presence of such a statue would definitely deter any and all visits by officials and/or friendly delegations to the University.  It should be pointed out that despite what may have happened in Beijing a year and a half ago, our Federal Government has not severed its relations with China, just as the City of Vancouver has not broken its sister-city relations with Guangzhou; and your University has not rescinded its twining relations with Chungshan University.

(c)  Most of the people in our community believe that it is really up to the people in China to deal with the incident of June 4, 1989.  If democracy is the concern for them, then they should decide on the form and degree of democracy that they should have and they are the only ones that should work out the time-table for the process to take place.  It is our position that for anyone else outside to China to get involved in those kinds of decisions really gets very close to be interfering with another country's affairs.  How would we Canadians feel if the people in China put up a statue in China for the purpose of highlighting the injustice done to the Chinese Canadians due to the head Tax and the Chinese Exclusion Act?

(d)  If the aims and objectives of the applicants in this instance is to promote more democracy in China, it would seem only logical that the forum for their efforts should be in China, not Canada and definitely not in a setting such as yours.

..../2

---

Dr. David W. Strangway
Page 2
January 23, 1991

Finally, we would like to inform you that we are strongly opposed to what the group is trying to do and we have many community organizations and individuals who share the same views as we do.  It is hoped that you would consider what we have submitted very seriously and if needed, our Society would be happy to arrange a delegation to appear before you to sepak to this matter.

We thank you for your attention in this matter.

Yours truly,

Yee
President

Mw/tt

cc. Chancellor, Dr. Lesie R. Peterson
    Board of Governors - Chairman Kenneth Bagshaw

First museum exhibit the Chinese Canadian Museum. Museum director, retired judge, and advisor to the Premier of BC, Bill Yee, claimed Uyghur genocide in China are 'lies' according to media reports.

© *Ina Mitchell*

United Front allies have made great strides in gettng assigned to projects where they have an advisory role, job as political aide, or appointed to government commitees; from here they have reshaped Canadian historical narrative in relation to China.

© *Ivy Li*

Announcement made in China on CCP government website announcing that wealthy businessman Jin Pingliang spent ¥60 million (about CAD$10 million) to buy the Greater Vancouver Zoo.

CREDIT: *Zhejiang Federation of Returned Overseas Chinese*

The Greater Vancouver Zoo is neighbour to the Royal Canadian Navy's primary communications relay site for Maritime Forces Pacific. The owner of the Zoo, Jin Ping Liang, is a National Commitee of the Chinese People's Political Consultative Conference (CPPCC) member. In the background on a shelf is a book on "FBI Psychological Influence."

Aerial Map of the Aldergrove receiving site is the Royal Canadian Navy's primary communications relay site for Maritime Forces Pacific. It is close to the USA border and shares space with USAF HAARP Bounce Station. The Zoo owned by Jin Ping Liang, a National Commitee of the Chinese People's Political Consultative Conference (CPPCC) member is seen in proximity to the site in this map.

MAP DATA: ©2023 Google / Astrium, Maxar Technologies

Commanding-level org. "Chinese Benevolent Association of Canada" has been co-opted by Beijing friendly members in recent years. They are listed as on United Front websites in the PRC.

New east-west United Front strategy in Canada calls for the establishment of a Canada-wide propaganda communication system as part of an eight-point consensus agreement between the two east and west hubs.

CREDIT: *CACA / WeChat*

Liang Muxian is a former agent for the CCP's United Front is seen escorted from Tenth Church in Vancouver, BC where she was praying for students protesting in Hong Kong. The church was surrounded by pro-CCP students, many of whom studied at the Justice Institute of BC (JIBC), and also volunteer for the local Chinese consulate as well as at the Chinese community police station in Vancouver.

© *Ina Mitchell*

**"THE LIST":** All-China Federation of Returned Overseas Chinese (ACFROC) list of agents dispatched around the world. These agents are often engaged in influence operations under the pretext of 'culture'. These agents have had remarkable success in gaining access to high levels of government. Seen here is Mayor of Vancouver (2008-18), Gregor Robertson, Harjit Sajjan Minister of National Defence (2015-21) and Prime Minister of Canada, Justin Trudeau, with two agents on the list (#20 and #23). The PRC Consul General from China in Vancouver is also in both photos.

© *Ina Mitchell Atribution for website: All-China Federation of Returned Overseas Chinese*

**#13 ON THE "LIST":** Wang Dianqi President of the Canada Chinese Peaceful and Unification Association. Wang Dianqi supports Beijing's annexing Taiwan by force, and has donated C$400,000 to China's military

CREDIT: *CACA / WeChat*

**INSET:** Front page of Vancouver Province shows alleged money launderer Paul King Jin and a headline that he was given standing at the Commission of Inquiry into Money Laundering. **UNDER:** Website screen grab of Commission of Inquiry into Money Laundering in British Columbia shows Paul King Jin in British Columbia through his lawyer. Interrogating officials thought by many to be a form of intimidation through proxy.

**ESPIONAGE GAMES:** On December 1, 2018, CFO of Huawei, Meng Wanzhou was arrested at Vancouver International Airport on extradition to USA. The USA charged her under bank and wire fraud, as well as conspiracies to commit such, in relationship to financial transactions conducted by Skycom, which had functioned as Huawei's Iran-based subsidiary, in violation of U.S. sanctions. **ABOVE:** Seen here is video still of Meng Wanzhou doppelganger in a video created by a new security firm that was seeking government approval for a license to operate a personal guard and private investigation services based at Paul Kin Jin's gym in Richmond, BC. Was this a message being sent to the Canadian Government? **BELOW:** The real Meng Wanzhou, CFO of Huawei.

CREDIT: *Video screen gab / Blackcore Security*

**LEFT:** S.U.C.C.E.S.S. board of directors holds meeting with PRC Consul General and various consular officials including consul in charge of United Front activities in the province of BC. The PRC Consulate has a significant amount of control over S.U.C.C.E.S.S. even though it is funded by the Canadian Government.

S.U.C.C.E.S.S. runs an Overseas Chinese Service Center that is part of the United Front—the Communist Party's domestic and interNational influence apparatus.

CREDIT: *S.U.C.C.E.S.S.*

**BELOW:** The RCMP investigating Chinese 'police' stations in Canada. More than 50 exist worldwide, including 3 in Greater Toronto Area. On the west coast of Canada, the Wenzhou Friendship Society operates one. China also operates a center under the pretext of it being a community police center providing translation services to all of Vancouver's Chinese diaspora. Seen here is Chief Constable Adam Palmer, COM, of the Vancouver Police with CCPC volunteer Guang "Eileen" Chen who is also an events coordinator for the Chinese Consulate. She was an assistant for ex-Liberal MP Joe Peschisolido.

*Images: CCPC / © Ina Mitchell / Eileen Chen-WeChat*

Chen Zhichen was a police cadet who received training at the Justice Institute of BC (JIBC) in 2017. Did she return back to China after being trained in Canada or was she dispatched to the US? The FBI arrested Zhichen as an alleged Chinese agent in 2023 along with others. Charged with working inside the US to silence dissidents.

China's police cadet students seen in shirts with image Panda and Nutria, from the Justice Institute of BC (JIBC) have been issued orders by the Chinese Consulate to engage in pro-Beijing protesting against pro-democracy activists in Canada. They also provide security at consular events. These cadets also volunteer at the Chinese Police Center in Vancouver's Chinatown.

**REVEALING CONNECTIONS**: 1) PRC Consular Officials; 2) JIBC instructor; 3) Wenkang Wang (#1 on "The LIST") is the father of Alex Wang, a director with the Chinese Police Center in Vancouver. Seen in insert with Chief Constable Adam Palmer, COM, of the Vancouver Police.

Hu Jun is the president of the hometown association, the Guizhou Association of Canada and designer of Panda and Nutria image custom designed for the Chinese Consulate in Vancouver. Seen here are pro-Beijing protestors outside the Vancouver Consulate. The same protestors that circled Tenth Street Church. As an artist, Hu Jun is known for hosting and engaging in United Front exchanges related to culture and art related to his city, Burnaby, BC.

**COVERT GLOBAL OPERATION:** Operation Fox Hunt reveals Chinese Nationals in other countries escorted off planes with hoods on their heads. Their capture aided by overseas police, mobile Chinese police, and other 'asset' recovery experts. Propaganda photos show Police Officer, Yin Zehuan, who is a member of the Operation Fox Hunt mobile team of the Ministry of Public Security is seen exhausted in the hospital and on train as he hunts for humans.

Vice President Xie Yuan met with Mr. Duncan McIntosh, Executive President of Canada China Friendship and Goodwill Association (CCFGA) on Oct. 31, 2016.

**INFLUENCE OPS:** Duncan McIntosh, partner of the Premier of P.E.I., Wade MacLauchlan (2015–19), set up a proxy united front NGO called the Canada China Friendship and Goodwill Association (CCFGA). The CCFGA falls under the umbrella of the Chinese People's Association for Friendship with Foreign Countries (CPAFFC); a united front organization in the united front system used to influence and co-opt political and industrial elites to promote the interests of the Chinese Communist Party (CCP) while downplaying its association with the CCP. Seen here is background image is Duncan and Frank Zhou meeting with VP of CPAFFC in 2016.

**INSET:** In 2018, while Wade was Premier of PEI, he took part in an Atlantic Canadian leader's summer gathering where elite leaders influence each other's ideas on regional and global matters. Seen in photo are attendees, President Bill Clinton (1993-2001), Premier Wade MacLauchlan (2015-19), Duncan McIntosh, and UK Prime Minister Tony Blair (1997- 2007).

The Premier of BC, John Horgan (2017–22), meets with Xu Minghua who has held a variety of top-ranking positions connected to the Politburo of the Chinese Communist Party, including the Zhejiang Provincial Supervision Commission. In 2018, Duncan McIntosh, partner of PEI's Premier at the time, arranged a meeting between Xu Minghua and Premier Horgan. Officially, the BC Government did not mention the meeting with Xu Minghua. Instead, they only mentioned Mr. Wen Zhang, Director of the Foreign Affairs Department for Oceania and The America's for the Province of Zhejiang, China.

© *Province of British Columbia / Flickr*

**CONFLICTING ALLEGIANCES:** MP George Chow, Minister of State for Trade in BC joined in a celebration of the new Shantou Overseas Talent Work Liaison Station together with fellow United Front agents Hilbert Yiu and Franco Feng. The purpose of talent stations is to take talent from Canada for the purpose of Xi's great rejuvenation of the Motherland.

**"THE LIST" — Franco Feng:** Franco, while living in Canada, made it clear that his priority was admited that he was going to introduce more overseas talents, and continuously work to advance technology and talents for the purpose of helping build Shantou's' infrastructure." The Thousand Talents Plan, this was one of Franco Feng's commitments as a United Front agent to the Motherland. **INSET:** Franco with then Director of the OCAD of the United Front Work Department (UFWD) of the Chinese Communist Party (CCP).

CREDIT: *WeChat*

**"THE LIST" — Grant Lin:** Grant Lin is a real estate developer responsible for large sections of Richmond's' condo skyline. One time vice-chair of S.U.C.C.E.S.S. and chair of China's only United Front University. Grant is listed as a united front agent on "List". He is seen here with Qiu Yuanping, director of the Overseas Chinese Affairs Office of the State Council (OCAO) and Conservative MP, Alice Wong.

*Atribution: WeChat*

Sherman Jen is owner of Maple Leave Education Systems and philanthropist, donating to local universities in Canada. He is an active participant in Chinese People's Political Consultative Conference (CPPCC), which is a political advisory body in the People's Republic of China and a central part of the Chinese Communist Party (CCP) United Front System. Maple Leaf Schools provide education to overseas Chinese Nationals.

CREDIT: *Maple Leaf Educational Systems*

### 2022 Canada Mitacs Undergraduate Internship Cooperation Scholarship Selection Notice

According to the Memorandum of Understanding between the China Scholarship Council (hereinafter referred to as the China Scholarship Council) and Canada's Mitacs on co operative undergraduate internships, in 2022, the China Scholarship Council will send 200 outstanding undergraduate students to Canadian universities for scientific research intern ships. The relevant matters are hereby notified as follows:

**1. Basic requirements for applicants**

(1) Support the leadership of the Communist Party of China and the path of socialism with Chinese characteristics. love the motherland, have a sense of responsibility to serve the country, the society, and the people, and have a correct world outlook, outlook on life, and values.

(2) Have a good professional foundation and development potential, have outstanding performance in work and study, and have the professionalism and sense of mission to ret urn to China after graduation to serve the country's construction.

(3) Have the nationality of the People's Republic of China and do not have the right of permanent residence abroad.

(4) Applicants must be at least 18 years old at the time of application (born before January 1, 2003), and will be a full-time third-year student of a four-year undergraduate progr am in a "double first-class" university after September 2021, or a five-year undergraduate student fourth graders.

**ABOVE AND RIGHT:** MLA Teresa Wat seen here giving a scholarship to a student on behalf of the Chinese government. An MoU between China Scholarship Council Canada's Mitacs requires all applicants to support the Communist Party of China.

**LEFT:** The Chinese Students and Scholars Association (CSSA) has a student association at every major campus in North America. They have been co-opted by the CCP and are active in carrying out overseas Chinese operations consistent with Beijing's United Front strategy. Local PRC consulates fund these activities as well as control these interNational students through government sponsorships. PRC Consular officials also control the student's movement in exchange for services. The photo shows students at TRUCSSA goose stepping on campus.

CREDIT: *TRUCSSA*

**BELOW:** Canadian Senator Victor Oh personally presented Queen's Jubilee medals and certificates to a group of united front compatriots. Numbers correspond with images on right where they attended official Chinese government and CCP-inspired events.

Map of major active Canadian and US Navy bases, stations and other facilities in close proximity to a State controlled research center located in remote area of BC's west coast.

MAP DATA: *©2023 Google / Astrium, Maxar Technologies*

**TOP:** Mayor Ken Sim with tycoon and philanthropist, Johnny Fong (CTG Brands Inc.) Reports from Chinese media Ken Sim is said to have congratulated the first council of the Teochew Federation for supporting his election win.

© *Ina Mitchell*

**MIDDLE:** Bernard "Bernie" Chan was the Hong Kong Deputy to National People's Congress of the People's Republic of China advising Carrie Lam. Hei s the cousin of Ken Sim, Mayor of Vancouver. Bernard is a "Patron" of the China–United States Exchange Foundation (CUSEF), an organization that is a central part of the Chinese Communist Party's united front strategy of influence in the U.S. CUSEF is classified as a "foreign principal" with the Foreign Agents Registration Act (FARA).

© *Bernard Chan*

**BOTTOM:** Mayor of Vancouver, Gregor Robertson (May 17, 2005 – July 15, 2008)

© *We Chat*

**BELOW:** Images surfaced showing Edward Hong Tao, a frequent associate of the PRC Consulate and Mayor Ken Sim. Photos also show him holding his hands in a "pay me" symbol at Vancouver Police HQ. As well as a graphic of a voter box together with the Vancouver Police Foundation logo. The Vancouver Police Union endorsed Mayor Ken Sim, who promised one hundred new officers.

**INFLUENCE OPS:** All three levels of government capitulated to the demands of the united front during the middle of Covid epidemic: (Center Front from L-R) Mayor of Vancouver, Minister of Health for Canada, Minister of Health for the Province of BC. Seen in background from left to right is Paul Tam, owner of Intelli group whose client is the Liberal Party of Canada. He is also on the ICONNBC. Paul was the understudy of Hilbert Yiu who is a leader with the commanding level CBA and united front agent. Alex Wang is on the board of directors of the Chinese Community Police Center. In front of him is Queenie Choo, CEO of S.U.C.C.E.S.S. which is tied to the police center as a founding organization.

PRIME MINISTER · PREMIER MINISTRE

**10th Anniversary of the Quanzhou Friendship Society**

It is with great pleasure that I welcome you to the celebration of the 10th anniversary of the Quanzhou Friendship Society.

Since its establishment in 2006, the Quanzhou Friendship Society has dedicated their efforts towards establishing deeper trade and cultural ties between Canadian and Chinese business communities, as well as providing community support for those Canadians who proudly trace their roots to the city of Quanzhou. Trade and investment links between Canada and China will undoubtedly grow in the coming years, which is why organizations like the Quanzhou Friendship Society are necessary to ensure that our economic relationship is forged on a stable, strong, and mutually beneficial foundation.

Tonight, we gather to celebrate the achievements of the Quanzhou Friendship Society and recognize the contributions of those who have a connection with Quanzhou. This community organization has not only supported vital links within our Chinese-Canadian community, but has also deepened the connections between Canadians of all backgrounds.

Thank you to the organizers of this amazing event and to all of you who are present tonight. Please accept my warmest welcome and best wishes for a successful night.

Ottawa
2016

**(ABOVE) MURDER:** Wu Shumin was a leader with the Quanzhou Friendship Society. She was seen at events that mixed members of her hometown association, consular officials and Canadian politicians. Wu Shumin was seen here with Malcolm Brodie, Mayor of Richmond. She had organized crime connections and was murdered in 2022. She is seen here with the Mayor of Richmond at a United Front event.

**LEFT:** Letter from Justin Trudeau, Prime Minister of Canada to the organization Wu Shumin was a leader of. Political letters and certificates are often used by the United Front to legitimize operations.

# APPENDIX

## OPERATION DRAGON LORD SUMMARY AND APPENDIX 1.4

**FOIA Request**
36850.42443 HUDACK DRAGON LORD - CHINESE INVOLVEMENT IN U.S. OR CANADA

The Operation Dragon Lord (ODL) Appendix 1.4 extracts were provided to the authors by a former Canadian crown prosecutor. According to the document, ODL was a Department of Justice operation which involved multiple US agencies. Part of the report focused on the 'Unholy Trinity.' The task force needed to better understand the potential impact on US national security. Both the United States and Canada were the targets for the operation.

The summary indicates multiple agencies provided information and toe on to thank both Canadian and Australian agencies for their help and participation in the report's findings. 5 Eyes regularly shared data amongst partners. As for the ODL Summary, we had passages reviewed and confirmed by Canadian intel analysts who shared their own observations and data with the US regarding the Unholy Trinity at the time of the operation, which commenced in 1998.

The full report is archived in the CIA's public vault directory. To our knowledge, no one except those on the task force has read the full report.

Various media and interested parties have the Freedom of Information Act (FOIA) requests previously starting in 2001. Our most recent requests have yet to be answered.

## APPENDIX 1.4-------Extracts from 'DragonLord'

```
Operation: Dragon Lord
(Section 14-12 to 14-18)
Ref: FBI- C-3467034 C-34671 14
C-271 1002
C-271 1333
C-271 1174
Ref: NSA- Requires requisition
C-3467 122
C-3467035
C-271 1467
C-271 1003
```

(U.S.J.D.T.S.) Section 14-12: Foreign Advances (Canada)
Power Corp, Chairmen Paul Desmarais (see attachcd FBI bio. C-3467034)
Peter Munk (see attached FBI bio. C-3467122) Jack Austin (see attached
FBI bio. C-3467114) re: (China Canada Busines Council. Desmarais/Munk
export and development within China include gold mining and
transportation sales connection to Chincse Pulp investment (British
Columbia) and high level introductions. Further introduction and
devclopment in high tech market sector (see section 16-9 this report)
and media development. (U.S.T.S.)


(U.S.J.D.T.S.) Section 14-13: Foreign Advances (Canada)
Power Corp., President Andre Desmarais (see attached FBI bio. C-
3467035)
associated as board membcr to China International Trust & Investment
Corp. (CITIC) Pacific. Wang Jung (see attached FBI bio. C-27 11002),
chairman CITIC subsidiaries include Norinco And Polytechhologies (see
scetion 7-4 this report) Identificd Arms/marketer/smuggling. Robert
Kuok
(see attached FBI bio. C-271 1467) associate Lo Hsin Han (see attached
FBI bio. C-271 1333) have directed investments as per this association.
Desmarais/Chtretien relationship (see Section 14-22 this report) allows
for extraordinary influence at administrative levels. (U.S.T.S.)

)U.S.J.D.T.S. ) Section 14-14: Foreign Advances ( Canada )

OPERATION DRAGON LORD


With the rapid and sensational demise of the Soviet Union, the focus of
intelligence agencies in the United States began to shift in the mid to
late 1990s.

While the Communist threat dissipated in Eastern Europe as regime afler
regime fell in quick succession, U.S. intelligence agencies and the
U.S.
Justice Department were mandated to concentrate their intelligence
gathering efforts and pro secutorial energies increasingly on China's
Communist regime.

This coordinated effort marked a new and exciting era of co-operation between the agencies involved. That spirit of cooperation and mutual respect has propelled and marked the entire Dragon Lord investigation.

Drawing on the extraordinaiy and unrivalled resources and manpower of several U.S. intelligence and law enforcement agencies, including thc Ccntral Intelligence Agency, the National Security Agency, the Defense Tntel ligence Agency, the Federal Bureau of Investigation and others, a taskforce was struck in January, 1998 to investigate the ties between the PRC, its intelligence agencies, and ethnic-Chinese criminal gangs known as triads.

The central and guiding directive of the taslcforce, led by the U.S. Justice Department, was to investigate and report on the multi-faceted threat posed, but not limited to, vital U.S. national security interests
by the political and criminal nexus emerging between PRC military intelligence and ethnic-Chinese triads.

Earlier, intelligence agencies in Canada and Australia produced reports of a similar naturc, which were shared with taskforce members. These reports provided a useful and authoritative foundation for the work of the taskforce.

During the research and writing of this report, Canadian and Australian intelligence officers were repeatedly consulted and provided critical information which helped guide our understanding of the nature and scopc
of the threat posed by what we have called: China's unholy trinity.

A deep debt of gratitude must be paid to our brethren in Canada and Australia for their extraordinary assistance in the writing of this report.

THE UNHOLY TRINITY

China's unholy trinity, the marriage between PRC intelligence agencies, triads and influential Chinese business tycoons, pose a real, clear, and
mushrooming threat to U.S. Canadian and Australian security interests

This is the central and undeniable finding of this study.

This threat manifests itself, the taskforce found, in sometimes insidious ways. Indeed, the insidious nature of these powerful relationships often proved difficult to hurdle
when mapping out how far the tentacles of the trinity reached into U.S.,
Canadian and Australian politics, business, media and financial institutions.

Nonetheless, we found that the trinity's reach is now deep-rooted and wide-ranging.

For example, a detailed examination of contributions to established federal and state political parties in the U.S., Canada and Australia, found that triad-controlled firms have repeatedly made generous donations to high profile, and often-successful political candidates.

Triad controlled financial institutions have also successfully
engineered control over some of the key lcvcrs of the U.S., Canadian
and
Australian economies. In particular, triads, working in concert with
high-profile Chinese expatriate businessmen, have assumed control of
dominant media and financial institutions in the U.S. and Canada.

This, in turn, has permitted Beijing to exercise some control over the
assets and revenue of these institutions in return for immunity from
prosecution for triad leaders, who are deeply involved in the
multi-billion dollar drug and people smuggling trade.

Of serious concern, is the growing presence of the trinity in military
related industries in the U.S., Canada and Australia. Intelligence
reports indicate that PRC controlled businesses and triads have worked
in tandem to flood North American markets with relatively cheap
automatic weapons.

Moreover, PRC intelligence have exploited their triad ties to
successfully intimidate and recruit foreign Chinese nationals employed
in sensitive military related industries to illegally obtain highly
classified information about weapons of mass destruction.

While these worrying relations can bc demonstrated, the insidious
nature
of the Chinese threat has, in the past, encouraged a sense of disbelief
among senior intclligence and political officials who are often
confronted with sometimes ambiguous evidence pointing to the trinity's
activities in North America.

Regrettably, this has allowed even well documented intelligence to be
summarily dismissed as so-called "conspiracy theories." Chinese
authorities, anxious to deflect attention away from the growing power
of
the trinity, have welcomed these misguided assessments and used them to
disparage and undermine other attempts to reveal their intelligence
operations.

But by employing human and signals intelligence gathered particularly
by
NSA and CSE, access to higher than top secret reports on key Chinese
figures who havc bcen instrumental in engineering the trinity, and the
successful infiltration of key triad organizations, has permitted us to
brcach the wall of secrecy which previously thwarted efforts to chart
the trinity's far-reaching influence.

That stealthy influence is infecting and eroding the key financial and
political underpinnings of U.S., Canadian and Australian society and
therefore poses an unprecedented and powerful threat that needs to
addressed, monitored, and where possible, must be dismantled.
CANADA - THE TRINITY'S GATEWAY TO THE WORLD


Another major and undeniable finding of this report points to the
worrying and potentially destabilizing presence in Canada of the
Chinese

trinity.

Canadian Security Intelligence Service officers have long fretted over
the trinity's growing influence and presence in their country.

At first. Canadian intelligence officials believed that the trinity was
using Canada as a fertile, and easily accessible testing ground for its
operations. Rut now, regrettably, it is apparent that Canada has become
the gateway for the trinity's operations throughout North America.

Exploiting Canada's lax immigration laws, border patrols, and generous
social welfare system, triad leaders and their associates have been
able
to establish a well nourished base of operations in Canada.

As such, Canada has now become one of the pre-eminent security concerns
of the U.S. government.

Triad organizations have established operations in large Canadian
cities, which border the U.S. and offer these criminal gangs easy
access
to major U.S. cities and financial institutions, to promote their
illicit activities.

The Royal Canadian Mounted Police launched several undercover
operations
in the early 1 990s to infiltrate triad organizations operating in
Canada. And in the late 1990s attempted to set up a task force with
CSIS to monitor thc brcadth of the trinity's operations in Canada. The
task force, unfortunately, was not established. This was a missed
opportunity.

The Dragon Lord taskforce has, in effect, picked up that fallen baton.

Aggressive and long-overdue steps must be taken by U.S. authorities,
including the U.S. Justice Department, State Department and
intelligence
officials within the executive branch to make it abundantly clear to
their counterparts in Canada that the U.S. government can no longer
tolerate such a threat emanating principally from within Canada's
borders.

The trinity's flourishing operations in Australia must also be
addressed
swiftly.


THE COMING WAR

The threat posed by the Chinese trinity to U.S. national security
interests cannot be underestimated.
It is not an overstatement to suggest that the very security and
stability of America's financial and political system will, in large
measure, be tested by our resolve to combat the trinity's growing
strength.

To date, there has been too much delay and prevarication. The time is

ripe for the U.S. government to attack, not by using traditional weapons
of war, but to mount a broad, well-financed intelligence and law-enforcement campaign to infiltrate and dismantle the trinity's operations, particularly in North America.

The campaign must be fought the same resolve and determination that has always defined America when it wages war. And make no mistake, this is a
war.

Our failure to attack will cost America and Americans dearly. The time to act is now.

# ACKNOWLEDGEMENTS

*E tenebris lux*

The authors would like to thank all those who have contributed to this book in many ways from inspiration to expert insight, research, and more. We thank you:

- The 4th pillar of democracy-media; for giving us a voice and platform to create public awareness on the issue of hybrid warfare.
- The nameless operatives of the intelligence services who worked in the shadows, risking their livelihoods for their guidance and support as we wrote this book.
- OSINTers and translators for digging in and finding data most people did not believe existed.
- All of the people interviewed and quoted for their openness and honesty in giving their perspectives and experiences including pro-democracy activists, victims of the Chinese Communist Party (CCP), and agents and allies of the United Front Work Department of the CCP.

A special call-out to the following people:

Calvin Crustie, Carolyn Bartholomew, Anne-Marie Brady, Cory Bernardi, Charles Burton, Tom Blackwell, Daphne Bramham, Kim Bolan, Michael Chong, Garry Clement, Gordon Chang, Bernard Charnwut Chan,

# ACKNOWLEDGEMENTS

Anders Corr, Sam Cooper, Nicholas Eftimiades, Bethany Allen-Ebrahimian, David Eby, Dave Formosa, Richard Fadden, Gerry Groot, Omid Ghoreishi, Peter German, Clive Hamilton Alex Joske, Jan Jekielek, Tasha Kheiriddin, Michel Juneau-Katsuya, Philip Lenczycki, Bethany Lindsay, Catherine Lévesque, Ivy Li, Finn Lau, Natalie Liu, Kirk LaPointe, Brock Martland, Bob Mackin, Scott Newark, Jonathan Manthorpe, Mareike Ohlberg, Michael Pompeo, Cleo Paskal, Alexander Panetta, Doug Quan, Benedict Rogers, Nathan Ramos, Graeme Smith, Lieutenant-Colonel Jennifer Stadnyk, Bob Stewart, Fenella Sung, Judy Trinh, David Vigneault, Christopher Wray, Graeme Wood, Emily Weinstein, Bob Young, RS, M, H, LP, P, TJ, BR, LM, CB and the Project Mosaic Investigation Team.

♡ to our family and friends for their patience and understanding.

Sincere gratitude to our editor "L" and our publisher Dean Baxendale for his enduring commitment to ensuring democracy by going where few would in order to make this world a better place.

Appreciation to the following organizations for their assistance; Global Affairs Canada, The Canadian Security Intelligence Service (CSIS), The Federal Bureau of Investigation (FBI), The Department of National Defence, Canadian Armed Forces, Project Seshat.

# ENDNOTES

## INTRODUCTION

1. Government of Canada, Public Safety Canada, "Foreign Interference and Hostile Activities of State Actors," Feb. 25, 2021, https://www.publicsafety.gc.ca/cnt/trnsprnc/brfng-mtrls/prlmntry-bndrs/20210625/08-en.aspx.

2. David E. Pozen, *The Mosaic Theory, National Security, and the Freedom of Information Act*, 115 Yale L. J. 628 (2005). Available at: https://scholarship.law.columbia.edu/faculty_scholarship/573.

## CHAPTER ONE

1. This 1999 document was given to us by a highly credible source, and the information in it has recently been corroborated by a former CSIS agent with direct knowledge of the US operation. The document has been assessed as not coming from the operation itself. Support for the information contained in the document can be found in Five Eyes files, the declassified Sidewinder report, and testimony provided to the US government by experts on the threat emanating from the CCP. The actual Dragon Lord report is believed to be archived in the CIA's public vault directory. To our knowledge, only those on the task force have seen the report. Our attempts to acquire the report through freedom of information requests have been unsuccessful.

2. Michel Juneau-Katsuya, appearing before the Special Committee on Canada-China Relations, Parliament of Canada, House of Commons, 43rd Parl., 2nd sess., April 19, 2021, https://www.ourcommons.ca/DocumentViewer/en/43-2/CACN/meeting-23/evidence.

3. Gerry Shih, "China's Backers and 'Triad' Gangs Have a History of Common Foes. Hong Kong Protesters Fear They Are Next," *Washington Post*, July 23, 2019, https://www.washingtonpost.com/world/asia_pacific/chinas-backers-and-triad-gangs-have-history-of-common-foes-hong-kong-protesters-fear-they-are-next/2019/07/23/41445b88-ac68-11e9-9411-a608f9d0c2d3_story.html.

4.   Frederic Dannen, "Partners in Crime: Gangs of Hong Kong," *New Republic*, June 14, 1997, https://newrepublic.com/article/90738/partners-in-crime.

5.   Peter Beaumont, "Stanley Ho, Flamboyant 'Godfather' of Macau Casinos, Dies Aged 98," *Guardian*, May 26, 2020, https://www.theguardian.com/business/2020/may/26/stanley-ho-the-billionaire-macao-casino-tycoon-dies-aged-98.

6.   Don Butler, "The McAdam File: Bribery, Chinese Gangsters and Betrayal," *Ottawa Citizen*, November 18, 2016, https://ottawacitizen.com/news/local-news/the-mcadam-file-bribery-chinese-gangsters-and-betrayal.

7.   Don Butler, "Jobless and Devastated: Brian McAdam's Grim Reward for Blowing the Whistle," *Ottawa Citizen*, Nov. 18, 2016, https://ottawacitizen.com/news/local-news/jobless-and-devastated-brian-mcadams-grim-reward-for-blowing-the-whistle.

8.   Jeff Sallot and Andrew Mitrovica, "Mounties Blamed CSIS for Sanitizing Sidewinder," *The Globe and Mail*, May 6, 2000, https://www.theglobeandmail.com/news/national/mounties-blamed-csis-for-sanitizing-sidewinder/article18422995/.

9.   Sallot and Mitrovica, "Mounties Blamed CSIS for Sanitizing Sidewinder."

10.  The original Sidewinder report can be found at various sites online, including https://www.primetimecrime.com/Articles/RobertRead/Sidewinder%20page%201.htm and https://www.scribd.com/document/34328956/Chinese-Intelligence-Services-and-Triads-Financial-Links-in-Canada.

11.  Judi McLeod, "In Canada Spies Are Us," *Canada Free Press*, Jan. 26, 2005, https://canadafreepress.com/2005/cover012605.htm.

12.  Cleo Paskal, "In U.S. Backyard: How China Embedded Itself in Canada," *Sunday Guardian*, Jan. 2, 2021, https://www.sundayguardianlive.com/news/u-s-backyard-china-embedded-canada.

13.  Jonathan Manthorpe, *Claws of the Panda: Beijing's Campaign of Influence and Intimidation in Canada* (Toronto: Cormorant Books, 2019).

14.  Konrad Yakabuski, "Like Father, Like Sons?" *The Globe and Mail*, May 26, 2006, https://www.theglobeandmail.com/report-on-business/like-father-like-sons/article25677391/.

15.  Manthorpe, *Claws of the Panda*, pp. 127–28."

16.  "Some Politicians Under Foreign Sway: CSIS," CBC News, June 22, 2010, https://www.cbc.ca/news/politics/some-politicians-under-foreign-sway-csis-1.909345.

17.  "What Richard Fadden Told the CBC," *The Globe and Mail*, June 25, 2010, https://www.theglobeandmail.com/news/national/what-richard-fadden-told-the-cbc/article4322968/.

18.  "Chinese-Canadians Demand Explanation from CSIS Head," CTV

News, July 2, 2010, https://bc.ctvnews.ca/chinese-canadians-demand-explanation-from-csis-head-1.528698.

19. Wendy Stueck, "Chinese-Canadians Request Meeting with CSIS Head," *The Globe and Mail*, July 2, 2010, https://www.theglobeandmail.com/news/british-columbia/chinese-canadians-request-meeting-with-csis-head/article1212147/.

20. https://royalpacific.com/realtors.html/davidchoi/.

21. *Report on Canadian Security Intelligence Service Director Richard Fadden's Remarks Regarding Alleged Foreign Influence of Canadian Politicians* (Report of the Standing Committee on Public Safety and National Security, March 2011), https://www.ourcommons.ca/DocumentViewer/en/40-3/SECU/report-8/.

22. Xinhua, "Xi meets representatives of overseas Chinese," *China Daily*, Updated May 28, 2019, http://www.chinadaily.com.cn/a/201905/28/WS5ced49c9a3104842260be51f_1.html.

23. Wikidata, "China Overseas Friendship Association (External name of the 9th bureau of the United Front Work Department)," Accessed Aug. 23, 2023, https://www.wikidata.org/wiki/Q97159112. See also: "Gathering the Hearts of Overseas Chinese, Bringing Overseas Chinese Power, Xi Jinping Talks about 'Overseas Chinese,'" China News Network, Sept. 27, 2019.

24. See, for example, Catherine Fiankan-Bokonga, "A historic resolution to protect cultural heritage," *The UNESCO Courier*, October–December, 2017, https://en.unesco.org/courier/2017nian-di-3qi/historic-resolution-protect-cultural-heritage. See also Ien Ang, "Chinatowns and the Rise of China," Modern Asian Studies 54(4):1-27, December 2019, https://www.researchgate.net/publication/337872400_Chinatowns_and_the_Rise_of_China.

25. Zhuang Guotu, "The Overseas Chinese: A long history," April 2021, *The UNESCO Courier: Many Voices, One World*, https://en.unesco.org/courier/2021-4/overseas-chinese-long-history.

26. City of Vancouver, *Chinatown Transformation: Cultural Heritage Assets Management Plan (CHAMP) Strategic Framework and UNESCO World Heritage Site Process*, RTS No. 13710, June 2022, https://vancouver.ca/files/cov/chinatown-cultural-heritage-assets-management-plan.pdf.

27. Central Radio and Television Station, "Talk about overseas Chinese work in this way with 'overseas Chinese' bridge," May 30, 2019, Central Video Station, Central Radio and Television Station, Accessed Aug. 14, 2023, https://www.gqb.gov.cn/news/2019/0530/46213.shtml.

28. Steven Chase and Robert Fife, "CSIS head tells MP Michael Chong that he and family were targeted by China," *The Globe and Mail*, May 2, 2023, https://www.theglobeandmail.com/politics/article-csis-confirms-mp-michael-chong-and-family-targeted-by-china/.

29. Spencer Van Dyk, "Chong says it's 'astonishing' that PM never saw re-

ports of foreign threats to an MP," CTV News, May 7, 2023, https://www.ctvnews.ca/politics/chong-says-it-s-astonishing-that-pm-never-saw-reports-of-foreign-threats-to-an-mp-1.6387600.

30. Canadian Press, "Decision on Chinese diplomat being made 'very, very carefully:'Trudeau," CBC News, May 7. 2023, https://www.cbc.ca/news/politics/trudeau-china-diplomat-expulsion-decision-1.6835193.

31. Embassy of the People's Republic of China in Canada website, "Remarks of the Spokesperson of the Chinese Embassy in Canada," May 4, 2023, http://ca.china-embassy.gov.cn/eng/sgxw/202305/t20230505_11070695.htm.

32. Government of Canada, Statement from Global Affairs Canada, "Canada declares Zhao Wei persona non grata," May 8, 2023, https://www.canada.ca/en/global-affairs/news/2023/05/canada-declares-zhao-wei-persona-non-grata.html.

33. Philip Lenczycki, "Dems Cry 'Racism' After DCNF Bombshells Expose Rep. Judy Chu and Biden Appointee's Ties to Alleged Chinese Intel," Daily Caller News Foundation, Feb. 24, 2023, https://dailycaller.com/2023/02/24/gooden-chu-jeffries-goldman-krishnamoorthi-schiff-tiffany-lamalfa-dominic-ng/.

34. https://twitter.com/LenczyckiPhilip/status/1631476625497022465?s=20.

35. Bethany Allen-Ebrahimian, "Meet the U.S. Officials Now in China's Sphere of Influence," *Daily Beast*, Jul. 23, 2018, Updated Nov. 21, 2018, https://www.thedailybeast.com/meet-the-us-officials-who-now-lobby-for-china.

36. Hadley Newman (2022), *Foreign information manipulation and interference defence standards: Test for rapid adoption of the common language and framework 'DISARM,'* (PDF), Nov. 29, 2022, p. 60. ISBN 978-952-7472-46-0 – via European Centre of Excellence for Countering Hybrid Threats. Accessed Aug. 29, 2023, https://stratcomcoe.org/publications/foreign-information-manipulation-and-interference-defence-standards-test-for-rapid-adoption-of-the-common-language-and-framework-disarm-prepared-in-cooperation-with-hybrid-coe/253..

37. Bob Mackin, "NDP Incumbent George Chow's Silence Alarms Anti-CCP Human Rights Campaign," theBreaker.news, October 18, 2020, https://thebreaker.news/news/horgan-chow-united-front/.

38. Kelvin Gawley, "Liberal Richard Lee Drops Out of Burnaby South Election, as Wife Faces Illness," *Burnaby Now*, May 16, 2019, https://www.burnabynow.com/local-news/liberal-richard-lee-drops-out-of-burnaby-south-election-as-wife-faces-illness-3099836.

39. Sam Cooper, "B.C. Politician Breaks Silence: China Detained Me, Is Interfering 'in Our Democracy,'" Global News, November 29, 2019, https://globalnews.ca/news/6228973/b-c-politician-richard-lee-china-detained-interfering-democracy/.

## CHAPTER TWO

1.    Embassy and Consulates General of the People's Republic of China in Canada–2011-04-26, http://ca.china-embassy.gov.cn/.

2.    https://www.canadianaffair.com/blog/how-big-is-canada/.

3.    Graeme Wood, "Huawei-Sponsored Event Draws Flag-Waving B.C. Politicians," *Business in Vancouver* (*BIV*), October 5, 2021, https://biv. com/article/2021/10/huawei-sponsored-event-draws-flag-waving-bc-politicians.

4.    Philip Lenczycki, "Dem Rep Listed As 'Co-Chair' Of Yet Another Non-profit With Ties To Chinese Communist Party, "Rep. Judy Chu accepted a letter of appointment from UCCC in December 2014," Daily Caller News Foundation, April 16, 2023, https://dailycaller.com/2023/04/16/judy-chu-ufwd-ccp-uccc/.

5.    Bob Mackin, "Alleged foreign police station a major concern for Richmond, country, says councillor," BIV, Dec. 11, 2022, https://biv.com/article/2022/12/alleged-foreign-police-station-major-concern-richmond-country-says-councillor.

6.    The term commanding-level organization simply refers to an organization that oversees other, subordinate organizations in a hierarchical network.

7.    Susan Lazaruk, "Lytton has played an important role in the history of British Columbia," *Vancouver Sun*, July 2, 2021, https://vancouversun. com/news/local-news/lytton-has-played-an-important-role-in-the-history-of-british-columbia.

8.    British Columbia, government website, "Building the Railway," undated story within the "Chinese Legacy BC" page, https://www2.gov.bc.ca/gov/content/governments/multiculturalism-anti-racism/chinese-legacy-bc/history/building-the-railway#:~:text=Chinese%20railway%20workers%20were%20brought%20by%20ship%20from,the%209%2C000%20rail-way%20workers%2C%206%2C500%20were%20Chinese%20Canadians.

9.    Tessa Vikander, "All 1,600 artifacts in Lytton's Chinese history museum destroyed by fire 'can't be replaced,'" CTV News Vancouver, July 5, 2021, https://bc.ctvnews.ca/all-1-600-artifacts-in-lytton-s-chinese-history-museum-destroyed-by-fire-can-t-be-replaced-1.5496262.

10.   Maryse Zeidler, "Wildfire that decimated B.C. town was likely human-caused, says official," CBC News, July 4, 2021, https://www.cbc.ca/news/canada/british-columbia/lytton-fire-likely-human-caused-1.6089991.

11.   Black Press Media Staff, "B.C. Chinese community raises over $50,000 for museum destroyed in Lytton fire," Saanich News, March 31, 2022, https://www.saanichnews.com/news/b-c-chinese-community-raises-over-50000-for-museum-destroyed-in-lytton-fire-313372.

12.   Canadian Alliance of Chinese Associations website, "Liden [sic] was devoured by the fire, and the joint emergency donation rescued the victims," 2021, Accessed Aug. 23, 2023, https://ca-ca.ca/zh/news/2021/464-litton-

was-engulfed-in-fire,-and-the-caca-made-an-emergency-donation-to-help-the-victims.html.

13. Ritchie B. Tongo, "Taiwan's rocky road to independence and democracy," *The Conversation*, Aug. 10, 2022, https://theconversation.com/taiwans-rocky-road-to-independence-and-democracy-188378.

14. Sylvie Kerviel, "Genghis Khan exhibition defies Chinese censorship at Nantes history museum," *Le Monde*, December 8, 2022, https://www.lemonde.fr/en/culture/article/2022/12/08/genghis-khan-defies-chinese-censorship-at-nantes-h-museum_6007034_30.html#:~:text=-Canceled%20in%20October%202020%20after,in%20Nantes%2C%20western%20France.

15. Canadian Alliance of Chinese Associations website, "Canadian Chinese Association supports the Taiwan issue and the new era of China's unified cause,"2022, Accessed Aug. 15, 2023, https://tinyurl.com/wj6j68jb.

16. Personal interview, Ina Mitchell and Viviane Gosselin at Chinese Canadian Museum, Aug. 13, 2021.

17. Arlene Chan, "Chinese Immigration Act," The Canadian Encyclopedia, March 7, 2017, https://www.thecanadianencyclopedia.ca/en/article/chinese-immigration-act.

18. Vivian Luk, "100 years after Exclusion Act, anti-Chinese racism in Canada remains," CBC Radio, July 1, 2023, https://www.cbc.ca/radio/100-years-after-exclusion-act-anti-chinese-racism-in-canada-remains-1.6882957.

19. Bethany Lindsay, "Developer Gets Earful from Judge for 'Evasiveness,' Wins $1 in Defamation Suit," CBC News, Dec. 3, 2018, https://www.cbc.ca/news/canada/british-columbia/developer-gets-earful-from-judge-for-evasiveness-wins-1-in-defamation-suit-1.4931063.

20. "Shaughnessy Heritage Mansion Damaged by Fire Must Be Repaired, Says City," CBC News, Feb. 22, 2018, https://www.cbc.ca/news/canada/british-columbia/shaughnessy-mansion-fire-slavageable-heritage-status-1.4548080.

21. "CCSPE," accessed Feb. 26, 2023, https://www.51vote.org/introduce.

22. Lindsay, "Developer Gets Earful from Judge."

23. Kathleen Harris, "Justin Trudeau Insists Fundraiser Attendees Hold No Special Sway on Policy," CBC News, Dec. 12, 2016, https://www.cbc.ca/news/politics/trudeau-news-conference-2016-fundraising-1.3892600.

24. Doug Quan, "HQ Vancouver's 'success stories' suspect as Asian companies sputter or fall under scrutiny," *Financial Post*, Dec. 31, 2019, https://financialpost.com/news/vancouver-outreach-success-stories-suspect-as-asian-companies-sputter-or-fall-under-scrutiny.

25. Simon Little, "Ottawa 'Screwed Up' When It Greenlit Sale of B.C. Retirement Homes to Chinese Company: UBC Prof," Global News, Feb. 26, 2018, https://globalnews.ca/news/4049411/anbang-retirement-homes-bentall-centre-chinese-government/.

26.    Zhejiang Federation of Returned Overseas Chinese website, "Canadian overseas Chinese Pan Miaofei donated millions to help build his hometown," Oct. 10, 2020, Accessed Aug. 15, 2023, http://www.zjsql.com.cn/index.php?m=content&c=index&a=show&catid=16&id=45209.

27.    Graeme Wood, "Surrey Assailant Feared COVID-19 Is a 'Biological Weapon,' Court Hears," *North Shore News*, October 22, 2021, https://www.nsnews.com/bc-news/surrey-assailant-feared-covid-19-is-a-biological-weapon-court-hears-4543297.

28.    Zhejiang Federation of Returned Overseas Chinese website, "Canadian overseas Chinese Pan Miaofei donated millions to help build his hometown," Oct. 10, 2020, http://www.zjsql.com.cn/index.php?m=content&c=index&a=show&catid=16&id=45209.

29.    Bob Mackin, "China's Top West Coast Diplomat Announces Departure from Vancouver Consulate," *Business in Vancouver* (*BIV*), August 3, 2022, https://biv.com/article/2022/08/chinas-top-west-coast-diplomat-announces-departure-vancouver-consulate.

30.    Graeme Wood, "China's New Envoy to B.C. Marks National Day, Met with Protest," *Vancouver Is Awesome*, October 3, 2022, https://www.vancouverisawesome.com/bc-news/chinas-new-envoy-to-bc-marks-national-day-met-with-protest-5904359.

31.    China News Network, "Chinese associations in eastern and western Canada signed a mutual aid and cooperation agreement to help each other," Baidu, June 14, 2022, https://baijiahao.baidu.com/s?id=1735594550724131106&wfr=spider&for=pc.

32.    Dawa News, "Proposals for senators and representatives to unite and rejuvenate the country to sign a contract with the eastern Chinese community to watch and help each other - the joint tour group's eastern trip," Archive Today. June 13, 2022, https://archive.ph/2022.08.31-172205/http:/dawanews.com/dawa/node3/n5/n18/u1ai50108.html#selection-205.0-205.200.

33.    Toronto Chinese Group Federation website, Access attempted Aug. 29, 2023 (site partially opened but hung up on translation request), https://ccmedia.news/ctcco/.

34.    Snow Goose Media website, Accessed Aug. 29 2023, https://www.snowgoosemedia.com/.

35.    "About Us," Canadian Alliance of Chinese Associations, accessed February 27, 2023, https://www.ca-ca.ca/zh/about-us/organization.html.

36.    Easy Canada website, "Canada's East-West China Agency signed a mutual aid and cooperation agreement to help each other, recover the economy, resist discrimination, and unite and prosper" Easyca.ca, June 6 2022, https://easyca.ca/archives/308955.

37.    "Overseas Chinese Vancouver Spend 60 Million Yuan Overseas to Buy the Only Zoo in Vancouver" (translated), Zhejiang Federation of Returned Overseas Chinese, August 16, 2017, http://www.zjsql.com.cn/

index.php?m=content&c=index&a=show&catid=13&id=33093.

38. Bao Miaomiao, "See how Wenzhou business enterprises on the "Belt and Road" tell the world the "Chinese story"," News 66WZ, September 10, 2021, https://news.66wz.com/system/2021/09/10/105401344.shtml.

39. "Look at how Wenzhou business enterprises on the 'Belt and Road' tell the 'Chinese story' to the world," News Center-Wenzhou.com (66wz.com), Attempted access Aug. 29, 2023, site hung up on translation, https://news.66wz.com/system/2021/09/10/105401344.shtml.

40. http://www.zjsql.com.cn/index.php?m=content&c=index&a=show&catid=13&id=33093.

41. http://wztz.66wz.com/system/2012/04/11/103115412.shtml.

42. ttp://ww.703804.com/thread-16395921-1-1.html.

43. Naval Radio Section (NRS) Aldergrove—Bing Maps, https://www.bing.com/maps?q=Naval+Radio+Section+%28NRS%29+Aldergrove&FORM=HDRSC6&cp=49.073788%7E-122.436045&lvl=13.8. See also,

44. http://jproc.ca/rrp/aldergrove.html.

45. Dragon Lord report.

46. Graeme Smith and Gerry Groot, "How to Make Friends and Influence People: Inside the Magic Weapon of the United Front," *Little Red Podcast*, April 2018, https://open.spotify.com/episode/6KvibA7g6vZIOw5IjhzhSo.

## CHAPTER THREE

1. Lin Yi, "Chinese Writer Regrets Her Communist Past," *The Epoch Times*, April 6, 2012 (updated July 10, 2017, https://www.theepochtimes.com/article/chinese-writer-regrets-her-communist-past-1486927. Original link: https://www.epochtimes.com/gb/12/3/29/n3553196.htm.

2. "China 'Orders Christians to Destroy Crosses on Their Churches and Take Down Images of Jesus in Intensifying Crackdown on Religion,'" *Daily Mail*, July 21, 2020, https://www.dailymail.co.uk/news/article-8544835/China-orders-Christians-destroy-crosses-churches-images-Jesus.html.

3. Bob Mackin, "We're in a Free Country and They Want to Stop People from Praying. It's Just Mind Boggling," theBreaker.news, August 20, 2019, https://thebreaker.news/news/china-mob-at-church/.

4. "About," Tenth Church, https://www.tenth.ca/pages/about.

5. Nick Cohen, "Why Do Muslim States Stay Silent Over China's Abuse of the Uighurs?" *Guardian*, July 4, 2020, https://www.theguardian.com/commentisfree/2020/jul/04/why-do-muslim-states-stay-silent-over-chinas-uighur-brutality.

6. Jorge Barrera, "Chaos Agent," CBC News, Feb. 5, 2022 https://www.cbc.ca/newsinteractives/features/yuri-bezmenov-soviet-defector-canada.

7. Adam B. Ellick, Adam Westbrook, and Jonah M. Kessel, "Meet the KGB Spies Who Invented Fake News," *The New York Times*, November 12,

2018, https://www.nytimes.com/video/opinion/100000006210828/russia-disinformation-fake-news.html.

8. Epoch Times Staff, "Canadian Group Denies Being Front for Chinese Regime," *Epoch Times*, June 21, 2007, https://www.theepochtimes.com/canadian-group-denies-being-front-for-chinese-regime_1416742.html.

9. We originally located this information in Charlie Gillis, "Talking to the Great Wall," *Maclean's*, July 9, 2007, but when we tried to confirm the details of the article in 2023, it appeared to have been scrubbed from the internet. We were only able to find traces of Gillis's article in online subject bibliographies, such as this one: "Links relating to Charles Burton's DFAIT report Assessment of the Canada-China Bilateral Human Rights Dialogue and related Parliamentary Committee Hearings," Accessed July 11, 2023, https://docs.google.com/document/d/1vwyw5e2pYa0SV-loWJPyt07PDjaNeEm2HT80Vypv6zMY/preview. This source lists Gillis's article, but without a hyperlink, and says it also appeared in the Canadian Encyclopedia as "Canada's Fruitless Human Rights Dialogue with China," http://www.canadianencyclopedia.ca/index.cfm?PgNm=TCE&Params=M1ARTM0013115. The Canadian Encyclopedia page turned up a 404 warning for a "Page Not Found." See also Matthew Little, "Friends of Chinese Regime Back New Wave of Liberal MP Hopefuls," *Epoch Times*, September 19, 2014, https://www.theepochtimes.com/friends-of-chinese-regime-back-new-wave-of-liberal-mp-hopefuls_933395.html.

10. "Canadian Group Denies Being Front for Chinese Regime."

11. Hua Zheng ("responsible editor"), "Canadian Chinese leader Chen Chengding's biography in Beijing," Source: People's Political Consultative Conference, Xinhuanet, June 25, 2015, https://www.xinhuanet.com/politics/2015-06/25/c_127946830.htm.

12. Hua Zheng ("responsible editor"), "Canadian Chinese leader Chen Chengding's biography in Beijing."

13. Alert readers may note small discrepancies between the names of similar-sounding hometown and friendship associations referred to in this book. Every effort has been made to distinguish between groups. Group names tend to change without notice or explanation, and translations vary, so that the names used are often slightly different.

14. Committee of Legal Advisers of the Chinese Overseas Chinese Federation. All Federation of Returned Overseas Chinese. August 1, 2016.

15. "Annual meeting of the Overseas Chinese Lawyers Legal Advisory Committee on Sept. 4, 2020 in Beijing," Silk Council, Nov. 26, 2020, https://www.silkcouncil.org/post/annual-meeting-of-the-overseas-chinese-lawyers-legal-advisory-committee-on-sept-4-2020-in-beijing.

16. Reuters, "China Theft of Technology Is Biggest Law Enforcement Threat to US, FBI Says," *Guardian*, February 6, 2020, https://www.theguardian.com/world/2020/feb/06/china-technology-theft-fbi-biggest-threat.

17. Zak Vescera, "Local Chinese Groups Take Out Pro-Communist Party Ads Amidst Hong Kong Protests," *Vancouver Sun*, June 26, 2019, https://vancouversun.com/news/local-news/local-chinese-groups-take-out-pro-communist-party-ads-amidst-hong-kong-protests.

18. Rena Li, "Chinese Canadian Groups Support Security Law for HK," *China Daily Global*, May 29, 2020, https://www.chinadaily.com.cn/a/202005/29/WS5ed0c2e0a310a8b24115981a.html.

## CHAPTER FOUR

1. https://www.chinaqw.com/m/hqhr/2019/10-15/234069.shtml.

2. http://www.gd.chinanews.com.cn/2019/2019-10-15/405231.shtml.

3. Guo Shujiao, "Overseas advisory groups offer suggestions and implement them," SOHU.com, Jan. 16, 2019, https://www.sohu.com/a/295129580_801776. See also, "Xu Qun meets with guests from Canada Shandong Chamber of Commerce," Jian Innovation Zone, June 5, 2017, http://innovation.jinan.gov.cn/art/2017/6/5/art_16571_977073.html.

4. Invitation letter from Montreal Consulate and Jia Ming: "Invitation letter to Shandong (Montreal) Talents Cooperation and Entrepreneurship Exchange Meeting in Canada," April 11, 2016, http://montreal.china-consulate.gov.cn/kjhz/201604/t20160411_5368103.htm.

5. "Phase 9 Program Helps Nearly 200 Professionals Get Career Advancement The ninth CPAC-TD Leadership Training Program was successfully held," CPAC, Nov. 28, 2019, https://cpac-canada.ca/%E4%B9%9D%E6%9C%9F%E9%A1%B9%E7%9B%AE%E5%8A%A9%E8%BF%91%E4%B8%A4%E7%99%BE%E5%90%8D%E4%B8%93%E4%B8%9A%E4%BA%BA%E5%A3%AB%E8%8E%B7%E5%BE%97%E8%81%-8C%E5%9C%BA%E6%99%8B%E5%8D%87-%E7%AC%AC%E4%B9%9D%E6%9C%9Fc/?lang=zh-hans.

6. Zhejiang Federation of Returned Overseas Chinese, "Introduction of the leader," 2018, http://www.zjsql.com.cn/index.php?m=content&c=index&a=lists&catid=45.

7. Canadian Federation Corporation, "One Belt and One Road Canada Promotion General Association," July 17, 2017, https://opengovca.com/corporation/10325724.

8. "Lin Zhiyong, the former chairman of the Hualian Association, was expelled: what did he do," March 6, 2020, VanPeople.com.

9. "Lin Xingyong attended the 'National Two Sessions' on behalf of overseas Chinese," SOHU.com, March 4, 2019. Link unavailable.

10. "Canada prepares to build a memorial to the victims of the Nanjing Massacre," Montreal Chinese Community United Centre website, June 22, 2018, Accessed Aug. 29, 2023, https://www.mccuc.ca/canada_monument_of_nanjing_massacre_ch/.

11. Fengqi Qian and Guo-Qiang Liu, "Remembrance of the Nanjing Massacre in the Globalised Era: The Memory of Victimisation, Emotions and the Rise of China," China Report, Volume 55, Issue 2. Abstract accessed through Sage Journals website, Sept. 14, 2023, https://journals.sagepub.com/doi/abs/10.1177/0009445519834365?journalCode=chra.

12. Closing of the 10th National Congress of Returned Overseas Chinese Family Members Wang Huning attended—All-China Federation of Returned Overseas Chinese—People's Network. Sept. 1, 2018, Xinhua.com.

13. Clive Hamilton and Alex Joske, "Australian Universities Are Helping China's Military Surpass the United States," Sydney Morning Herald, October 27, 2017, https://www.smh.com.au/world/australian-universities-are-helping-chinas-military-surpass-the-united-states-20171024-gz780x.html.

14. Evan Dyer, "Experts Call on Canadian Universities to Close Off China's Access to Sensitive Research," CBC News, Sept. 15, 2020, https://www.cbc.ca/news/politics/china-canada-universities-research-waterloo-military-technology-1.5723846.

15. Christopher Wray, "The Threat Posed by the Chinese Government and the Chinese Communist Party to the Economic and National Security of the United States" (speech, Hudson Institute, Washington, DC, July 7, 2020), https://www.fbi.gov/news/speeches/the-threat-posed-by-the-chinese-government-and-the-chinese-communist-party-to-the-economic-and-national-security-of-the-united-states.

16. David Vigneault, "Message from the Director," CSIS Public Report 2020, April 2021, https://www.canada.ca/en/security-intelligence-service/corporate/publications/2020-public-report/message-from-the-director.html.

17. Xander Vagg, "Resources in the South China Sea," American Security Project, Dec. 4, 2017, https://www.americansecurityproject.org/resources-in-the-south-china-sea/.

18. Natural Resources Canada, "Canadian Nuclear Technology Contributes to China's Clean Energy Growth Plans," press release, June 6, 2017, https://www.canada.ca/en/natural-resources-canada/news/2017/06/canadian_nucleartechnologycontributestochinascleanenergygrowthpl.html.

19. Central Intelligence Agency, The United Front in Communist China: A Technique for Controlling, Mobilizing, and Utilizing Non-Communist Masses, May 1957 (released August 1999), https://www.cia.gov/readingroom/docs/CIA-RDP78-00915R000600210003-9.pdf.

20. "Zhejiang Economic and Trade Group visited BC province. This rooftop person became the chief representative of the Liaison Office in Canada," Sept. 26, 2018, Taizhou News, http://tz.zjol.com.cn/tzxw/201809/t20180925_8350276.shtml

21. "Zhejiang Economic and Trade Delegation visited BC Province to discuss trade and investment," Sept. 22, 2018, https://ttnews.zjol.com.cn/ttxw/system/2018/09/22/031160853.shtml

22. "Zhejiang Economic and Trade Delegation Visits BC Province to Discuss Trade and Investment-Tiantai News Network," (zjol.com.cn), Sept. 22, 2018, http://ttnews.zjol.com.cn/ttxw/system/2018/09/22/031160853.shtml.

23. "Zhejiang Council for the Promotion of International Trade," (ccpitzj.gov.cn), http://www.ccpitzj.gov.cn/jrobotfront/search.do?websiteid=330000000000065&tpl=2788&p=1&Municipal_name=%E8%B4%B8%E4%BF%83%E4%BC%9A&q=%E7%8E%8B%E5%85%B8%E5%A5%87.

24. "The opening ceremony of the Canada Liaison Office of Zhejiang Council for the Promotion of International Trade and the Zhejiang Chamber of Commerce of the China Chamber of International Commerce was held in Vancouver," (ccpitzj.gov.cn), http://www.ccpitzj.gov.cn/art/2018/10/10/art_1229621732_24632.html.

25. Zhong Nan, "CCPIT to Step Up Trade Facilitation Measures in Overseas Markets," *China Daily*, Sept. 30, 2019, https://www.chinadaily.com.cn/a/201901/30/WS5c51002ba3106c65c34e73f5.html.

26. "CCPIT Global," China Council for the Promotion of International Trade, https://en.ccpit.org/infoById/8a8080a94fd37680014f-d3e115a80017/5.

27. Lily Kuo and Niko Kommenda, "What Is China's Belt and Road Initiative?" *Guardian*, undated explainer from the Cities of the new Silk Road series, https://www.theguardian.com/cities/ng-interactive/2018/jul/30/what-china-belt-road-initiative-silk-road-explainer.

28. "Wang Dianqi: For 33 consecutive years, he has regarded supporting the army as a career," zjtz.gov.cn, Aug. 31, 2021, http://tyjrswj.zjtz.gov.cn/art/2021/8/31/art_1229454535_449.html.

29. Andrew Greene and Andrew Probyn, "One Belt, One Road: Australian 'Strategic' Concerns Over Beijing's Bid for Global Trade Dominance," ABC News, Oct. 22, 2017, https://www.abc.net.au/news/2017-10-22/australian-concerns-over-beijing-one-belt-one-road-trade-bid/9074602.

30. Martin Hála and Jichang Lulu, "The CCP's Model of Social Control Goes Global," Asia Research Institute, University of Nottingham, Dec. 20, 2018, The CCP's model of social control goes global—Asia Dialogue (theasiadialogue.com).

31. British Columbia Government News, Office of the Premier, "Premier strengthens relationship with Guangdong province of China," May 9, 2016, https://news.gov.bc.ca/releases/2016PREM0053-000742.

32. Mike Howell, "Vancouver Mayor Suspends Meetings with Chinese Government Officials," *Vancouver Is Awesome*, April 8, 2021, https://www.vancouverisawesome.com/local-news/vancouver-mayor-suspends-meetings-with-chinese-government-officials-3614998.

33. "CSIS said 'nobody' was paying attention to alleged election meddling: former Vancouver mayor," March 16, 2023, CBC News, https://www.you-

tube.com/watch?v=a1CweJ0aXOg.

34. Dan Fumano, "David Eby 'troubled' by reported election interference, while Chinese consulate pushes back," *Vancouver Sun*, March 17, 2023, https://vancouversun.com/news/local-news/eby-troubled-by-reported-election-interference-while-chinese-consulate-pushes-back.

35. Consulate General of the People's Republic of China in Vancouver, "Remarks of the Spokesperson of the Chinese Consulate General in Vancouver on some Canadian Politicians and Media's Accusations of 'Interference' by China in Canadian Elections," March 16, 2023, http://vancouver.china-consulate.gov.cn/eng/news/202303/t20230317_11043375.htm.

36. Mike Howell, "Chinese Consulate Lashes Back at Vancouver Mayor," *Business in Vancouver (BIV)*, April 12, 2021, https://biv.com/article/2021/04/chinese-consulate-lashes-back-vancouver-mayor.

37. BC United Caucus, "MLA Wat's Letter to the Premier and Minister Eby on Anti-Racism Action Items," May 27, 2021, https://www.bcliberalcaucus.bc.ca/mla-letters/3767-2/.

38. Mike Howell, "Chinese Consulate Lashes Back at Vancouver Mayor," *Business in Vancouver (BIV)*, April 12, 2021, https://biv.com/article/2021/04/chinese-consulate-lashes-back-vancouver-mayor.

## CHAPTER FIVE

1. Credit Suisse website, "Global Wealth Report, 2023," https://www.credit-suisse.com/about-us/en/reports-research/global-wealth-report.html.

2. Joanne Lee-Young, "Vancouver Is the Third Least-Affordable City in the World: Survey," *Vancouver Sun*, April 19, 2022, https://vancouversun.com/news/local-news/vancouver-third-least-affordable-city-demographia.

3. Elaine O'Connor, "Sports Cars Worth $2 Million Impounded from Richmond Teenagers Amid Suspected Street Racing," *Richmond News*, Sept. 2, 2011, https://www.richmond-news.com/local-news/sports-cars-worth-2-million-impounded-from-richmond-teenagers-amid-suspected-street--racing-2946078.

4. Mike Hager, "Incomeless Students Spent $57-Million on Vancouver Homes in Past Two Years," *The Globe and Mail*, Sept. 15, 2016, https://www.theglobeandmail.com/news/british-columbia/incomeless-students-spent-57-million-on-vancouver-homes-in-past-two-years/article31892652/.

5. David Eby, "Fix the Housing Crisis," press conference, video, Sept. 14, 2016, https://www.facebook.com/watch/live/?ref=watch_permalink&v=1180783485315331.

6. Cassidy Olivier, "$31.1-million Point Grey mansion owned by 'student,'" *Vancouver Sun*, May 12, 2016, https://vancouversun.com/business/real-estate/31-1-million-point-grey-mansion-owned-by-student.

7. Olivier, *Vancouver Sun*, May 12, 2016.

8. https://peterbrowncapital.com/full-biography/.

9. Olivier, *Vancouver Sun*, May 12, 2016.

10. Olivier, *Vancouver Sun*, May 12, 2016.

11. Jackie Northam, "Vancouver Has Been Transformed by Chinese Immigrants," NPR, *All Things Considered*, June 5, 2019, https://www.npr.org/2019/06/05/726531803/vancouver-has-been-transformed-by-chinese-immigrants.

12. Peter M. German, *Dirty Money: An Independent Review of Money Laundering in Lower Mainland Casinos*, March 31, 2018, https://news.gov.bc.ca/files/Gaming_Final_Report.pdf.

13. Bob Mackin, "Who Are the People in the Neighbourhood? Lonely West Van Mansions, Where a Forest Stood," theBreaker.news, June 7, 2018, https://thebreaker.news/news/west-van-empty-mansions/.

14. Jiayang Fan, "The Golden Generation," *New Yorker*, Feb. 14, 2016, https://www.newyorker.com/magazine/2016/02/22/chinas-rich-kids-head-west.

15. Jon Azpiri. "Metro Vancouver the Luxury Car Capital of North America," Global News, Jan. 11, 2016, https://globalnews.ca/news/2447804/metro-vancouver-the-luxury-car-capital-of-north-america/.

16. Peter German, *Dirty Money, Part 2: Turning the Tide: An Independent Review of Money Laundering in B.C. Real Estate, Luxury Vehicle Sales & Horse Racing*, March 31, 2019, https://icclr.org/publications/dirty-money-report-part-2/, p. 186.

17. German, *Dirty Money, Part 2*, p. 185.

18. "Chinese Bought $1.3B of Canadian Commercial Real Estate This Year," CBC News, June 30, 2016, https://www.cbc.ca/news/business/cbre-commercial-real-estate-chinese-1.3659847.

19. "Chinese Government Takes Over Troubled Insurance Giant Anbang," *Guardian*, Feb. 23, 2018, https://www.theguardian.com/world/2018/feb/23/chinese-government-anbang-insurance-giant.

20. Paul Willcocks, "How the Chinese Government Took Control of BC Seniors' Homes," *Tyee*, Feb. 28, 2018, https://thetyee.ca/Opinion/2018/02/26/Chinese-Government-Control-BC-Senior-Homes/.

21. China Minsheng Investment Group website, "CMIG—Gathering global intelligence, providing advices on the Belt and Road Initiative," Accessed: Aug, 25, 2023, https://www.cm-inv.com/en/ydyl/822.htm.

22. Frances Bula, "Firm with Chinese Ties Buys Vancouver's Grouse Mountain Resorts," *The Globe and Mail*, July 18, 2017, https://www.theglobeandmail.com/news/british-columbia/firm-with-chinese-ties-buys-vancouvers-grouse-mountain-resorts/article35728359/.

23. China Minsheng Investment Group website, cm-inv.com.

24. Transcript of Attorney General Barr's Remarks on China Policy at the Gerald R. Ford Presidential Museum, Grand Rapids, MI, July 17, 2020, https://www.justice.gov/opa/speech/transcript-attorney-general-barr-s-

remarks-china-policy-gerald-r-ford-presidential-museum.

25. Cuban Democracy Act of 1992, sec. 1703, https://1997-2001.state.gov/www/regions/wha/cuba/democ_act_1992.html.

26. "U.S. Trade Embargo Has Cost Cuba $130 Billion, U.N. Says," Reuters, May 8, 2018, https://www.reuters.com/article/us-cuba-economy-un-idUSKBN1IA00T.

27. Fabian Dawson, "Inside Vancouver's Battle of the Asian Property Tycoons," *Toronto Star*, Feb. 4, 2021, https://www.thestar.com/news/canada/2021/02/04/inside-vancouvers-battle-of-the-asian-property-tycoons.html#:~:text=Hong%20Kong%20tycoon%20Li%20Ka%2D-shing%2C%20a%20regular%20on%20the,in%201988%20for%20%24320%20million.

28. Dan Fumano, "A $75-billion snapshot of foreign-owned Vancouver real estate," *Vancouver Sun*, March 27. 2019, https://vancouversun.com/news/local-news/dan-fumano-a-75-billion-snapshot-of-foreign-owned-vancouver-real-estate/.

29. Northam, "Vancouver Has Been Transformed."

30. Dan Fumano, *Vancouver Sun*, March 27, 2019.

31. Northam, "Vancouver Has Been Transformed."

32. Website, "Maintaining the Integrity of Public Gaming in British Columbia," CFSE, https://cfseu.bc.ca/about-cfseu-bc/joint-illegal-gaming-investigation-team/

33. Sam Cooper, Stewart Bell and Andrew Russell, "High-roller targeted in RCMP's probe of alleged 'transnational drug trafficking' ring," Globalnews.ca, part of Fentanyl: Making a Killing series, Nov. 29, 2018, https://globalnews.ca/news/4658161/fentanyl-wealth-compound-british-columbia/.

34. Yvette Brend, "2 Key Names in B.C. Money-Laundering Probe Shot in Richmond Restaurant, 1 Fatally," CBC News, Sept. 21, 2020, https://www.cbc.ca/news/canada/british-columbia/richmond-shooting-jin-zhu-1.5732397.

35. Kim Bolan, "E-Pirate Money-Laundering Investigation: Leadership Problems, Missteps Proved Fatal," *Vancouver Sun*, Oct. 17, 2019, https://vancouversun.com/news/crime/leadership-problems-investigation-missteps-proved-fatal-to-e-pirate.

36. Office on Drugs and Crime, "Transnational organized crime facilitated through technology: the Phantom Secure case," https://www.unodc.org/unodc/en/untoc20/truecrimestories/phantom-secure.html

37. FBI News, "International Criminal Communication Service Dismantled: Phantom Secure Helped Drug Traffickers, Organized Crime Worldwide," https://www.fbi.gov/news/stories/phantom-secure-takedown-031618

38. Gordon Hoekstra, "Accused in alleged $220 million underground bank and money laundering scheme fighting forfeiture," *Vancouver Sun*, Jan. 3, 2021,

39. Peter German & Associates Inc., *Dirty Money–Part 2 (Turning the Tide— An Independent Review of Money Laundering in B.C. Real Estate, Luxury Vehicle Sales & Horse Racing)*, March 31, 2019, https://cullencommission. ca/files/Dirty_Money_Report_Part_2.pdf.

## CHAPTER SIX

1. British Columbia Gov News, "Billions in money laundering increased B.C. housing prices, expert panel finds," news release, May 9, 2019, https://news.gov.bc.ca/releases/2019FIN0051-000914.
2. "Billions in money laundering increased B.C. housing prices, expert panel finds," BC Gov News, Finance, May 9, 2019, https://news.gov.bc.ca/releases/2019FIN0051-000914.
3. German, *Dirty Money*, p. 37.
4. German, *Dirty Money*, p. 37.
5. Cullen Commission, proceedings at hearing, April 26, 2021, https://cullencommission.ca/data/transcripts/Transcript%20April%2026,%202021.pdf, p. 189. David Eby was the executive director of the BCCLA before he was elected an MLA.
6. Jessica Magonet, "Challenging Anti-Asian Racism at the Cullen Commission," BCCLA website, June 1, 2021, https://bccla.org/2021/06/challenging-anti-asian-racism-at-the-cullen-commission/.
7. Jason Proctor, "B.C. Supreme Court Rejects Class Action Suit Over Foreign Buyers Tax," CBC News, October 25, 2019, https://www.cbc.ca/news/canada/british-columbia/foreign-buyers-tax-housing-chinese-1.5336201.
8. Li v. British Columbia, [2019] BCSC 1819, https://www.bccourts.ca/jdb-txt/sc/19/18/2019BCSC1819.htm#_Toc22721539.
9. Cullen Commission, proceedings at hearing, Feb. 19, 2021, https://cullencommission.ca/data/transcripts/Transcript%20February%2019,%202021.pdf, p. 118.
10. Cullen Commission, proceedings at hearing, February 19, 2021, p. 30.
11. Vanessa Balintec, "2 Years into the Pandemic, Anti-Asian Hate Is Still on the Rise in Canada," CBC News, April 3, 2022, https://www.cbc.ca/news/canada/toronto/2-years-into-the-pandemic-anti-asian-hate-is-still-on-the-rise-in-canada-report-shows-1.6404034.
12. Honourable Teresa Wat, *Chinese Historical Wrongs Consultation Final Report and Recommendations*, British Columbia, https://www2.gov.bc.ca/assets/gov/british-columbians-our-governments/our-history/historic-places/documents/heritage/chinese-legacy/final_report_and_recommendations.pdf.
13. "Council Member Bios," British Columbia Government website, https://www2.gov.bc.ca/gov/content/governments/multiculturalism-anti-racism/chinese-legacy-bc/legacy-initiatives-advisory-council/council-members-bios.

14. Xiao Xu, "Two hundred Chinese citizens denied visas for Vancouver conference," *The Globe and Mail*, June 7, 2018, https://www.theglobeandmail.com/canada/british-columbia/article-two-hundred-chinese-citizens-denied-visas-for-vancouver-conference/.

15. Graeme Wood, "Huawei crisis spurs welcome rethink of Canada-China relations: expert," Business in Vancouver (biv.com), March 19, 2019, https://biv.com/article/2019/03/huawei-crisis-spurs-welcome-rethink-canada-china-relations-expert.

16. Government of British Columbia, *Chinese Historical Wrongs Consultation Final Report*, 2014, https://www2.gov.bc.ca/assets/gov/british-columbians-our-governments/our-history/historic-places/documents/heritage/chinese-legacy/final_report_and_recommendations.pdf.

17. "Premier Announces New Chinese-Canadian Community Advisory Committee," Office of the Premier, press release, Feb. 23, 2018, https://news.gov.bc.ca/releases/2018PREM0002-000269.

18. Email Correspondence from Brea Shaw, Brea Shaw, Research and Project Analyst, Crown Agencies and Board Resourcing Office, August 4, 2021. Email Correspondence from Lele Truong, executive advisor, communications and stakeholder relations, Office of the Premier, Government of British Columbia, Nov. 4, 2021.

19. "The inauguration ceremony of the first council of the Canadian Teochew Association was grandly held," World Chaoshang Media, July 24, 2023, https://www.sohu.com/a/705781551_481645.

20. Canadian Alliance of Chinese Associations website, "Joint visit to 2017 winning Chinese candidates," ca-ca.ca, https://ca-ca.ca/zh/news/2017%E5%B9%B4%E5%BA%A6/371-%E8%81%94%E5%B8%AD%E4%BC%9A%E6%8B%9C%E8%AE%BF2017%E8%83%9C%E9%80%89%E5%8D%8E%E8%A3%94%E5%8F%82%E9%80%89%E4%BA%BA.html.

21. Canadian Alliance of Chinese Associations website, "Chairman Wang Chengqi talked to the Director of Finance to discuss the 2017 budget," https://ca-ca.ca/zh/news/2017%E5%B9%B4%E5%BA%A6/377-%E7%8E%8B%E5%85%B8%E5%A5%87%E4%B8%BB%E5%B8%AD%E5%AF%B9%E8%AF%9D%E8%B4%A2%E6%94%BF%E5%8E%85%E9%95%BF%EF%BC%8C%E8%AE%A8%E8%AE%BA2017%E5%B9%B4%E5%BA%A6%E8%B4%A2%E6%94%BF%E9%A2%84%E7%AE%97.html.

22. Katie DeRosa, "NDP Hopes to Capitalize on B.C. Liberal Inaction on Money-Laundering," *Vancouver Sun*, June 16, 2022, https://vancouversun.com/news/ndp-hopes-capitalize-bc-liberal-inaction-on-money-laundering.

23. "Where the Money Goes," British Columbia Lottery Corporation, Accessed Jan. 15, 2023, https://corporate.bclc.com/community-benefits/where-the-money-goes.html.

24. German, *Dirty Money*, p. 209 and German, *Dirty Money 2*, p. 305..

25. "Strategy to Combat Transnational Organized Crime," White House, press release, July 25, 2011, https://obamawhitehouse.archives.gov/the-press-office/2011/07/25/fact-sheet-strategy-combat-transnational-organized-crime.

26. British Columbia New Democratic Party, "Working for You," party platform 2020, https://www.bcndp.ca/BCNDP_Platform_2020_FINAL.pdf.

27. Interview with Brock Martland. July 26, 2021.

28. Keith Bradsher, "China Tightens Controls on Overseas Use of Its Currency," *The New York Times*, Nov. 29, 2016, https://www.nytimes.com/2016/11/29/business/economy/china-tightens-controls-on-overseas-use-of-its-currency.html. Author Note: Chinese citizens are allowed to move only $50,000 a year overseas. To get around that limitation, many elites transfer money to criminal-controlled bank accounts in China before they travel to Vancouver. Once they've arrived, the criminals' associates provide them with their funds in Canadian dollars, using money likely collected from fentanyl sales. The money is then "snow-washed" through casino gambling.

29. Mark Hosak, "City Submits 'Vancouver Model' of Decriminalization Application to Health Canada," Forward Together website, March 2, 2021, https://www.forwardvancouver.ca/vancouver_model.

30. Kim Bolan and Gordon Hoekstra, "Deadly Shooting of Alleged Money Launderer Could Impact Ongoing Cases," *Vancouver Sun*, Sept. 22, 2020, https://vancouversun.com/news/deadly-shooting-of-alleged-money-launderer-could-impact-on-going-cases.

31. Bob Mackin, "More Charges in Killing of Richmond Underground Banker," theBreaker.news, April 30, 2022, https://thebreaker.news/news/more-charges-silver-international/.

32. Kim Bolan, "E-Pirate Money-Laundering Investigation: Leadership Problems, Missteps Proved Fatal," *Vancouver Sun*, Oct. 17, 2019, https://vancouversun.com/news/crime/leadership-problems-investigation-missteps-proved-fatal-to-e-pirate.

33. Commission of Inquiry into Money Laundering in British Columbia, Introductory Statement from Commissioner Cullen, 2019, https://cullen-commission.ca/introductory-statement/?ln=eng.

34. Commission of Inquiry into Money Laundering in British Columbia, *Final Report*, June 2022, https://cullencommission.ca/files/reports/CullenCommission-FinalReport-Full.pdf, p. 642.

35. Commission of Inquiry, *Final Report*, pp. 642–43.

36. Commission of Inquiry, *Final Report*, p. 1624.

37. Richard Racraft, "Johnston says no to public inquiry on foreign interference," CBC News, May 23, 2023, https://www.cbc.ca/news/politics/johnston-pubblic-inquiry-report-1.6851735.

38. Bob Mackin, "After Money Laundering Probe Heard Last Witness, NDP Installed Real Estate Exec as Casino Board Chair," theBreaker.news, May 29, 2021, https://thebreaker.news/business/new-bclc-chair/.

39. Joanna Chiu, "'Prime Targets': Are Canada's Local Politicians in the Sights of Beijing's Global PR Machine?" *Toronto Star*, August 8, 2020, https://www.thestar.com/news/canada/2020/08/08/are-canadas-local-politicians-a-target-for-beijings-global-pr-machine.html?rf.

40. Bob Mackin, "Exclusive: NDP minister unaware she posed for photo with Paul King Jin, target of civil forfeiture case," Aug. 27. 2019. theBreaker.news, https://thebreaker.news/news/beare-jin/.

41. Kim Bolan, "B.C. Wants Gym Linked to Alleged Money Launderer Forfeited," *Vancouver Sun*, August 13, 2020, https://vancouversun.com/news/b-c-wants-gym-linked-to-alleged-money-launderer-forfeited.

42. Chef Yang House website, https://chefyanghouse.com/.

43. Paul King Jin, interview with the authors and Bob Mackin, August 27, 2019.

44. Interview. Paul King Jin. August 27, 2019.

45. Bob Mackin, "NDP Minister Unaware She Posed for Photo with Paul King Jin, Target of Civil Forfeiture Case," theBreaker.news, August 27, 2019, https://thebreaker.news/news/beare-jin/.

46. "Canada-China-U.S.-Mexico Boxing Match Warms Up for Tokyo Olympics," *Sing Tao Daily*, September 15, 2018.

47. Bob Mackin, "NDP Minister Unaware She Posed for Photo with Paul King Jin."

48. Joanna Chiu, "'Prime Targets.'"

49. Sam Cooper (@scoopercooper), "Remember River Rock VIP and reported PLA honcho Tiger Yuan?" Twitter, Feb. 13, 2019, 2:48 p.m., https://twitter.com/scoopercooper/status/1095771766050484226?t=sMAVpKprS-fQqeXxz6sntAw&s=19.

## CHAPTER SEVEN

1. "What Does Xi Jinping's China Dream Mean?" BBC News, June 6, 2013, https://www.bbc.com/news/world-asia-china-22726375.

2. Nathan Vanderklippe, "Chinese Blacklist an Early Glimpse of Sweeping New Social Control," *The Globe and Mail*, Jan. 4, 2018, https://www.theglobeandmail.com/news/world/chinese-blacklist-an-early-glimpse-of-sweeping-new-social-credit-control/article37493300/.

3. Nicole Kobie, "The Complicated Truth About China's Social Credit System," *Wired UK*, June 7, 2019, https://www.wired.co.uk/article/china-social-credit-system-explained.

4. Kobie, "The Complicated Truth."

5. Vanderklippe, "Chinese Blacklist."

6.  Fan Yifei, "Thoughts on CDBD Operations in China," Yicai Global, April 8, 2020, https://www.yicaiglobal.com/news/thoughts-on-cbdc-operations-in-china.

7.  Frederick Kempe, "A Digital Dollar Would Help the U.S. and Its Allies Keep China in Check," CNBC, February 27, 2021, https://www.cnbc.com/2021/02/27/op-ed-a-digital-dollar-would-help-the-us-and-its-allies-keep-china-in-check.html.

8.  Jan Jekielek, "Kyle Bass: The 'Cancer' of China's Digital Currency," *American Thought Leaders Podcast*, July 15, 2021, https://www.theepochtimes.com/kyle-bass-the-cancer-of-chinas-new-digital-currency_3895862.html?&utm_medium=AmericanThoughtLeaders&utm_source=YouTube&utm_campaign=ATL-KyleBass&utm_content=7-10-2021.

9.  Roula Khalaf and Helen Warrell, "UK Spy Chief Raises Fears Over China's Digital Renminbi," *Financial Times*, Dec. 11, 2021, https://www.ft.com/content/128d7139-15d6-4f4d-a247-fc9228a53ebd.

10. "China Canceled H&M. Every Other Brand Needs to Understand Why," Bloomberg News, March 14, 2022, https://www.bloomberg.com/graphics/2022-china-canceled-hm/.

11. Scott McGregor and Ina Mitchell, "China's Social Credit Program Creeps into Canada," *Sunday Guardian*, April 17, 2021, https://www.sundayguardianlive.com/news/chinas-social-credit-program-creeps-canada.

12. McGregor and Mitchell, "China's Social Credit Program."

13. Krassi Twigg and Kerry Allen, "The disinformation tactics used by China," BBC News, March, 12, 2021, https://www.bbc.com/news/56364952.

14. "Drug Overdose Death Rates," National Institute on Drug Abuse, January 20, 2022, https://nida.nih.gov/research-topics/trends-statistics/overdose-death-rates.

15. Federal, Provincial, and Territorial Special Advisory Committee on the Epidemic of Opioid Overdoses, "Opioid and Stimulant-Related Harms in Canada," Public Health Agency of Canada, December 2022, https://health-infobase.canada.ca/substance-related-harms/opioids-stimulants.

16. Lenny Bernstein and Joel Achenbach, "Drug Overdose Deaths Soared to a Record 93,000 Last Year," *Washington Post*, July 14, 2021, https://www.washingtonpost.com/health/2021/07/14/drug-overdoses-pandemic-2020/. This 900,000 figure is deaths from all drugs, but most overdose deaths these days are from synthetic opioids. According to the CDC, 75 percent of ODs in the US in 2020 involved an opioid (https://www.cdc.gov/drugoverdose/deaths/index.html). The Chinese are currently operating in the cocaine, heroin, methamphetamine and synthetic drug realms.

17. Emily Feng, "'We Are Shipping to the U.S.': Inside China's Online Synthetic Drug Networks," NPR, Nov. 17, 2020, https://www.npr.org/2020/11/17/916890880/we-are-shipping-to-the-u-s-china-s-fentanyl-sellers-find-new-routes-to-drug-user.

18.  Joe Rogan, "Ben Westhoff Went Undercover to Visit a Chinese Drug Lab," *Joe Rogan Experience*, Nov. 7, 2019, https://www.youtube.com/watch?v=3G6K2FNLSgo.

## CHAPTER EIGHT

1.  RCMP, "Media Relations Officers, E Division Headquarters," https://bc-cb.rcmp-grc.gc.ca/ViewPage.action?siteNodeId=446&languageId=1&contentId=-1.

2.  Jimmy Quinn, "Congresswoman Defies Warnings from Pro-Democracy Groups to Attend Hong Kong–Sponsored Event," *National Review*, Aug. 22, 2023.

3.  Michael Pompeo, "U.S. States and the China Competition" (speech, National Governors Association Meeting, Washington, DC, Feb. 8, 2020), USC Annenberg, USC US–China Institute, https://china.usc.edu/mike-pompeo-us-states-and-china-competition-feb-8-2020.

4.  Michael Pompeo, "U.S. States and the China Competition."

5.  Anna Gronewold, "Pompeo to governors: China is watching you," Politico, Feb. 8, 2020, https://www.politico.com/news/2020/02/08/mike-pompeo-governors-china-112539.

6.  Beatrice Chao and Maya Liu, "Don Davies: MP Champion of the 10-Year Visa," *China Daily*, April 9, 2015, http://usa.chinadaily.com.cn/a/201504/09/WS5a2e164ba310eefe3e9a2827.html.

7.  Nicholas A. MacDonald, "Parliamentarians and National Security," *Canadian Parliamentary Review* 34, no. 4 (2011), http://www.revparl.ca/english/issue.asp?param=208&art=1460.

8.  Neil Moss, "Experts, Opposition MPs Divided on NSICOP's Value, as Debate on National Security Docs Handling Continues," *Hill Times*, Aug. 11, 2021, https://www.hilltimes.com/story/2021/08/11/experts-opposition-mps-divided-on-nsicops-value-as-debate-over-national-security-docs-handling-continues/229523/.

9.  Nick Boisvert, "O'Toole Pulls Conservative MPs from National Security Committee, Alleging Liberal Cover-Up Related to COVID-19," CBC News, June 17, 2021, https://www.cbc.ca/news/politics/otoole-nsicop-withdrawal-1.6070130.

10.  Video recording of Don Davies speech, Spring Festival, hosted by the People's Republic of China Consulate in Vancouver, Jan. 10, 2020, Bayshore Grand Foyer/Ballroom, Vancouver. Video in co-author Mitchell's private collection.

11.  Clive Hamilton and Mareike Ohlberg, "The Sad Case of John McCallum," *Toronto Sun*, July 20, 2020, https://torontosun.com/opinion/columnists/book-excerpt-the-sad-case-of-john-mccallum. This article is an excerpt from Hamilton and Ohlberg's book *Hidden Hand: Exposing How the Chinese Communist Party Is Reshaping the World* (Optimum Publishing, 2020).

12. Hamilton and Ohlberg, *Hidden Hand*, p. 54.

13. Matthew Pottinger, "Beijing's Long Arm: Threats to U.S. National Security" (statement before the Senate Select Committee on Intelligence, Washington, DC, Aug. 4, 2021), https://www.intelligence.senate.gov/sites/default/files/documents/os-mpottinger-080421.pdf.

14. "Two Innocents in Red China," CBC Radio Archives, Accessed Aug. 23, 2023, https://www.cbc.ca/player/play/1789346814.

15. Hilary Russell, "Norman Bethune," *The Canadian Encyclopedia*, published Aug. 8, 2010, https://www.thecanadianencyclopedia.ca/en/article/norman-bethune.

16. Marie-Danielle Smith, "In the First Hours of His Week-Long Visit to China, Justin Trudeau Hears a Lot About His Dad," *National Post*, Aug. 30, 2016, https://nationalpost.com/news/politics/in-the-first-hours-of-his-week-long-visit-to-china-justin-trudeau-hears-a-lot-about-his-dad.

17. "Montreal Olympics: The Taiwan Controversy," CBC Radio Archives, https://www.cbc.ca/player/play/1754413091.

18. "Tête à Tête: Alexandre Trudeau," CPAC, 2016, https://www.cpac.ca/episode?id=e4c4ff16-c79a-457b-8a84-4c7bf8608f86.

19. Alexandre Trudeau, *Barbarian Lost: Travels in the New China*, HarperCollins Publishers Ltd., 2016. See also, Confucius Institute in Edmonton website, "Mr. Alexandre Trudeau Visited the Confucius Institute in Edmonton," Posted April 11, 2017, http://confuciusedmonton.ca/mr-alexandre-trudeau-visited-the-confucius-institute-in-edmonton/.

20. Justin Trudeau, "Expanding Trade with Asia Is the Next Big Thing," *National Post*, Nov. 19, 2012, https://nationalpost.com/opinion/justin-trudeau-expanding-trade-with-asia-is-the-next-big-thing.

21. "CNOOC, COSCO Team Up in Oil Exploitation," *China Daily*, Sept. 24, 2007, http://www.chinadaily.com.cn/business/2007-09/24/content_6129857.htm.

22. "PRC Acquisition of U.S. Technologies," CNN, 1999, https://www.cnn.com/ALLPOLITICS/resources/1999/cox.report/acquisition/page7.html.

23. See email from Paul Andrew Mitchell to redacted recipients, sent June 25, 1997, and made available on his site at http://supremelaw.org/sls/email/box009/msg00923.htm.

24. Cain Nunns, "China's Poly Group: The Most Important Company You've Never Heard Of," *GlobalPost*, February 25, 2013, https://theworld.org/stories/2013-02-25/chinas-poly-group-most-important-company-youve-never-heard.

25. "Chinese Communist Company COSCO Is Threat to United States National Security," 143 Congressional Record, no. 42 (April 17, 1997), https://www.govinfo.gov/content/pkg/CREC-1997-04-17/html/CREC-1997-04-17-pt1-PgH1696.htm.

26. "Justin Trudeau's 'Foolish' China Remarks Spark Anger," CBC News,

Nov. 9, 2013, https://www.cbc.ca/news/canada/toronto/justin-trudeau-s-foolish-china-remarks-spark-anger-1.2421351.

27. Robert Fife and Steven Chase, "Trudeau Defends Fundraiser as Effort to Attract Chinese Investment," *The Globe and Mail*, November 22, 2016, https://www.theglobeandmail.com/news/politics/trudeau-defends-fundraiser-as-effort-to-attract-chinese-investment/article32996950/.

28. Fife and Chase, "Trudeau Defends Fundraiser."

29. Fife and Chase, "Trudeau Defends Fundraiser."

30. John Dotson, "China Explores Economic Outreach to U.S. States Via United Front Entities," *China Brief* 19, no. 12, June 26, 2019, https://jamestown.org/program/china-explores-economic-outreach-to-u-s-states-via-united-front-entities/.

31. Rachel Aiello, "Trudeau Foundation not used for foreign interference, PM's brother tells MPs," CTV News, May 3, 2023, https://www.ctvnews.ca/politics/trudeau-foundation-not-used-for-foreign-interference-pm-s-brother-tells-mps-1.6382495.

32. Aaron Wherry, "The Trudeau Foundation is a mere subplot in a much larger and more serious issue," CBC News, May 4, 2023, "https://www.cbc.ca/news/politics/alexandre-trudeau-foundation-wherry-analysis-1.6831669. Testimony by Alexandre 'Sacha' Trudeau to the House of Commons Access to Information, Privacy and Ethics Committee (ETHI), May 3, 2023.

33. Catherine Lévesque, "Sacha Trudeau denies Trudeau Foundation was target of foreign influence, says Chinese donor is 'honourable,'" *National Post*, May 3, 2023, https://nationalpost.com/news/sacha-trudeau-denies-trudeau-foundation-target-of-foreign-influence.

34. https://www.canada.ca/en/canadian-heritage/news/2022/02/government-of-canada-introduces-legislation-to-support-the-next-generation-of-canadian-artists-and-creators.html.

35. https://liberal.ca/wp-content/uploads/sites/292/2021/09/Platform-Forward-For-Everyone.pdf.

36. https://2023.liberal.ca/wp-content/uploads/sites/565/2023/05/Policy-Resolutions-2023-National-Convention_OFFICIAL_ENG.pdf.

37. Embassy of the People's Republic of China in Canada website, "Remarks of the Spokesperson of the Chinese Embassy on Canada's False Accusation of China's Interference in Its Internal Affairs," Feb. 4, 2023, http://ca.chinaembassy.gov.cn/eng/sgxw/202303/t20230305_11035939.htm.

## CHAPTER NINE

1. Yan Yan, He Changsong, "The 10th National Congress of Returned Overseas Chinese and Dependents of Overseas Chinese recruited the list of overseas members of the 10th Chinese Federation of Returned Overseas Chinese," China Federation of Returned Overseas Chinese (translat-

ed), September 1, 2018, Accessed March 1, 2023, http://www.chinaql.org/n1/2018/0901/c421026-30265666.html.

2. Yan Yan, He Changsong, "The 10th National Congress of Returned Overseas Chinese and Dependents."

3. Catherine Yuen profile, https://www.directory.gov.hk/details.jsp?dn=cn%3D1141005173%2Cou%3DCEDB%2Cou%3DPeople%2Co%3D-government%2Cc%3Dhk&lang=eng.

4. Jolson Lim, "Harjit Sajjan Criticized for Attending Event Celebrating Chinese Regime," iPolitics, September 30, 2019, https://ipolitics.ca/2019/09/30/harjit-sajjan-criticized-for-attending-event-celebrating-chinese-regime/.

5. Yang Kaiqi, "Overseas Chinese Affairs Office Unveiled the First Batch of 18 'Overseas Chinese and Chinese Mutual Aid Centers,'" China News Network, September 29, 2014.

6. Nathan Vanderklippe and Steven Chase, "Canada's Visa Application Centre in Beijing Run by Chinese Police," *The Globe and Mail,* February 8, 2021, https://www.theglobeandmail.com/world/article-canadas-visa-application-centre-in-beijing-run-by-chinese-police/.

7. Profile info on Robert Potter, https://wikitia.com/wiki/Robert_Potter.

8. Cameron Charters, "Chinese Spies Pose as Refugees in UK Visa Plot," *Times,* August 9, 2021, https://www.thetimes.co.uk/article/chinese-spies-pose-as-refugees-in-uk-visa-plot-g0fdfv37v.

9. Wang Qin, China News Network, "Five domestic overseas Chinese food prosperity bases gathered in Yangzhou to jointly promote Chinese food overseas prosperity", May 19, 2023 http://www.chinaqw.com/zh-wh/2023/05-19/358195.shtml.

10. Yan Yu Zhang Shiyu, "Overseas overseas Chinese projects take root: helping overseas Chinese and warming the hearts of overseas Chinese," China News Network, February 2, 2018, https://www.163.com/dy/article/D9L-8NC4E0514R9KD.html.

11. "Qiu Yuanping inaugurated the second batch of 12 overseas Chinese aid centers," Video No. 46376, September 28, 2015, Beijing, https://vs.cns.com.cn/video/detailTemp/46376.html?id=46376.

12. "Tan Tianxing, deputy director of the Overseas Chinese Affairs Office of the State Council, introduced the plan to benefit overseas Chinese: put the service of overseas Chinese in the most important position." Video No. 46652, October 5, 2015, Hong Kong, https://vs.cns.com.cn/video/detailTemp/46652.html?id=46652.

13. https://vs.cns.com.cn/video/detailTemp/75327.html?id=75327.

14. Interview with the authors, July 31, 2023. Email transcript, lightly edited by Philip Lenczycki. All quotes are from this interview.

15. Canada Revenue Agency, S.U.C.C.E.S.S. (quick view), Accessed March 1, 2023, https://apps.cra-arc.gc.ca/ebci/hacc/srch/pub/dsplyRprtngPrd?q.

bnRtNmbr=108152349&q.stts=0007&q.chrtyPrgrmTyp=13&selected-
CharityBn=108152349RR0001&dsrdPg=1.

16. "S.U.C.C.E.S.S. Selected to Provide Pre-Arrival Services," press release,
Immigration, Refugees and Citizenship Canada, January 3, 2019, https://
www.canada.ca/en/immigration-refugees-citizenship/news/2019/01/
success-selected-to-provide-pre-arrival-services.html.

17. [name redacted], "The Quasi Government: Hybrid Organizations with
Both Government and Private Sector Legal Characteristics, Congressional Research Service, June 22, 2011, https://www.everycrsreport.com/
reports/RL30533.html.

18. Government of Canada, Grants and Contributions. "Celebrate Canada
Together 2023 Recipient: National Congress of Chinese Canadians,"
https://search.open.canada.ca/grants/record/pch,016-2022-2023-Q4-
1358767,current.

19. "All-Canada Chinese Association (Ontario) held a press conference to
celebrate Canada's National Day," Fenghua Media, Canada China News
Network, June 17, 2023, https://www.ccpeople.ca/m/view.php?aid=8419.

20. "All-Canada Chinese Association (Ontario) held a press conference to
celebrate Canada's National Day," Fenghua Media, June 17, 2023, https://
www.ccpeople.ca/m/view.php?aid=8419.

21. Foreign Agents Registration Act Contact Page for Assistant Attorney
General for National Security Matthew G. Olsen, U.S. Department of
Justice website, https://www.justice.gov/nsd-fara.

22. Blackwell, Tom, "Trio of parliamentarians use Canada's racist history to
attack foreign agent registry for China," Post Media, June 20, 2023, https://
www.stthomastimesjournal.com/news/politics/trio-of-canadian-politicians-
linking-abandoned-chinese-exclusion-law-to-a-foreign-agent-registry.

23. Chuck Chiang, "Senator fears 'modern Chinese exclusion' but some re-
dress activists reject link," The Canadian Press, March 14, 2023, https://
www.ctvnews.ca/canada/senator-fears-modern-chinese-exclusion-but-
some-redress-activists-reject-link-1.6310556.

24. ACCT Foundation website. "Our Founding Members," updated 2022,
Accessed Aug. 2, 2023, https://acctfoundation.ca/our-founding-members

25. ACCT Foundation website. "About ACCT," updated 2023, Accessed
Aug. 2, 2023, https://acctfoundation.ca/summit/about-acct/.

26. Joan Bryden, "China's 'mouthpiece': Senator faces online backlash, calls to
resign after 2 Michaels, Meng tweet," Oct. 3, 2021, The Canadian Press,
https://globalnews.ca/news/8239522/senator-yuen-pau-woo-twitter-
backlash/.

27. "Minister Joly Announces Funding for the ACCT Foundation in Calgary." Canadian Heritage press release, Calgary, Dec. 6, 2017, https://
www.canada.ca/en/canadian-heritage/news/2017/11/minister_joly_an-
nouncesfundingfortheacctfoundationincalgary.html.

28. Immigration, Refugees and Citizenship Canada, Recipient: ACCT Foun-

dation, Calgary, Amendments for: 094-2021-2022-Q4-X228716006, Government of Canada Grants and Contributions website. March 1, 2022, https://search.open.canada.ca/grants/record/cic,094-2021-2022-Q4-X228716006,current?amendments.

29. Government of Canada, Grants and Contributions, Accessed Aug. 17, 2023, https://search.open.canada.ca/grants/?sort=agreement_start_date+-desc&search_text=ACCT+&page=1.

30. http://vancouver.china-consulate.gov.cn/chn/news/201802/t20180222_4891833.htm. Press release was changed to remove CCP.

31. Brennan MacDonald, "Senators decline to label China's treatment of Uyghurs a genocide," CBC News, June 29, 2021, https://www.cbc.ca/news/politics/senate-canada-vote-china-genocide-1.6084640.

32. Jennifer Kay Lee, "'Humiliation Day': July 1 has added meaning for some Chinese-Canadians," CBC, June 29, 2017, https://www.cbc.ca/news/canada/nova-scotia/humiliation-day-chinese-canadian-head-tax-exclusion-act-july-1-1.4175025.

33. ACCT Foundation website, "2023 Aspire to Lead Chinese Canadians Leaders' Summit June 23-25, Ottawa, Ontario," accessed Aug. 3, 2023, https://acctfoundation.ca/summit/.

34. Guy Lawson, "Trudeau's Canada, Again," *The New York Times Magazine*, Dec. 8, 2015, https://www.nytimes.com/2015/12/13/magazine/trudeaus-canada-again.html.

35. Douglas Quan, "Silence on Tiananmen Anniversary Could Be Sign of China's Influence on Canadian Community Groups: Critics," *National Post*, June 17, 2019, https://nationalpost.com/news/canada/silence-on-tiananmen-anniversary-could-be-sign-of-chinas-influence-on-canadian-community-groups-critics.

36. "Stories of Success," S.U.C.C.E.S.S. Society & Foundation, 2017-2018 Annual Report, https://successbc.ca/wp-content/uploads/2020/03/2017-2018-SUCCESS-Annual-Report.pdf.

37. Bob Mackin, "Ex-Richmond Casino Exec on High Rollers from China: 'These People Just Kept Flowing In,'" theBreaker.news, Feb. 9, 2021, https://thebreaker.news/business/walter-soo-cullen/.

38. Graeme Wood, "China paid $3.2 million to now-cancelled B.C. police academy program," Glacier News, Jul 23, 2021, https://www.vancouverisawesome.com/bc-news/china-paid-32-million-to-now-cancelled-bc-police-academy-program-3981740.

39. Sing Tao Media Group Canada, Oct. 1, 2018, https://www.singtao.ca/2437780/?variant=zh-cn.

40. http://www.chinaqw.com/kong/2015/11-18/70964.shtml.

41. China Overseas Chinese Network: Global List of Service Centres around the world including CDAC Vancouver, Accessed Aug. 18, 2023, http://www.chinaqw.com/hqhr/hzzx.shtml.

42. Council of Foreign Relations website, "Excerpt: *The Third Revolution: Xi Jinping and the New Chinese State*," https://www.cfr.org/excerpt-third-revolution.

43. Consulate-General of the People's Republic of China in Vancouver, "Overseas Chinese Affairs Office," April 17, 2007, http://vancouver.china-consulate.gov.cn/eng/overseachinese/.

44. National People's Congress of the People's Republic of China, Constitution of the People's Republic of China, posted Nov. 20, 2019, http://www.npc.gov.cn/englishnpc/constitution2019/201911/1f65146fb6104d-d3a2793875d19b5b29.shtml.

45. Cui Jiaming, "Visit Jiangsu Yangzhou Chinese Food Prosperity Base: Promoting Chinese Food Culture and Promoting the Prosperity of Chinese Food Overseas," Overseas Chinese Affairs Office of the State Council website, Dec. 1, 2022, https://www.gqb.gov.cn/news/2022/1201/55680.shtml.

46. Netherlands Huaxing Arts Group website, http://yw.huaxingnl.com/hly-sty/bk_21832631.html.

47. Philip Lenczycki, "Exclusive: Chinese Intel-Linked 'Service Centers' in US Cities Used Cultural Events to Push Communist Party Propaganda," July 12, 2023, The Daily Caller News Foundation, https://dailycaller.com/2023/07/12/ccp-chinese-intelligence-culture-propaganda/.

48. Xu Changan, "Toronto Huaxing Art Troupe's large-scale song and dance evening celebrates the Year of Cultural Exchange between China and Canada," China News Network, June 24, 2015, https://www.chinanews.com.cn/hr/2015/06-24/7362810.shtml.

49. "Toronto Huaxing Art Troupe hosted a large-scale gala to celebrate Canada's 150th National Day," China News Network, July 6, 2017, https://news.sina.com.cn/o/2017-07-06/doc-ifyhweua4087032.shtml.

50. Video: Festival of Spring—Brilliance of Huaxing, Feb. 12, 2022, Spring Festival Gala Canada, https://www.bilibili.com/video/BV1ER4y177qN/.

## CHAPTER TEN

1. Royal Canadian Mounted Police website, "Retired RCMP officer charged with foreign interference," Press Release, July 21, 2023, Montréal, Quebec, http://prod2.pub.rcmp-grc.gc.ca/en/news/2023/retired-rcmp-officer-charged-foreign-interference.

2. Gold Coast Tiger Bay Club website, "White Collar Crime, an International Mega-Problem," as told by FBI agent and International Forensic Executive Ross Gaffney. Event Announcement, April 13, (year unknown), https://myemail.constantcontact.com/The-Truth-About-White-Collar-Crime--an-International-Mega-Problem-.html?s-oid=1102010861425&aid=G2utjN2FnYs.

3. Xie Chuanjiao and Zhang Yan, "Canada to seize assets and extradite fugi-

tives: Envoy," May 26, 2015, *China Daily*, https://global.chinadaily.com.
cn/china/2015-05/26/content_20817730.htm.

4. In September, 2016, *The Globe and Mail* reported that the two sides had
signed an agreement on the sharing and return of forfeited assets. This
was described as a first for China, and the *Globe* quoted Xu Hong, a
director-general in China's foreign ministry, saying that the agreement
would provide a "powerful weapon for China to more effectively recover
the transferred state-owned assets and reinforce the global effort to fight
corruption." Meanwhile, a spokesperson for Global Affairs has since told
us that no such agreement is in force. The lack of transparency on this
issue speaks to shifts in public opinion about whether Canada should be
helping the Chinese government recover assets and repatriate citizens.
Nathan Vanderklippe, "China's Fox Hunt in Canada strains trust that an
extradition treaty is possible," *The Globe and Mail*, Sept. 23, 2016, https://
www.theglobeandmail.com/news/world/chinas-fox-hunt-in-canada-
strains-trust-that-an-extradition-treaty-is-possible/article32042306/.

5. "China 'takes advantage' of Canada: Former ambassador to China," CTV,
Power Play with Vassy Kapelos, May 2, 2023, https://www.youtube.com/
watch?v=WEz4eCA5jlE. Guy Saint-Jacques, "The diplomatic expulsions
could provide a welcome reset of Canada's relationship with China," *The
Globe and Mail*, May 10, 2023.

6. Guy Saint-Jacques, "The diplomatic expulsions could provide a welcome
reset of Canada's relationship with China," *The Globe and Mail*, May 10,
2023, https://www.theglobeandmail.com/opinion/article-the-diplomatic-
expulsions-could-provide-a-welcome-reset-of-canadas/.

7. Government of Canada, "Canada-China Law Enforcement and Ju-
dicial Cooperation," News Release, Feb. 9, 2012, https://www.canada.
ca/en/news/archive/2012/02/canada-china-law-enforcement-judicial-
cooperation.html.

8. Wang Shu, "China and Canada to sign Agreement on Sharing and Return of Recovered Assets," Beijing News, Dec. 2, 2014, https://news.
china.com/domesticgd/10000159/20141202/19035118_2.html.

9. Government of Canada, Prime Minister of Canada—Justin Trudeau,
"Joint Communiqué—1st Canada-China High-Level National Security
and Rule of Law Dialogue," Press Release, Sept. 13, 2016, Ottawa, Ontario, https://www.pm.gc.ca/en/news/backgrounders/2016/09/13/joint-
communique-1st-canada-china-high-level-national-security-and.

10. Email exchange with Rebecca Purdy, senior spokesperson with the Canada
Border Services Agency, Sept. 21, 2021. See also, Government of Canada,
Prime Minister of Canada—Justin Trudeau, "Joint Statement Between
Canada and the People's Republic of China," Press Release, Sept. 23, 2016,
Ottawa Ontario, https://pm.gc.ca/en/news/statements/2016/09/23/joint-
statement-between-canada-and-peoples-republic-china.

11. Email Correspondence, Patricia Skinner for Global Affairs Canada, Sept.
15, 2021.

12. Email Correspondence, Sgt. Caroline Duval for RCMP HQ Media Relations, Ottawa, Sept. 10, 2021.

13. RCMP, *Federal Policing: Annual Report 2021*, https://www.rcmp-grc.gc.ca/dam-gan/hq-dg/img/federal-policing-annual-report-rapport-annuel-police-federale/rcmp-federal-policing-annual-report-2021.pdf, pp. 32–33.

14. The Honourable Ralph Goodale, PC, MP, Minister of Public Safety and Emergency Preparedness, Royal Canadian Mounted Police Departmental Results Report, 2017–18, pp. 8 and 26, http://web.archive.org/web/20211128020952/https://www.rcmp-grc.gc.ca/wam/media/2983/original/020aef77844b2e404ed8cedc0c06e086.pdf. Accessed Aug. 3, 2023 via WayBack Machine.

15. House of Commons, Standing Committee on Foreign Affairs and International Development, Number 091, 1st Session, 42nd Parliament, March 27, 2018, https://www.ourcommons.ca/DocumentViewer/en/42-1/FAAE/meeting-91/evidence.

16. See, for example, Office of Public Affairs, Department of Justice, "Eight Individuals Charged With Conspiring to Act as Illegal Agents of the People's Republic of China," press release, Oct. 28, 2020, https://www.justice.gov/opa/pr/eight-individuals-charged-conspiring-act-illegal-agents-people-s-republic-china.

17. Zhang Yan and Qin Jize, "Canada to return illegal assets," *China Daily*, Updated April 25, 2013, accessed Aug. 10, 2023, https://www.chinadaily.com.cn/china/2013-04/25/content_16447007.htm.

18. RCMP Federal Policing, Annual Report 2021, https://www.rcmp-grc.gc.ca/dam-gan/hq-dg/img/federal-policing-annual-report-rapport-annuel-police-federale/rcmp-federal-policing-annual-report-2021.pdf, pp. 32–33.

19. Government of Canada, Forfeited Property Sharing Regulations—Seized Property Management Act, SOR/95-76 (1995), https://laws-lois.justice.gc.ca/eng/regulations/SOR-95-76/page-1.html#h-977132.

20. Email Correspondence, Melissa Gruber for Public Affairs and Issues Management, Department of Justice, Sept. 10, 2021.

21. Email Correspondence, Vincent Yang, June 14, 2022.

22. Email Correspondence, Vincent Yang, June 14, 2022.

23. Thierry Balzacq and Frédéric Charillon, (eds.), *Global Diplomacy: An Introduction* (Palgrave Macmillan, 2020). See Chapter 4, "Paradiplomacy," by Stéphane Paquin, https://doi.org/10.1007/978-3-030-28786-3_4, https://www.stephanepaquin.com/wp-content/uploads/2020/02/Paquin2020_Chapter_Paradiplomacy.pdf.

24. Government Public Safety Canada, Canada-China Relations Committee: Hot Issues Notes—Foreign Interference and Hostile Activities of State Actors, Feb. 25, 2021, https://www.publicsafety.gc.ca/cnt/trnsprnc/brfng-mtrls/prlmntry-bndrs/20210625/08-en.aspx.

25. Royal Canadian Mounted Police website, Protocol on foreign criminal investigators in Canada, Nov. 2, 2020 (date modified), https://www.rcmp-grc.gc.ca/en/protocol-foreign-criminal-investigators-canada.

26. "Ex-Interpol chief sentenced to 13 years in jail," AFP, Reuters, Deutsche Welle (DW), Jan. 21, 2020, https://www.dw.com/en/china-ex-interpol-chief-meng-hongwei-sentenced-to-13-years-in-jail/a-52082404.

27. Youtube, "More than 3,000 fugitives captured abroad in China's 'Fox Hunt' operation,'" CGTN, November 3, 2017, https://www.youtube.com/watch?v=xzsSwjrMO5s.

28. Judy Trinh, "Lawsuit alleges Ontario securities regulator put Canadian's safety at risk by co-operating with Chinese state police," CTV News, April 17, 2023, https://www.ctvnews.ca/canada/lawsuit-alleges-ontario-securities-regulator-put-canadian-s-safety-at-risk-by-co-operating-with-chinese-state-police-1.6359521.

29. Reuters staff, "China says using young, educated anti-graft officials as 'fox hunters,'" Reuters, April 18, 2015, https://www.reuters.com/article/us-china-corruption-idUSKBN0N909U20150418.

30. Marsh, Kim, *Cunning Edge: A 45-Year Journey Conducting Global Undercover Investigations* (Manitoba. The Ingram Book Company, 2022), p. 111.

31. Royal Canadian Mounted Police website, "RCMP IMET Special Advisory Group board members announced," Press Release, Nov. 12, 2021, Toronto, Ontario, https://www.rcmp-grc.gc.ca/en/news/2021/rcmp-imet-special-advisory-group-board-members-announced.

32. R. v. Rosenfeld, 2009 ONCA 307 (CanLII), https://www.canlii.org/en/on/onca/doc/2009/2009onca307/2009onca307.html?resultIndex=1.

33. Baines, David, "Too few charges, too many changes: IMET underdelivers," Investment Executive, Jan. 26, 2006, https://www.investmentexecutive.com/newspaper_/news-newspaper/news-32305/.

34. https://ca.linkedin.com/in/craighannaford.

35. Marsh, Kim, *Cunning Edge*, p. 144.

36. Marsh, Kim, *Cunning Edge*, p. 115.

37. Bill Majcher, "How Money is Laundered in Hong Kong," Foreign Correspondents' Club, Hong Kong, Club Lunch, Video, posted May 14, 2015, https://www.youtube.com/watch?v=NorhizJ66EQ.

38. Bill Majcher, "How Money is Laundered in Hong Kong."

39. Bill Majcher, "How Money is Laundered in Hong Kong."

40. Private interview with co-author Mitchell and Kim Marsh, 2017, Vancouver.

41. SUZZESS website, Management Profile: Robert "Beau" Hunter—Canada Associate, Senior Consultant. Updated: 2023. Accessed Aug. 2, 2023, https://www.suzzess.com/team-member-robert-hunter.html.

42. https://www.suzzess.com/about-us.html.

43. https://www.suzzess.com/team-member-yosh-wong.html.

44. https://www.cii2.org/board-members-and-officers

45. http://web.archive.org/web/20200814021109/https://successbc.ca/learn-about-us/organizational-support-team/.

46. "Gov't wants your laptop. Copyright Law: International agreement seeks to curb piracy," *The Province News*, May 27, 2008, Accessed Aug. https://www.pressreader.com/canada/the-province/20080527/281526516798529.

47. Flyer for Gold Coast Tiger Bay Club talk, "White Collar Crime: An International Mega-Problem," as told by FBI agent and international forensic specialist Ross Gaffney, Wednesday, April 13 (year not shown), https://myemail.constantcontact.com/The-Truth-About-White-Collar-Crime--an-International-Mega-Problem-.html?soid=1102010861425&aid=G2utjN2FnYs.

48. Graeme Wood, "Chinese Secret Police agent charged in US undertook training in BC," New Westminister Record, April 25, 2023, https://www.newwestrecord.ca/highlights/chinese-secret-police-agent-charged-in-us-undertook-training-in-bc-6906614.

49. Justice Institute of British Columbia website, "JIBC welcomes three new members to the Board of Governors," Press Release, Aug. 11, 2021, https://www.jibc.ca/news/article/jibc-welcomes-three-new-members-board-governors.

50. Graeme Wood, "Chinese police training in B.C. an espionage risk, critics say," Business in Vancouver (Glacier), Jan. 25, 2021, https://www.vancouverisawesome.com/bc-news/chinese-police-training-in-bc-an-espionage-risk-critics-say-3291155.

51. Xie Chuanjiao and Zhang Yan, "Canada to seize assets and extradite fugitives: Envoy."

## CHAPTER ELEVEN

1. Sebastian Rotella and Kirsten Berg, "Operation Fox Hunt: How China Exports Repression Using a Network of Spies Hidden in Plain Sight," ProPublica, July 22, 2021, https://www.propublica.org/article/operation-fox-hunt-how-china-exports-repression-using-a-network-of-spies-hidden-in-plain-sight.

2. Canada in the New Cold War (@Plan200_ca): "A new board of directors for Vancouver CCP United Front group Canada Fujian Industry & Commerce Association (CFICA) was sworn in last month. United Front Work Department bodies from Beijing and Beijing sent letters of congrats, and Vancouver UFWD station chief Hu Qiquan," Twitter, June 9, 2019, 6:42 p.m., https://twitter.com/Plan200_ca/status/1137852586730565632.

3. "Anne in China Inc.," Sunrise Group website, accessed March 1, 2023, https://en.sunriseltd.ca/anne-in-china-inc/.

4. Jim Day, "Entrepreneur Frank Zhou Building Business in P.E.I. and

China," SaltWire, Nov. 28, 2014, https://www.saltwire.com/prince-edward-island/news/entrepreneur-frank-zhou-building-business-in-pei-and-china-97838/.

5. "About Us: Sunrise Immigration," Sunrise Group website, accessed March 10, 2023, https://en.sunriseltd.ca/sunrise-immigration/.

6. "The Mighty Island: A Framework for Economic Growth," July 13, 2017, https://www.princeedwardisland.ca/sites/default/files/publications/economicframework-july13-2017-web.pdf.

7. David Parkinson, "Island of Boom," *The Globe and Mail*, January 19, 2018, https://www.theglobeandmail.com/news/pei-immigration-canada/article37671852/.

8. Parkinson, "Island of Boom."

9. Kevin Bissett, "If Departing Premier Has National Ambitions, He Isn't Saying," *Maclean's*, Feb. 20, 2015, https://macleans.ca/politics/if-departing-premier-has-national-ambitions-he-isnt-saying/.

10. Canadian Press, "Lawsuit Against Former Premier, P.E.I. Government, Refiled by Three Whistleblowers," Global News, June 12, 2019, https://globalnews.ca/news/5381248/lawsuit-against-former-premier-p-e-i-government-refiled-by-three-whistleblowers/.

11. Nicholas Keung, "Immigration pilot program aims to draw newcomers to Atlantic Canada," *Toronto Star*, Nov 25, 2017, https://www.thestar.com/news/immigration/2017 /11 /25/immigration-pilot-program-aims-to-draw-newcomers-to-atlantic-canada.html.

12. "The Premier of Nova Scotia, Honorable Stephen McNeill, Travels to China in the Autumn of 2018," press release, Sunrise Group, November 13, 2018, https://en.sunriseltd.ca/2018/11/13/the-premier-of-nova-scotia-honorable-stephen-mcneill-travels-to-china-in-the-autumn-of-2018/.

13. Lei's Real Talk, "Does immigration fraud on Canada's PEI cause U.S. concerns over security?" Published 9/30/2023 https://www.youtube.com/watch?v=MmxnyRFWtTg.

14. Duncan McIntosh, "Presentation Tonight in Charlottetown Focuses on Theatre," SaltWire, February 15, 2019, https://www.saltwire.com/prince-edward-island/news/presentation-tonight-in-charlottetown-focuses-on-theatre-284852/.

15. Ye Zi, The Chinese's People's Association for Friendship with Foreign Countries website, "Vice President Xie Yuan Meets with Duncan McIntosh," Aug. 31, 2016, https://web.archive.org/web/20210220000135/https://cpaffc.org.cn/index/news/detail/id/5784/lang/2.html.

16. Michael Pompeo, Secretary of State, "Designation of the National Association for China's Peaceful Unification (NACPU) as a Foreign Mission of the PRC," Press Statement, US Department of State, Oct. 28, 2020, https://2017-2021.state.gov/designation-of-the-national-association-for-chinas-peaceful-unification-nacpu-as-a-foreign-mission-of-the-prc/.

17. Government of Canada, *Foreign Interference Threats to Canada's Democratic*

*Process*, Canadian Security Intelligence Service Report, July 2021, https://www.canada.ca/en/security-intelligence-service/corporate/publications/foreign-interference-threat-to-canadas-democratic-process.html.

18. House of Commons, Special Committee on Canada-China Relations, No. 025, 2nd Session, 43rd Parliament, Lynette H. Ong, Associate Professor of Political Science, Munk School of Global Affairs & Public Policy, University of Toronto, May 3, 2021, https://www.ourcommons.ca/DocumentViewer/en/43-2/CACN/meeting-25/evidence.

19. Toshi Yoshihara and Jack Bianchi, "Uncovering China's Influence in Europe: How Friendship Groups Coopt European Elites," Center for Strategic and Budgetary Assessments, July 1, 2020, https://csbaonline.org/research/publications/uncovering-chinas-influence-in-europe-how-friendship-groups-coopt-european-elites, p. 12.

20. Duncan France, "Youxie—The Chinese Govt. dept. that arranges friendly relationships with other countries," New Zealand China Friendship Society website, May 8, 2014, https://nzchinasociety.org.nz/youxie-our-chinese-associate/.

21. "Lin Songtian: Chinese, Americans oppose war, conflict," *China Daily*, March 8, 2023, https://www.chinadaily.com.cn/a/202303/08/WS-64084a00a31057c47ebb31da.html.

22. Henry Austin and Alexander Smith, "Coronavirus: Chinese official suggests U.S. Army to blame for outbreak," NBC News, March 13, 2020, https://www.nbcnews.com/news/world/coronavirus-chinese-official-suggests-u-s-army-blame-outbreak-n1157826.

23. Hamilton and Ohlberg, *Hidden Hand*, p. 62.

24. Bethany Allen-Ebrahimian, "New book examines Neil Bush's China links," Axios, July 14, 2020, https://www.axios.com/2020/07/14/new-book-examines-neil-bush-china-links.

25. Zhao Huanxin, "Carter honored for China relations work," *China Daily*, June 13, 2019, http://global.chinadaily.com.cn/a/201906/13/WS5d025f-faa3103dbf14328126_1.html.

26. "Zhou Xuan, Chairman of Canada Sunrise Group and Secretary General of the Canada-China Friendship and Goodwill Exchange, Came to Inspect" (translated), press release, Jinhua Foreign Office, May 9, 2016, http://swb.jinhua.gov.cn/art/2016/5/9/art_1229168148_58849056.html.

27. Normalization is a process by which ideas and behaviours that fall outside of social norms come to be viewed as acceptable. People often point to Donald Trump, for instance, as a figure who normalized racist and misogynistic attitudes that most Americans would once have refused to accept, especially from the highest office in the land. Jessica Brown, "The powerful way that 'normalisation' shapes our world," BBC News, March 19, 2017, https://www.bbc.com/future/article/20170314-how-do-we-determine-when-a-behaviour-is-normal.

28. Chinese People's Association for Friendship with Foreign Countries,

"Vice President Xie Yuan Meets with Duncan McIntosh," Aug. 31, 2016, https://cpaffc.org.cn/index/news/detail/id/5784/lang/2.html.

29. Chinese People's Association for Friendship with Foreign Countries (CPAFFC) website, Ye Zi, "Vice President Xie Yuan Meets with Duncan McIntosh, Department of American and Oceanian," Aug. 31, 2016, https://cpaffc.org.cn/index/news/detail/id/5784/lang/2.html.

30. Lee Edwards, "China's 'Soft' War Against America," The Heritage Foundation, Feb. 22, 2021, https://www.heritage.org/asia/commentary/chinas-soft-war-against-america.

31. Lee Edwards, "China's 'Soft' War Against America."

32. Don Craig (Creator), Government Communications, Province of British Columbia, Flickr—Nov. 14, 2018, https://flickr.com/photos/bcgov-photos/44970829965/in/photolist-2bvVfZk-fJgtWJ-9J8cms-P9uTvn-QLSdkb-pFZn3h-QVAKzc-2cQeAKs-9J5nxR-8SsPHN-fcVtMb-bESqJk-2did2V2-aEEjSV-2did4mi-2jmSrVc-fcVtZE-fcFbcp-9J8eG7-AGaDA3-9J5m5c-fcVu55-hMDqGs-9J8cJd-QVAKMX-bEkEhn-2jw3B5K-9J8fvo-9J8fZG-aDqVxs-aDqVjy-o1rbyd-aDnbX4-ai8KWh-dafbzF-PLZSGJ-9J8cwQ-2did31T-brqiQo-2did374-9J5ot6-9J8dg3-rA SCy7-atc97P-2bNCfPw-brqiEw-9VF3sm-9J5nKP-9J5mTB-zSnKoa.

33. Xu Minghua Biography, baike.baidu.com, Accessed Aug. 21, 2023, https://baike.baidu.com/link?url=5t4G02ppehtoD3vuOY6ikXeVw-GYe_CoM807JFxHVG3ajLLRYh8MmmyKX-eAxdIVDkS_fbw4xjzilN9yT4tlkXblxvzMJNyvsU-LhWUQXY8BmhJcwZj_dZPx0Y-9jMqnpp. See also: "The delegation from Zhejiang Province visited Canada to introduce the economic and social development" Dawa news, Nov. 18, 2018, http://www.dawanews.com/dawa/node3/n5/n18/u1ai23349.html.

34. Response Package, Open Information, Government of British Columbia, http://docs.openinfo.gov.bc.ca/Response_Package_MIT-2017-71726.pdf.

35. "Henan Acrobatic Group launched overseas listing, Puyang Acrobatics fully entered the North American market!"Puyang Morning Post, Oct. 15, 2016.

36. BC Government News, Minister of State for Trade, "Trade missions fostered new investment, business deals in 2016", Jan. 10, 2017, https://news.gov.bc.ca/releases/2017MIT0001-000036.

37. The Municipal Federation of Returned Overseas, "Overseas consultant of Weinan Federation of Returned Overseas Chinese," Aug. 5, 2011.

## CHAPTER TWELVE

1. Department of Justice, "Harvard University Professor and Two Chinese Nationals Charged in Three Separate China-Related Cases," Jan. 28, 2020, https://www.justice.gov/opa/pr/harvard-university-professor-and-two-chinese-nationals-charged-three-separate-china-related.

2. "In a Boston Court, a Superstar of Science Falls to Earth," *The New York Times*, Dec. 21, 2021. Retrieved December 22, 2021, https://www.ny-times.com/2021/12/21/science/charles-lieber.html.

3. "Threats to the U.S. Research Enterprise: China's Talent Recruitment Plans," Permanent Subcommittee on Investigations, US Senate, November 18, 2019, https://www.hsgac.senate.gov/imo/media/doc/2019-11-18%20PSI%20Staff%20Report%20-%20China's%20Talent%20Recruitment%20Plans.pdf. When we tried to check this link on Aug. 4, 2023, the page could not be found. The error appeared on the Homeland Security Governmental Affairs website.

4. Alanez and Andersen, "Harvard Scientist Charged with Lying."

5. "About Us," Canada Research Chairs, accessed March 2, 2023, https://www.chairs-chaires.gc.ca/about_us-a_notre_sujet/index-eng.aspx.

6. Alex Joske, "Hunting the Phoenix: The Chinese Communist Party's global search for technology and talent" (policy brief, Australian Strategic Policy Institute, August 2020), https://www.aspi.org.au/report/hunting-phoenix, p. 3.

7. Joske, "Hunting the Phoenix," p. 12.

8. Ken Dilanian, "Scientists at America's top nuclear lab were recruited by China to design missiles and drones, report says," NBC News, Sept. 21, 2022, https://www.nbcnews.com/news/world/scientists-americas-top-nuclear-lab-recruited-china-design-missiles-dr-rcna48834.

9. Dilanian, "Scientists at America's top nuclear lab were recruited by China."

10. "Chinese National Sentenced for Economic Espionage Conspiracy," press release, Department of Justice, April 7, 2022, https://www.justice.gov/opa/pr/chinese-national-sentenced-economic-espionage-conspiracy.

11. Joske, "Hunting the Phoenix," p. 45.

12. "Hawaii Man Indicted for Selling National Defense Secrets to the People's Republic of China," press release, Department of Justice, November 9, 2006, http://honolulu.fbi.gov/dojpressrel/pressrel06/defensesecrets110906.htm. When we tried to access this source again on Aug. 4, 2023, the page could not be found.

13. Joske, "Hunting the Phoenix," p. 8.

14. Joske, "Hunting the Phoenix," p. 9.

15. Joske, "Hunting the Phoenix," p. 12.

16. Joske, "Hunting the Phoenix," p. 12.

17. Sam Cooper, "Chinese vaccine company executives worked in program now targeted by Western intelligence agencies," Global News, December 2, 2020, https://globalnews.ca/news/7483970/cansino-nrc-covid-vaccine/.

18. Xi Jinping, "Speech at the Celebration of the 100th Anniversary of the European and American Alumni Association," speech (translated), October 21, 2013, http://cpc.people.com.cn/n/2013/1021/c64094-23277634.html.

19. Joske, "Hunting the Phoenix," p. 10.

20. Joske, "Hunting the Phoenix," p. 4.

21. See, for example, Xinxiang University website, "Xinxiang College held a 2023 demonstration school key implementation project construction promotion meeting," News Express, Aug. 25, 2023, https://www.xxu.edu.cn/jiansuo.jsp?wbtreeid=1029.

22. This posting was on a UBC website that linked to Huaqiao University in Quanzhou.

23. Xinhua News, "Top leaders attend congress of returned overseas Chinese ," www.news.cn, Aug. 29, 2018, http://www.xinhuanet.com/english/2018--08/29/c_137428195.htm .

24. Zhang Kem, "The Guangdong Association for the Promotion of Peaceful Reunification of China and the second National Conditions Study Class of the Guangdong Huangpu Military Academy Alumni Association were successfully completed in our institute," Meipian.cn, May 20, 2019, https://www.meipian.cn/24jvcelr.

25. "Representatives of overseas Chinese of Chaozhou origin went to Beijing to participate in the 10th National Overseas Chinese Representative Conference," Sohu.com, Aug. 30, 2018, https://www.sohu.com/a/250993814_759709.

26. Joske, "Hunting the Phoenix," p. 18.

27. "About Us," Innovation & Entrepreneurship International Competition, Accessed March 5, 2023, http://www.itcsz.cn/info-1-aboutus-3.shtml.

28. Startupheretoronto.com, "Toronto Mayor John Tory to Officially Open Sci Innovation Centre," Oct. 5, 2018, https://www.startgbc.com/toronto-mayor-john-tory-to-officially-open-sci-innovation-centre/.

29. Canadian Press, "Tory Senator Should Face Censure for Accepting Free China Trip: Ethics Committee," Global News, June 18, 2020, https://globalnews.ca/news/7083748/victor-oh-china-trip-senate-ethics/.

30. Senate of Canada, "Committee report concerning Senator Victor Oh," News Release, Standing Committee on Ethics and Conflict of Interest for Senators, June 18, 2020, https://sencanada.ca/en/newsroom/conf-committee-report-concerning-senator-victor-oh/.

31. Steven Chase, "Alberta Rewriting Rules to Safeguard University Research with China, Other Countries," *The Globe and Mail*, Oct. 11, 2022, https://www.theglobeandmail.com/politics/article-alberta-china-university-research/.

32. Jacob Sowers, "Texas A&M Shuts Down Collaboration with Chinese on Climate Research Over National Security Concerns," Free Speech Project, May 2, 2022, https://freespeechproject.georgetown.edu/tracker-entries/texas-am-shuts-down-collaboration-with-chinese-on-climate-research-over-national-security-concerns/.

33. Dilanian, "Scientists at America's Top Nuclear Lab Were Recruited by China."

34. *Threat Overview*, Canadian Security Intelligence Service, Briefing Material for the Minister of Public Safety and Emergency Preparedness, Date modified: Feb. 25, 2022, https://www.canada.ca/en/security-intelligence-service/corporate/transparency/briefing-material/2021-transition-binder/threat-overview.html.

35. "UBC and Chinese universities sign landmark agreements on research, joint degrees and student exchange," UBC News, April 10, 2015, https://news.ubc.ca/2015/04/10/ubc-and-chinese-universities-sign-landmark-agreements-on-research-joint-degrees-and-student-exchange/.

36. "UBC-China at a Glance," UBC China Council, August, 2016, https://chinacouncil.sites.olt.ubc.ca/files/2016/10/UBC-China-data-Aug25_2016.pdf.

37. "Overview," The UBC China Council, https://chinacouncil.ubc.ca/ubc-china/overview/.

38. "China's Digital Ambitions: A Global Strategy to Supplant the Liberal Order," The National Bureau of Asian Research, Report #97, March 2022, https://www.nbr.org/wp-content/uploads/pdfs/publications/sr97_chinas_digital_ambitions_mar2022.pdf.

39. Canadian Press, "University of Waterloo to end research partnership with Chinese tech giant Huawei," with files from CBC News, May 4, 2023, https://www.cbc.ca/news/canada/kitchener-waterloo/university-waterloo-ends-partnership-with-huawei-1.6831971.

40. "Xi Jinping thought added into curriculum: Ministry of Education," *Global Times*, Aug. 21, 2023, https://www.globaltimes.cn/page/202108/1232364.shtml.

41. Zou Shuo, "2 plans detail China's goals for education," *China Daily*, Updated Feb. 25, 2019, https://english.www.gov.cn/policies/policy_watch/2019/02/25/content_281476537597482.htm. (www.gov.cn).

42. "Evolution of China's Education System," *China Daily*, June 28, 2021, https://govt.chinadaily.com.cn/s/202106/28/WS60e2c32b498e-02b3aaaae4dd/evolution-of-chinas-education-system.html.

43. Zou Shuo, "2 plans detail China's goals for education," *China Daily*, February 25, 2019, https://english.www.gov.cn/policies/policy_watch/2019/02/25/content_281476537597482.htm#:~:text=Two%20development%20plans%20were%20issued%20on%20Feb%2023,the%20education%20modernization%20drive%20from%202018%20to%202022.

44. Australian Government website, "China's education modernisation plan towards 2035," accessed April 1, 2020, https://internationaleducation.gov.au/International-network/china/PolicyUpdates-China/Pages/China's-education-modernisation-plan-towards-2035-.aspx.

45. "The CPC Central Committee and the State Council issued China's Education Modernization 2035," Xinhua News, Feb. 23, 2019, http://www.gov.cn/xinwen/2019-02/23/content_5367987.htm.

46. Australian Government website: "China's education modernisation plan towards 2035."

47. Ministry of Education website: "Ministry of Education: Comprehensively promote the joint construction of the 'Belt and Road' education action," Feb. 20, 2019, http://www.gov.cn/xinwen/2019-02/20/content_5367017. htm.

48. Australian Government website: "China's education modernisation plan towards 2035."

49. Office of the Spokesperson, U.S. Department of State website, "'Confucius Institute U.S. Center' Designation as a Foreign Mission," Fact Sheet (Archived Content: 2017-2021), Aug. 13, 2020, https://2017-2021.state. gov/confucius-institute-u-s-center-designation-as-a-foreign-mission/ index.html.

50. Overseas Chinese Affairs Office of the State Council, "Qiu Yuanping: Serving Overseas Chinese Action Year Comprehensively implement eight plans to benefit overseas Chinese," March 9, 2015, https://www.gqb.gov. cn/news/2015/0312/35240.shtml.

51. China Cultural Industry Association website: "Leaders – Zhang Bin," 2013, http://www.chncia.org/en/leaders.php?mid=2.http://www.chncia. org/en/leaders.php?mid=2.

52. Chuck Chiang, "Chinese dairy moguls target Mandarin-language market," Business in Vancouver, May 23, 2017, https://biv.com/article/2017/05/chinese-dairy-moguls-target-mandarin-language-mark.

53. *Chinese and Chinese American Philanthropy* (Report), Global Chinese Philanthropy Initiative, https://www.international.ucla.edu/media/files/ GCPI_Report_Single-Pages-jn-hn5.pdf, p. 14.

54. Kuo, V., Miao, J., Feng, T., & Hu, M., *Chinese and Chinese American Philanthropy*, report of the Global Chinese Philanthropy Initiative, 2017, https://www.international.ucla.edu/media/files/GCPI_Report_Single-Pages-jn-hn5.pdf, p. 37.

55. *Certification Inspection Report: British Columbia Program*, Maple Leaf International Schools, https://www2.gov.bc.ca/assets/gov/education/ administration/kindergarten-to-grade-12/internationaleducation/inspectionreports/10396936_mlis-x_fall2020insprpt_post.pdf.

56. UNESCO website, Silk Roads Programme, "Xi'an," accessed Aug. 2, 2023, https://en.unesco.org/silkroad/content/xian.

57. Sun Zhenghao, Zhang Chenjun, Zhang Sijie, Cai Xinyi, "How Belt and Road has changed an ancient Chinese city," Xinhua News, Aug. 10, 2022, https://en.imsilkroad.com/p/329430.html.

58. *Certification Inspection Report: British Columbia Program*, Maple Leaf International Schools, https://www2.gov.bc.ca/assets/gov/education/ administration/kindergarten-to-grade-12/internationaleducation/inspectionreports/10396815_mlis-c_fall2020insprpt_post.pdf, p. 2.

59. Signum International Educational Services Inc. website, Professional

Background of James W. Beeke, assessed Aug. 3, 2023, https://www.sig-numeduservices.com/content/j_beeke.html.

60. Royal Roads University website, "Sherman Jen, Honorary Degree, Spring 2013 Convocation," https://www.royalroads.ca/sherman-jen.

61. Government of Canada, *First Report - The Right Honourable David Johnston, Independent Special Rapporteur on Foreign Interference*, May 23, 2023, https://www.canada.ca/en/democratic-institutions/services/reports/first-report-david-johnston-independent-special-rapporteur-foreign-interference.html.

62. Maple Leaf Schools website, "Dr. Sherman Jen, The Winner of Cognia's 2021-2022 Excellence in Education Award," June 14, 2022, https://www.mapleleafschools.com/sherman-jen-the-winner-of-cognias-2021-2022-excellence-in-education-award#:~:text=Cognia%20is%20pleased%20to%20announce%20that%20the%20winner,CEO%2C%20and%20Chairman%20of%20Maple%20Leaf%20Educational%20Systems.

63. "10 Hurun Report," Ren Shuliang wealth ranking, Baidu.com, Oct. 10, 2019, https://baike.baidu.com/reference/4708566/8beeBdE98_GVPcLK2Vff0i9RD_mbOt6BBwiNAHoNFiroEWfRSwD2jhAN3Z_yDPumnG_oKpyxjqU_tRRhtOYQuToYQvIx3fIh5YmYVQ.

64. Interview with the authors, May 11, 2023.

65. Maple Leaf Education Group website, Accessed Aug. 12, 2023, https://www.mapleleafschools.com.

66. Maple Leaf website, "Sherman Jen—Founder, President and Chairman of Maple Leaf Education Systems," Accessed Aug. 2, 2023, https://www.mapleleafschools.com/corporate/about-us/founder.

67. Thompson Rivers University website, "University gift is largest ever," press briefing, Oct. 5, 2017, https://inside.tru.ca/2017/10/05/jen-gift-is-largest-ever/.

68. OurKids.net website, Maple Leaf World Schools-Canada Tuition and Financial Aid, Accessed Aug. 3, 2023, https://www.ourkids.net/school/maple-leaf-education-north-america/1257/tuition-fees.

69. "A Chinese company opens a private school in Richmond. It is expected that teachers will understate issues such as Tibet," *Xingdao Comprehensive Newspaper*, May 10, 2021, Accessed Aug. 6, 2023, http://bit.ly/3Kw46ge.

70. Daphne Bramham, "New Richmond private school to 'tread lightly' on China concerns," *Vancouver Sun*, May 10, 2021, https://vancouversun.com/opinion/columnists/daphne-bramham-new-richmond-private-school-to-tread-lightly-on-china-concerns.

71. Huaqiao University website, Accessed Feb. 28, 2018, https://en.hqu.edu.cn/.

72. Alex Joske, Australian Strategic Policy Institute, "The Party Speaks for You: Foreign Interference and the Chinese Communist Party's united front system," Policy Brief Report No. 32/2020, June 9, 2020, https://www.aspi.org.au/report/party-speaks-you.

# ENDNOTES

# ENDNOTES

73. Email correspondence with co-author Ina Mitchell, June 12, 2022.

74. Yuanheng website, "Our Projects," Accessed Aug. 3, 2023, http://yuanheng.ca/en/projects/.

75. Canadian Fujian Hometown Association website (Archived 2013), 福建同乡联谊会十年期会长寻根华夏行基金简章 (Fujian Hometown Friendship Association Root Seeking Travel Fund), http://web.archive.org/web/20180812035134/http://fujiancanada.org/?page_id=50.

76. Alyshah Hasham, "Toronto mayor's race polls show Olivia Chow with narrow lead," *Toronto Star*, April 28, 2023, https://www.thestar.com/news/gta/olivia-chow-leads-latest-toronto-election-polls-but-the-most-popular-choice-for-mayor-isn/article_c5071011-9436-5bc3-97f7-b2cd24ebfa98.html.

77. Canadian Chinese Association website, Accessed Aug. 6. 2023, https://www.concn.ca/.

78. Huaqiao University website, "Zhang Bin, Vice Chairman Lin Square, led the delegation of the Canadian Fujian Hometown Association to visit BGI," Sept. 13, 2011, https://www.hqu.edu.cn/info/1212/74589.htm.

79. "Canadian Fujian Hometown Association Vancouver held the first "Straits Cup—Belt and Road" Golf Invitational Tournament," June 5, 2019, Soho.com, https://www.sohu.com/a/318720684_100253941.

80. BC Government FOI: Minister George Chow's personal trip to China, http://docs.openinfo.gov.bc.ca/Response_Package_JTT-2018-87909.pdf.

81. Derrick Penner, "UBC 'continuing to evaluate its position' on Huawei research support," *Vancouver Sun*, May 9, 2023, https://vancouversun.com/news/local-news/ubc-continuing-to-evaluate-its-position-on-huawei-research-support.

82. Beijing Forestry University website, "Interim provisions on the Administrative Measures for Sino-foreign Cooperation in Running Schools of Beijing Forestry University," January 2013, http://hzbx.bjfu.edu.cn/zcfg/265147.html.

83. University of British Columbia website, Faculty of Forestry, Accessed Aug. 2, 2023, https://give.ubc.ca/faculty-of-forestry/.

84. British Columbia Government, 2021 BC Forest Sector—Statistics Summary, https://www2.gov.bc.ca/assets/gov/farming-natural-resources-and-industry/forestry/forest-industry-economics/economic-state/2021_bc_forest_sector_-_statistics_summary.pdf.

85. "We signed a contract with the College of Forestry at the University of British Columbia (UBC)," Soho.com, Aug. 1, 2018, https://www.sohu.com/a/244536512_816215.

86. University of British Columbia website, Faculty of Forestry, Asia Forestry Research Centre—Partner Universities and Active Members, Accessed Aug. 2, 2023, https://afrc.forestry.ubc.ca/partnership/.

87. Family Enterprise Canada website, Accessed Aug. 6, 2023, https://access.familyenterprise.ca/members/?id=59099078.

88. "We signed a contract with the College of Forestry at the University of British Columbia (UBC)," Soho.com.

89. Henan Capital Construction Science Experimental Research Institute (Group) Co., Ltd. Website, Group Profile, Accessed Aug. 2023, https://www.jbjsjc.com/gywm/1.html.

90. University of British Columbia website, UBC Faculty of Forestry, Faculty Profiles, Frank Lam, Accessed Aug. 6,. 2023, https://forestry.ubc.ca/faculty-profile/frank-lam/.

91. Beijing Forestry University website, "The 2021 Sino-foreign Cooperative Education New Student Meeting and UBC-UBG Scholarship Award Ceremony was held in our university," Accessed Aug. 2, 2023, http://hzbx.bjfu.edu.cn/xwsd/381997.html.

92. Laura Oliver, World Economic Forum, "China has sent 60,000 soldiers to plant trees," Feb. 16, 2018, https://www.weforum.org/agenda/2018/02/china-army-soldiers-plant-trees/.

93. Beijing Forestry University website, Beijing Forestry University-University of British Columbia undergraduate cooperative education program, Jan. 10, 2018, http://hzbx.bjfu.edu.cn/bxts/265088.html.

94. Robert Kozak, University of British Columbia website, UBC Faculty of Forestry—Message from the Dean, Accessed Aug 2, 2023, https://forestry.ubc.ca/about/deans-message/.

95. Beijing Forestry University website, Beijing Forestry University-University of British Columbia undergraduate cooperative education program.

96. Beijing Forestry University, 2012 Military Training—Leave method for student military training, April 28, 2013, http://xsc.bjfu.edu.cn/gfjy/xsjx/148083.html.

97. Beijing Forestry University, "Our university held the 2020 undergraduate student military training kick-off mobilization conference," Ministry of Armed Forces, May 9, 2021, http://news.bjfu.edu.cn/ztbd/2020jbks-jxzt/369824.html.

98. "The Canadian Fujian Hometown Association and the Chinese Overseas Chinese Mutual Aid Association held an award ceremony for international student," Chinaqw.com: China Overseas Chinese Network, April, 13, 2015, http://www.chinaqw.com/hqhr/2015/04-13/45096.shtml.

99. Grizzly Bear Institute of Canada, Event Notice: "One Belt, One Road," North American Forum, May 21 2017, http://www.grizzlybearinstitute.org/en/%e4%b8%80%e5%b8%a6%e4%b8%80%e8%b7%af%e5%80%a1%e8%ae%ae%e5%9c%a8%e5%8c%97%e7%be%8e%e7%9a%84%e5%ae%9e%e8%b7%b5/.

100. Guoren Zhang, "Trudeau Government and China's Billionaires," Grizzly Bear Institute of Canada website, Feb. 2, 2018, http://www.grizzlybearinstitute.org/%e7%89%b9%e9%b2%81%e5%a4%9a%e6%94%bf%e5%ba%9

c%e5%92%8c%e4%b8%ad%e5%9b%bd%e7%9a%84%e4%ba%bf%e4%b8%87%e5%af%8c%e8%b1%aa%e4%bb%ac/.

101. Upwell Canada website, "Committed to biological science research and development, Serve human health," https://upwellcanada.com/.

102. Kenneth Chan, "Vancouver education company looking to spin off $1.4 billion of student housing", Daily Hive, Aug 27 2020, https://dailyhive.com/vancouver/cibt-global-education-city-vancouver-portfolio.

103. https://investerest.vontobel.com/en-ch/articles/9571/the-belt-and-road-initiative--the-most-ambitious-infrastructure-and-investment-plan-in-history/.

104. China Council for the Promotion of International Trade website, "CCPIT Provides COVID-19 Force Majeure Certificates and Other Services," March 13, 2020, Accessed Aug. 6, 2023, https://en.ccpit.org/infoById/40288117668b3d9b0170d2952a7f0799/2.

105. Government of Canada, Immigration, Refugees and Citizenship Canada, "New pathway to permanent residency for over 90,000 essential temporary workers and international graduates," News Release, April 14, 2021—Ottawa, https://www.canada.ca/en/immigration-refugees-citizenship/news/2021/04/new-pathway-to-permanent-residency-for-over-90000-essential-temporary-workers-and-international-graduates.html.

106. Government of Canada, Marco Mendicino, Minister of Citizenship and Immigration, "Temporary public policy to facilitate the granting of permanent residence for foreign nationals in Canada, outside of Quebec, with a recent credential from a Canadian post-secondary institution," Public Policy, April 12, 2021, https://www.canada.ca/en/immigration-refugees-citizenship/corporate/mandate/policies-operational-instructions-agreements/public-policies/trpr-international-graduates.html.

107. Akshay Kulkarni, "Nearly half a million B.C. residents can't vote. Here are some of their voices," CBC, Sept. 13, 2021, https://www.cbc.ca/news/canada/british-columbia/b-c-residents-who-can-t-vote-1.6172891.

108. Daphne Bramham, "Maple Leaf schools go global, but they are as much about China as Canada," *Vancouver Sun*, May 24, 2021, https://vancouversun.com/opinion/columnists/daphne-bramham-maple-leaf-schools-go-global-but-they-are-as-much-about-china-as-canada.

## CHAPTER THIRTEEN

1. Graeme Wood, "China is paving its 'belt and road' to British Columbia," Syndicated news agencies, Aug. 17, 2020, https://www.newwestrecord.ca/bc-news/china-is-paving-its-belt-and-road-to-british-columbia-4683428.

2. State Council Information Office of the PRC, "Wang Huning meets overseas Chinese entrepreneurs," Xinhua, Updated Nov. 19, 2019, http://english.scio.gov.cn/topnews/2019-11/19/content_75422530.htm.

3. All China Federation of Overseas Chinese, "List of Overseas Mem-

bers of the Tenth Committee of the All-China Federation of Returned Overseas Chinese Members Employed by the Tenth National Congress of Returned Overseas Chinese and Their Families," September 1, 2018, Para 4 Sub-para 13 (Canada) http://www.chinaql.org/n1/2018/0901/c421026-30265666.html.

4. Alex Joske, "The party speaks for you: Foreign interference and the CCPs United Front system," Australian Strategic Policy Institute, June 1, 2020, Pages 19 to 30, https://www.jstor.org/stable/resrep25132.12.

5. Anne-Marie Brady, "Magic Weapons: China's political influence activities under Xi Jinping," Wilson Center, September 18, 2017, https://www.wilsoncenter.org/article/magic-weapons-chinas-political-influence-activities-under-xi-jinping.

6. World / North America Commerce Valley, Company Background, "Shing Kee Godown (CANADA) Holding Ltd. Was founded in 2015 by Taicheng Guo, Hongyi (Sunny) Wu and other board of directors." 2022 https://nacvglobal.com.

7. Graeme Wood, "Chinese government launches 'Belt and Road' warehouse in Surrey," Vancouver is Awesome, August 17, 2022, https://www.vancouverisawesome.com/bc-news/chinese-government-launches-belt-and-road-warehouse-in-surrey-5708258.

8. Wayback Machine, "Practice and Prospect of Chinese Merchant Ships Opening up Polar Routes," International Shipping Network , Dec. 27, 2018, https://web.archive.org/web/20190603033829mp_/http://www.ishipoffshore.com/html/7/2018-12-27/8608.htm

9. Chuck Chiang, The Canadian Press, "Northern premiers say Canada can't have Arctic security without infrastructure," CBC, Updated July 5, 2023, https://www.cbc.ca/news/canada/north/northern-premiers-arctic-security-1.6879517.

10. Prime Minister of Canada Stephen Harper website: "PM announces signing of new investment agreement with China," September 2012—Vladivostok, Russia, http://web.archive.org/web/20141216194015/http://www.pm.gc.ca/eng/node/21916.

See also, "Canada Ratifies Investment Agreement with China," Sept. 12, 2014, Ottawa, Ontario, Foreign Affairs, Trade and Development Canada, http://web.archive.org/web/20140913235615/https://www.international.gc.ca/media/comm/news-communiques/2014/09/12a.aspx?lang=eng.

11. Canada China Chamber of Industry and Commerce Association (CCCICA) website, "The 2nd Canada China Investment Summit Successfully Concluded," Nov. 28, 2014, http://www.cccica.com/en/the-2nd-canada-china-investment-summit-successfully-concluded/.

12. "The groundbreaking ceremony of the Canada-China Trade City, the World Commodity Trading Base, was held in Vancouver," Ningxia Daily, Yindi, October 11, 2018, http://www.yindi.cn/html/xwzx/jtyw/4289.html.

# ENDNOTES

13. Marquis, Christopher and Qiao, Kunyuan, *Mao and Markets: The Communist Roots of Chinese Enterprise* (New Haven: Yale University Press, 2022), p. 91.

14. BC United Caucus, "Get to Know Teresa Wat," https://www.bcunitedcaucus.ca/team/teresa-wat/.

15. BC Government News, "Premier strengthens relationship with Guangdong province of China," May 9, 2016, https://news.gov.bc.ca/releases/2016PREM0053-000742.

16. Willy Lam, '*Hu Jintao Picks Core Sixth-Generation Leaders*,' China Brief, The Jamestown Foundation, May 15, 2009, page 2, https://jamestown.org/wp-content/uploads/2009/05/cb_009_01.pdf.

17. BC Government News, "Premier strengthens relationship with Guangdong province of China," May 9, 2016, https://news.gov.bc.ca/assets/releases/2016PREM0053-000742/VIDEO_Premier_podium01.mov.

18. BC Government News, "Premier strengthens relationship with Guangdong province of China," May 9, 2016, https://news.gov.bc.ca/assets/releases/2016PREM0053-000742/VIDEO_Premier_podium02.mov.

19. Steven Chase and James Griffiths, "Ottawa halts participation in China-led development bank," *The Globe and Mail*, June 14, 2023 https://www.theglobeandmail.com/politics/article-ottawa-launching-review-of-canadas-membership-in-china-led-development/.

20. Julie Davidson, Correspondence Services JTT:EX, "Subject: CLIFF logs for Hu Chunhua's visit, Guandong–BC economic trade conference," compiled Nov. 27, 2018, Accessed July 27, 2023, http://docs.openinfo.gov.bc.ca/Response_Package_JTT-2018-87287.pdf, pp. 49–60.

21. Julie Davidson, Correspondence Services JTT:EX, "Subject: CLIFF logs for Hu Chunhua's visit."

22. Julie Davidson, Correspondence Services JTT:EX, "Subject: CLIFF logs for Hu Chunhua's visit," p. 49.

23. https://biv.com/article/2020/08/china-paving-its-belt-and-road-british-columbia.

24. Julie Davidson, Correspondence Services JTT:EX, "Subject: CLIFF logs for Hu Chunhua's visit," p. 60.

25. BC Government, '*The Pacific Gateway Transportation Strategy 2012 – 2020: Building Markets, Growing Jobs*,' https://www2.gov.bc.ca/assets/gov/driving-and-transportation/reports-and-reference/reports-and-studies/planning-strategy-economy/gateway_strategy.pdf#:~:text=B.C.%20is%20Canada's%20Pacific%20Gateway%2C%20the%20preferred%20gateway,-for%20special%20focus%20in%20the%20BC%20Jobs%20Plan.

26. OECD, *China's Belt and Road Initiative in the Global Trade, Investment and Finance Landscape*, https://www.oecd.org/finance/Chinas-Belt-and-Road-Initiative-in-the-global-trade-investment-and-finance-landscape.pdf, page 3.

27. Bennett Jones, "Only Canadian Based Firm to Advise China's Ministry of

Commerce," Dec. 16, 2013 https://www.bennettjones.com/Publications-Section/Announcements/Bennett-Jones-Only-Canadian-Based-Firm-to-Advise-Chinas-Ministry-of-Commerce.

28. Teo Chew Society of Vancouver, "Chaoshan People in Canada.".

29. China Info Services, "Qinhuangdao Economic and Technological Development Zone," *China Daily*, Dec. 20, 2018, https://govt.chinadaily.com.cn/s/201812/20/WS5d08a17c498e12256565dfd8/qinhuangdao-economic-and-technological-development-zone.html.

30. Kaperoni Business Financial Group, "World Commerce Valley,"2014–2023, http://www.kaperonigroup.com/about-us/world-commerce-valley/.

31. Xinhua Silk Road Information Services, "FAQ: What is Beijing-Tianjin-Hebei (Jing-Jin-Ji)?" https://en.imsilkroad.com/p/313554.html.

32. China Briefing, Map: Jing-Jin_Ji at a glance, 2018, https://www.china-briefing.com/news/wp-content/uploads/2018/04/CB-Jing-Jin-Ji-at-a-Glance-002.jpg.

33. Wayback Machine, "The 'two sessions' of Hebei Province kicked off, focusing on the coordinated development of Beijing, Tianjin and Hebei," Jan. 7, 2016, https://web.archive.org/web/20190318053538/http://www.shijieshanggu.com/media/show/16.html.

34. Andrew Kurjata, "A Hail Mary pass: how the Port of Prince Rupert became a player in the world of global trade," CBC, Aug. 29, 2017, https://www.cbc.ca/news/canada/british-columbia/prince-rupert-port-ten-years-1.4267502.

35. "Overseas Chinese Communities-Hand in Hand on 'the Belt and Road,' Heart to Heart for the 20th CPC National Congress," Video, China.com, Cultural Development Center, Sept. 13, 2022.

36. Vancouver Overseas Chinese Network, "The establishment of the Cantonese Chamber of Commerce in Canada, the inauguration ceremony of the Canadian Federation of Guangdong Associations and the dinner to celebrate the 70th anniversary of the founding of New China were held," Sept. 11, 2019, https://tinyurl.com/yc5y4wcr.

37. Elections BC, "Financial Reports and Political Contributions Search Results for Lin Shaoyi and Canada Chaoshan Business Association," Oct. 6, 2014, https://tinyurl.com/muypc8mz.

38. Taisheng International Investment Services Company Ltd, "In the zone: Terrace's connection to China's Qinhuangdao Economic Development Zone," Feb. 5, 2014, https://taishenginvest.com/%E5%8A%A8%E6%80%81%E6%9B%B4%E6%96%B0/352-in-the-zone-terrace-s-connection-to-china-s-qinhuangdao-economic-development-zone.

39. City of Terrace, "Community Update: Qetdz/Taisheng Property at Skeena Industrial Development Park," May 3, 2016, https://www.terrace.ca/sites/default/files/docs/business-development/news_release_taisheng_may_2016_final.pdf.

40. The Wayback Machine—Chaoren Online, "Canadian tide businessman Lin Shaoyi took the lead in establishing Songshan thermal power plant in Shantou," Nov. 1, 2008, https://web.archive.org/web/20140701064831/ http://www.chaoren.com/news/chaoxun/globle/2013-10-30/2041.html.

41. Chuck Chiang, The Canadian Press, "Northern premiers say Canada can't have Arctic security without infrastructure," CBC, Updated July 5, 2023, https://www.cbc.ca/news/canada/north/northern-premiers-arctic-security-1.6879517.

42. Municipal Information Network, "City Signs Friendly Exchange Agreement with Qinhuangdao, China," Dec. 3, 2015, https://municipalinfonet. com/article/municipal/category/economy/63/555716/city-signs-friendly-exchange-agreement-with-qinhuangdao-china.html.

43. Terrace Standard, "Terrace, B.C. city council wrong in holding meeting in private," Dec. 17, 2015, https://www.terracestandard.com/opinion/terrace-b-c-city-council-wrong-in-holding-meeting-in-private/.

44. Josh Massey, "In the zone: Terrace's connection to China's Qinhuangdao Economic Development Zone," *Terrace Standard*, Feb. 5, 2015, https:// www.terracestandard.com/news/in-the-zone-terraces-connection-to-chinas-qinhuangdao-economic-development-zone.

45. Zarrin Gull, "Belt and Road Initiative—a Canadian perspective," *China Daily*, Aug. 9, 2018, http://www.chinadaily.com.cn/a/201808/09/WS5b-6b9449a310add14f384c28.html.

46. Julie Davidson, Correspondence Services JTT:EX, "Subject: CLIFF logs for Hu Chunhua's visit," compiled Nov. 27, 2018, accessed July 27, 2023, http://docs.openinfo.gov.bc.ca/Response_Package_JTT-2018-87287.pdf.

47. Julie Davidson, Correspondence Services JTT:EX, "Subject: CLIFF logs for Hu Chunhua's visit, Guandong–BC economic trade conference," compiled Nov. 27, 2018, accessed July 27, 2023, http://docs.openinfo.gov. bc.ca/Response_Package_JTT-2018-87287.pdf, p. 48.

48. China International Economic and Trade Arbitration Commission, "The Unveiling Ceremony of China International Economic and Trade Arbitration Commission North America Arbitration Center was held in Vancouver, Canada," July 4, 2017, http://www.cietac.org/index.php?m=Article&a=show&id=15467.

49. Cheryl Jahn, "Prince George A Foreign Trade Zone," Feb. 23, 2018, https://ckpgtoday.ca/2018/02/23/prince-george-a-foreign-trade-zone/.

50. Andrew Kurjata, "Companies can skip Canadian taxes if shipping goods through new Prince George trade zone," CBC, Feb. 23, 2018, https://www.cbc.ca/news/canada/british-columbia/foreign-trade-zone-bc-1.4549622.

51. The Wayback Machine, "The 'two sessions' of Hebei Province kicked off, focusing on the coordinated development of Beijing, Tianjin and Hebei," China News Network, Jan. 7, 2016, https://web.archive.org/web/ 20190318053538/http://www.shijieshanggu.com/media/show/16.html.

52. China Daily, "Beijing-Tianjin-Hebei Integrated Development Plan," (story expands to: "Five things you need to know about Beijing-Tianjin-Hebei integrated development," China Services Info, April 18, 2019), https://govt.chinadaily.com.cn/index/specials/jingjinjiintegration.

53. Government of Canada, "Prince George Receives Foreign Trade Zone Designation and Investment in Clean Tech Sector," News Release, Feb. 23, 2018, https://www.canada.ca/en/western-economic-diversification/news/2018/02/prince-george-receives-foreign-trade-zone-designation-and-investment-in-clean-tech-sector.html.

54. The Wayback Machine, "B.C. and Guangdong Work Together To Open Doors For Businesses, Create Good Jobs In B.C.," Destination BC, Jan. 23, 2018, https://www.destinationbc.ca/news/b-c-and-guangdong-work-together-to-open-doors-for-businesses-create-good-jobs-in-b-c/.

55. The Wayback Machine, "Li Qingwu, Chairman of Hong Kong Shengji Warehouse, met with representatives from the Prince George Airport Authority in Canada (Prince George Airport Authority)," Zhonghai Shanggu of China Ltd, Nov. 19, 2019, https://web.archive.org/web/20210302130332/http://www.shijieshanggu.com/activity/show/24.html.

56. Taisheng International Investment Services Company Ltd, "In the zone: Terrace's connection to China's Qinhuangdao Economic Development Zone," Feb. 5, 2014, https://taishenginvest.com/%E5%8A%A8%E6%80%81%E6%9B%B4%E6%96%B0/352-in-the-zone-terrace-s-connection-to-china-s-qinhuangdao-economic-development-zone.

57. The Canadian Press, "Port of Prince Rupert set to master 2021 challenges with 2022 upgrades, improvements," City News Everywhere, Jan. 18, 2022, https://toronto.citynews.ca/2022/01/18/port-of-prince-rupert-set-to-master-2021-challenges-with-2022-upgrades-improvements/.

58. Meng Jiangbo, "Side Notes on China-Canada Trade Cooperation Ministerial Roundtable," People's Daily Online, June 19, 2015, http://zgbx.people.com.cn/n/2015/0619/c347569-27183664.html.

59. Meng Jiangbo, "Side Notes on China-Canada Trade Cooperation."

60. Office of the Premier, "Premier strengthens relationship with Guangdong province of China," May 9, 2016, https://news.gov.bc.ca/releases/2016PREM0053-000742.

61. BC Legislature, April 24, 2018, Morning, Statements (Standing Order 25B), Vancouver International Trade Forum and Trade with China, Teresa Wat—speaker.

62. BC Legislature, April 24, 2018, Morning, Statements (Standing Order 25B). See also, Fan Xiaolong, Huang Xuruiping, and Chen Hong, "Xiaolong interviewed Huang Xuruiping, president of the North American Investment Chamber of Commerce," Oct. 19, 2020, https://www.sohu.com/a/425816801_496050.

63. Hua News Agency, "2018 Vancouver International Trade Forum

successfully concluded ," Lahoo.ca, March 21, 2018, https://lahoo.
ca/2020/08/28/19072.

64. North American Investment Association website, Message from the
President, 2017, https://naiacanada.com/en/about/message-from-the-
president. She writes, "This association will do its utmost to organize
more Canadian food companies and actively engage this project to expand
the food export channels along the Belt and Road and promote more
Canadian food exports."

65. Daisy Xiong, "Richmond business owners concerned about 'unclear'
Canada-China situation," *Richmond News*, Dec. 13, 2018, https://
www.richmond-news.com/local-business/richmond-business-owners-
concerned-about-unclear-canada-china-situation-3089814.

66. Chuck Chiang, "Province signals support for B.C. food exporters," BIV,
Jan. 16, 2018, https://biv.com/article/2018/01/province-signals-support-
bc-food-exporters.

67. North America Investment Association website (see certificate of appreciation, three pages down on home page), Accessed Aug. 22, 2023, https://
naiacanada.com/en/news.

68. North America Investment Association website, "Message from the
President," 2017, https://naiacanada.com/en/about/message-from-the-
president.

69. Sarah Hall, "Geographical imaginations of the Belt and Road Initiative,"
Asia Research Institute, University of Nottingham, Jan. 31, 2019, https://
theasiadialogue.com/2019/01/31/geographical-imaginations-of-the-belt-
and-road-initiative/.

70. British Columbia Government News, Office of the Premier, "Premier
strengthens relationship with Guangdong province of China," News Release,
May 9, 2016, https://news.gov.bc.ca/releases/2016PREM0053-000742.

71. British Columbia, "Premier strengthens relationship with Guangdong province of China," Archived version of press release, May 9.
2016, https://archive.news.gov.bc.ca/releases/news_releases_2013-
2017/2016PREM0053-000742.htm.

72. British Columbia, Response Package, (Draft) Protocol Itinerary, Version
2.6, Visit of His Excellency Hu Chunhua, May 8–9, 2016, http://docs.
openinfo.gov.bc.ca/Response_Package_GCP-2016-63673.pdf.

73. Yusen Logistics, "Our one-stop e-fulfillment solutions provide e-retailers
a competitive edge," https://www.yusen-logistics.com/ca_en/services/
supply-chain-solutions/success-stories/discover-key-to-growing-your-e-
commerce-business.

74. Yusen Logistics, "Yusen Logistics Expands Operation in Surrey, B.C.
Canada," Aug. 22, 2022, https://www.yusen-logistics.com/ca_en/insights-
news/press-releases/8096.

75. Peter Bryant, "Chinese Missions along the Belt and Road," *ChinaSource
Quarterly* (Summer, 2020), June 8, 2020, Accessed Aug. 22, 2023, https://

www.chinasource.org/resource-library/articles/chinese-missions-along-the-belt-and-road/.

76. Back to Jerusalem website, "What Is 'Back to Jerusalem?'" Accessed Aug. 22, 2023, https://backtojerusalem.com/about/.

77. Huang Zhenlin, "One Belt One Road and Mission Opportunity: Evangelistic Seminar," Chinese Annual Conference, The Methodist Church of Malaysia, Sept. 20, 2017, http://web.archive.org/web/20171105054805/www.methodist.org.my/2017/09/%E4%B8%80%E5%B8%A6%E4%B8%80%E8%B7%AF%E4%B8%8E%E5%AE%A3%E6%95%99%E5%A5%91%E6%9C%BA%E5%B8%83%E9%81%93%E8%AE%B2%E5%BA%A7%E4%BC%9A/.

78. Huang Zhenlin, "One Belt One Road and Mission Opportunity: Evangelistic Seminar."

79. China International Commercial Court, "Directory of Third Party Arbitration Institutions," June 28, 2022, https://cicc.court.gov.cn/html/1/219/399/406/index.html.

80. China International Economic and Trade Arbitration Commission, "The CEO of Vancouver Economic Commission of Canada visited CIETAC and signed a memorandum of cooperation between the two parties," March 31, 2021, http://www.cietac.org/index.php?m=Article&a=show&id=14164.

81. China International Economic and Trade Arbitration Commission, "The Mayor of Vancouver, Canada led a delegation to visit CIETAC," September 6, 2017, http://www.cietac.org/index.php?m=Article&a=show&id=14425.

82. Central University of Finance and Economics website, "Profile: Qikun Zhang," June 14, 2019, http://mba.cufe.edu.cn/english/info/1165/5017.htm.

83. Central University of Finance and Economics website, http://www.cufe.edu.cn/.

84. Yen Nee Lee, "China wants a seat in an international tribunal for maritime disputes. The U.S. is against it," CNBC, Aug. 3, 2020, https://www.cnbc.com/2020/08/04/us-is-against-china-seeking-a-seat-in-tribunal-that-settles-maritime-dispute.html.

85. James Rogers and Charlotte Hornby, "International Arbitration Report, Development and reform of CIETAC Q&A with Dr. Wang Wenying, Secretary General of CIETAC Hong Kong," Norton Rose Fulbright, p. 2, https://www.nortonrosefulbright.com/-/media/files/nrf/nrfweb/knowledge-pdfs/international-arbitration-report---issue-12.pdf?revision=&revision=4611686018427387904.

86. Sabrina Lee with Wilmer Cutler Pickering Hale and Dorr LLP, "Arbitrating Chinese Disputes Abroad: A Changing Tide?" Kluwer Arbitration Blog, April 7, 2016, http://arbitrationblog.kluwerarbitration.com/2016/04/07/arbitrating-chinese-disputes-abroad-a-changing-tide/.

87. Email from Attorney General, Government Communications and Public Engagement, to co-author Ina Mitchell, July 4, 2023.

## CHAPTER FOURTEEN

1. Jason Schreurs, "Hummingbird Cove shellfish hatchery opens," Glacier Media Group–Powell River Peak, Sept. 21, 2016, https://www.prpeak.com/local-business/hummingbird-cove-shellfish-hatchery-opens-3400279.

2. Food business network, "Rich and colorful Canadian seafood," July 20, 2020, https://news.21food.cn/2901/2897381.html.

3. Sing Tao Daily, "Chinese company invests 40 million in British Columbia to introduce marine seedling technology," Van People.com, https://info.vanpeople.com/608692.html.

4. National Advanced Worker, The title of outstanding laborer awarded by the Central Committee of the Communist Party of China, https://www.baike.com/wikiid/1662988297792074090?from=wiki_content&prd=innerlink&view_id=48f1zeuz5ju 000.n

5. Ding Yi, "Innovation-driven development Talents win the future] Zhou Zunchun: Bi Haiqin's hard work and innovation have yielded fruitful results," Dalian Tianjin Network, August 12, 2020, https://dalian.runsky.com/2020-08/12/content_6069148.html.

6. Ryan D. Martinson, "The 13th Five-Year Plan: A New Chapter in China's Maritime Transformation," The Jamestown Foundation, China Brief – Volume 16 Issue 1, January 12, 2016, https://jamestown.org/program/the-13th-five-year-plan-a-new-chapter-in-chinas-maritime-transformation.

7. Research and development of aquatic products and precision nutrition, BGI Marine, http://www.bgimarine.com/en/special/1.

8. BGI Marine, "Biological Exploration] Interview with Xu Junmin, Chairman of Huada Marine: To be the 'foundation builder' for the development of the marine pharmaceutical industry," BGI Marine News, Sept. 11, 2021, http://www.bgimarine.com/news/detail/212.

9. Fresh Products, "Hairy crab," BGI Marine, http://www.bgimarine.com/product/17.

10. See, for example: https://en.genomics.cn/en-project-dzwyjs-6185.html; http://www.lnshky.com/scientific_research/show-123.html; http://www.lnshky.com/scientific_research/show-149.html; https://baike.sogou.com/v53236117.htm;jsessionid=7388A4456F95133D9ECB462D434F4522 16; http://www.lnshky.com/; https://apnews.com/article/ap-top-news-international-news-ca-state-wire-genetic-frontiers-health 4997bb7aa36c-45449b488e19ac83e86d; and https://www.statnews.com/2018/11/25/china-first-gene-edited-babies-born/.

11. Elizabeth Mosier 2017 SFU. A Case for Land-Based Aquaculture for First Nations.

12. Interview with Mayor Dave Formosa, July 26, 2022.

13. Email from Strategic Media Relations Advisor, Fisheries and Oceans Canada, Pacific Region to co-author Ina Mitchell, July 18, 2022.

14. Caishen Group blog, Hummingbird Cove Lifestyle Hatchery, http://web.archive.org/web/20160314190413/http://www.caishengroup.com/blog/project/hummingbird-cove lifestyle-hatchery/. Citation is based on a version of the website that was archived before being removed from the internet.

15. Caishen Group, Hummingbird Cove Lifestyle Hatchery website (archived).

16. Meng Jiangbo, "Side Notes on China-Canada Trade Cooperation Ministerial Roundtable," People's Daily Online, June 19, 2015, http://zgbx.people.com.cn/n/2015/0619/c347569-27183664.html.

17. Bob Mackin, "Inside the Chinese government's "immoral, embarrassing" cocktail party for municipal politicians and bureaucrats," theBreaker.news, Sept. 26, 2019, https://thebreaker.news/news/ubcm-prc-party/.

18. https://powellriver.civicweb.net/document/65658/.

19. https://ca.linkedin.com/in/victor-h-gao-6521185a?original_referer=https%3A%2F%2Fwww.bing.com%2F.

20. https://www.avweb.com/recent-updates/experimentals/murphy-resurgent/; http://en.doofgroup.com/chairman-message; http://www.chinadaily.com.cn/a/202207/01/WS62be42a6a310fd2b29e69ada.html.

21. http://en.doofgroup.com/chairman-message; http://en.doofgroup.com/company-news/99.

22. Deocode39, "Behind the deal: China buys Italian-made helicopters," June 30, 2022 https://decode39.com/3712/deal-china-italy-helicopters/.

23. http://en.doofgroup.com/company-news/261.

24. https://www.kitplanes.com/want-to-own-a-kit-company-murphy-aircraft/.

25. https://tc.canada.ca/en/aviation/aircraft-airworthiness/recreational-aircraft-airworthiness/eligible-amateur built-aircraft-kits; http://www.china.org.cn/china/2022-01/07/content_77976548.htm.

26. http://sn.ifeng.com/a/20191015/7758804_0.shtml.

27. https://www.nwpu.edu.cn/xxgk/xxjj.htm; https://k.sina.com.cn/article_3464714474_ce8358ea00100xyje.html#/.

28. http://www.mo-fly.cn/about/.

29. "New Powell River Seaplane Service Launches March 7!" Harbour Air Ltd., Jan. 18, 2022, https://harbourair.com/new-powell-river-seaplane-service-launches-march-7/.

30. Fraser Valley College, "Regular Minutes," October 16, 1984, https://ufv. civicweb.net/document/23640/.

31. Siobhan Gorman, August Cole and Yochi Dreazen, "Computer Spies Breach Fighter-Jet Project," April 21, 2009, https://www.wsj.com/articles/ SB124027491029837401.

32. "BC Flight Training Center intends to train pilots for AVIC," Sohu.com, August 7, 2018, https://www.sohu.com/a/245635244_739899.

33. U.S. Department of Defense, "DOD Releases List of People's Republic of China (PRC) Military Companies in Accordance With Section 1260H of the National Defense Authorization Act for Fiscal Year 2021," October 5, 2022, https://www.defense.gov/News/Releases/Release/Article/3180636/dod-releases-list-of-peoples-republic-of-china-prc-military-companies-in-accord/.

34. https://new.qq.com/rain/a/20220812A04SZ900; https://wzb.bzu.edu.cn/.

35. https://fly.bzu.edu.cn/11611/list.htm
https://www.guet.edu.cn/info/1161/28597.htm
https://www.bzu.edu.cn/_t209/2016/0314/c15a18869/page.htm
https://www.sohu.com/a/498652430_121123770
http://www.gliet.edu.cn/info/1161/28599.htm
https://www.kmust.edu.cn/info/1011/4010.htm
https://mhhk.kust.edu.cn/info/1016/2332.htm
https://www.bzu.edu.cn/_t209/2016/0314/c15a18869/page.htm.

36. Fact Sheet, "Forced Labor in China's Xinjiang Region," Office to Monitor and Combat Trafficking in Persons, US Dept of State, July 1, 2021, https://www.state.gov/forced-labor-in-chinas-xinjiang-region/.

37. With files from Belle Puri, "Chinese airline doubles Vancouver flights," CBC, July 19, 2013, https://www.cbc.ca/news/canada/british-columbia/chinese-airline-doubles-vancouver-flights-1.1336356.

38. EAA, "An S-LSA From China," July 28, 2016, https://www.eaa.org/airventure/eaa-airventure-news-and-multimedia/eaa-airventure-news/eaa-airventure%20oshkosh/07-28-2016-an-s-lsa-from-china.

39. https://web.archive.org/web/20111015155815/http://www.tritonaircraft.com/about.php and https://www.zhaopin.com/companydetail/CZ141471710.htm.

40. Military + Aerospace Electronics, "DARPA funds heliplane design for combat search and rescue," Nov. 9, 2005, https://www.militaryaerospace.com/home/article/16712829/darpa-funds-heliplane-design-for-combat-search and-rescue.

41. Baidu, "The producer of the anti-famine gift film 'Lonely Smoke in the Desert' signed a cooperation agreement for aerial photography of the film in Canada," Nov. 7, 2018, https://baijiahao.baidu.com/s?id=1616541213251384461&wfr=spider&for=pc and https://baijiahao.baidu.com/s?id=1578505146316855541&wfr=spider&for=pc.

42. https://www150.statcan.gc.ca/n1/pub/61-517-x/61-517-x2019003-eng.htm.

https://www.163.com/news/article/AS9SB0H000014AED.html.
http://www.zongshen.cn/news/jtxw/.

43. State Council of the PRC, "China unveils 5-year plan to advance civil aviation development," Xinhua News, Jan. 7, 2022, https://english.www.gov.cn/statecouncil/ministries/202201/07/content_WS61d8386ac-6d09c94e48a34f4.html.

44. Office of the US Trade Representative, "Findings of The Investigation Into China's Acts, Policies, and Practices Related to Technology Transfer, Intellectual Property, And Innovation Under Section 301 of The Trade Act Of 1974," Executive Office of the President, March 22, 2018, p. 17, https://ustr.gov/sites/default/files/Section%20301%20FINAL.PDF.

45. News Release, "AVIC International concludes the acquisition of Aritex to become market leader worldwide for automatic assembly systems," Airframer, April 29, 2016, https://www.airframer.com/news_story.html?release=33443.

46. http://mobile.zongshen.cn/founder/csrjj/.

47. BC Government News, Office of the Premier, "New framework for natural gas development puts focus on economic and climate targets," Press Release, March 22, 2018, https://news.gov.bc.ca/releases/2018PR-EM0012-000480.

48. Taj Mitha, "BCIT signs training agreements in China," Isamilimail, Dec. 22, 2013, https://ismailimail.blog/2013/12/22/taj-mitha-bcit-signs-training-agreements-in-china/.

49. BC Gov News, "BC releases international trade mission costs," Minister of State for Trade, May 3, 2016, https://news.gov.bc.ca/releases/2016MIT0010-000712.

50. http://thecapeonbowen.ca/developer-story.php.

51. Globe Newswire, "ElectraMeccanica Strategic Partner Zongshen Industrial Group Validates Company's Go Forward Strategy With The Exercise of 1.4 Million Warrants," ElectraMeccanica Vehicles Corp, Nov. 1, 2021, https://www.globenewswire.com/news-release/2021/11/01/2324423/0/en/ElectraMeccanica-Strategic Partner-Zongshen-Industrial-Group-Validates-Company-s-Go-Forward-Strategy-With-The-Exercise-of-1-4-Million-Warrants.html.

52. Yvette Brend, "Pair claims they didn't know mansion was being used as illegal gambling den," CBC News, Nov. 29, 2017, https://www.cbc.ca/amp/1.4425040.

53. "Cui Ge's dinner has an artistic taste," Sohu, July 12, 2019, http://www.sohu.com/a/326274030_737753.

54. "[Hundred Years Dream Chaser] Riding the wind and waves, let the domestic aircraft have a 'Chinese heart,'" Sohu, July 29, 2021, http://www.sohu.com/a/480159767_121106884.

55. Chongqing Evening, "Zongshen's drones will be mass-produced in September," China News.com, June 17, 20015, http://www.chinanews.com.cn/auto/2015/06-17/7349589.shtml.

56.  Sina Military News, "The media said that the pterodactyl drone has been," Nov. 15, 2012http://mil.news.sina.com.cn/2012-11-15/1519706886.html.

57.  Liu Xuanzun, "China's first vessel-borne lightweight helicopter drone makes maiden flight," *Global Times*, Dec. 3, 2020, https://www.global-times.cn/page/202012/1208896.shtml.

58.  Army Recognition, "Chinese AR500C unmanned helicopter performs its maiden flight," May 24, 2020, https://armyrecognition.com/may_2020_news_defense_global_security_army_industry/chinese_ar500c_un-manned_helicopter_performs_its_maiden_flight.html, and "China's AR-500B shipborne unmanned helicopter made its first flight," China's New Military Weapons, Dec. 3, 2020, https://www.china-arms.com/2020/12/ar500b-unmanned-helicopter-first-flight/.

59.  Hualong Net-Chongqing Daily, "Driving Aircraft Manufacturing Through Aircraft Operations," 163.com, June 17, 2015, https://www.163.com/news/article/AS9SB0H000014AED.html.

60.  China Meteorological Administration, "50th Anniversary of Fengyun Satellite Program," China Meteorological News Press, Sept. 10, 2020, https://www.cma.gov.cn/en2014/news/News/202009/t20200930_564281.html.

61.  Robert Fife and Steven Chase, "Former Canadian fighter pilots face RCMP probe over training work in China" *The Globe and Mail*, Sept. 5, 2023, https://www.theglobeandmail.com/politics/article-canadian-pilots-china-training-rcmp/.

62.  Dirk van der Kley, Twitter, July 13, 2022, https://twitter.com/dvanderkley/status/1547119255388246016.

63.  https://townfolio.co/bc/powell-river/demographics.

64.  Chris Bolster, "City of Powell River confirms start of Wildwood development," Sept. 20, 2017, https://www.prpeak.com/local-news/city-of-powell-river-confirms-start-of-wildwood-development-3404256.

65.  Chris Bolster, "City of Powell River halts Olive Devaud renovations," June 7, 2017, 2017, https://www.prpeak.com/local-news/city-of-powell-river-confirms-start-of-wildwood-development-3404256.

66.  Asia Pulp and Paper, "Sustainable Innovations for Our Future – Humble Beginnings," https://asiapulppaper.com/about-us.

67.  Paper Excellence website, https://paperexcellence.com/paper-excellence-canada-welcomes-catalyst-paper/.

68.  Black Press Media, "Catalyst Paper to sell U.S. mills to Chinese company," Victoria News, May 25, 2018, https://www.vicnews.com/news/catalyst-paper-to-sell-u-s-mills-to-chinese-company-39006.

69.  Ellen Barry, "A Maine Paper Mill's Unexpected Savior: China ," Jan. 23, 2020, *The New York Times*, https://www.nytimes.com/2020/01/15/us/maine-mill-china.html.

70.  Nine Dragons Paper holding Limited, "Company Profile," http://www.

ndpaper.com/sc/about/profile.php.

71. Waste360 Staff, "Could Nine Dragons Save an Old New England Mill Town?" Waste360, Jan. 16, 2020, https://www.waste360.com/paper/could-nine-dragons-save-old-new-england-mill-town.

72. Women in Leadership, "Personal introduction of Zhang Yin, Chairman of Nine Dragons Paper," m.jingliren.org, Aug. 17, 2021, https://m.jin-gliren.org/ldl/nxldl/248845.html.

73. All-China Federation of Industry and Commerce Bulletin, "Zhang Yin: Become bigger and stronger on the 'Belt and Road,'" Nov. 20, 2019.

74. China News Network, "How can Chinese businessmen contribute to the construction of the 'Belt and Road'? Listen to what Chinese business-men have to say," Sina Finance, April 20, 2021, https://baijiahao.baidu.com/s?id=1697570952640016697&wfr=spider&for=pc

75. "Nine Dragons Paper Celebrates Restart of Pulp Mill in Old Town, Maine Old Town, Maine," Aug. 14, 2019, https://doc.irasia.com/listco/hk/ndpaper/press/cp190814.pdf.

76. Paper Excellence website, "Paper Excellence Announces Indefinite Cur-tailment of Catalyst Paper Tiskwat Mill In Powell River, BC," News Release, Dec. 1, 2021, https://paperexcellence.com/paper-excellence-announces-indefinite-curtailment-of-catalyst-paper-tiskwat-mill-in-powell-river-bc/.

77. Black Press Media, "Catalyst Paper to sell U.S. mills to Chinese company," Victoria News, May 25, 2018, https://www.vicnews.com/news/catalyst-paper-to-sell-u-s-mills-to-chinese-company-39006.

## CHAPTER FIFTEEN

1. Personal Video, Ken Sim in Vancouver City Hall chamber, Nov. 17, 2022.

2. CSIS Report, *Foreign Interference Threats to Canada's Democratic Process*, July 2021, https://www.canada.ca/content/dam/csis-scrs/documents/pub-lications/2021/foreign-interference-threats-to-canada%27s-democratic-process.pdf.

3. Team Ken, "ABC Vancouver today announced that it will accept cryp-tocurrency donations," ABC Vancouver Campaign website, April 27, 2022, https://abcvancouver.ca/2022/04/abc-vancouver-today-an-nounced-that-it-will-accept-cryptocurrency-donations/.

4. Overseas Chinese Affairs Office of the State Council, "Chen Youqing, a famous overseas Chinese leader, passed away, and the Hong Kong chief executive expressed deep condolences," China News Network, April 21, 2022, https://archive.ph/Jgqii#selection-245.0-245.121.

5. Grace Shao, "To bring Hong Kong back to normal, violence must stop, politician says ahead of weekend protests," CNBC, Oct. 18, 2019, https://www.cnbc.com/2019/10/18/hong-kong-protests-bernard-chan-says-violence-has-to-stop.html.

6. Personal Interview, Audio recorded.

7. Robert Fife, Steven Chase, Nathan Vanderklippe, "China's Vancouver consulate interfered in 2022 municipal election, according to CSIS," *The Globe and Mail*, March 16, 2023, https://www.theglobeandmail.com/politics/article-chinas-vancouver-consulate-interfered-in-2022-municipal-election/.

8. Tristin Hopper, "B.C. property titles bear reminders of a time when race-based covenants kept neighbourhoods white," *National Post*, May 16, 2014, https://nationalpost.com/news/canada/b-c-property-titles-bear-reminders-of-a-time-when-race-based-covenants-kept-neighbourhoods-white.

9. Personal video, Ken Sim, Chinese-only roundtable, Floata Restaurant, Vancouver, BC, Aug. 29, 2022.

10. CCS100 website, Biographical information of directors, Accessed Aug. 28, 2023, http://ccs100.ca/portfolio/.

11. CCS100 website, About Canada Committee, 100 Society, Accessed Aug. 29, 2023, https://web.archive.org/web/20220629164605/http://ccs100.ca/views-of-chinese-canadians-on-the-rule-of-law-in-relation-to-mengwanzhous-extraditioncase-a-survey-report/.

12. Found in Translation blog, "Pro-Beijing community leader said Chinese Canadians will 'punish bad politicians with votes,'" Aug. 1, 2023, https://foundintran.substack.com/p/pro-beijing-community-leader-said.

13. Ding Guo "The silent majority will punish bad politicians with their votes," April 19, 2023, http://web.archive.org/web/20230724203425/https://riseweekly.com/dingguo-2023-4-18/.

14. Email exchange between co-author Ina Mitchell and Tung Chan, Oct. 29, 2021.

15. Online Seminar: Anti Racism Media Training, May 1, 2021. Email Exchange, Tung Chan to co-author Ina Mitchell, Oct. 29, 2021.

16. MLARA Press Release, "MLARA setting the record straight—About Maple Leafs Anti-Racism Action Association (MLARA)," June 1, 2020, https://mlara.org/2021/05/13/press-release-june-1-2020.

17. Sam Cooper, "United Front groups in Canada helped Beijing stockpile coronavirus safety supplies," Global News, April 30, 2020, https://globalnews.ca/news/6858818/coronavirus-china-united-front-canada-protective-equipment-shortage/.

18. Vikki Hui, "Richmond resident starts petition against foreign influence registry," Richmond News, April 21, 2023, https://www.richmond-news.com/local-news/richmond-resident-starts-petition-against-foreign-influence-registry-6892693.

19. Personal video, Ken Sim, Chinese-only roundtable, Aug. 29, 2022.

20. Vancouver Police Union, "Vancouver Police Union Endorses Ken Sim for Mayor," Safetyisaright.ca, Oct. 5, 2022, https://safetyisaright.ca/2022/10/

vancouver-police-union-endorses-ken-sim-for-mayor/ https://safe-tyisaright.ca/2022/10/vancouver-police-union-endorses-ken-sim-for-mayor/.

21. Private Interview, Recorded, Tom Stamatakis, Canadian Police Association, Aug. 28, 2023.

22. Personal emails between Jordan Eng and co-author Ina Mitchell, Aug. 30, 2023.

23. Kristen Robinson, "Vancouver delegation to tour San Francisco's Chinatown to learn how it's being revitalized," Global News, Aug. 28, 2022, https://globalnews.ca/news/9090884/vancouver-leaders-vpd-officers-san-francisco-chinatown/.

24. Email from Vancouver Police Foundation to co-author Ina Mitchell, April 14, 2023.

25. Dion Lim, "Tech billionaire funding network of 1,000 security cameras around SF addresses privacy concerns," ABC 7 News, July 16, 2020, https://abc7news.com/chris-larsen-sf-crime-applied-video-solutions-robbery/6320899/.

26. City of Vancouver, Members' Motion B.3, Urgent Measures to Uplift Vancouver's Chinatown.

27. Li Ming, "WeChat and TikTok Help the CCP Spread Its Thought Control Overseas," Falun Dafa—Minghui.org, Dec. 30, 2020, https://en.minghui.org/html/articles/2020/12/30/189173p.html.

28. Seth Kaplan, "China's Censorship Reaches Globally Through WeChat," *Foreign Policy*, Feb. 28, 2023, https://foreignpolicy.com/2023/02/28/wechat-censorship-china-tiktok/.

29. Personal video, Vancouver City Council meeting, Nov. 15, 2022.

30. City of Vancouver's website, "View names on the Reserve List," Accessed Aug. 28, 2023, https://vancouver.ca/your-government/view-names-on-the-reserve-list.aspx.

31. City Manager, "Council Report," City of Vancouver, Jan. 6, 2023, https://council.vancouver.ca/20230117/documents/r1.pdf Report - Uplifting Chinatown Action Plan - Council - January 17, 2023 (vancouver.ca).

32. ACCT Foundation website, $5 Canadian Bill Petition, April 28, 2022, https://acctfoundation.ca/5-canadian-bill-petition.

33. Steve Scherer, "Canada's Trudeau denies report that Liberals told to drop candidate over China ties," Reuters, Feb. 28, 2023.

34. Sam Cooper, "Liberals ignored CSIS warning on 2019 candidate accused in Chinese interference probe: sources," Feb. 24, 2023, https://globalnews.ca/news/9504291/liberals-csis-warning-2019-election-candidate-chinese-interference/.

35. Kenneth Chan, "58% of Vancouver voters support a ward system of selecting City Council," Daily Hive News, June 21, 2022, https://dailyhive.com/vancouver/vancouver-city-council-ward-system-at-large.

36. Telephone interview between Baldwin Wong and co-author Ina Mitchell, 2021.

37. Ji Yuqiao, "China's support and contribution to UNESCO," *Global Times*, Sept. 14, 2020, https://www.globaltimes.cn/content/1202025.shtml.

38. Jon Hernandez, "Cultural sites 'under constant attack,' director says, as graffiti and vandalism blight Vancouver's Chinatown," CBC, Jan. 25, 2022, https://www.cbc.ca/news/canada/british-columbia/chinatown-attacked-with-graffiti-1.6327709.

39. Ji Yuqiao, "China's support and contribution to UNESCO," *Global Times*, Sept. 14, 2020, https://www.globaltimes.cn/content/1202025.shtml.

40. ICONNBC Business Association website; https://iconnbc.com/.

41. Karin Larsen, "'Rampant' spread of coronavirus misinformation causing businesses to suffer: health minister, mayor," CBC News, Feb. 17, 2020, https://www.cbc.ca/news/canada/british-columbia/coronavirus-patty-hajdu-kennedy-stewart-adrian-dix-vancouver-chinatown-misinformation-1.5466333.

42. Peninsula Canada Holding Group Website, Accessed August 31, 2023, http://web.archive.org/web/20180606114909/http://www.bandao.ca/%E6%8E%A7%E8%82%A1%E9%9B%86%E5%9C%98/.

# DIGITAL INDEX

An index of people and subjects is available for this book online.

Please visit us at:

optimumpublishinginternational.com/operationdragonlord